The Complete Idiot's Reference Card

State Motorcycle Requirements

The Motorcycle Industry Council Government Relations Office releases a report each summer listing motorcycle laws in all 50 states and the District of Columbia. The information contained here is the most recent as of this writing.

State	Safety Helmet Required?	Eye Protection Required?	Daytime Headlight Use Required?
Alabama	Yes	No	No
Alaska	Yes[2]	Yes[11]	No
Arizona	Yes[1]	Yes[10]	No
Arkansas	Yes[3]	Yes	Yes
California	Yes	No	Yes
Colorado	No	Yes	No
Connecticut	Yes[1]	Yes[10]	Yes
Delaware	Yes[5]	Yes	No
District of Columbia	Yes	Yes[10]	No
Florida	Yes	Yes	Yes
Georgia	Yes	Yes[10]	Yes
Hawaii	Yes[1]	Yes[10]	No
Idaho	Yes[1]	No	No
Illinois	No	Yes	Yes
Indiana	Yes[1,4]	Yes[1]	Yes
Iowa	No	No	Yes
Kansas	Yes[1]	Yes[10]	Yes
Kentucky	Yes	Yes	No
Louisiana	Yes	Yes[10]	No
Maine	Yes[6]	No	Yes
Maryland	Yes	Yes[10]	No
Massachusetts	Yes	Yes[10]	No
Michigan	Yes	Yes[10]	No
Minnesota	Yes[1,4]	Yes	Yes
Mississippi	Yes	No	No

continues

alpha
books

State Motorcycle Requirements

State	Safety Helmet Required?	Eye Protection Required?	Daytime Headlight Use Required?
Missouri	Yes	No	No
Montana	Yes[1]	No	Yes
Nebraska	Yes	No	No
Nevada	Yes	Yes[10]	No
New Hampshire	Yes[1]	Yes[10]	No
New Jersey	Yes	Yes[10]	No
New Mexico	Yes[1]	Yes[10]	No
New York	Yes	Yes[10]	No
North Carolina	Yes	No	Yes
North Dakota	Yes[1]	No	Yes
Ohio	Yes[7]	Yes[10]	No
Oklahoma	Yes	Yes[10]	No
Oregon	Yes	No	Yes
Pennsylvania	Yes	Yes	Yes
Rhode Island	Yes[8]	Yes	No
South Carolina	Yes[2]	Yes[3,10]	No
South Dakota	Yes[1]	Yes[10]	Yes
Tennessee	Yes	Yes[10]	No
Texas	Yes[9]	No	Yes
Utah	Yes[1]	No	Yes
Vermont	Yes	Yes[10]	No
Virginia	Yes	Yes[10]	No
Washington	Yes	Yes[10]	No
West Virginia	Yes	Yes	Yes
Wisconsin	Yes[1,4]	Yes[11]	Yes
Wyoming	Yes[1]	No	Yes

[1]Operators under 18 years of age

[2]Operators under 18 years of age and all passengers

[3]Operators under 21 years of age

[4]Those with learner's permits

[5]Possession by all; those under the age of 19 and those with learner's permit must wear helmets

[6]All passengers under the age of 15, operators with a learner's permit, and all riders for one year after obtaining their license

[7]Novice-license holders

[8]All passengers, operators under 21 years of age, and all riders for one year after obtaining their license

[9]Except for riders over the age of 21 who have completed a rider's education course or who maintain at least $10,000 health-insurance coverage for motorcycle-related injuries

[10]Except if the bike is equipped with a windshield

[11]Except if the bike is equipped with a windshield 15 inches or taller

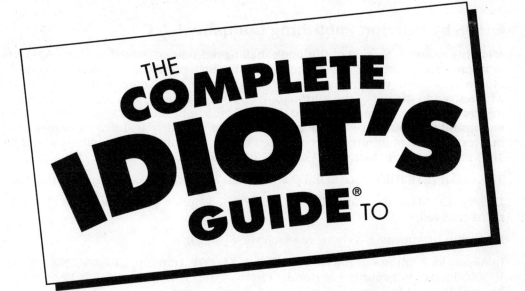

THE

COMPLETE
IDIOT'S
GUIDE® TO

Motorcycles

*by the Editors of Motorcyclist™ Magazine
with Darwin Holmstrom*

alpha
books

A Division of Macmillan General Reference
A Simon & Schuster Macmillan Company
1633 Broadway, New York, NY 10019-6785

International Standard Book Number: 0-02-862416-5
Library of Congress Catalog Card Number: 98-85424

00 99 98   8 7 6 5 4 3 2 1

Interpretation of the printing code: the rightmost number of the first series of numbers is the year of the book's printing; the rightmost number of the second series of numbers is the number of the book's printing. For example, a printing code of 98-1 shows that the first printing occurred in 1998.

Printed in the United States of America

Note: This publication contains the opinions and ideas of its author. It is intended to provide helpful and informative material on the subject matter covered. It is sold with the understanding that the author and publisher are not engaged in rendering professional services in the book. If the reader requires personal assistance or advice, a competent professional should be consulted.

ALPHA DEVELOPMENT TEAM

Publisher
Kathy Nebenhaus

Editorial Director
Gary M. Krebs

Managing Editor
Bob Shuman

Marketing Brand Manager
Felice Primeau

Senior Editor
Nancy Mikhail

Development Editors
Phil Kitchel
Jennifer Perillo
Amy Zavatto

Editorial Assistant
Maureen Horn

PRODUCTION TEAM

Production Editor
Mark Enochs

Copy Editor
Fran Blauw

Cover Designer
Mike Freeland

Photo Editor
Richard H. Fox

Illustrator
Jody P. Schaeffer

Graphics Coordinator
John Hunt

Graphic Conversion Technician
Oliver Jackson

Designer
Glenn Larsen

Indexer
Ginny Bess
Tim Tate

Layout/Proofreading
Angela Calvert
Kim Cofer
Mary Hunt
Megan Wade

Contents at a Glance

Contents

22 How to Become a Motorcycle Road Racer 283

Foreword

I have these really vivid visual images of bikes from when I was very young. I remember when I was about five years old, my aunt was going with a guy who had a bike. He came over to the house with his Harley. It had the two-tone tinted windshield like they had in the '50s, and on the bottom part of the windshield there was a sticker of a girl in a two-piece bathing suit. And I remember my mother going, "Get away from there!" And I said, "I'm not looking at the girl, I'm looking at the bike." And she said, "I know what you're looking at. Get out of there." "I'm not, I want to look at the bike." So I remember my mother having a huge fit over this pornographic motorcycle!

The first bike I ever got was a Honda 350 back in 1971. I bought it from a Harley-Davidson dealer in Everett, Massachusetts. I remember I went down and just bought it. You didn't have to have a license in those days. You didn't even have to know how to ride. You bought a motorcycle like you buy an air rifle. The salesman says, "Hey, okay, good luck," and you're off.

I remember getting on the freeway, not knowing what I was doing. I turned my head to see if a car was coming and my glasses blew off. So now I'm on something I've never ridden, in the rain, no helmet of course, and I can't see. But I still remember thinking, "This is fun!"

Another time I was on that bike, still not very familiar with it, and I got caught in some rain grooves. The tires just wanted to follow the grooves, you know? I thought, "How do I get out of this?" I remember just sailing past my exit, and thinking maybe I'll run out of gas or something. I had no idea what to do. So that's why I think training is important. Back then, I learned by *almost* having accidents.

Riders today shouldn't have to learn the way I did. My advice to newcomers to motorcycling is this:

➤ Take a motorcycle safety course. That's the first thing.

➤ Lie down on the ground and have a friend put the bike gently on top of you. (Just kidding, folks, don't try this at home) Okay, now magnify that feeling by a thousand, because that's what it's like when you fall off a bike. Everybody falls off, at some point, and you have to be willing to accept that.

➤ Never take the bike when you're in a hurry, because that's when you have an accident. If work is ten minutes away and I got up an hour early, I'll take the bike. If work is ten minutes away and I've got to be there in ten minutes, I'll take the car.

The motorcycling world is different now than when I got started. It's less cohesive than it used to be. The simplest poll to take is to ride down the street and wave, and see how many riders wave back. I'm probably the last generation of guys who waves at everybody. Owning a motorcycle used to be a lifestyle. Now, it's more a lifestyle accessory, like a cell phone or a fanny pack.

Today, people have a lot more money to spend, and they're not learning how to ride. I'm amazed at the number of people who just don't know. It's like you just buy this rocket ship that you sit on. But you have to prepare for motorcycling like it's a sport, because it is.

The editors at *Motorcyclist*™ and Darwin Holmstrom have pulled together a lot of great advice and information on the sport of motorcycling. As both an idiot and a motorcyclist, I found this book very helpful.

—Jay Leno

Motorcycle enthusiast, comedian, and host of *The Tonight Show*

Introduction

Me and My Motorcycle

Motorcycles represent different things to different people. For some folks, they represent basic transportation. To others, they represent the exhilaration of power and speed. To the humorless, they represent a societal irritation.

To me, motorcycles represent pure freedom.

Growing up on an isolated farm in northern Minnesota, I had a rather lonely childhood. Our nearest neighbor was several miles away, and I could go weeks or even months without seeing another kid once school let out for the summer. That changed during my eleventh summer, when I got my first motorcycle. My life has never been the same.

That was more than 20 years ago, and since then, I've traveled hundreds of thousands of miles on a dozen different motorcycles. I've visited every contiguous state west of the Mississippi, and a bunch to the east. I've lived in different cities, held different jobs, but the one thing that has remained constant is my devotion to the sport of motorcycling. As I write, the exhaust pipes on my motorcycle are cooling in my garage, having just returned from a 150-mile ride. (I ride year-round—no small feat, considering I live in North Dakota).

I never feel more alive than when I'm riding a bike. For me, traveling in a car is too much like watching television: I feel as if I'm viewing my surroundings through the end of a glass tube. When I'm on a bike, I feel as though I am actually there, experiencing the world. Not only do I see my surroundings, but I feel them, smell them, taste them. I feel a part of something larger, something complete, and not just an uninterested voyeur.

I derive great comfort from that feeling. Sometimes when I haven't ridden for awhile, I start to feel disconnected. I don't notice it while it's happening, but when I finally get back out on the road, when I run my bike through the gears and watch the city disappear in my rear-view mirror, I realize how out of touch with myself I've been. When I start to feel that way, I know it's time to go for a ride.

Because the sport of motorcycling has brought me so much pleasure and satisfaction, I want to share this activity with others; my goal is to bring as many people into the motorcycling community as I can. But it is not a community to be entered into lightly. As rewarding as motorcycling is, it comes with risks. This is especially true for new riders—your chances of getting in trouble decrease as you become more experienced.

But motorcycling can be a safe sport, even when you are just starting out. The key is proper training. Such training has not always been easy to obtain. Back when I was learning to ride, I had absolutely no guidance. The dealer who sold me my first bike explained how to shift the gears, then sent me on my way. That was the extent of my training. I was eleven years old.

Times have changed. Thanks to the work of such organizations as the Motorcycle Safety Foundation (MSF), rider training is available in most parts of the United States. In this book, I've gathered as much information from the best sources and combined it with my own experience to create what I hope will be one of the best books available for a beginning rider.

I've also included a lot of practical and fun information unavailable anywhere else to help make this book the most complete beginner's resource you can buy. In addition to basic and advanced riding techniques and general motorcycle maintenance, I've covered the history of motorcycling, the types of bikes available, and the general workings of a bike.

In this book, you'll learn how to buy a bike. You'll learn about motorcycle racing and how you can become a racer. I'll show you what accessories will make your motorcycle more enjoyable to ride and where you can find those accessories. Perhaps most importantly, I'll teach you about the motorcycling community itself.

And of course there are plenty of pictures. If you're anything like me, you enjoy looking at motorcycles almost as much as riding them.

How to Use This Book

This book follows a linear, step-by-step structure and takes you through the entire motorcycle experience from start to finish. This book is structured this way to help you minimize the risks associated with motorcycling, to help make your entry into the sport safe and enjoyable.

This book is divided into five parts, each designed to take you to a new level of enjoyment in a safe, orderly fashion.

Part 1, "Biker Basics," sets the stage for the adventure you are about to embark on, providing a general overview of why we ride, the history of motorcycling, and the types of bikes available.

Part 2, "So You Want to Buy a Bike...," helps you identify what type of motorcycle you need and teaches you how to buy your first motorcycle. You get detailed discussions about the parts of a motorcycle, and more important, how those parts relate to you, the rider.

Part 3, "On the Road," is probably the most important part of this book. It helps you actually get out and ride. This is where you put your knowledge to the test, where theory translates into reality.

Part 4, "Living with a Motorcycle," condenses the entire spectrum of the motorcycle-ownership experience into chapters that cover maintenance, repair, customization, and collecting.

Part 5, "The Motorcycling Community," provides an overview of the world you are getting into. When you buy a motorcycle, you are not just buying an object; you're investing in a lifestyle. This part discusses the many places in which you'll meet fellow motorcycle enthusiasts, including motorcycle clubs, races, and rallies.

I've also included five appendices that you'll find useful. Appendix A lists all the new streetbikes for sale in the United States, along with the bikes that are best suited for beginners and the bikes I believe are best buys. Appendix B features a comprehensive list of used bikes that make ideal first motorcycles. Appendix C highlights useful motorcycle-related resources, and Appendix D is a glossary of the terms you'll encounter in this book.

Extras

Throughout this book, you'll find tips and information that will help you ride better and safer, without looking like a dork in the process. This information is highlighted in sidebars:

Motorcycle Moments

Anecdotes of historical and personal moments in the history of motorcycling.

Motorcycology
Tips and inside information providing insights into safe, enjoyable motorcycling.

Cycle Babble
Definitions of technical motorcycling terms that pop up throughout the book.

Steer Clear
Advice on practices and hazards to avoid if you want to keep the shiny side up—which means not falling down.

Acknowledgments

I would like to thank all the people who helped with this book. Judy and Dan Kennedy at Whitehorse Press have been incredibly helpful, providing me with much information at the exact moment I needed it. It's as if they read my mind, at times. I found their excellent book, *The Motorcycling Safety Foundation's Guide to Motorcycling Excellence*, to be the single most-useful resource I used in writing this book. Whitehorse's *Street Smart* video series also proved to be an essential source of information.

I would also like to thank the Motorcycle Safety Foundation itself, partly because without the ground-breaking work they have done in the field of motorcycle safety, this book could not have been written, and partly because of all the lives they have saved.

I received a great deal of last minute help getting items I needed for photo shoots from several people and companies, especially Ron Harper at Chase Harper, Ann Willey at National Cycle, and Fred Wyse at Vanson. Over the years, I have used products from all three companies, which is why I chose them for the photos—I know they are of the highest quality. It was nice to discover that the folks making those products are of the same high quality.

I want to thank the photographers who supplied me with last-minute photography: Brian J. Nelson, Timothy Remus, and Rick Menapace. I'd also like to thank the people who helped with the photo shoot: Jennifer and Dave Berger and Ed Ostoj.

Dan Keenen at Dynojet Research helped me put some technical information into terms anyone can understand, for which I am grateful. I'd also like to thank all the other individuals and groups who helped me write this book.

I'd like to thank all the motorcycle journalists who inspired me to not only ride, but to write about my experiences. The work of Phil Schilling, Cook Neilson, Gordon Jennings, Art Friedman, Kevin Cameron, Peter Egan, David Edwards, Ed Hertfelder, Clement Salvadori, Steven Jon Thompson, Steve Anderson, Bob Carpenter, and countless others helped me get through many long winters in the Northern Plains. I'd like to give a special thanks to those journalists who write about safety issues, writers like David Hough and Lawrence Grodsky. Not only have they helped me learn what I needed to know to write this book, but they may have saved my life a time or two.

I'd also like to thank my wife, Patricia, whose support (and tolerance) helped make this book possible.

I'd especially like to thank *Motorcyclist*™ editor Mitch Boehm, who connected me with this project.

The publisher thanks the staff of *Motorcyclist*™ magazine and the Petersen Publishing Company for bringing this project together. Special thanks to Dick Lague, vice president and executive publisher; Kevin Smith, editorial director; Chris Hobson, product manager; and Jeremy Kove, director of sales.

This book is dedicated to the great riders and racers who have taught me about the art of motorcycling, people like Jerry Stageberg, Al Burke, Denny Kannenberg, and many others. And to the late Ricky Graham. I had the privilege of watching Mr. Graham win the Grand National Championship in 1993, and regret that I won't see that again.

Special Thanks to the Technical Reviewer

The Complete Idiot's Guide to Motorcycles was reviewed by an expert who not only checked the historical and technical accuracy of everything you'll learn here, but also provided valuable insight to help ensure that this book tells you everything you need to know about the sport and art of motorcycling. Our special thanks are extended to Robert S. Griffith.

Robert is the Feature Editor at *Motorcyclist*™ magazine and has been riding motorcycles for more than 10 years. During his editorial tenure, he has had the enjoyable opportunity to test just about every streetbike made in the last six years.

Part 1
Biker Basics

Congratulations! As a beginning biker, you are about to embark on an adventure that will change your life. No other hobby will affect you at such a fundamental level as motorcycling. It will start subtly—at work, you'll find yourself daydreaming about going for a ride while you stare at the gibberish on your computer screen; in meetings, you'll look right through your boss and instead see the road outside the window. In your mind, you'll be riding on that road. Before you know it, you'll have a pet name for your motorcycle, which of course you'll tattoo on some hidden part of your body.

In other words, you will become a biker.

You are about to enter the community of motorcyclists. In this part of the book, you'll learn about that community, its history, and all it has to offer you—including an introduction to the joys of motorcycling.

Chapter 1

The Motorcycle Mystique

In This Chapter

➤ Why motorcyclists love to ride

➤ Motorcycles as chicken soup for your soul

➤ The cultural impact of motorcycles

➤ How motorcycle films have shaped generations of motorcyclists

➤ The advantages of owning a motorcycle

Perhaps one word best sums up the appeal of motorcycles: *fun*. Fun is what I had the first time I rode my neighbor's minibike nearly three decades ago. It's what I had this morning when I took my bike out for a ride.

But it's a complex fun, composed of many facets. Part of the pleasure of riding comes from the freedom and mobility the machine gives you. The exhilaration you feel as you power effortlessly up to cruising speed provides a portion of the fun. Part of your enjoyment comes from developing your riding skills—your ability to control the beast.

In this chapter, I'll show you why motorcycle riding can be such a rewarding, exhilarating, and liberating experience.

The Thrill of the Open Road

The sun creeps over the treetops, its warm rays driving the chill from your limbs as you open the garage door and wheel your motorcycle out onto the driveway. You prop the bike up and check to make certain everything is OK, which it will be since you take good care of your machine. You don your helmet and jacket and pull on your gloves, then start your engine. The beast jumps to life, then settles into a lumpy, powerful idle. You look over the bike one last time, then mount up and ride away. Now the fun begins.

It's early and traffic is light. Soon you've left the city behind. Twenty minutes down the interstate, exit, and you're on your favorite road. You have a vague destination, a coffee house on the other side of the mountain about 45 miles away, but riding is not about destinations—it's about journeys. And this road is your journey.

You take it easy at first, waiting for your tires to warm up. You shift the transmission through the gears, feeling the satisfying mesh of the cogs, and breath in the cool, clean morning air. An eagle soars over the road. You look up briefly as it disappears behind the next ridge, then get back to the ride. The vibration through the handlebars and footpegs feels reassuring, making you aware of your machine's mechanical presence.

As your tires warm, you push the envelope a bit, accelerating harder through each curve. You're riding well within your limits, but each turn you lean into gets your heart rate up a little higher. You snake through a series of S-curves, settling into a rhythm among you, the road, and your bike, engaged in a dance as elegant as any ballet. This is what it's all about.

It doesn't matter if you're riding a cutting-edge sportbike, a heavyweight cruiscr, or a big touring bike—the thrill of the ride is what draws you out again and again. Whatever emotional baggage you may have accumulated you leave behind on the open road. When you're participating in a dance with your bike and the road, it doesn't matter if your boss is a pointy-headed sociopath, your spouse shouts at you, or your kids act like juvenile delinquents. There's no room for such worries on a bike, because the activity at hand requires your total, undivided attention.

Bikes Are Beautiful

Most of us find motorcycles themselves gratifying—objects of art with an innate beauty that fills some need within us.

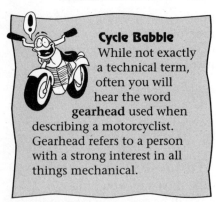

Cycle Babble
While not exactly a technical term, often you will hear the word **gearhead** used when describing a motorcyclist. Gearhead refers to a person with a strong interest in all things mechanical.

Motorcyclists tend to be *gearheads*. We love looking at our motorcycles almost as much as we love riding them. (In fact, some folks seem to be more enamored of viewing their machines than they are of riding them; legions of people trailer their motorcycles to different events around the country instead of riding them.)

Motorcycles possess a raw mechanical beauty. You'll be seeing all kinds of beautiful bikes throughout this book, but for starters, I think no bike better illustrates this visceral look than Harley-Davidson's Sportster. While Sportsters are Harley's smallest bikes, they are by no means small. They're mid-sized bikes, weighing around 525 pounds with a full tank of gas. Visually, the 1998 model is little changed from the original Sportster introduced in 1957, and many people agree that that's a good thing.

Harley's Sportsters, like this 1200 Sport, represent the elemental motorcycle. Consisting of an engine, a couple of tires, and a gas tank, you'll find nothing superfluous here. (Photo courtesy Motorcyclist™ *magazine)*

Sportsters are dinosaurs in every respect: they are not very powerful, they're uncomfortable, they don't handle exceptionally well, and they shake like unbalanced washing machines, yet Harley sells as many of them as it can build.

I believe that's because Sportsters possess the honest, brutal look that, to many eyes, is how a motorcycle should appear. Many riders are willing to overlook or correct a Sportster's flaws just to ride the archetypal motorcycle.

The looks of most Harleys, not just Sportsters, elicit strong, mostly favorable, responses from motorcyclists and non-motorcyclists alike. No other motorcycle company has had the appearance of its products elevated to near-art status the way Harley-Davidson has.

As you'll see in Chapter 18, "Creative Customizing and Collecting," the customized machines of such builders as Arlen Ness, Mallard Teal, and Donnie Smith often resemble metallic sculptures more than motorcycles. A visit to any custom-bike show can take on the trappings of a visit to a museum.

All of this provides a good example of how important the look of a motorcycle is. That's as true of a Yamaha,

Motorcycology

The demise of an entire motorcycle company can in part be traced to its producing one motorcycle the public found visually unappealing. BSA attempted to enter the modern motorcycle market by producing a three-cylinder motorcycle—the BSA Rocket 3. The bike showed promise, but its styling, created by an industrial-design firm with no experience in the motorcycle market, received such a dismal public reception that the resulting low sales caused BSA to implode.

Triumph, Laverda, BMW, or Ural as it is of a Harley. Motorcyclists love the way bikes look, and for every bike, there is someone who loves its appearance.

I learned this the hard way. A while back, in an article on motorcycle style, I poked fun at a bike that was generally accepted as being one of the uglier machines to have been produced during the past 20 years. I wrote that these motorcycles were probably very nice bikes, but they were so butt-ugly no one ever found out, because no one would be seen on one. I thought this was a fair assessment, since the bike had been a sales disaster.

Fair or not, at least one reader took issue with my critique and wrote in suggesting my head was deeply embedded in a place that defied all laws of physics. The man owned one such "ugly motorcycle," and it had given him more than 100,000 miles of enjoyment. I felt bad about that situation, not because the reader questioned my hygienic habits and insulted my ancestors, but because I had belittled a motorcycle that obviously meant a great deal to him.

The Tao of Two Wheels

Some time ago, a colleague of mine, a reporter who covered religious topics at a newspaper, asked me why I didn't go to church. I told her I did go to church, every day, when I went out riding my motorcycle.

For many motorcyclists, the ceremony of going for a ride provides the same spiritual sustenance other people find through the ceremonies conducted by organized religions. The similarities are striking. We wear our leathers and riding suits as vestments, we have a prescribed ritual for starting our engines, and our favorite roads compose our liturgy.

The very nature of riding a motorcycle forces the rider into a spiritual state. Think of it this way: Most religious systems encourage some form of meditative technique. Christians have prayer. Native Americans meditate inside sweat lodges, and Eastern spiritual systems advocate elaborate chanting techniques. All these methods have as their common general goal the transcendence of the self or ego in order to get in touch with some greater force.

Motorcycling forces riders to transcend their egos—to empty themselves and exist in the world around them. The consequences of not being totally aware of their actions and environment, of becoming distracted by the baggage of their everyday lives, are too great. When you're out in the world on a bike, you must be completely in the moment, completely aware of your surroundings, or you may find yourself meeting your concept of God earlier than you might have hoped.

But when everything is working, when you and your bike are totally in sync and the road rushing under your feet feels like an extension of your body—at those times, you get in touch with divinity.

Biker Chic

Not all that long ago, motorcycles were considered the domain of leather-clad hood-lums—guys you didn't want your daughter to be seen with. But that stereotype has always been inaccurate, and most people now realize that.

Motorcycle Moments

While most people realize that motorcyclists are respected members of society, a few holdouts still cling to the image of the outlaw biker. During the summer of 1997, the BMW Riders Association held a rally at Fontana Village in Graham County, North Carolina. Citing Graham County Sheriff's Office reports that 14,000 outlaw bikers were about to invade the county, law-enforcement agencies from across the state descended on the rally. They set up road blocks, searched motorcycles for drugs and weapons, and generally harassed rally-goers. Apparently, intelligence gatherers failed to inform officials that BMW riders tend to be the most conservative segment of the motorcycling community and that there probably aren't 14,000 outlaw bikers left in the entire country.

Motorcycling began to gain social acceptance in the 1960s, when the Japanese began exporting small, nonintimidating motorcycles to the United States, but only in recent years has motorcycling been elevated to the status of high fashion.

Celebrities have always ridden motorcycles. Clark Gable terrorized Los Angeles on his Ariel Square Four. Marlon Brando used his own personal motorcycle in the film *The Wild One*. James Dean rode bikes from the time he was in high school. Steve McQueen's real-life racing antics made the jump scene in *The Great Escape* look feeble.

But these were Hollywood's bad boys—sexy rebels who knew no fear. You wouldn't find a nice woman like Donna Reed or a respectable fellow like Jimmy Stewart straddling a motorcycle.

Sometime during the 1980s, that changed. This shift in our collective perception began slowly—photos of businessman Malcolm Forbes touring the world on his Harley-Davidson appeared in mainstream magazines and Juan Carlos, the King of Spain, could be found touring his domain on a Harley. Soon, Hollywood's bad boys, people like Mickey Rourke, Sylvester Stallone, Bruce Willis, and Arnold Schwarzenegger, came out of the closet and proclaimed themselves bikers.

But it didn't stop there. Nice, respectable folks like Jay Leno and Mary Hart let the world know they were motorcyclists. Country boy Lyle Lovett began appearing on magazine covers aboard his hot-rod Ducati. Rosie O'Donnell seldom appeared in the tabloids without her Suzuki Intruder. Even *Friend*-ly Courtney Cox appeared in public-service ads riding her Ninja.

Now motorcycles are must-have fashion accessories for celebrities and celebrity wannabes, much like nipple rings were *de rigueur* for Seattle grunge rockers in the early 1990s.

The Art of Motorcycles

Although the motorcycle-as-nipple-ring is a fairly recent development, bikes have always had a strong influence on popular culture. In turn, popular culture has played a strong role in developing the motorcycle community.

The appeal of motorcycles to actors is no coincidence. Because riding a bike is a high-profile activity, motorcycles have always been an excellent method for studios to show-case and draw attention to their stars.

The history of motorcycles in film is as old as the history of motion pictures itself. Motor-cycles appeared in some of the earliest silent films, like *Mabel at the Wheel* (1914), in which Charlie Chaplin drops Mabel off the back of his motorcycle and into a mud puddle.

And films about motorcycle riders appeared early on, such as *No Limit* (1935), in which English actor George Formby played a motorcycle-riding hero battling a gang of biker toughs.

While motorcycles played many roles in Hollywood films, the medium of film played an even more influential role in shaping motorcycle culture. As motorcycle films became more popular, increasing numbers of riders tried to emulate their screen heroes. When Marlon Brando portrayed Johnny in *The Wild One*, he portrayed a very atypical motorcy-clist. After a generation of bikers grew up with Brando's Johnny as a role model, though, the image of the leather-clad motorcycle-riding hood, while still an aberration, became much more common.

Because of the influence of films, portrayals of motorcyclists became self-fulfilling proph-esies. The myriad outlaw biker B movies Hollywood cranked out during the 1960s and 1970s spawned a subculture of motorcyclists who modeled themselves on the bikers in those films. When Peter Fonda portrayed the philosophical Wyatt in *Easy Rider*, he gave birth to the real-life hippie poet-biker stereotype. When Arnold Schwarzenegger came back as promised in *Terminator 2: Judgment Day*, he did so on a Harley Fat Boy. Soon a Harley and a cigar were the fashion accessories of the 1990s.

Motorcycle Moments

The event that inspired the film *The Wild One*, the so-called Hollister Invasion, was actually more of a non-event. On the Fourth of July of 1947, about 3,500 motorcyclists rode to Hollister, California (a town of about 4,500) to attend an American Motorcycle Association (AMA) race meeting, and another 500 or so riders showed up just to have a little fun. A few bikers got a bit out of hand, and by noon the next day, 29 of them had been cited for drunkenness, indecent exposure, and traffic violations. The real importance of the event involved its press coverage; newspapers ran hyperbolic tales of anarchy and debauchery as thousands of bikers ran amuck, and *Life* magazine printed an infamous photo of a beer-guzzling rider stretched out on his customized Harley amid a pile of beer bottles. (The photo was staged by the *Life* photographer.) The myth of the outlaw biker was born.

According to legend, the term *one-per-center*, used to describe outlaw bikers, was created after the Hollister Invasion, when an AMA official blamed the trouble on the one percent of motorcyclists who belonged to the outlaw contingent.

From a Wild One to an Easy Rider

The films *The Wild One* and *Easy Rider* marked the beginning and the end of Hollywood's most influential period on motorcycling and are the two most important motorcycle films ever made.

The Wild One became the archetypal biker flick because it was the first to portray the unique breed of bikers that sprang up in post–World War II America.

This film marked the beginning of a decades-long period of mistrust between motorcyclists and the general public. Johnny and his buddies seem pretty tame by today's standards; compared to bikers portrayed in later flicks, they're about as nice a bunch of boys as you'll ever meet. But back in 1953, Johnny represented the anti-Christ to Middle America.

The Wild One gave birth to a new genre: the B biker movie. In the 1950s and 1960s, Hollywood cranked out a pile of low-budget biker flicks. Each of these films tried to outdo the others in portraying the wild outlaw biker. *Easy Rider*, starring Peter Fonda, Dennis Hopper, and Jack Nicholson (in his first major film role) shattered that stereotype.

Easy Rider, directed by Dennis Hopper, changed everything. No longer was the anti-hero biker a confused Neanderthal, mindlessly lashing out at whatever got in his way. Instead, *Easy Rider* presented the biker as a sensitive, thoughtful enigma.

With the film Easy Rider, producers Dennis Hopper and Peter Fonda turned the Hollywood biker image upside down. (Photo courtesy Motorcyclist™ *magazine)*

Motorcycle Moments

While Peter Fonda was an accomplished motorcyclist prior to filming *Easy Rider*, costar Dennis Hopper was anything but. Before making the film, Hopper's motorcycle experience was confined to a scooter he had owned in the 1950s, and he had crashed that machine in a rather spectacular fashion. After finishing the film, Hopper admitted to having been scared silly by his Harley.

The financial success of *Easy Rider* ensured a host of imitators, but the biker-flick genre's success was short-lived. The problem seemed to be that there was no new ground to break: *Easy Rider* was such an encompassing film that all following flicks seemed to be pale imitations by comparison.

Easy Rider: The Convenience of Bikes

Given the influence motorcycles have had on film and on our general culture, it's easy to argue the more esoteric appeal of motorcycling, but the sport has some practical benefits as well.

The relatively low price of motorcycles makes them attractive as practical transportation. While prices have risen dramatically during the past couple of decades, for the most part, bikes are still much less expensive than cars. You can buy a motorcycle in "like-new" condition in the $2,500 price range. For that money, you can pick up a bike that will deliver years or even decades of trouble-free transportation. Try finding a car for the same amount that is not ready for the crusher.

In congested urban areas, the small size and mobility of a motorcycle provide real advantages over a car. An experienced rider can zip through traffic, and in places where the practice is legal (like California), you can ride between lanes on the freeways. While this practice, known as *lane splitting*, may sound dangerous, some studies indicate that it may actually be safer than idling along in a traffic jam.

And with a motorcycle, you will never have to worry about a parking spot. You can always find a space to back into, because you'll only require a fraction of the space a car requires.

Another practical benefit of motorcycles is their fuel efficiency. Even the biggest touring bike or fastest sportbike gets as many miles to the gallon as most econo-cars, and when ridden prudently, a smaller motorcycle can get 60 miles to the gallon or better. My wife once got 79 miles to the gallon on a small motorcycle she rode through the mountains of Colorado.

Cycle Babble
Lane splitting refers to the practice of riding between lanes of traffic on a freeway. While this practice may sound dangerous, studies indicate that it might actually be safer than idling along in a traffic jam.

This might not seem that great an advantage these days, when we have cheap gas and suburban parents haul their kids to school in sport-utility vehicles that get less than 10 miles to the gallon, but that cheap gas may soon be a thing of the past.

If global climate change really is caused by the burning of fossil fuels, as the majority of respected scientists now believe it is, we may soon be facing the prospect of dramatically increased fuel prices. While this does not bode well for motorsports in general, because of the fuel-efficient nature of motorcycles, we could be poised for a new boom of motorcycles as a form of practical transportation. This has been the case for years in Europe.

The Least You Need to Know

➤ You get from motorcycling what you put into it.

➤ Like meditation, motorcycling requires your undivided attention.

➤ Biker flicks have shaped motorcycle culture as much as motorcycle culture has shaped biker flicks.

➤ Motorcycles can be practical as well as fun.

Chapter 2

A Brief History of Bikes

In This Chapter

➤ How motorcycling developed from cheap transportation into a passionate hobby

➤ The myth of the outlaw biker

➤ How the baby boomers changed the face of motorcycling

➤ Harley-Davidson's role in today's motorcycle market

Motorcycling offers more pleasure than any other activity a person can engage in (well, okay, not *any* other activity, but almost). It also extracts a high penalty for making mistakes. If you're going to be a motorcyclist, you'll need as much knowledge as you can get to survive out there, and a solid understanding of the history of the sport is part of that knowledge.

But knowing how we got here from there serves as an ego boost as well. Motorcyclists are gearheads, people with an almost unnatural attraction to things mechanical. Like every other group, we have our inside secrets, status symbols that tell if a person is a hardcore rider or just another dork with a motorcycle. Few of these clues scream "Dork!" as loud as a rider poorly versed in the history of motorcycles. In this chapter, I'll give you the inside info you'll need to become a true motorcyclist.

Humble Beginnings

Almost as soon as the modern bicycle appeared toward the end of the nineteenth century, some inspired individual decided to strap an internal-combustion motor to the contraption. By the turn of the century, a variety of motorized bicycles was available to the general public.

The motorized-bicycle experiments of two young men, William S. Harley and Arthur Davidson, would prove to be more influential to American motorcycling than all the rest combined.

The pair realized their experiments had commercial potential, and along with Arthur's brothers, Walter and William, they formed the Harley-Davidson Motor Company in 1903 to manufacture motorized bicycles. From this humble beginning sprang the longest continuously-running motorcycle manufacturing firm in the world, affectionately known as The Motor Company.

Motorcycle Moments

Gottlieb Daimler, the German inventor who produced the first functional four-stroke engine, may well have created the first gasoline-powered motorcycle. After his early experiments using an engine to power a four-wheeled horseless carriage produced less than satisfactory results (probably due to the whopping .5 horsepower the motor cranked out), Daimler built his *Einspur*, or single-tracked test vehicle, in 1885. Although crude, this vehicle incorporated many features still found on motorcycles today, such as a cradle frame and twist-grip controls on the handlebars.

But even that wasn't the first motorcycle. The Smithsonian Institute's National Museum of American History displays a two-wheeled powered vehicle built in about 1868 by Sylvester H. Roper, a Massachusetts resident. The main difference between Roper's and Daimler's machines was Roper's use of a steam engine.

But Mr. Harley and the Davidson boys weren't the only people conducting such experiments.

In 1902, one year before the formation of The Motor Company, a German engineer named Maurice (Mauritz) Johann Schulte designed a motorcycle, the first to be produced by Triumph Cycle Co. Ltd. of England. This machine was still very much a motorized bicycle with a Belgian-produced engine fitted to its frame.

The early years of the twentieth century saw hundreds of similar companies form. The low power output of the engines available made them better suited to power small, two-wheeled vehicles than larger, carriage-type machines, and motorcycles thrived as forms of personal transportation. Plus, cars were still too expensive for most people to own; motorcycles were cheaper and more plentiful.

Like all technology of that time, motorcycle development proceeded at a frantic pace. Soon, the early motorized bicycles were supplanted by machines designed from the start to be operated by some form of engine. By the end of World War I, most of the technical innovations we see today had been tried with varying degrees of success. Since other technologies, such as *metallurgy*—the study of metals—had not kept pace with such innovations, by the 1920s, motorcycle designers had settled on relatively simple designs. The brilliant ideas of those early designers proved to be ahead of their time, and many would have to wait until the 1970s or 1980s to finally find acceptance.

Although the sport of motorcycling thrived initially, the same technological advances that drove its success led to the first of the sport's many crises. As internal-combustion engines became more powerful and efficient, they became more practical as power sources for horseless carriages. And with the advent of affordable automobiles like Henry Ford's Model T in 1913, average people could afford to buy cars. Clearly, it was easier to haul the entire family to church in an automobile; you could only haul three or four family members on a motorcycle, and then only if it was equipped with a sidecar.

By the end of World War I, many of the companies manufacturing motorcycles had either gone out of business or switched to the manufacture of some other product. Motorcycles might have become extinct but for some clever marketing moves on the part of the remaining manufacturers.

Motorcycling survived by positioning itself as a sport, a leisure activity, rather than trying to compete with automobiles as practical transportation. The move made sense. People had been racing motorcycles all along; promoting riding in general as a sport was a logical extension of that activity.

This market positioning helped motorcycling survive its second great crisis: the Great Depression. This worldwide economic disaster finished off many of the remaining motorcycle-manufacturing firms that had survived the advent of the inexpensive, reliable automobile, and again, those companies that survived did so by promoting motorcycling as a sport.

Cycle Babble
Sidecars are small carriages attached to the side of a motorcycle to provide extra carrying capacity and extra stability in low-speed, low-traction conditions. Sidecars usually consist of a tube-like cockpit area resting on a frame that attaches to the motorcycle on one side and is held aloft by a wheel on the opposite side.

The Wild Ones: The Outlaws' Conveyance

Motorcycling in America entered the modern era following World War II. Important technological advances had been made prior to the war, but most people were too busy struggling to survive the Depression to pay much attention.

World War II changed all that. After the war, a lot of restless people came back from Europe and Asia, people not content to go back to the way things were. They could afford transportation, and they had an elaborate new highway system to explore. Many of them decided to explore those new roads via motorcycles.

As you saw in the last chapter, the film *The Wild One* played an important role in the formation of the post-war motorcycling community. It was a difficult time for many Americans. We'd won the war, but afterward, nothing seemed quite the same. To the general public, Johnny, Marlon Brando's character in the film, represented everything that was wrong with the country. Like Communism, the stereotype of the outlaw biker become a focal point for their fears.

When Marlon Brando roared into small-town America in The Wild One, *he used his own motorcycle, a 650cc Triumph Thunderbird very much like this 1953 example. (Photo ©1998 Timothy Remus)*

But not everyone feared Johnny. Some people wanted more out of life than the latest automatic appliances in the kitchen and a new Plymouth sedan parked in the driveway. For them, Johnny represented an escape from the mind-numbing conformity of McCarthy-era America. In Johnny, Brando created a role model for these disaffected young people—a figure that jelled in America's psyche as the archetypal outlaw biker.

The Japanese Invasion

Throughout the 1950s, motorcycling remained the domain of extreme gearheads and one-per-centers (outlaws). Nice people did not ride a bike. Nice people didn't even associate with those who did ride, whether they were upstanding members of the American Motorcycle Association (AMA) or hardcore outlaws.

The reason for this involved more than just the perceived danger of the sport or of motorcyclists' outlaw image. There were practical reasons for the marginality of motorcycling as well.

Part of the problem was that the machines themselves demanded a great deal from their owners. The technological advancements of motorcycling had not kept pace with automobiles. By the 1950s, cars were relatively reliable, easily-maintained devices, and the experience of owning one was not all that different than it is today.

Bikes were another story.

The reason only gearheads owned motorcycles back then was because you had to be a gearhead to own one. There was nothing easy about riding a bike. Even starting the beast was a traumatic experience in those pre–electric-start days. Glance at the starting procedure of a mid-1950s Triumph as outlined in its owner's manual, and you'll be instructed to tickle carburetors, retard the spark, and align the piston according to the phase of the moon. Once you'd accomplished all this, it was time to kick the starting lever. If all was in sync and the gods were smiling on you, the machine would start without backfiring and smashing your ankle into hundreds of tiny bone shards (which happened more frequently than you might imagine).

And all this just to *start* the bike. Keeping it running was just as difficult. Riders who put a lot of miles on their machines knew the inner workings of their bikes intimately. They saw them frequently, sometimes even when they hadn't intended to: More than one rider saw pistons, valves, and connecting rods flying from their engines as they exploded like grenades between the riders' legs.

You Meet the Nicest People on a Honda

Part of the reason for the stagnation in motorcycle design at this time was lack of competition. The Indian Motorcycle Company (the first American motorcycle company, preceding Harley-Davidson by two years) had quit building motorcycles by the mid-1950s, and even before it gave up the ghost, it had long ceased being competitive with Harley-Davidson. The British manufacturers only had to keep up with one another, and as long as none of them raised the stakes too high, none of them had to try too hard. There were interesting developments taking place in other European countries, but those countries were still in such turmoil from the war that manufacturers there concentrated on producing cheap transportation for their own people and weren't interested in exporting motorcycles to the rest of the world.

That was soon to change. In only a few years, these complacent manufacturers would find themselves up against some very serious competition from a most unlikely source: Japan.

Like Italy and Germany, Japan was in ruins following World War II. Unlike those countries, Japan's manufacturing infrastructure had been completely destroyed. After the war, Japan had to start from scratch. The Japanese rose to the challenge, and rather than rebuilding the past, they looked to the future for their inspiration.

17

Like European countries, Japan's post-war motorcycle industry emerged to service society's need for cheap transportation. That industry had a humble beginning, with many manufacturers building clones of bikes from other countries.

Motorcycle Moments

While most early Japanese motorcycles were small bikes, the bikes manufactured by the Rikuo company were big exceptions. That company manufactured large V-twin Harley-Davidson replicas, built under a licensing agreement with The Motor Company. Soon, Rikuo was improving on the Harley design, introducing telescopic forks in 1948, a year before Harley introduced the innovation. This was followed by the introduction of a foot-operated gearshift (Harley still used a cumbersome, hand-operated system) and automatic spark advance (for easier starting). By this time, Rikuo believed it had modified its design to the point where it no longer had to pay for the license agreement. Harley disagreed and made its displeasure known to the Japanese government, which in turn withdrew its orders for police bikes from Rikuo, forcing the company out of business.

Motorcycology

Prior to becoming a manufacturer of motorcycles, Soichiro Honda, the founder of Honda, operated a series of businesses that were less than successful. In fact, he once described his life as "Nothing but mistakes, a series of failures, a series of regrets." But he credited those failures for his success. "Success can be achieved only through repeated failure and introspection. In fact, success represents 1 percent of your work and results from the 99 percent that is called failure."

Americans had little use for the more-or-less overgrown mopeds coming out of Japan, nor did any other country for quite a few years. But by the late 1950s, Japanese motorcycles began to make their way into Europe and then into the United States. By this time, Japanese bikes had evolved into distinctive, original machines with innovations that made riders take note. These were elegant, reliable, nimble, and fast bikes, and cheap to boot.

The innovation people most took note of was the inclusion of electric starters on many of these machines. No longer did riders need the legs of mules to kick start their bikes; they simply pushed a button and rode off.

Unlike other manufacturers, the Japanese realized the sales potential of motorcycles that were convenient to use, and no Japanese company capitalized on convenience as a selling point as well as Honda. In an ad campaign designed to highlight the utility of its machines, Honda set the sport of motorcycling on the path toward respectability.

That campaign was the famous "You meet the nicest people on a Honda" series of ads, and it single-handedly undid much of the damage done to the image of motorcycling by films like *The Wild One*. The ads, which featured "normal" people doing non–outlaw-type things on Honda motorcycles, appeared in 1961 and were so effective that they made the sport of motorcycling seem acceptable to society as a whole. The ads had such a powerful effect that for years afterward, the word *Honda* became synonymous with small motorcycles, much like the name *Xerox* is used as a verb meaning "to photocopy."

This Honda ad proved so effective at getting people to buy motorcycles, it's still studied in advertising classes today. (Photo courtesy Vreeke and Associates)

The Japanese Hit the Big Time

Because the Japanese were only producing small motorcycles and not "real" bikes, the other major manufacturers didn't consider them a serious threat and paid little attention to them. That proved to be a mistake—a fatal mistake for many of the more marginal manufacturers—because the Japanese were dead serious.

As the 1960s progressed, the bikes coming from Japan increased in size and capabilities, but the other manufacturers still paid them little heed. By 1965, when Honda introduced its CB 450, the competition had wised up. This bike, known as The Black Bomber for its racy black bodywork, handled like a European machine and could outrun a stock Harley-Davidson with more than twice its engine displacement.

Finally, Japan's competitors realized what they were up against and found the motivation to respond to the threat. The British manufacturers BSA and Triumph began to jointly develop a large-displacement, multicylinder machine in an attempt to preserve their advantage in sporting bikes, and Harley grafted an electric starter onto its big twin engine in an attempt to provide Japanese-style convenience.

Both these projects proved to be too little too late. By the time the British unveiled their triples, which proved to be flawed machines with styling only a mother or designer could love, Honda had unveiled its big gun: the four-cylinder CB750.

Perhaps the most significant motorcycle in history, the 1969 Honda CB750 changed the face of motorcycling. (Photo courtesy Vreeke and Associates)

It's impossible to overstate the impact this bike had on the motorcycling world.

What Honda did by introducing the CB750 was the equivalent of a car company producing a high-quality sports car equal to or better than the best machines produced by Porsche or Mercedes, and then selling it for the price of a Hyundai. Here was a machine capable of outrunning any mass-produced motorcycle on the road and able to do so all day long without any mechanical problems. Plus, people could afford it.

Given the success of the big Honda, it was only a matter of time before other manufacturers followed suit and produced big bikes of their own. Kawasaki jumped into the four-cylinder arena, with its mighty Z1, and after a couple of false starts, Suzuki joined the fray, followed by Yamaha.

These big-bore motorcycles devastated the competition. For the British, hampered by management unable to let go of pre-WWII motorcycle designs, the competition proved to be too much. Harley-Davidson managed to survive, partly due to the fanatical loyalty of its customers, but entered into a long period of decline. For a while in the 1970s, it looked like the Japanese would be the only people left in the motorcycling business.

Baby Boomers on (Two) Wheels

The success of the Japanese manufacturers in the United States provides one of history's best examples of being in the right place at the right time. The Japanese caught a wave, a wave caused by the baby-boom generation, and this massive influx of young people provided the fuel to propel the Japanese invasion.

While some restless individuals returning from the war spent their newfound wealth on motorcycles and raising hell, most used that money to pursue the American dream—a dream that included raising a family. And raise families they did, prolifically, creating a new generation so large that their whims would dictate trends for the rest of their lives and probably shape our culture for generations to come. The impact of the so-called baby-boom generation will still be felt long after the last baby boomer has moved on to that great salvage yard in the sky.

The Boomer Boom

Just as the first small Japanese motorcycles began to appear on the West Coast, the first wave of baby boomers was getting its collective driver's license. It didn't take an advanced degree in economics to see the profit potential of providing these kids, products of unprecedented affluence, with fun, affordable, and reliable motorcycles.

The maturation of the Japanese motorcycle industry mirrors the maturation of the baby-boom generation. As these kids grew in size, so grew the Japanese bikes. By the 1970s, most baby boomers were entering adulthood. They roamed farther, rode faster, and were physically larger than when Mr. Honda first started importing his small Dream motor-cycle into the country. They no longer needed small, inexpensive motorcycles to ride to football practice or down to the beach.

What they needed were full-sized motorcycles with enough power to satisfy their adven-turous spirits, bikes comfortable enough for cross-country trips. And the Japanese were happy to oblige.

By this time, these young people had become accustomed to the convenience and reliability of Japanese motorcycles. Harley-Davidsons of the 1970s were only incremen-tally improved over those built during the 1930s. Compounding these problems, Ameri-can Machine and Foundry (AMF), Harley's parent company at that time, was more interested in turning a quick buck than in long-term development. Even Willie G. Davidson, a direct descendant of one of the company's founders, Arthur Davidson, admits that their bikes suffered quality-control problems during this period as a result of AMF's desire to get as many bikes as possible to the market.

Problems were even worse over in England. During the 1950s and 1960s, the British bike industry was run in large part by the same people who had brought the industry to prominence in the 1930s and 1940s. These people tended to oppose even the slightest change.

Motorcycology
While the Italians produced mechanically brilliant motorcycles during the 1960s and 1970s, cosmetically, they left much to be desired. The bikes were beautiful from a distance, but upon closer inspection, the quality of paint and bodywork was abysmal. One well-known example of this was *Cycle* magazine's 1974 Ducati 750SS test bike, which came with an actual fly embedded in the fiberglass of the fuel tank.

The result was that the British motorcycle industry was in complete disarray and unable to cash in on the demographic trends taking place in the United States. It could not even develop a functional electric-starting system that didn't explode through the engine cases on every ninth or tenth starting attempt.

For the bulk of this massive new generation of Americans, British or American motorcycles were not an option. The German firm BMW produced spectacular bikes that were as reliable and convenient as Japanese machines, but cost more and were not as widely marketed in the United States. The Italians also produced motorcycles in many ways equal to or superior to the Japanese bikes, but these too came at a premium price. Add to this the peculiar Italian penchant for designing and developing spectacular machinery but then showing total disinterest in producing or marketing those same bikes, and the Italians were an even smaller blip than the Germans on the radar of most motorcyclists. For most riders, the only real option was to buy Japanese.

The Bust

Whenever something is going well, those profiting from it convince themselves that it will go well forever. That's just human nature. The Japanese manufacturers imagined their lock on the American motorcycle market was secure. But they were wrong.

In hindsight, it makes sense. As the baby boomers grew older, many of them lost interest in the adventuresome activities they engaged in during their youth. Even if they were still interested in pursuing sports such as motorcycling, their lives were changing in ways that limited the available time they had to do so. After they graduated from college, their careers began demanding ever-increasing amounts of their time. And when they started families, those families cut into both the free time they had to ride and the amount of cash available to spend on toys like motorcycles.

You would think the motorcycle manufacturers would have seen this trend coming, but they didn't. By the time the tail end of the baby-boom generation entered the workforce in the early-to-mid–1980s, a time when the manufacturers could have logically expected a market downturn, the Japanese had instead increased production to record levels. And when the bust hit, American distributors found themselves with warehouses filled with unsold Japanese motorcycles.

Throughout most of the 1980s, the American distributors concentrated on eliminating this surplus, selling three-, four-, and even five-year-old carryover bikes at a fraction of their original cost. The cost of carrying these machines for nearly half a decade drove many dealers out of business, and the lost profits from having to sell the motorcycles below cost almost bankrupted at least one of the Japanese manufacturers.

The effects of this debacle are still felt today. Those few people who had bought motorcycles at list price during the early 1980s were not too pleased to come back to trade those machines a year or two down the road and see the exact same bikes sitting on showroom floors priced at less than half of what they paid. Not only was this insulting, it made it impossible for them to sell their own used bikes and further enhanced Japanese bikes' reputations for being "disposable motorcycles." This, in turn, made prospective buyers leery of investing in new Japanese bikes. It is only in the last few years that the Japanese motorcycle industry has regained the respect of the motorcycle-buying public.

Motorcycle Moments

While the 1980s surplus of unsold motorcycles proved an expensive mistake for the sellers of those bikes, bargain hunters had a field day. In 1985, I purchased a brand-new carryover 1982 Yamaha Seca 650, a bike that listed for $3,200 new in 1982, for $1,399 right out of the crate. Many riders still use those bargain bikes on a daily basis, racking up hundreds of thousands of miles on them.

The Risen Hog: The Resurrected Motorcycle Market

Once again, the future of the sport of motorcycling appeared uncertain, but help was coming. The cavalry was on its way, only this time it had chosen a most unlikely mount: Harley-Davidson motorcycles.

In 1981, a group of 13 senior Harley-Davidson executives purchased Harley-Davidson from AMF. Work commenced on a new engine, and the introduction of that engine, known as the *Evolution*, opened up an entirely new market for Harley-Davidson.

Prior to 1981, Harleys were still motorcycles of the old school, meaning that to own one, you had to have the mechanical acumen to overhaul the beast on the side of the road in the middle of the night with nothing but a Zippo lighter, an adjustable wrench, and an intimate familiarity with the motorcycle's internals to guide you. Harleys just were not practical, reliable machines for the majority of riders.

The Evolution engine ended that sorry state of affairs and proved to be a reliable, long-life engine. For the first time, an owner didn't have to be a grease monkey to ride a Harley.

Cycle Babble
Harley's big twin engines have always had names. Prior to the introduction of the **Evolution**, or *Evo*, these names related to the engine's appearance. The first overhead-valve big twin, introduced in 1936, was called the **Knucklehead**, because the valve covers included large nuts that looked like knuckles. This was followed by the **Panhead** in 1948, so named because the valve covers looked like upside-down cake pans. The **Shovelhead**, introduced in 1966, had valve covers that looked like shovels.

Harley's image as an unreliable, stone-age artifact prevented the new machine from gaining immediate marketplace acceptance, so to get a bit of breathing room, Harley petitioned the Reagan administration to impose a temporary tariff on imported motorcycles with engine displacements over 700 cubic centimeters.

In the end, Harley's successful comeback proved to be a blessing for everyone and contributed much to the rebounding of the industry as a whole. So successful was the new Evo engine that Harley asked the federal government to remove the tariff a year before it was originally scheduled to be lifted. By the early 1990s, Harley was selling every motorcycle it could make, with people waiting months and even years to be able to purchase one.

As you saw in Chapter 1, Harley's newfound success permeated every aspect of American culture. Soon, you could buy everything from official Harley-Davidson underwear to Harley-Davidson toilet-seat covers and Harley-Davidson cigarettes.

Ironically, the one thing that was tough to find was an actual Harley-Davidson motorcycle. Weary of the quality-control problems it had during the AMF days, Harley was careful not to expand its production beyond its capabilities.

As Harley's increasing popularity fueled a new interest in motorcycles, the lack of available Harley-Davidsons created a vacuum. Once again, the Japanese stepped up to fill this vacuum.

And once again, the baby boomers were the driving force behind this new interest in motorcycling. These were the same people who bought all those little Hondas in the 1960s, who terrorized the highways on thundering Kawasakis in the 1970s, and who spent the 1980s raising kids and making money.

Now their kids are growing up, and they once again find themselves with some free time and money on their hands. They miss the fun they used to have on their motorcycles, so they're getting back into the sport.

Today motorcycling's popularity is once again increasing. Sales for the four Japanese manufacturers—Honda, Yamaha, Kawasaki, and Suzuki—have been on the rise since 1992, Harley-Davidson sells every bike it can build, and the European manufacturers are experiencing unprecedented popularity in the United States. BMW, Ducati, and Moto Guzzi are a larger part of the American market than they ever were in the past. Triumph began producing bikes in 1991, after being out of action for nearly a decade. MZ, an Eastern European manufacturer, and Laverda, an Italian manufacturer, recently began importing bikes to the United States.

We even have some homegrown competition for Harley-Davidson for the first time since the demise of Indian. Polaris, an American manufacturer of snowmobiles and all-terrain vehicles, is introducing a large cruiser-type bike in 1998. Excelsior-Hendersen, one of the three main American motorcycle builders prior to the Great Depression, also expects to resume production in the near future.

Today's motorcyclists can select from a larger variety of motorcycles than ever before, and every one of these motorcycles provides levels of reliability and performance that were unimaginable 30 years ago. There has never been a better time to be a motorcyclist.

The Least You Need to Know

- ➤ Motorcycles have been around nearly as long as the modern safety bicycle.
- ➤ The Japanese took the sport of motorcycling to new heights of popularity with their small, non-intimidating, reliable, and fun machines.
- ➤ The fate of motorcycling since World War II has mirrored the fate of the baby-boom generation.
- ➤ The rebirth of Harley-Davidson, following the introduction of the Evolution engine, proved so strong, it helped pull the entire motorcycle industry out of an economic slump.
- ➤ Today's motorcycle buyers have more choices today than at any time since the first part of the 20th century.

Chapter 3

Street Squid or Dirt Donk? Types of Motorcycles

In This Chapter

➤ The difference between types of motorcycles

➤ Doing it in the dirt: types of dirtbikes and dual-sport bikes

➤ Which street standards are endangered species

➤ Cruisers: the ultimate American bikes

➤ Touring machines

Unlike motorcycles of the past, modern bikes are convenient transportation devices: You don't have to have legs strong enough to kick bricks out of walls or the ability to grind valves in a parking lot to ride them. But for that convenience, we had to give up something. We gave up simplicity.

Back in the bad old days, one bike pretty much served every purpose. You could buy a BSA Gold Star, for example, and use it as everyday transportation on public roads. That bike could also be adapted to dirt use, too; just remove the front fender, change the tires, and bolt on a higher pipe. And should you want to go racing, with a little work on the engine, your Gold Star could be competitive on any track in the world.

This was true of just about any motorcycle made.

Life was much simpler then. Today a new rider is confronted with a disorienting variety of motorcycle types to pick from. In this chapter, I'll show you the different types of bikes and how to choose the best type for you.

Split Personalities: Dual Sports

Many riders want to travel off the beaten path, but at the same time they need a motor-cycle they can legally drive on public roads to get to that non-beaten path. Motorcycle manufacturers have long recognized this need; that's why they make dual sports. During the 1960s and 1970s, every maker, from Yamaha to Ducati, offered *dual-purpose motorcycles*—bikes that went by names like Enduro or Suzuki's more imaginative Bearcat.

> **Cycle Babble**
> Dual-sport motorcycles (sometimes called **dual-purpose** bikes) are street-legal motorcycles with varying degrees of off-road capabilities.

These bikes were primarily road bikes with some off-road capabilities thrown in. They were a blast to ride down logging roads, and they made great commuter bikes.

As the baby boomers aged, they lost interest in these versa-tile and fun machines, and their popularity declined. But now the breed seems to be gaining in popularity once again. Each of the big four Japanese companies, as well as several European firms, manufactures some form of dual sport, as they are now called.

➤ Honda makes the XR650L, probably the most off-road-worthy of the big dual sports coming out of Japan.

➤ Kawasaki builds its KLR650, an excellent light-weight street bike that will get you down some trails, provided the going doesn't get too hairy.

➤ Splitting the difference is Suzuki's DR650, a better streetbike than the Honda and a better dirtbike than the Kawasaki.

➤ Yamaha's U.S. entry into the big dual-sport market is the XT600. A decent enough bike, this machine is not really competitive with the entries from the other Japanese manufactures.

➤ BMW's main entry in the dual-sport market is its gigantic R1100GS (which we will discuss shortly), but it also builds the terrific F650, that, while not technically a dual-sport, is at least as capable off road as Kawasaki's KLR650.

➤ KTM, a small European manufacturer, makes the 620 R/XCe, a worthy (but pricey) entry into this category.

➤ MZ recently introduced its Baghira, a dual sport that, while a bit on the heavy side for serious off-road work, is faster than just about any other single-cylinder dual sport on the street.

Any of these bikes makes an ideal first motorcycle. In addition to having varying degrees of dirt-worthiness, each makes a nimble, forgiving streetbike. They're all fantastic city bikes. Their light weight and easy handling make them excellent bikes for a learner, but their all-around capability means a rider won't outgrow them after learning to ride. (If you want to check out these and other dual sports, see Appendix A.)

Not only is Kawasaki's KLR650 the lowest priced of all the big dual-sports, it's also a terrific all-around motorcycle. (Photo courtesy Motorcyclist™ magazine)

The only drawback these bikes have is that they're tall machines. Part of the reason they work so well both on and off the road is becasue they have long-travel suspensions, which place the seat high off the pavement. While this lets riders see traffic, it also presents some challenges for those with shorter inseams.

In the last decade or so, another type of dual sport has appeared: the *leviathans*. These are large-displacement machines based on streetbikes. In a way, they're throwbacks to earlier times, when a single machine was used for all purposes.

BMW introduced the first of the leviathans in 1980, when it brought out the R80GS, an 800cc, twin-cylinder bike with high fenders and exhaust pipes. This versatile bike proved popular, especially in Europe, but it might have remained an anomaly, one of a kind, had it not been for one event—the Paris Dakar Rally.

The Paris Dakar Rally is an off-road race across thousands of miles of desert along the west coast of Africa, and it is here that the leviathans really shine. The event's popularity generated the production of Dakar-style replicas from most of the major motorcycle manufacturers.

> **Cycle Babble**
> The term **leviathan** originally referred to a Biblical sea monster, but has come to mean something of immense size and power, a good description of these big, multi-cylinder dual sports, which can weigh almost twice as much as the largest single-cylinder dual sports.

These were bikes like the original R80GS, basically streetbikes with a bit of off-road equipment, but with bodywork resembling the Dakar racers—bikes like the Ducati/Cagiva Elefant and Triumph Tiger. Honda made something called the Africa Twin, and Yamaha produced its own Dakar-style bike, the Super Tenere, but these were never imported into the United States.

Most single-cylinder dual sports have modest off-road capabilities, but these leviathans are best suited to graded dirt roads; they are just too heavy for off-road work. You probably don't want to take them up a mountain trail. But these big buggers make very good streetbikes, in part because of their long-travel suspensions, relatively light weight (at least when compared to, say, a Harley-Davidson), and nimble handling. You could do worse than to buy one.

Cruisers: The American Bikes

Choppers, customs, cruisers—whichever term you use, you are referring to a distinctly American style of motorcycle. The American landscape, both social and geographical, shaped this style of motorcycle into its present form.

As mentioned in Chapter 2, many of the restless soldiers returning from Europe and Asia after World War II chose to explore the United States on motorcycles, but the motorcycles available didn't suit them all that well. Outlaw bikers called the big Harley-Davidson touring bikes of that time "garbage wagons," because they considered all the accessories and extras mounted on them garbage. In fact, Bylaw Number 11 of the original Hell's Angels charter states: An Angel cannot wear the colors (club insignia) while riding on a garbage wagon... The first thing most outlaws did was chop off all superfluous parts, which to them was anything that didn't help the bike go faster: fenders, lights, front brakes, whatever. Hence, the term *chopper.*

Choppers like these may look cool, but by altering the supension compo-nents, owners also alter handling characteristics, often rendering the machines nearly impossible to ride. (Photo ©1998 Darwin Holmstrom)

Choppers came to symbolize the outlaw motorcycle contingent, the infamous one-per-centers. By the 1960s, these bikes had evolved into radical machines far removed from the intent of the original customized bikes, which was improved straight-line performance. Anyone seeking outright performance would ride a Japanese or British bike. Harley had long since given up the pretense of producing sporting motorcycles.

People rode Harleys to look cool, and nothing looked cooler than a Harley chopper. The extended forks and modified frames of these motorcycles made them nearly impossible to ride, but the owners didn't seem to mind. Riding a motorcycle with unsafe handling characteristics seemed to be another way of letting society know the rider didn't care if he or she lived or died.

Over the years, such machines gained in popularity—even as they declined in practicality—but manufacturers seemed not to notice. It wasn't until the 1970s, after decades of watching American riders customize their bikes, that the manufacturers got into the act and began offering custom-styled bikes.

Cycle Babble

A **chopper** once referred to a custom motorcycle that had all superfluous parts "chopped" off in order to make the bike faster. Today it refers to a type of custom that usually has an extended fork, no rear suspension, and high handlebars.

The birth of the factory custom can be in large part attributed to one man: Willie G. Davidson. Willie G., as he is known, worked in Harley's styling department, but he was also an avid motorcyclist who knew what people were doing to their bikes. One popular customizing technique was to take the fork off of a Sportster and graft it onto a stripped-down big-twin frame, so Willie G. did just that at the factory. The result was the original Super Glide.

The Super Glide model, offered in 1971, was not a screaming success, due in part to a funky boat-like rear fender (known as the *Night Train* fender). The next year, Harley gave the bike a more conventional rear fender and sold thousands of Super Glides.

Harley wasn't the only company working on a custom-styled bike. The British manufacturer Norton also developed a cruiser in the early 1970s. Unfortunately, its cruiser, the ungainly High Rider, wasn't well received. The bike only contributed to the company's eventual demise.

Kawasaki was the first Japanese company to test the factory-chopper waters, introducing its KZ900LTD in 1976. The bike featured pull-back buckhorn handlebars, a teardrop-shaped gas tank, a seat with a pronounced step between the rider and passenger portion, and a liberal dousing of chrome plating. These bikes forced the rider into a backward-leaning riding position (raising unbridled hell with his or her lower back), but otherwise, they were still functional, useful machines.

As the decade progressed, the Japanese stuck to this formula. This approach had a limited future; the real future of cruisers was being forged elsewhere, by Willie G.

Two of Willie G.'s creations in particular proved to be the models for today's cruisers: the Low Rider, introduced in 1977, and the Wide Glide of 1980. Study these bikes, and you'll see elements of every cruiser now produced. The bobbed fender of the Wide Glide can be found on cruisers from Honda, Suzuki, and Kawasaki. The kicked-out front end and sculpted fenders of the Low Rider hint at the shape of Yamaha's Virago. These two bikes are arguably the most influential factory customs of all time.

Harley-Davidson's original Super Glide, with its fiberglass "Night Train" rear fender, was a sales failure when introduced, but today original examples command a premium price. (Photo ©1998 Darwin Holmstrom)

What of the Japanese? As the 1980s progressed, Japanese manufacturers got closer and closer to building motorcycles that looked like Harley-Davidsons. But they have taken cruiser styling in new directions, too. Honda now builds its Valkyrie, a massive, six-cylinder cruiser. Yamaha's Royal Star looks as much like a classic Indian motorcycle as it does a Harley-Davidson. And BMW's cruiser, the R1200C, doesn't resemble any other motorcycle on the planet. (See Appendix A to get a good look at these bikes.)

This segment of the market is thriving, and for good reason: Cruisers are easy bikes to live with. Many of them are nearly maintenance-free. They look good, and when outfitted with a windshield, are comfortable out on the road. They may not handle as well as sportbikes, nor haul as much gear as touring bikes, but in many ways, they fulfill the role of a standard, all-around motorcycle. Many riders don't ride a motorcycle to get from point A to point B as quickly as possible. They just like to ride. If that describes you, you might be cruiser material.

Harley's Wide Glide was one of the most influential cruisers ever built. Just about every cruiser now being produced displays some elements of Wide Glide styling. (Photo courtesy Motorcyclist™ magazine)

Sportbikes

If, on the other hand, you are not the laid-back, easy-rider type, you might be interested in something with a little more sporting capability. Well, you are definitely in the right place at the right time; the range of sporting motorcycles available has never been better.

When British bikes began to appear in the United States in appreciable numbers following World War II, it became obvious that while Harleys may be faster in a straight line, the British models could run circles around a Harley when the road began to wind. This gave the British a reputation as producers of highly-sporting motorcycles. The British managed to maintain this reputation until the early 1970s, with bikes like Norton's 850 Commando.

When the Japanese began producing large, four-cylinder motorcycles, these became the new leaders in straight-line performance. The term *Universal Japanese Motorcycles* (UJMs) was coined to describe them.

While they were wicked-fast, most UJMs of the 1970s did not handle all that well, mostly because of inferior suspension components and flimsy frames. They out-handled Harleys (which tended to be about as nimble as a freight train), but they could not keep up with a properly-functioning Norton Commando.

The real breakthrough in the development of sportbikes from Japan was Honda's 750cc Interceptor, introduced for the 1983-model year. This bike, with its revolutionary V-four engine, was Japan's first purpose-built sporting motorcycle.

The Interceptor revolutionized sportbikes. It started off a technology war between the Japanese manufacturers that still continues to this day. Kawasaki brought out its original 900 Ninja, a bike in many ways as groundbreaking as the Interceptor. Yamaha introduced its five-valve FZ 750, a bike so influential that Ferrari adopted some of its technology for its cars. And Suzuki blew the world away by introducing its GSX-R series, bikes that really were racers with headlights.

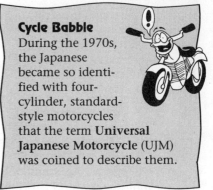

Cycle Babble
Sportbikes are motorcycles designed to handle well at high speeds. Out-of-control sportbike riders are sometimes called **squids**.

Cycle Babble
During the 1970s, the Japanese became so identified with four-cylinder, standard-style motorcycles that the term **Universal Japanese Motorcycle** (UJM) was coined to describe them.

The Italians are another prominent force in the sportbike scene. When they started building large-displacement sportbikes in the 1970s, bikes like Moto Guzzi's V7 Sport and Ducati's 750SS, the Italians raised the ceiling on riders' expectations from their machines. While never exported in numbers large enough to become a real presence in the American market, these bikes influenced the direction sporting motorcycles would take.

Today's sportbikes cover nearly the entire spectrum. Yamaha's YZF 600, while being a more capable sporting motorcycle than the pure race bikes of just a few years ago, is so comfortable and versatile, it could almost be considered a sport-tourer. Suzuki's latest generation of GSX-R has such high-performance limits that only a few experienced riders can ever approach them. The razor-sharp handling of Ducati's 916 is just slightly removed from that of the bike Carl Fogarty won two World Superbike Championships on. And the next generation of sportbikes looks like it will raise current standards even higher.

Pure Dirt

The motorcycles manufactured for purely off-road use today tend toward the extreme end of the motorcycle spectrum. These are machines like the screaming race bikes leaping through the air in arenas around the country during Supercross races.

These bikes usually don't make good beginner bikes. In fact, many of them are intended as strictly racing machines. Almost all of them have two-stroke engines, which means that you will have to mix oil into your gas before you fill your tank, which is a messy, time-consuming process. And inconvenient, should you find yourself miles from home without a can in which to mix fuel.

> **Cycle Babble**
> Dirtbikes are machines intended for off-road use and aren't legal to ride on public roads. Sometimes the term **pure-dirt** is used to distinguish a dirtbike from a dual-sport motorcycle. Dirtbike riders are sometimes referred to as **dirt donks**.

Adding to this inconvenience is the fact that pure-dirt bikes aren't legal to ride on public roads.

Dirtbikes also feature an extremely abrupt power delivery. When the engine starts, it unleashes a whole bunch of horsepower in a most-surprising fashion. Riders inexperienced in handling these machines commonly suffer from broken bones in their hands. This is because the power catches the rider by surprise, causing the bike to flip over backward, crushing his or her hands with the handlebars. I've seen it happen more than once.

There are alternative bikes available for those who want to do serious off-road riding. The bikes I'm referring to are four-stroke trailbikes (you'll look at four-stroke engines in Chapter 5, "Anatomy of a Motorcycle"). Honda has long been a proponent of such motorcycles, and its XR series (not to be confused with the XR-L series—this gets confusing) offers terrific alternatives. Yamaha has also jumped on the four-stroke bandwagon with its YZF400 and WR400.

With four-stroke dirtbikes, you won't have to premix fuel, plus you'll find that they have smooth, easily-controllable power. Unless your ultimate goal is to race, and you have some familiarity with off-road riding, these bikes may make a better choice for your first dirtbike.

Probably the biggest disadvantage of a pure-dirt motorcycle is that it's not legal to drive on public roads (hence the term *pure-dirt*). This means you'll have to transport the machine from your garage to the place you intend to ride—for example, in a pickup truck or a trailer. These bikes don't meet the emissions or noise requirements for street legal vehicles, nor do they have the electrical equipment, like turn signals and horns, required in most states. In some states, it is possible to manipulate the legal system enough to license an off-road bike for use on public roads, but by doing so, you may be setting yourself up for future legal problems.

Street Standards: An Endangered Species

Because Japanese motorcycles were so influential to motorcyclists who entered the sport in the 1960s and 1970s, the look of these bikes became imprinted in our psyches as the way a motorcycle should look.

These were pretty basic bikes: Back then, function dictated form. The gas tank sat above the engine to allow the gas to run down into the carburetors. The way the human body bends pretty much dictated the placement of the rest of the parts.

As motorcycles became more specialized in the 1980s, the look of motorcycles changed. Motorcyclists were so excited by new developments that we didn't realize we were losing something in the process. Then one day in the late 1980s, we realized that the basic bike no longer existed. Motorcyclists began complaining about this situation, and soon the Japanese designed bikes that embodied the virtues of those older models.

Unfortunately, while the inclusion of the older styling features contributed to a retro look for these new machines, it also detracted from their overall versatility. Suzuki and Kawasaki were the first to come to the market with standard motorcycles. Kawasaki's entrance into this new/old market segment was the Zephyr 550, a four-cylinder UJM-type bike introduced for the 1990 model year. The bike did not sell well in the United States. Very few of these machines found their way to the public highways, and they were soon dropped from Kawasaki's lineup.

Suzuki's entrant, the VX800 of the same year, did slightly better in the market. This was a full-sized, competent machine that fulfilled the promise of the versatile standard. In fact, it is a bike I highly recommend, whether to a beginner or a long-time motorcyclist. But it was never a sales dynamo and was imported to U.S. shores for only four years.

Neither Kawasaki nor Suzuki gave up on the concept of standard bikes after the lukewarm reception of their initial efforts. Kawasaki imported increasingly larger Zephyrs, but they came with increasingly larger price tags. None of the Zephyr series offered anything a rider couldn't find in a used GPz 900 Ninja—and for a fraction of the Zephyr's price.

Motorcycle Moments

After failing to sell many Zephyrs, Kawasaki tried to capitalize on the appeal of its original 900 Ninja, a groundbreaking motorcycle when introduced in 1984, by bringing out the GPz 1100 in 1995. This very good (and reasonably priced) motorcycle also failed to find buyers, probably because as good as it was, it still wasn't any better than the original.

Suzuki, in an attempt to recapture the sales success it had enjoyed with its big GS series of the 1970s and 1980s, brought out the GSX1100G, a big, 1980s-style standard with a modern, single-shock rear suspension. On paper, the Suzuki fulfilled every requirement those clamoring for standard bikes claimed to need from a bike.

But the GSX was even less successful than the VX. The reason probably involved the bike's appearance. At the risk of offending loyal GSX riders, many people considered the bike to be goofy-looking. One magazine wag even suggested they take the coloring crayon away from the designer who conceived the machine. (For the record, I kind of like the bike's look, if you get rid of the screwy high-rise handlebars and clean up the busy-looking front end.)

Honda was the first Japanese manufacturer to find relative success in the standard bike market, with its Nighthawk CB750. Here was a bike that offered the versatility UJMs were known for and looked good doing it. Perhaps the factor that contributed most to the bike's success was its low price. In this case, you really did get your money's worth.

Cycle Babble
The devices mounted at the front of a motorcycle to protect the rider from the elements are called **fairings**. These range from simple, Plexiglas shields mounted to the handlebars to complex, encompassing body panels that shroud the entire front half of the bike. Bikes without any type of fairing are known as **naked bikes**.

These were, and still are, great values for the money. My wife bought one of these bikes as her first full-sized motorcycle, and one of my greatest regrets is selling that bike.

While the Nighthawk was the first modern Japanese standard to hold its own in the marketplace, it never set any kind of sales records. It seemed the standard might once again disappear from the market, had a couple of manufacturers not rethought the concept.

First Yamaha introduced the Seca II 600. At first glance, this nimble, fun bike might not be considered a standard, since it included a small, frame-mounted *fairing* (a device that protects riders from the elements).

But riders didn't care; the fairing just added to the bike's practicality. It seemed that being naked (without fairing) was not a prerequisite for a standard. Suzuki also realized this and brought out its Bandit series. These bikes are comfortable motorcycles that incorporate the best technology available, a useful fairing, and a reasonable price. So far, they have been sales successes.

Suzuki finally got the modern standard formula right with its successful Bandit series. (Photo courtesy Motorcyclist™ magazine)

The Ultimate Behemoths: Touring Bikes

Another category of specialized motorcycle to appear over the last several decades is the purpose-built *touring bike*, a bike equipped for longer rides on the road.

Harley started this trend by offering a fairing and luggage as optional equipment on its Electra Glide back in the 1960s, but other companies were slow to pick up on the trend.

In the late 1970s, BMW introduced its first factory *dresser* (the preferred name for a touring bike), the R100RT, a bike that met with market success.

Honda had been producing a bike specifically for touring: the Gold Wing. In time, Honda began offering fairings and luggage as accessories, but these were still add-on parts, equipment for which the machines hadn't been specifically designed.

Other companies offered touring packages for their standard bikes, too, but there's a problem with this approach: Accessories affect the handling of a machine, often adversely. Large fairings and luggage can really make a bike get squirrelly.

Yamaha decided to make its mark on the touring-bike market and in 1983 introduced the Venture, Japan's first bike designed from the ground up to have an

> **Cycle Babble**
> A **touring bike** is a bike equipped for longer rides with fairings and lockable saddle bags. While early bikers looked on motorcycles equipped for touring with scorn, calling them **garbage wagons**, over time they began to see their appeal. They began to refer to garbage wagons as **baggers** and finally **dressers**, the term many Harley riders use today.

integrated fairing and luggage. The approach of designing a machine from the ground up with this much bodywork produced a seamless motorcycle and sent Honda back to the drawing board.

Honda did not like being sent back to the drawing board, and when it returned, it did so with a vengeance. The 1984 Gold Wing 1200 set new standards in functionality and comfort. The Gold Wing 1500, a six-cylinder behemoth introduced for the 1988 model year, blew away even its predecessor. The Gold Wing proved to be such a perfect touring machine that the other Japanese manufacturers simply gave up trying to compete in that market segment.

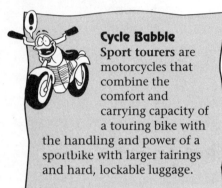

Cycle Babble

Sport tourers are motorcycles that combine the comfort and carrying capacity of a touring bike with the handling and power of a sportbike with larger fairings and hard, lockable luggage.

The success of the Gold Wing has meant that the ultimate-behemoth class of touring bikes has seen relatively little change over the past decade, but there have been some exciting developments in other types of touring motorcycles during that time, especially in the *sport-touring* segment of the market. Sport tourers combine the comfort and carrying capacity of a touring bike with the handling and excitement of a sportbike. You can think of these machines as sportbikes with larger fairings and hard, lockable luggage.

This class existed for a long time without having a proper name; in fact, almost every BMW built in the last quarter of the century falls into this group.

Although the term "sport touring" is fairly new, BMW has been building such bikes for decades.

Kawasaki produced the first purpose-built Japanese sport tourer with its Concours, introduced in 1986. Honda followed suit, bringing out its ST1100 in 1991. Over on the other side of the world, manufacturers like Ducati and Triumph also offer BMW competition in the sport-touring arena.

These bikes represent a compromise, giving up a bit of sporting capability to the smaller, more agile sportbikes while sacrificing some luggage-carrying capability when compared to the ultimate behemoths. It seems a compromise many riders are willing to make. If you like to crank up the throttle in corners and cover huge expanses of geography in a single sitting, but you don't need to carry everything you own with you on a trip, these bikes may be a good compromise for you, too.

Lately, the *touring cruiser*, another subcategory of touring bike, has also been developed. The touring-cruiser bikes combine the looks of cruisers with the functionality of touring bikes. With their windshields and hard luggage, they are more comfortable and convenient than cruisers, yet they retain the American look that makes cruisers so popular.

The Least You Need to Know

➤ Dual-sport motorcycles make excellent all-around bikes, especially for beginners.

➤ Cruiser styling reflects the unique tastes and needs of American motorcyclists.

➤ Sportbikes are high-performance motorcycles designed to go fast and handle well. They usually have full-coverage bodywork and cramped riding positions, although there are some exceptions.

➤ Pure-dirt bikes look like dual-sports but are designed strictly for off-road use—and illegal to ride on the street.

➤ Standard-style motorcycles are characterized by comfortable riding positions and minimal body work.

➤ Touring bikes are (usually) large motorcycles with fairings, hard, lockable luggage, and other touring amenities.

Part 2
So You Want to Buy a Bike...

Now comes the most exciting part of your entire adventure: getting your first bike. There's nothing quite like going out to the garage and seeing a new bike parked inside. It's fun just to go out and look at it, admire its combination of form and function. You'll soon be able to visualize its details, the curves in its bodywork, the way it smells when you park it after a ride on a warm summer day. You'll grow to recognize the slight ticking sound as the oil cools when you shut the engine off. The machine will become a part of you.

But your first bike will be as demanding as it is exciting. To keep your bike in the condition you brought it home in, you'll need to have a basic understanding of its mechanical nature.

And just buying a bike in the first place can be a traumatic event. Like any form of commerce, people sell motorcycles to make money, and if you walk into a dealership unprepared, you will be their cash cow.

In this part of the book, you'll learn what kind of bike is right for you, what that bike is made of, how different bikes work, how to buy your first motorcycle without getting ripped off, and what extra gear you'll need after you buy the bike.

Choosing the Right Bike

You are about to enter into a relationship with a mechanical object unlike any you have had before. Owning a motorcycle is a much more intimate experience than owning a car or pickup truck, perhaps because you meld into the machine when you ride, your body encasing the mechanical heart of the bike. You become part of the machine. You ride just inches away from the engine, the source of your bike's power, and you feel and hear the internal-combustion event more directly than is possible in an enclosed vehicle.

And you control the direction in which you travel with your body, leading the bike down the road with your own movements just as you would lead a dance partner. This provides a much more immediate experience than sitting inside a glass bubble, turning a steering wheel vaguely connected to some invisible mechanism.

Given the nature of this intimate relationship, it is vital that you choose the right partner. With the dizzying array of motorcycles available, choosing that partner might seem daunting at this stage, but it's really not as confusing as it might seem. You don't have to know every detail of every bike ever made; you only need to know yourself and your own needs.

What Do You Want to Do?

Before you select a type of bike, first you need to determine what kind of riding you want to do (as discussed in Chapter 3). If you have no interest in riding on public roads, if you just want a bike to ride through the swamps and forests, you should probably consider getting a strictly off-road dirtbike.

But you will probably want something you can ride on the road. Riding off-road is great fun, but by getting a bike that is not street-legal, you cut off a lot of your future options. Unless you already have friends who are into serious off-road riding, you'll probably want a machine you can legally ride to the local hangout to visit old friends and make new ones.

Or maybe you don't give a rip about riding off-road. You might have visions of riding through corners on a high-performance sportbike, leaned over so far your knees skim the surface of the asphalt. Or perhaps you envision yourself making epic road trips aboard the biggest touring rig available. Maybe you dream of conquering the jungles on a dual-sport machine.

On the other hand, you may not even know what you want out of a bike just yet.

Whether you know exactly what you want out of the sport or you are still trying to figure that out, it's best to keep your options open. Just because you want to see the world doesn't mean you have to buy an ultimate-behemoth luxo-tourer. And just because you want to be the next speed racer doesn't mean you have to buy the bike that won at Daytona this year.

While bikes have grown increasingly more specialized over the last 15 years, they still remain remarkably versatile machines.

Any bike can be a tourer if you take it on a trip. I've put 1,000-mile days on a hard-edged sportbike. I've traveled the entire United States on a big V-twin cruiser. My wife once rode a 500cc thumper from the Canadian border to Mexico and back.

And in the right hands, any bike can be a sportbike. While riding an 18-year-old, 650cc Japanese bike, I've shown my tail to testosterone-crazed *squids* (sportbike racers) on the latest sporting hardware. And while riding a modern sportbike, I've been embarrassed on a twisty road by an old dude on a Harley that was older than I was.

While any bike can be used for nearly any purpose, there is a reason certain types of motorcycles are used for certain tasks more frequently than others. I still suffer from wrist problems from touring on a sportbike, and my wife bought a larger bike within weeks of returning from her trip on the thumper. And that guy who smoked me on his old Harley would probably love riding a modern sportbike, if he ever tried one.

Choosing a Versatile Motorcycle

You might think you know what you want to do before you start riding, but after you've been at it a while, you might discover an interest in an entirely different form of riding.

You might get a Harley Sportster thinking you'll only use it to ride to the lake on the weekends, for example, and then develop an itch to ride to the farthest corners of North America.

That's why it's a good idea to get as versatile a motorcycle as possible for your first bike. As I said in Chapter 3, the big dual sports are about as versatile as a bike can get. They can handle unpaved roads and worse, and they can be set up for touring.

However, you might not be interested in this type of bike. You might be turned off by the looks of the machine. Another disadvantage of the dual-sport bikes is their height: They are tall machines. While sitting up high is an advantage, because it lets you see over traffic (and, more important, helps other drivers see you), it presents some challenges to those with shorter inseams. To fit on one, you need to be of at least average height, or you may find these bikes a bit of a handful in stop-and-go traffic.

Suzuki's DR650SE is an example of a dual-sport. This popular, versatile bike was voted "Best Dual-Sport Single" by Motor-cyclist™ in 1996 and 1997. (Photo courtesy Motorcy-clist™ magazine)

If dual sports aren't your thing, that doesn't mean you're out of luck. There are many versatile pure-street bikes to choose from, too.

Browse Appendix A, "Biker's Buying Guide to New Bikes," to learn more about the many types of dual-sport or pure-street bikes that might be right for you.

Getting a Good Fit

A big factor in versatility is comfort. If you are comfortable on a bike, you can ride it harder and farther. And different bodies fit on different bikes. You can't really tell by looking at it if a bike is going to fit you, either. For example, I fit nicely on Yamaha's YZF 600 and could ride one from coast to coast without needing wrist surgery. But Honda's

CBR600F3 puts my hands to sleep within minutes. Yet a new rider would be hard-pressed to see a noticeable difference between the two bikes if they were parked side by side, and many other riders find the Honda just as comfortable as the Yamaha.

Cycle Babble
The science of **ergonomics**, or human engineering, is used to design devices (including everything from cars to chairs) that conform to the human body. Ergonomics is a prime consideration when designing motorcycles; the idea is to provide maximum efficiency while keeping operator fatigue to a minimum.

Motorcycle *ergonomics*—the science of designing motorcycles that conform to the human body—receives much attention in the motorcycling press these days. Ergonomic considerations influence all aspects of motorcycle design, from the riding position to the placement of the controls, which in turn contributes to the overall versatility of a motorcycle. The better a motorcycle fits you, the more comfortable you will be. The more comfortable you are, the more useful your motorcycle will be.

Because choosing a motorcycle is as much an emotional process as it is an intellectual one, in the end, only you will know what type of motorcycle will be right for you. But once you've selected a type of bike, getting a versatile bike that fits your body will make your entire motorcycle experience much more rewarding. (I'll talk more about trying out and buying bikes in Chapter 7, "Buying Your First Bike.")

Starting Out Small

Probably the most common mistake new riders make when choosing their first bike is buying a bike that's too large for them to learn to ride easily.

Cycle Babble
Using the handlebar as a lever to lean the bike into a turn is called **countersteering**, because you do it backward: If you want to turn right, you push the handlebars to the left. This makes the motorcycle lean to the right, which in turn makes the bike move to the right.

I'll discuss the basics of riding in Chapter 10, "Preparing to Hit the Road," but I'd like to explain a little about how motorcycles work here so you'll understand this important point. By nature, motorcycles are unstable vehicles: If you don't hold them up some way, they fall over. When you ride, your bike is held up by its own inertia; its spinning tires create gravitational energy.

But anytime your motorcycle is not traveling in a perfectly straight line, its weight shifts around in a manner you may be totally unused to. When traveling, a motorcycle doesn't follow its front wheels around a corner like a car does; instead, the bike leans around corners, rotating around a central axis, much like an airplane.

Because of this, you don't steer a motorcycle the way you drive a car. Instead, you *countersteer* it, using the handlebar to lever the motorcycle into a lean and initiate a turn.

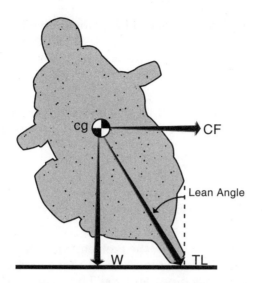

Rather than turning like a car, motorcycles lean into a turn rotating on the machine's central axis like an airplane.

The point I'm trying to make here is that on the road, motorcycles move around a lot, in weird ways. This takes some getting used to, even on a lightweight motorcycle. On a heavier bike, this can be so disconcerting, it scares a new rider into never learning to steer the motorcycle properly.

The people who seem to run into the most trouble are those who choose a heavyweight cruiser or a big touring motorcycle for their first bike.

Perhaps it's a Freudian thing, but size seems to be some sort of a status symbol for cruiser riders. As a popular T-shirt slogan says, *Size does matter*. Unfortunately, for a new rider, it matters in a negative way.

For one thing, the heavy weight makes the motorcycle tend to ride in a straight line, even when you attempt to negotiate a turn. The more bike weight you have, the more you have to wrestle the machine through every turn. In addition, excessive weight can be especially problematic in cruisers because of certain handling characteristics common to the breed. Because of the steering geometry required to give cruisers their chopper-like look, they tend not to be the best-handling bikes on the road. To many novice riders, the bikes feel as if they are going to flop over. This feeling is unsettling enough for an experienced rider; it's a distraction a novice does not need.

Trying to master a large touring bike is also usually a mistake for a novice. I've seen the enthusiasm of a lot of new riders nipped in the bud after they bought an ultimate behemoth-type touring bike before they were ready. When you get in over your head on one of these machines, their heavy weight is going to hurt you. When things start to go wrong on an 800-pound motorcycle, they go wrong fast.

We all fall into the "bigger is better" trap. For years, I rode a Honda ST1100, a 700-pounder and one of the finest sport-touring motorcycles in the world. I enjoyed it so much, I may never have ridden anything else, had fate not intervened. A balloon payment coming due on my condo forced me to sell the big ST1100 and get a small, cheap motorcycle. I missed the big Honda, but in the process, I rediscovered the pleasure of riding a small, nimble motorcycle. Now, if I were forced to only have one bike, I would choose a lightweight sporty motorcycle over a larger machine.

But you can go to the other extreme, too. While selecting a motorcycle that is too large can ruin your enthusiasm for the sport, if you select one that is too small, you will soon outgrow the bike.

Starting Out Slow

New sportbike riders tend not to have weight-related problems, because sportbikes are light, maneuverable motorcycles.

While they are not physically large machines, the problem with sportbikes has to do with power—specifically, the fact that they have too much of it for a novice rider. Grab a handful of throttle on one of these machines, and you'll be traveling at over 100 miles per hour before your brain even has a chance to register your change in velocity. The slowest of these bikes is a wicked-fast machine, and before you buy one for your first bike, you should honestly assess your self-control. These bikes present a challenge for even the most experienced rider; for a beginner, they are expensive forms of suicide.

Best Bets for New Bikers

So the trick is to find the right compromise: a bike small and safe enough to learn to ride, but competent enough to keep up with you as your skills grow. There are machines in each bike category that fulfill these requirements. As I mentioned earlier, any of the dual sports makes a great first bike, if you physically fit it and like its style. And most of the standard-style motorcycles are easy to learn to ride, and you can live with them for a very long time. Most of these bikes have high sporting capabilities, too, should you find yourself drawn to sportbikes.

The middleweight cruiser class teems with good choices for a first bike, if your taste runs toward custom-style motorcycles. Just about any of the 500cc–800cc cruisers are bikes you will enjoy riding for a long time.

If you're adamant about getting a Harley-Davidson for your first bike, things can get a bit sticky. The big twins are physically large bikes and will probably be uncomfortable for most novice riders. They also cost as much as most new cars.

Harley makes its Sportster series for people looking for a bike smaller than a big twin. While these attractive motorcycles represent good values for the money, they have some inherent drawbacks that limit their usefulness as all-around motorcycles.

Harley's ultimate behemoth, the Electra Glide Ultra Classic ($18,065), shown on the left, dwarfs Harley's entry-level bike, the 883 Sportster ($5,245). (Photos courtesy Motorcyclist™ *magazine)*

Because Sportsters have solidly-mounted engines (which I'll discuss in Chapter 6, "Start Your Engines"), the bikes shake worse than any other motorcycle you can buy. Period. At freeway speeds, this becomes a serious problem. As if that weren't bad enough, the heat generated by the rear cylinder will roast your inner thighs on a warm day. For these reasons, Sportsters are best suited for short trips around town.

If you hanker to see the world on your bike, you're in luck, even if you're a beginner. Any bike that fits you and has enough power to keep up with traffic can be outfitted for touring. You can tour on a dual sport, standard, cruiser, or sporty bike; you don't need an ultimate behemoth. Don't get me wrong; the big touring bikes are fantastic machines. I own one myself and use it more than any other bike. They are just too heavy for a novice rider.

New or Used?

Once you've selected a type of motorcycle, you need to decide whether you want to buy a new bike or a used one.

Price is probably the prime determining factor in this decision. If money is no object, you can just waltz into a dealership and buy any bike that strikes your fancy. You can buy two or three of them if you're that well off, so you don't even have to make any choices.

But most of us have to make prudent decisions when it comes to expenditures, especially when it comes to spending money on recreational activities like motorcycling. If you're on a budget, buying a used bike can be a wise decision.

We will go into the details of buying a used bike in Chapter 7, "Buying Your First Bike." In general, though, modern motorcycles are pretty tough to destroy, and unless the previous owner really went out of his or her way to trash the thing, most used bikes are in fairly good condition. This is especially true of motorcycles that appeal to more mature riders, such as touring bikes, cruisers, and standards. It is less true of sportbikes, which tend to lead harder lives than other types of motorcycles. Dual sports can go either way. They are usually in fair condition, unless the owner has attempted to do serious off-road riding on them.

Motorcycology
We won't discuss buying used off-road motorcycles, since these are primarily race bikes, or bikes that have been ridden by expert riders under extremely stressful conditions. If you choose to purchase a used off-road motorcycle, you should be prepared to entirely rebuild it.

Motorcycology
As I write this, I already see signs that the used Harley market has peaked. The same day I saw the used Sportster advertised in the newspaper for $13,000, I saw the identical machine sitting on my local Harley dealer's showroom floor. With a few accessories added by the dealer, the list price was $8,900. If the individual advertising the bike for $13,000 managed to sell his machine for that price, he deserves the extra $4,000 for his marketing skills.

One disadvantage of buying a used bike is that you are never quite certain what you are getting. Another disadvantage of buying used is that you don't usually get a warranty. I'll show you how to minimize your risks in Chapter 7.

But given the reliable nature of modern bikes, these disadvantages are fairly insignificant. The advantage of buying used is that used bikes are less expensive than new ones. This is especially true of Japanese motorcycles, which historically have had fairly poor resale value. For example, Kawasaki's 1998 Ninja 500R retails for $4,999. At that price, the little Ninja represents one of the best values in motorcycling. But you can find a used fixer-upper for as little as $1,000. Nice, clean, used models can be found for as little as $1,500 to $2,000. These bikes may be 10 years old or more, but they are the same basic motorcycle as the new model.

Harley-Davidsons prove the exception. Because people have been waiting months or even years to buy new Harleys, the used market has gone insane. I recently saw a 1998 Sportster 1200 Custom, a bike that lists for $8,700, advertised in a newspaper for $13,000. A premium of $4,300 is quite a price to pay for being impatient. I strongly recommend waiting to buy a new one, given the current market climate.

Fortunately for buyers (and unfortunately for those looking to turn a quick buck), that climate seems to be changing. The current market boom, caused by demand exceeding supply, appears to be waning. Harley plans to step up production dramatically over the next few years. This means the future supply of new Harleys will meet demand. Already, you can find new Harleys sitting for sale on showroom floors, a situation unheard of a couple of years ago. When supply and demand equalize, only a fool would pay more for a used bike than a new bike.

While buying a used bike may make the most sense from a pure dollars-and-cents point of view, buying a new bike has its advantages, too. When you buy a new bike, you get a warranty. While the odds of a modern bike breaking down are slim, it does happen, and when it does, that warranty is nice to have.

Another benefit of buying a new bike is that it can be easier to finance. Often the dealer will be able to finance the machine, saving you the hassle of procuring financing yourself. And many manufacturers offer attractive low-interest financing packages.

Buying a new bike frees you from some of the worries of buying a used bike. Knowing the machine's complete history has certain benefits. When you are a bike's only owner, you can break it in properly yourself, and you know the bike has been properly maintained.

Plus, there's the intangible benefit of riding a brand-new motorcycle. There's nothing quite like the feeling of riding away from a dealership on your brand-new bike.

The Costs of Cycling

The most obvious (and largest) cost of motorcycling is the cost of the bike itself. New streetbikes range from a low of around $3,000 for a Kawasaki 250 Ninja to a high of almost $23,000 for a Bimota SB8R. Most new bikes will fall into the $5,000–$10,000 range.

Used bike prices can vary even more than new bike prices. I'll tell you where to find price references for specific bikes in Chapter 7, "Buying Your First Bike," but expect to spend at least $2,500–$5,000 for a good used motorcycle (unless you're a skilled bargain hunter).

No matter what type of bike you buy, or whether you buy new or used, you will find some unexpected costs. Some of these costs, like buying insurance, will become apparent soon after you write the check for the bike. Others, like the cost of basic maintenance, will rear their ugly heads only after you've racked up a few miles.

These costs aren't obvious to a new rider, and a little knowledge ahead of time can influence your choice of a bike. As you will learn, that choice will in turn influence those hidden costs.

Insurance Costs

Some insurance companies simply will not insure a motorcycle. Those that do usually use a completely arbitrary method of determining insurance premiums based on engine displacement. Basically, the smaller your engine, the lower your insurance costs are likely to be, and any bodywork will add to your premium. This may seem logical to someone who knows absolutely nothing about bikes, but once you understand more about engines (which I'll discuss in Chapter 6), you'll realize that engine size means little.

But that's the way things are, so it's a good idea to take insurance costs into account when selecting a motorcycle. Check insurance prices in your area before buying a bike. Rates for the same bike from the same company can double from one location to the next. For example, my wife, who has a spotless driving record, paid about $260 per year for full-coverage insurance on her Honda ST1100 when she lived in North Dakota. When she moved to Minneapolis, her insurance premiums (using the same policy) doubled, shooting up to nearly $600 per year.

Maintenance Costs

Even less obvious than insurance costs are maintenance costs. While modern bikes don't require an annual overhaul like many older models do, they still require more mainte-nance than most cars. This is partly because motorcycles are so technologically advanced.

Motorcycle designers have to use sophisticated mechanisms to get a relatively small motorcycle engine to generate so much power. Thus, these engines require more routine maintenance than less highly-stressed engines. Add in the other procedures your bike will require, such as carburetion adjustments and chain and tire replacements (which I'll discuss in Chapter 17, "Rx: Repair"), and you can expect to fork out some serious cash for tune-ups over the years.

And if you don't do your own basic maintenance and instead take your bike in for things such as oil and tire changes, you can add a significant amount to your overall total. But there are some things you can do to minimize these expenses. The less you abuse your motorcycle in general, the less money you will have to spend maintaining it.

The Least You Need to Know

➤ The perfect bike for one rider may be ill-suited for the next rider.

➤ When choosing a type of bike, consider the type of riding you want to do, the versatility of the bike, and the comfort of the bike.

➤ While a big bike may impress your buddies, it may also hamper your growth as a motorcyclist.

➤ There are valid reasons for choosing to buy either a new bike or a used bike. Used bikes are generally cheaper than new bikes and can be in good enough condition to ride; however, new bikes often come with financing and warranties and are in perfect condition when you buy them.

➤ Different types and sizes of motorcycles have different hidden costs, such as the cost of insurance and the cost of maintenance.

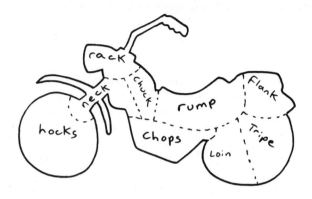

rack
neck
chuck
Flank
rump
hocks
chops
Tripe
Loin

Chapter 5

Anatomy of a Motorcycle

In This Chapter

➤ Understanding the mechanical bits that make your bike tick

➤ How the top and bottom end of the engine make your motorcycle go

➤ How the carburetor and induction system work

➤ The importance of the frame, wheels, and tires

➤ The uses of bodywork

Many riders love motorcycles for their elegant lines, lines disrupted by the least-possible amount of mechanical components. Yet the simple appearance of the motorcycle belies a complex mechanical system, or rather, set of systems.

In *Zen and the Art of Motorcycle Maintenance*, author Robert M. Persig writes that it is a mistake to see the motorcycle as simply a collection of parts. Rather, he describes motorcycles as a collection of ideas, and he describes working on bikes as "…working on concepts." He writes: "That's all a motorcycle is, a system of concepts worked out in steel."

To get a complete understanding of a motorcycle, you'll need a little mechanical background, a basic understanding of Persig's "system of concepts." In this chapter, I'll give you a guided tour of the inner workings of a bike.

The Nature of the Beast

Motorcycles are mechanical devices. Bikes that have tried to hide their mechanical nature have usually failed to win over the motorcycling public. Philip Vincent, founder of the

Vincent-HRD motorcycle company, discovered this in 1954 when he tried to sell versions of his magnificent Vincent motorcycles cloaked in fiberglass bodywork. The failure of the Black Prince and Black Knight helped seal Vincent's fate, and the last Vincent motorcycle was constructed at Vincent's Stevenage factory in 1955.

Subsequent fully-enclosed motorcycles have fared little better than the Vincent. Ducati marketed a fully enclosed series of bikes, the Pasos and 907 I.E., in the late 1980s and early 1990s, but these never set motorcycle buyers on fire. As a result, Ducati now offers several models with small half *fairings* (the devices mounted at the front of a motorcycle to protect the rider from the elements) or no fairings at all to better showcase its engines. Honda tested the market for shrink-wrapped bikes when it introduced the Pacific Coast in 1989. This model did so poorly that it was withdrawn from the market; it was such a competent all-around motorcycle, though, that it rose from the dead and is now back in production.

Other designers learned from the lack of success of these bikes, and newer designs, like the recent wave of sporting twins from Japan, highlight rather than hide their engines. Motorcyclists appreciate a bike's mechanical nature, and any biker worth his or her leather jacket is well-versed in the anatomy of a motorcycle.

Meeting the Motor

The motor seems a logical place to start when dissecting a bike. Motorcycles are, after all, named for their engines. The engine, more than anything else, gives a motorcycle its character and personality. Looks may stir you to buy a bike, but it is the characteristics of the engine that keep you riding it year after year. As Philip Vincent said, "Motorcycles are supposed to be ridden, and one cannot see the model when one is riding it," (Vincent, *An Autobiography*, 1976).

In the next chapter, you'll examine the different types of engines and how the type of engine and its state of tune affect the character of the motorcycle. In this chapter, you'll just focus on the different parts of the engine and what each one does.

The engine proper is usually divided into two parts—the lower portion, called the *bottom end*, which includes the parts that transmit power to the rear wheel, and the upper portion, called the *top end*, which is where the internal-combustion process takes place. The engine also includes a system to introduce a fuel charge into the chambers where combustion takes place. This is called the *induction system*, and consists of either a carburetor (or more likely carbure-tors), or else fuel injectors, and it works in conjunction with a series of valves that are part of the engine's top-end.

Cycle Babble
The **bottom end** of a bike refers to the bottom part of the engine, where the crankshaft and (usually) the transmission reside. The **top end** refers to the upper part of the engine, which contains the pistons, cylinders, and valve gear, and the **induction system** consists of the apparati that mix an air-and-fuel charge and inject it into the combustion chamber, located in the top end.

The Belly of the Beast: The Bottom End

I like to compare motorcycle components to the human body to make it easier to envision. The bottom end is the entrails of a bike. This is where all the commotion in the engine is converted into forward motion.

The two clam-shell–like metal halves that surround the bottom end are called *cases*. All motorcycle engine bottom ends contain at least one *crankshaft* (on certain designs, two crankshafts occupy the space within the engine cases, but these are rare, especially in the United States).

The crankshaft is connected via *connecting rods* to the *pistons*, which are the slugs moving up and down within the *cylinders* (the hollow shafts in the top end inside which internal combustion occurs). The connecting rods attach to the crankshaft on *eccentric journals*, or *metal shafts*, and their up-and-down movement is converted into a circular motion through the design of these journals.

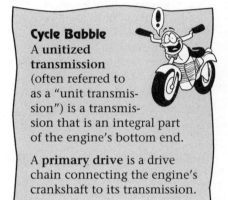

Cycle Babble
A **unitized transmission** (often referred to as a "unit transmission") is a transmission that is an integral part of the engine's bottom end.

A **primary drive** is a drive chain connecting the engine's crankshaft to its transmission.

As you'll see in the next chapter, the design of the crankshaft does much to give the engine its character; for example, it's the design of the crankshaft that gives Harley-Davidsons their characteristic rumbling sound (it's what also makes Harley engines vibrate like washing machines with unbalanced loads).

The Transmission

On most modern motorcycles, the circular motion created by the crankshaft setup is transmitted to the transmission through a series of gears or by a chain.

For all practical purposes, you can think of the transmission of a modern motorcycle as part of the bottom end. The crankshaft and the gearset usually reside inside the same cavity within the cases. This is called a *unitized transmission*, and since the 1950s and 1960s, it has been a part of just about every motorcycle engine designed.

One notable exception is Harley-Davidson, the only company still manufacturing motorcycles that use separate engines and transmissions, connected by a *primary drive*. The primary, as it is called, consists of a sprocket attached to the crankshaft that rides outside the engine cases, in a case of its own (called the primary case). This case is connected to the transmission, which is located behind the engine, via a primary chain.

Harley's primary drive system presents added maintenance chores: The primary chain must be periodically adjusted, a rather difficult process that creates more opportunities for things to go wrong. The exposed components are also more vulnerable to damage than components protected within the cases. No one knows for certain why Harley continues to use this archaic setup, but if I had to guess, I'd say it's purely for looks.

Cycle Babble
A **manual transmission** is a device consisting of a set of gears (the gearset), that enable an operator to get up to speed. All motorcycles now being produced have manual transmissions. In a motorcycle, the gears within the gearset are moved around with devices called **shifting forks**.

The transmission is an integral part of the bottom end on most motorcycles, but it is really a separate system. Transmission design varies from bike to bike, but most share some basic characteristics. Each transmission contains a *gearset*, which, as you might have guessed from the name, is a set of gears. Designers use complex mathematical equations between the diameter of these gears and a variety of other parts on the motorcycle to give a bike certain characteristics.

These gears are engaged by shifting a lever with your left foot, which moves *forks* inside the transmission, which in turn move the gears within. If you have any trouble with the transmission, the odds are it will involve those forks.

Harley-Davidson is the last major manufacturer still using an external primary drive on its motorcycle engines. (Photo ©1998 Darwin Holmstrom)

Valve Clatter: The Top End

The top end of a motorcycle is where the internal-combustion process takes place. The top end consists of the *pistons*, the *cylinder block*, and the *head*, which contains the *valve train*. As mentioned earlier, *pistons* are metal slugs that move up and down in the cylinders. The energy created by burning the fuel charge (a mixture of gasoline and air) acts on the tops of the pistons (known as the *crowns*) to make your bike move. Pistons are both simple and complex devices, but for the sake of this discussion, I'll stick with this simple definition.

The *cylinder block* is a rather simple device, too—a hunk of aluminum with holes bored through it, inside which the pistons move up and down. This hunk serves two purposes:

1. It channels the pistons' energy and forces them to move up and down (rather than flying all over the place, which would not help make your motorcycle move).

2. It dissipates the intense heat created by the burning fuel charge and the friction caused by the motion of the pistons. This is done by some sort of coolant circulating throughout the block, by cooling oil being sprayed on the hot spots on the piston, or by air flowing over the outside of the block. Usually, some combination of the three methods effectively cools the engine.

Cycle Babble
The area at the top of the cylinder where the fuel charge burns and pushes the pistons down is called the **combustion chamber**. The head sits atop the cylinder block and houses the **valve train**, the system of valves that let the fuel charges in and let the exhaust gases out.

The *valve train* is the most convoluted and confusing system in the top end. It consists of a *cam*, which is a rod with lobes on it that opens the valves. *Valves* are devices consisting of metal stems with flat disks on one end. They ride in metal tubes, called *valve guides*, and open and close at precise moments to let unburned fuel charges into the combustion chambers and to let the waste gases created during the combustion process exit the combustion chambers.

There are two basic types of valve trains: *overhead cam systems* and *pushrod systems*. There are several varieties of each system, but they all share some common traits.

Most modern bikes use overhead cams. In this type of valve train, the cams are located above the valves and act on them through a system of rocker arms, or the cam lobe acts directly on the valve. *Rocker arms* are metal levers that rotate on a small shaft like an upside-down teeter-totter; the cam lobes push one side of the rocker up, causing the other side of the rocker to push the valves down, opening them up.

The *pushrod system* has cams located below the combustion chambers, usually in the engine cases, that act on *pushrods*, long, metal rods connected to the rocker arms located above the valves. Harley-Davidson and Moto Guzzi are the only two major manufacturers still using this method of valve actuation in its traditional form. BMW uses a hybrid *cam-in-head system*, which locates the cam in the cylinder head but below the valves. This system uses short pushrods to open the valves.

Overhead cams have a more positive action (less slop in the system) and allow the engine to operate at a higher rate of *revolutions per minute* (RPM) than can pushrod engines. The

Cycle Babble
RPM stands for **revolutions per minute** and refers to the number of times the crankshaft spins around per minute. Often, the term **revs** is used, especially in conversation.

term *RPM* refers to the number of times a crankshaft spins around each minute. Being able to run at higher RPMs means an engine will put out more overall power—the faster your crankshaft can spin, the faster your rear wheel will turn, and the faster you will be able to go.

One advantage of Harley's pushrod system is easy maintenance. Harleys use hydraulically-adjusted *tappets* (small metal slugs between the cams and the pushrods) that eliminate the need for periodic valve adjustments. Some overhead-cam designs also use hydraulic-valve adjustments, but most require periodic manual adjustments.

Harley-Davidson is one of the last remaining motorcycle manufacturers to still use a pushrod-operated valve system. (Photo ©1998 Darwin Holmstrom)

To Inject or Not to Inject? Induction Systems

Since Gottlieb Daimler constructed the first gasoline-powered motorcycle back in 1885, motorcycles have had *carburetors*—complex devices that mix gasoline and air into the fuel charge squirted into the combustion chamber. Carburetors, or *carbs*, as they are usually called, rely on their shape to create the vacuum pressure that provides the energy for this squirt. Although modern carbs are remarkably efficient devices, they share many similarities with the crude device old Gottlieb bolted onto his half-horsepower engine way back when.

Today, most motorcycles have one carburetor for each cylinder, with a few exceptions.

The carburetor's century-long supremacy as the ultimate form of motorcycle induction system has been challenged in the last decade by *fuel injection*. Fuel injection refers to a system that forces the fuel charge into the combustion chamber with an electronic or mechanical pump of some sort.

The first reliable motorcycle fuel-injection system appeared on BMW's first four-cylinder motorcycle, the K100 of 1984. Now every engine BMW builds sports fuel injection.

Other makers are jumping on the fuel-injection bandwagon, too. Ducati introduced its first production fuel-injected bike in 1988, the 851 Superbike. Suzuki now offers a couple of models with fuel injection. Honda recently introduced its new, fuel-injected 800 Interceptor, and even Harley-Davidson offers fuel injection on some models.

With the universal acceptance of fuel injection in the automotive world, it might seem odd that motorcycles have been slower to adopt the technology. Fuel injection offers certain benefits, such as greater control over the ratio of the fuel charge and less dependence on atmospheric conditions, but for some reason, motorcycle fuel-injection systems have so far provided less than satisfactory results. The biggest problem seems to be a surging in the engine, which makes it difficult to maintain a steady RPM level.

Such jerky power delivery on a sportbike can be dangerous, since these bikes are often ridden close to their handling limits. When you're riding right on the edge, an unexpected surge in power while heeled over in a hard corner can lead to a trip to the emergency room.

The problems with fuel-injection systems on motorcycles seem to involve cost and size. Automotive systems incorporate many computerized controls not found on systems used on motorcycles. However, automotive systems tend to be too large to work in the compact space available on a motorcycle, and they are also quite expensive.

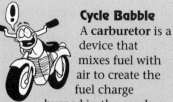

Cycle Babble
A **carburetor** is a device that mixes fuel with air to create the fuel charge burned in the combustion chamber.

Fuel-injection systems mix the fuel-air charges and forcibly inject them into the combustion chambers.

Motorcycology
BMW sells one model without fuel injection—the F650—but it doesn't actually build that bike. Aprilia, an Italian manufacturer, builds the bike for BMW, and even it doesn't build the bike's engine. Instead, it buys the engines from Rotax, an Austrian firm. With a pedigree like this, the bike might seem like some kind of mutt, but in reality, it is a fine, unique motorcycle.

The Clutch

One of the major obstacles designers of early motorcycles faced was creating a system for engaging and disengaging the power transmitted to the back wheel. This wasn't a problem as long as you were moving, but once you decided to stop, it quickly became important.

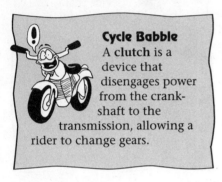

Cycle Babble
A **clutch** is a device that disengages power from the crank-shaft to the transmission, allowing a rider to change gears.

Most early motorcycles used a leather belt to transmit power from the engine to the rear wheel. This belt connected directly to the crankshaft. To give the rider some control over the flow of power, a pulley mounted on a lever was used to tighten the belt.

This system proved to be marginally effective, even on the underpowered machines of the time, and it soon became clear that a better system was needed. That system was the *clutch*. The clutch is a series of spring-loaded plates that, when pressed together, transmit power from the crankshaft to the transmission.

Early clutches were operated by a foot pedal, like on an automobile, with levers mounted to the gas tank to shift gears in the transmission. This setup proved to be cumbersome and awkward. When the British began exporting motorcycles to the United States with hand-operated clutches and foot-operated shifters, U.S. riders soon realized the benefits of such a system, forcing Harley-Davidson to adopt hand clutches and foot shifts for its motorcycles.

Nearly every full-sized motorcycle built since World War I uses a clutch, with a couple of notable exceptions. Honda experimented with a clutchless, or automatic, transmission on its CB 750 in the mid-1970s, and Moto Guzzi marketed an automatic bike at about the same time. Neither was a sales success. Unless you run across an example of one of these rare bikes, you should probably resign yourself to learning to use a clutch.

Rotating the Rubber: Drive Systems

You now have a fair idea about what all that commotion taking place down below your legs is all about, but really, it means nothing if you have no way of transmitting that commotion to the back wheel of your bike.

As with many other aspects of motorcycle technology, the three final-drive systems most commonly used today—chain, shaft, and belt—had all been tried before the European squabbling that started World War I got out of hand.

In Chains

In the early years of the sport, the crude belt system mentioned earlier was employed, but by the end of World War I, most manufacturers had settled on a *chain-drive system* (although a few opted for drive shafts). The simplicity and ease of repair of a chain-driven system made it a logical choice back then.

In this system, a sprocket mounted to an output shaft in the transmission is connected to a sprocket attached to the rear wheel of the motorcycle by the drive chain. Although such a setup requires periodic maintenance (the rear wheel needs to be adjusted to take up the slack created in the chain as it stretches over time), the benefits of this system make it popular to this day.

Unlike shafts, chains absorb much of the impact created during acceleration (which is the main reason they stretch over time). Shafts, which are much more rigid than chains, feed that energy back into the frame, causing all kinds of funky motion that a rider feels. This motion is called *shaft jacking*, and while it's not a serious problem in most real-world riding conditions, it detracts from a bike's handling.

Probably the biggest drawback of chain drives is that they are messy. In addition to needing to be tightened, they need to be cleaned and lubricated on a regular basis. The solutions used to do this are sticky and greasy, and they tend to fly off chains and onto a rider's jacket and clothes.

Getting the Shaft

Shaft drives do affect handling: They transmit the energy a chain absorbs directly to the *chassis* (the combined frame and suspension), causing the rear of the motorcycle to move up when it should move down and vice versa. Still, shaft drives are popular because they are so convenient and low-maintenance, especially when traveling. It's hard enough packing a motorcycle for an extended trip without having to put cans of lube and cleaning solvent in your duffel bag next to your shirts and underwear. Because of this, the most popular touring and sport-touring bikes have shaft drives.

A couple of clever companies (BMW and Moto Guzzi) have all but eliminated the antics associated with shaft systems by using creative rear-suspension geometry. By arranging suspension components in a parallelogram-type position, the rear suspensions on these bikes feed

Cycle Babble
Chain-drive final-drive systems transmit the power to the rear wheel via a chain.

Motorcycology
While they're messy, the lubes and solvents now available are much cleaner and easier to use than in earlier days. When I first started riding, we used motor oil to lubricate our chains. Back then, you could always tell a motorcyclist by the oil-splatter pattern on the back of his or her jacket.

Cycle Babble
Shaft-drive final-drive systems transmit the power to the rear wheel via a drive shaft. The chassis refers to the combined frame and suspension on a motorcycle.

the shaft-jacking motion into the frame along a horizontal axis rather than a vertical axis, converting the up-and-down motion into a forward-and-backward motion. The rider hardly notices this sort of movement.

While the shaft's acrobatics can be overcome by clever designers, another drawback of shaft systems cannot be overcome so easily: their weight. Shaft drives are heavy, and that weight is *unsprung*, meaning that it is not supported by the suspension. Unsprung weight tends to decrease the bike's capability to switch directions more than the same amount of weight carried by the suspension. Because it is more directly connected to the road than weight supported by the suspension, unsprung weight has a disproportionate (and negative) effect on handling.

The drawbacks of both shaft and chain systems led some companies to explore an old alternative: belt drives.

Belt It Out

Although *belt drives* were abandoned early on, by the beginning of the 1980s, advances in materials had once again made them a viable alternative. Harley-Davidson was the first to reintroduce the concept, equipping special-edition bikes (like its original Sturgis model) with both primary and final drive belts. The primary belt system never caught on, but the final drive belt did, and today every Harley made comes standard with such a belt.

Cycle Babble
Belt-drive final-drive systems transmit the power to the rear wheel via a drive belt.

Kawasaki also experimented with belts on some of its small displacement bikes.

The advantages of belts over chains are that belts are much cleaner, requiring neither messy lube nor cleaning solvents. While they do need periodic adjustments, they need such attention less frequently than chains.

The advantages of a belt system over a shaft is that belts, like chains, do not transmit unwanted motion into the chassis. They also do not come with the unsprung-weight penalty of a shaft system.

The disadvantages of belt systems, at least in the case of Harley-Davidson's application, is that they are true buggers to replace when they do go bad, especially on the big twins. Except for certain models, most big twins require that you partially disassemble the frame in order to replace a belt. And to replace a belt on all big twins, you must remove the primary drive and clutch assembly, which is no small job.

Harley's belt-drive system has many of the benefits of both shaft- and chain-drive systems. Its main drawback is that changing a belt when a failure occurs is a complex (and expensive) task. (Photo ©1998 Darwin Holmstrom)

Putting It All Together: Frame, Suspension, Wheels, and Tires

The frame, suspension, wheels, and tires on a motorcycle are basically the things that hold a bike together and keep it from falling down. In the past, that was pretty much all they did, but modern designers use them for much more.

The *frames* on early motorcycles were just a collection of tubes holding all the parts together. In the 1970s, however, designers began to realize that the stiffness of the frame affected overall handling characteristics and began experimenting with stiffer designs.

Motorcycle frames looked more or less the same from the time Harley and the Davidson boys built their first motorcycle until the mid-1980s. As a result of developments over the past 15 years, the twin-spar aluminum frames found on most modern sportbikes resemble the single- or double-cradle designs of the past about as much as an F-16 fighter jet resembles the Wright brothers' Flyer.

Suspension, which refers to the combination of forks, shocks, and to a degree, tires, also has come a long way during the same time period. Just having a suspension was quite an innovation at one time. Early bikes relied on sprung girder forks up front and a soft saddle in

Motorcycology
Designers have made modern motorcycle frames so stiff that today some designers are purposely trying to make frames less stiff, in pursuit of even better handling. Honda is a leader in designing a bit of flexibility into its frame on purpose (called "tuned flex"), although so far, results have been mixed.

back. It wasn't until the 1940s and 1950s that most motorcycle manufacturers began offering the hydraulic front forks and swinging-arm rear suspensions we now accept as the industry standard.

Once accepted, this setup became engraved in stone; it didn't change for the better part of 30 years.

During the 1970s, dirtbike manufacturers developed a variation of the swinging-arm rear suspension that used a single shock, and that system found its way onto streetbikes in the 1980s. The advantage of these systems is that they allow the wheel to travel farther up and down when the bike strikes a bump or other surface irregularity before the shock reaches the end of its travel and transmits a jarring thump to the rider. By incorporating variable-rate linkage into such a system, designers have introduced even more suspension travel into the shocks. This type of system is the most common in use today.

Cruisers usually use the older dual-shock setup. Because of this, cruisers tend to be a bit harsher to ride than other types of bikes, but this setup also gives these bikes the retro look cruiser buyers want.

A few manufacturers have attempted to market alternatives to the hydraulic fork front suspension, most notably Bimota, with its Tesi model, and Yamaha, with its GTS, but neither bike has sold well.

BMW, ever the innovator, produces the most successful alternate front suspension—the *Telelever system*. This takes the shock-absorption function of a hydraulic fork and transfers it to a shock absorber located behind the steering head. This brilliant system solves many of the chassis-dynamic problems associated with a traditional fork, but I believe that part of its success can be attributed to the fact that it still looks like a traditional fork.

Cycle Babble
Suspension refers to the forks, shocks, and to a degree, tires, of a motorcycle. It's the springs and fluids in these items that "suspend" the motorcycle frame off of the ground.

Wheels and tires have also seen a surge of development since the early 1970s. The first technological advancement was the advent of cast wheels in the 1970s. These allowed bikes to use automotive-like tubeless tires, which provide a tremendous safety advantage because they are less likely to blow out than a tube-type tire. If you have ever had a tire blow out on a car, you know you don't want it to happen to you when you're riding a bike.

The tires themselves have come a long way, too. When I started riding in the 1970s, we were lucky to get 5,000 miles on a set of tires. Today's touring tires can last three times that long. And today's radial street tires provide grip unheard of even in racing tires back then.

What all this means is that you have access to motorcycles that ride better, handle better, last longer, and are safer than anything a motorcyclist could have imagined possible just a few years ago.

It's Electric

The system most likely to cause trouble in your motorcycle is the electrical system. While the electrical systems on modern bikes are vastly improved compared to those of older bikes, they still lag behind their automotive counterparts in reliability.

The function of the electrical system is to:

1. Provide current to the ignition to burn the fuel charge.
2. Power all the electrical devices on your bike, like the headlight. This has always been a trouble spot on motorcycles.

The electrical system consists of a battery, some form of electrical-generation device, and an ignition system to provide spark to the combustion chamber. I'll discuss this system in greater detail in Chapter 16, "Zen and the Art of Motorcycle Maintenance."

Bodywork

Bodywork, a major component on most motorcycles today, didn't even exist on most motorcycles 15 years ago. For the first 95 years of motorcycling, *bodywork* just meant some sort of container mounted to the frame to store the gasoline.

The Europeans deserve much of the credit (or blame, depending on your own preferences) for making bodywork such a pervasive part of motorcycle design. BMW, Moto Guzzi, and Ducati all marketed motorcycles with *fairings* in the 1970s. (As you learned in Chapter 3, fairings are the devices mounted at the front of a motorcycle to protect the rider from the elements.) By the end of the 1970s, the Japanese manufacturers were starting to do the same.

BMW was one of the first companies to offer fairings as standard equipment on certain models. Shown here is the R1100RS. (Photo courtesy Motorcyclist™ magazine)

The only really surprising thing about this development was that it took the manufacturers so long to get in on the act. Perhaps the manufacturers were still haunted by the failure of the Vincent enclosed motorcycles discussed at the beginning of this chapter.

As the 1980s progressed, bodywork became more and more encompassing. Soon, many streetbikes came with not only fairings, but also *cowlings* that covered the engine. These items were designed to integrate with the rear portions of the bike, resulting in clean-looking bikes that have an almost automotive appearance. In addition to visual appeal, this full-coverage bodywork has the practical benefit of protecting the rider from the elements.

Cycle Babble
A cowling is a piece of bodywork that covers the engine area.

As long as the bike still looks like a motorcycle, riders appreciate the look of such bodywork, as well as the additional weather protection it provides.

Like everything, though, those benefits come at a price. As I mentioned in Chapter 4, the price of bodywork is higher than insurance premiums and higher repair costs. Even routine maintenance becomes more expensive on a bike with bodywork.

Yamaha's R-1 features such attractive bodywork, at first glance some observers mistake it for an Italian motorcycle. (Photo courtesy Motorcyclist™ magazine)

The Least You Need to Know

➤ The engine, more than anything else, gives a motorcycle its character and personality.

➤ The bottom end of the engine is where all the commotion in the engine is converted into forward motion.

➤ The top end of the engine is where the internal-combustion process takes place.

➤ The drive systems used today are chain, shaft, and belt.

➤ Bodywork, such as fairings and cowlings, help protect motorcycle riders from the elements.

Start Your Engines

In the last chapter, you took an in-depth technical look at the parts of a motorcycle. Now you're going to venture into a more esoteric, subjective area: the engine, the soul of a motorcycle.

You might wince at this bit of anthropomorphism, thinking a motorcycle has as much of a soul as a toaster or an electric screwdriver, but motorcyclists who have ridden for a while know the truth: Motorcycles posses a distinct essential spirit, and while the word *soul* doesn't exactly describe it, it comes closer than any other word in the English language. If bikes don't have souls, someone forgot to tell that to my motorcycles.

A variety of characteristics give each bike its unique identity, but none so clearly defines a bike's personality as its engine. And each type of engine has different characteristics, which is why certain types are used for specific motorcycles.

Many of the internal differences that give an engine its soul involve complicated mathematical and geometrical relationships between components such as the crankshafts, the pistons, and the flywheel; or, they involve the design of peripheral equipment, like the ignition system. These are technical details beyond the scope of this book. But knowing the basic types of engines and what you can expect from each will help you select the bike best suited for you.

The types of engines so strongly affect the entire motorcycling experience that you should take a bit of time to review the various types individually.

Engineering

All engine types get their characteristics from a combination of *horsepower* and *torque*. While closely related, horsepower and torque are not the same thing: Each is a measure of a different characteristic of an engine's power. Their relationship is complex, but Dan Keenen of Dynojet Research, a company that builds machines used to measure horsepower and torque, explains it in a way even I can understand. Keenen describes horsepower as a measure of how fast you can go, and torque as a measure of an engine's *snap*, or how fast it can get to its maximum speed.

Cycle Babble
Horsepower is a measure of an engine's strength. It is called horsepower because it was originally calculated by measuring how much weight a horse could lift in a certain period of time. **Torque** is a twisting force, and in a motorcycle, it is a measure of the leverage the engine exerts on the rear wheel.

In the real world, torque is usually more usable than prodigious amounts of peak horsepower. The benefits of lots of horsepower tend to be most apparent at speeds well beyond what local law-enforcement officials will allow; you can use torque at speeds that won't land you in jail.

There are two basic types of motorcycle engines in use today: the *two stroke* and the *four stroke*. Over the following pages, you'll look at each one.

The Four Stroke

Anyone who has ever added oil to a car has experience with four-stroke engines; the vast majority of road-going vehicles ever to turn a wheel on U.S. streets have four-stroke engines.

Cycle Babble
The **four-stroke engine** is sometimes called the **Otto cycle**, in honor of its inventor, Nikolaus August Otto. It's called a "four stroke" because the piston makes four strokes, or movements along the length of the cylinder, per cycle.

The four stroke gets its name from the number of strokes the piston makes during each *power cycle* (each series of events that produces power). The piston first moves down, drawing in the fuel charge (intake stroke), then moves up (compression stroke), at which time the fuel-and-air charge ignites and burns, pushing the piston down (power stroke). The fourth stroke occurs when the piston moves back up, forcing out the burned gasses (exhaust stroke).

The Single

The *single*, the most basic of engines, once powered most motorcycles on the road. In the old days, motorcycles were such problematic beasts, the general philosophy held that the fewer moving parts you had, the less chance those parts would break. And what could have fewer moving parts than a motorcycle with but one cylinder?

As designs and materials advanced, along with production techniques, manufacturers were able to create ever more complex motorcycles, with two, three, four, six, and even eight cylinders. Generally speaking, the more cylinders you have, the smoother the engine runs. Clever designers have produced twin-cylinder engines that run almost as smoothly as four-cylinder engines, but there is no way to make a single cylinder do so, and as a result, single-cylinder streetbikes have steadily lost popularity since the very beginning of the sport.

Today's big singles use *counterbalancers* (weights inside the engine) to cancel out some of the vibration to a certain degree, but you can't take the thump completely out of a *thumper* (a bike with a large-displacement, single-cylinder, four-stroke engine, so called because of the thumping sound of its exhaust).

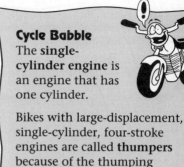

Cycle Babble
The **single-cylinder engine** is an engine that has one cylinder.

Bikes with large-displacement, single-cylinder, four-stroke engines are called **thumpers** because of the thumping sound of their exhaust.

MZ's Skorpion Replica represents a modern interpretation of the sporting single-cylinder motorcycle, once the most common type of bike. (Photo courtesy Motorcyclist™ magazine)

Another drawback of single-cylinder engines is that they don't make a lot of power.

But singles have advantages, too. Because they have few parts, they tend to be light power plants (engines), which is why they are so popular in the big dual sports. And while they may not generate a lot of power, they still provide satisfying amounts of torque.

Suppose that you are riding a BMW F650ST single. Beside you, your companion rides a Suzuki GSX-R 600, a four-cylinder bike that makes more than twice as much horsepower as your Beemer, but roughly the same torque. You pass the city limits, and the speed limit rises to 65. Say, for the sake of argument, that you're both running at roughly 2500 RPMs. You both whack open the throttle at the same time. You'll pull away first—even though the Suzuki has twice as much horsepower—because at 2500 RPMs, you have about 34 foot pounds of torque available to you, while the Suzuki only has about 22 foot pounds of torque available (torque, the force the engine exerts on the rear wheel, is measured in foot pounds).

69

Motorcycology
While there is no avoiding some degree of vibration in a single-cylinder bike short of adding more cylinders, modern thumpers with counter-balancers are smooth enough for many riders, provided they keep their speeds under 80 miles per hour or so. Even then, they vibrate less at speed than a stock Harley-Davidson Sportster.

Of course, within a few seconds, the Suzuki will have rocketed away from you when all that horsepower kicks in, but by then you are both going faster than the powers that be will allow anyway. And should the Suzuki rider drop the shifter down a few gears, she will have left you behind from the moment you hit the throttle. Either way, she will have accelerated to go-to-jail speeds quicker than you can process the sound of the sirens on Officer Bob's police cruiser as he begins high-speed pursuit.

The point of this hypothetical scenario is that while single-cylinder bikes offer less overall power than multicylinder bikes, the power they do offer is often more usable in the real world, a world populated by traffic lights, stray dogs, pedestrians, senior citizens, and law-enforcement officials. The same is true of many twin-cylinder motorcycles.

The V-Twin

The V-twin design found widespread support even in the early days of motorcycle development, largely because it fit the shape of the bicycle-style frames used on motorcycles at the time.

By 1907, Harley and the Davidson boys displayed a prototype V-twin engine for their motorcycles. When Philip Vincent decided to add another cylinder to his Comet and create the first Rapide, the two cylinders together formed a traditional V. And when the Japanese got serious about building American-style cruisers, their engine of choice was the V-twin.

Modern manufacturers build V-twin motorcycles for a variety of reasons; some are practical and objective, while others, like tradition and style, are purely subjective.

Cycle Babble
A V-Twin engine is a two-cylinder engine with its cylinders splayed out in a V shape.

V-twin engines vary widely in their characteristics. Some designs, like Harley-Davidson's 45-degree V-twin, vibrate excessively. Some Harley touring models, as well as the Dyna Glide series, compensate for that vibration with elaborate rubber-mounting systems. Other models, like the Sportsters and Softails, just shake away, rider be damned. The reason for this involves the crankshaft design used in all Harley V-twins, but the vibration is also caused by the narrow angle of the V.

Other V-twin cruisers use narrow-angle V engines but also use some sort of system for reducing vibration. Honda uses a staggered crankshaft, which fools the engine into thinking the V angle is a wider 90 degrees. Other manufacturers, like Kawasaki, use heavy counterbalancers.

One characteristic common to most V-twin engines (and all successful ones) is ample torque, especially in the larger models. Riders of high-revving sportbikes often comment on the lack of peak horsepower V-twin bikes usually display, but they're missing the point. While V-twins usually give away a lot of power up at the top of the power band (which, in the real world, means at triple-digit speeds), they make up for it by offering tremendous usable power at lower RPMs.

On a cruiser with a large V-twin engine, you can probably forget about riding all day at 145 miles per hour, but when you whack open the throttle at lower speeds (like the 65 to 70 miles per hour you'll usually find yourself riding), you are rewarded with jet-like thrust that sets you back in the saddle.

The Boxer

In 1923, Max Friz, an engineer working for BMW, built a motorcycle engine, the R32, a 500cc opposed twin, using basic principles still in use today. This engine earned the nickname *Boxer* because the pistons thrust outward, away from each other, like fists.

This was not the first opposed engine, but Friz's execution was unique, and the effectiveness of his design makes BMW's Boxer engines popular to this day. By opposing each other, the pistons cancel out primary vibration, creating a remarkably smooth twin-cylinder engine. And by locating the pistons on the side of the engine, Fritz placed them in the cooling airstream, leading to a cool-running, and thus long-lasting, engine. It's not uncommon to find BMWs with 200,000 or more miles showing on the odometer.

The success of Friz's design was not lost on manufacturers from other countries. During World War II, Harley-Davidson used his Boxer design for a military motorcycle, and in 1941, Ural began manufacturing a Beemer clone in Russia. Harley ditched this idea soon after World War II, but Ural is still at it, and you can now buy Ural motorcycles in the United States.

Many people find that the Boxer design offers an ideal compromise between twin-cylinder torque and multicylinder smoothness. Like the V-twin, a Boxer's primary characteristic is abundant torque rather than massive peak horsepower. This torque is usually found a bit higher in the RPM range than a V-twin's, but it still comes on early enough to be useful in the real world. In return, Boxers tend to have more top speed than V-twins. That, combined with the engine design's inherent smoothness, allows Boxer riders to cruise for extended periods at elevated speeds. You can get yourself thrown in jail on a Beemer without much effort on your part.

> **Cycle Babble**
> Opposed twins (two-cylinder engines with the pistons opposing each other) are called **Boxers** because the pistons look like fists flying away from each other.

Edward Turner's Speed Twin

In 1927, a young man in Britain named Edward Turner, working alone in his own shop, designed and built a 350cc single-cylinder motorcycle. The British motorcycle industry took note of this achievement, and he soon landed a job designing bikes. By 1936, he'd worked his way up to General Manager and Chief Designer at Triumph Engineering Co.

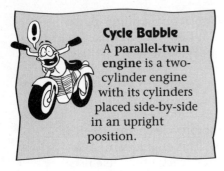

Cycle Babble
A **parallel-twin engine** is a two-cylinder engine with its cylinders placed side-by-side in an upright position.

In July of 1937, Turner introduced the 500cc Speed Twin, which featured a 27-horsepower parallel-twin engine that formed the basis of most Triumph motorcycle engines well into the 1980s. This engine, and its imitators from companies like BSA and Norton, became the power plant of choice for sporting motorcycles for decades to come.

Because of the design of its crankshaft, along with certain dynamic problems inherent in the parallel-twin design, these engines vibrated much more than a Boxer engine, but they vibrated less than a V-twin. Plus, they were light and powerful for their day. Their compact size enabled engineers to create compact motorcycles that could run circles around the big Harleys and Indians of that era, and their power output nearly equaled that of the big twins, which displaced as much as 1200cc.

Although the parallel twin has long since ceased being the power plant of choice for superbikes, the design still has enough appeal to keep it in production. Modern versions, with redesigned crankshafts and counterbalancers to tame vibration, power a variety of mid-sized bikes from manufacturers like Suzuki and Kawasaki. Kawasaki produces parallel twins in both cruiser and sportbike form. Any of these motorcycles make ideal first bikes. I'm especially fond of Kawasaki's EX500/Ninja 500 series; these are comfortable, good-handling, nimble motorcycles with enough power to keep a rider amused for decades.

The parallel twin seems to be making a comeback in the hard-core sportbike market, too. Yamaha produces the TDX for the European market with an 850cc parallel-twin engine. I haven't sampled the bike, but its predecessor, the TDM850, had what may be my all-time-favorite motorcycle engine. That bike is no longer imported into the United States, but if you can find a good used TDM, buy it. Also, the Italian company Laverda recently began importing a line of parallel-twin sportbikes that looks promising.

The British Triple

Eventually, the British responded to the Japanese invasion and introduced a new engine design, the *inline triple*. In many respects, this was just a Speed Twin with an extra cylinder grafted on, but it featured some unique characteristics, notably its compactness. British twins gained their reputation for being fine-handling motorcycles in large part because their compact engines allowed designers to tuck everything in, leaving very few hard parts to scrape the pavement during high-speed antics. With the triples, designers went to great lengths to retain that compactness.

Although promising, these bikes had too many problems to save the British motorcycle industry. Anyone who wants to learn how not to conduct business would do well to study the development of the Triumph Trident and BSA Rocket 3. A design firm with no experience in motorcycles was hired to style the bikes, resulting in bizarre-looking machines. Mechanically, the new bikes also failed. Although the engines were powerful, they proved unreliable in service, victims of underdevelopment.

Cycle Babble
A inline triple is an engine with three cylinders placed in a row.

After the styling of the new bikes was universally rejected by motorcycle buyers, Triumph redesigned the Trident (BSA had gone out of business by that time) and gradually worked out the mechanical bugs, but it was a waste of time. By then, Honda had already introduced its CB750 four-cylinder bike, and in doing so, effectively stripped the British of any influence in the motorcycle market.

Honda CB750: A Four for the Masses

The effect Honda's CB750 Four had on the motorcycling world can be compared to the effect the introduction of Microsoft's Windows operating platform had on the personal-computer industry. Sure, the old DOS system retained a few die-hard adherents, as did the British motorcycle industry, but just as the vast majority of computer users prefer Windows to DOS, the vast majority of the motorcycling public wanted four-cylinder bikes.

Although twin-cylinder bikes have experienced a resurgence in popularity in the past several years, riders still want four-cylinder motorcycles, which makes sense: The benefits of four-cylinder bikes can't be denied.

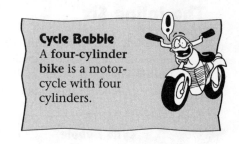

Cycle Babble
A four-cylinder bike is a motorcycle with four cylinders.

The primary benefits of a four-cylinder engine in a motorcycle are smoothness and a capability to run at higher RPMs than a comparable twin. (Higher RPMs is why almost all sportbikes use four-cylinder engines.) Fours tend to make their power higher up in the power band than twins and produce less torque at lower RPMs, but all but the most highly-tuned Fours (such as the Suzuki GSX-R 600) make adequate torque down low. Some Fours aimed at a more general audience, such as Suzuki's 1200 Bandit, make more torque than many twins.

The downside of four-cylinder motorcycles is that the engines tend to be rather bulky, although designers are working to rectify this situation. For example, Yamaha has moved the water pump inside the engine cases on its latest big-bore sportbike in an attempt to make the engine more compact. These engines are also more complex than twins and singles. More parts means more expensive maintenance.

The odds are you'll end up with a four-cylinder engine, not because it's better (or worse) than any other type, but because it is such a common design. This is especially true if you buy a used bike.

Honda's groundbreaking CB750, introduced in 1969, was perhaps the most influential motorcycle in history. (Photo courtesy Vreeke and Associates)

The Inline Six

For a few years in the mid-1970s and early 1980s, a few manufacturers fooled around with *inline six-cylinder* motorcycle engines, but these proved to be oddities, footnotes in the motorcycle history books. The odds of you stumbling across one of these beasties by chance are slim; most such machines are now the property of collectors.

Cycle Babble
An **inline six-cylinder engine** is an engine with six cylinders in a row.

A **V-four engine** is an engine with four cylinders arranged in a V-shaped configuration.

The Italian company Benelli produced a 750cc six-cylinder bike, but like many Italian bikes, this is one you'll probably only see in pictures. More common were the big Sixes produced by Honda and Kawasaki. These were functional motorcycles, but both were victims of their own excess. The width of those six-cylinders just proved to be more bulk than would comfortably fit down in the engine bay, and handling suffered, especially on the water-cooled Kawasaki, which weighed nearly as much as a small car. And if four-cylinder engines are complex to maintain, sixes are absolute nightmares.

The V-Fours

When Honda introduced its water-cooled *V-four* engine bikes for the 1982 model year, pundits predicted the demise of the inline four. It seemed reasonable at the time. These engines have exceptional power characteristics, providing good torque figures and more than adequate horsepower. Plus they are one of the smoothest engine designs in existence.

This engine design has become something of a standard—powering a variety of sportbikes, cruisers, and touring bikes—but it never came close to replacing the inline four. That was probably due to the expense of manufacturing such a complex engine design rather than any inherent flaws with the concept. In service, these have proven to be remarkably reliable motorcycles.

If you are in the market for a used motorcycle, a bike with a V-four engine is a safe bet. These bikes have been nearly indestructible. I have a friend who has 125,000 miles on his 1985 Honda 700 Magna as I write this. By the time you read it, he will probably hit 150,000 miles.

The Gold Wing

The engine Honda uses in its Gold Wing touring bikes is so unique, it doesn't fit into any other category. The only thing comparable to the four-cylinder version is the engine Subaru uses in its cars. This is a flat, Boxer-type engine, with four or six liquid-cooled cylinders, rather than two air-cooled cylinders, like BMW uses. The flat-four- and flat-six-cylinder engines used in Honda's Gold Wings are called *flat* because their cylinders are arranged in a flat, opposing configuration.

When Honda introduced its Gold Wing in 1975, it created a new class of motorcycle: the luxury tourer. (Photo courtesy Vreeke and Associates)

These are the smoothest engines used in motorcycles, period, and are a major part of the Gold Wing's appeal to the touring crowd. They also have a fairly centralized mass, which makes the entire motorcycle easier to maneuver. I've seen Gold Wing riders whip their bikes around as if they were riding sportbikes instead of ultimate behemoths weighing twice what the average sportbike weighs.

The L-Twin

Italian manufacturers have developed a unique take on the V-twin concept; by opening up (widening) the angle of the V to 90 degrees (changing the shape from a "V" to an "L," thus giving the configuration its name), they have created a smoother, more balanced twin-cylinder engine. Ducati's engines, which are longitudinal (they are positioned lengthwise in the frame), most obviously display the "L" configuration, but Moto Guzzi's engines, which are transverse (arranged crosswise in the frame), are also angled at 90 degrees.

The Two Stroke

The other common type of motorcycle engine is the two stroke, so called because its cycle consists of only two strokes: the piston moves down, drawing in the fuel-and-air charge, then moves up, at which point the charge ignites, forcing it back down and starting the process all over again. To provide lubrication for such an engine, oil must be mixed in with the fuel charge. This is what gives two strokes their characteristic smoky exhaust.

While this type of combustion cycle creates a high-revving, powerful little motor, it also creates a lot of pollution. Today, strokers are found mainly on off-road bikes and Grand Prix racing bikes, banished from public roads by the Environmental Protection Agency. But this was not always the case.

The Stroker Age: The Japanese Two Strokes

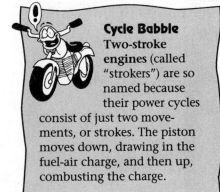

Cycle Babble
Two-stroke engines (called "strokers") are so named because their power cycles consist of just two movements, or strokes. The piston moves down, drawing in the fuel-air charge, and then up, combusting the charge.

With the exception of Honda, Japanese manufacturers originally invaded the U.S. market with small, two-stroke motorcycles.

Japan produced mainly strokers, as two-stroke engines are called, ranging from small, 50cc mopeds to Suzuki's GT750 and Kawasaki's infamous three-cylinder 750cc H2. Although some of these bikes continued in production until the late 1970s, by the early 1970s, it was clear that increasingly stringent air-quality rules would make the strokers extinct, at least in the United States. Other than Yamaha, which continued to develop its popular RD series of strokers throughout the decade, most manufacturers quit developing strokers for the U.S. market. By the early 1980s, you couldn't buy a brand-new street-legal two stroke in the United States.

Many of us grew up riding these fast, lightweight, cheap machines, and our memories of them are probably clouded by all the fun we had on them (and perhaps all that exhaust smoke has damaged our memories).

Yamaha was the last Japanese company to import a stroker streetbike into the United States with its popular RD/RZ series. (Photo courtesy Motorcyclist™ magazine)

Strokers are still out there, although they become tougher to find every year. Their inherent unreliability accounts for much of the reason they are not as plentiful as their four-stroke counterparts. Because these bikes relied on the proper amount of oil being mixed in with their fuel, they could easily be starved of lubrication, leading to a seized engine. Most of the later bikes had automatic oiling systems, but they still seized their engines more frequently than four-stroke engines.

Even if you can find one intact, strokers tend not to be practical motorcycles. They generate a lot of power for their size, but that power usually comes on only at the very top of the RPM range. Often, this power hits like a switch has been turned on. Before that switch is turned on, these bikes can hardly get out of their own way. I've found it takes a special type of lunatic to make good use of a stroker, a crazed motorcyclist who rides with the throttle wide open and controls his or her speed with the shifter. Every ride is a Grand Prix event for these folks, even a simple trip to the local convenience store. While you may be just the sort of lunatic I'm describing, this is not a good way to learn to ride.

Motorcycology

In the mid-1980s, Yamaha managed to sneak a two-stroke streetbike past the sensitive noses of the EPA, with the help of a catalytic converter. The RZ350 was a nice little sportbike, but it was underpowered. It could really be made into a road burner with a little work and an aftermarket pipe, but this eliminated the catalytic converter and made the bike illegal to drive on most public roads.

The Least You Need to Know

➤ The engine is where you'll find a motorcycle's soul.

➤ The combination of torque and peak horsepower shape an engine's personality.

➤ The shape and design of an engine contribute to its power-delivery characteristics.

➤ Four-stroke engines have broader ranges of power than two-stroke engines and make better bikes for beginners. The number of cylinders also influences power-delivery characteristics.

➤ Two strokes tend to have power-delivery characteristics best suited for experienced, slightly insane motorcyclists.

Chapter 7

Buying Your First Bike

In This Chapter

- ➤ Where to find a bike
- ➤ What to look for in a bike
- ➤ What's it worth?
- ➤ Wheeling and dealing

By now, you're so well-versed in motorcycle lore, you can entertain friends and family for hours with tales of Rollie Free's exploits aboard a Vincent Black Lightning, you're so familiar with the workings of the engine, you can tell a Kawasaki from a Suzuki just by the sound, and you know exactly what kind of bike you want. What's next?

Getting your first bike. The time has come to lose your moto-virginity.

Like your first lover, you will remember your first bike as long as you live. Although you will always enjoy the freedom motorcycling brings you, nothing quite compares to the heady exhilaration of those first rides. At this point, the best way to ensure that those rides are as pleasurable as possible is to get a good, dependable motorcycle.

Where to Buy Your Bike

Shopping for a motorcycle differs from shopping for a car in every aspect. For the most part, cars are appliances, like washing machines, bought and sold by staid, sensible people.

Motorcycles are expressions of passion, and the people buying and selling them tend to be passionate people. (Should you doubt this, ask yourself when you last saw someone covered with Chevrolet tattoos, wearing a T-shirt stating he'd rather see his sister in a brothel than his brother in a Toyota.)

Just finding a motorcycle differs from finding a car. You can find motorcycles in several places, some obvious, others less so.

Motorcycology
Finding a good motorcycle shop is a challenge in itself, but if you find a truly great one, you may have found a fun place to hang out, drink coffee, and absorb moto-culture. A good dealer knows that hardcore motorcyclists tend to spend every cent they have on bikes and accessories and will go to great lengths to make you feel at home in his or her shop.

Dealerships

The most obvious—and perhaps the easiest—place to find a bike is at a dealership. If you're buying a new bike, you'll have no choice but to buy from a dealer, but even if you're buying used, buying from a reputable shop can be the best way to get your first bike.

Physically locating a motorcycle dealership can present a challenge if you're not familiar with an area. People selling motorcycles don't have the kind of cash flow car dealers have, so usually you won't find motorcycle shops amid the endless car lots, strip malls, and office buildings in the sprawl suburban America has become. Motorcycle dealerships tend to be hidden in out-of-the way locations, like inner cities and industrial parks, where leases are lower. Check the Yellow Pages under "Motorcycle" to find dealers and repair shops in your area.

Choosing a Dealer

Not all dealerships are created equal. The quality of the staff makes or breaks a shop.

When you're buying your first motorcycle, it's tough to know if you are being taken advantage of. My first experience with a dealer turned out badly. I wanted to buy a 100cc Kawasaki dirtbike, but my father distrusted Japanese products (this was the early 1970s in rural Minnesota), so he took me to a shop selling American-made minibikes. He liked the minibikes because they were powered by snowmobile engines, which he believed to have been built right there in Minnesota. Actually, these engines were manufactured in Japan and were wholly unsuited for summertime operation. The second day I owned the bike, I seized a piston.

The dealer fully expected us to be back the next day; he knew these bikes were unfit, but he had a plan. He traded me the trashed minibike for a new 80cc Yamaha motorcycle. It ended up costing about 20 percent more than the 100cc Kawasaki would have cost, but it was either that or keep the blown-up minibike.

If that wasn't bad enough, the dealer lied to me about the model year of the bike. I was too naive to know where to check the date of manufacture and ended up buying a two-year-old carryover motorcycle for more than the price of a new one.

But I was only 11 years old, and I didn't have this book. Here are some tips to keep this from happening to you:

➤ Learn as much about the motorcycle as possible. Check Appendix A, "Biker's Buying Guide to New Bikes," and Appendix B, "Biker's Buying Guide to Used Bikes," to see if it's listed there. Go to the library and read back issues of motorcycle magazines that have tested the bike.

➤ Make sure your salesperson knows motorcycles. Ask good questions, and by the answers, you can tell if the person is uninformed, unscrupulous, or both. (See Chapter 8 for examples of questions you should ask.)

➤ Check the mileage on the odometer against the mileage on the title, and check the model year on the title against the date of manufacture on the frame, usually located on a plate riveted either to the steering head or the lower frame tube or beam. If something's not kosher, chances are neither is the shop selling the bike.

The date of manufacture is usually stamped either on the steering head or on the frame of a motorcycle. (Photos ©1998 Darwin Holmstrom)

Buying a motorcycle from a salesperson who knows bikes and whom you can trust can be fun, the beginning of a productive relationship, but getting ripped off can poison you for life. Generally, you're more likely to have a bad experience at a shop where motorcycles are just a sideline, like a car dealership that also carries a line of bikes, or a dealership devoted primarily to snowmobiles, watercraft, or some other type of recreational vehicle, and just carries motorcycles because its franchise requires it. Your best bet is to find a shop specializing in motorcycles.

But like any generalization, there are exceptions. The best salesperson I've ever dealt with worked at a Chrysler shop that carried Honda motorcycles. If you can find just one person at a shop who knows and cares about motorcycles, that's a good shop.

How's Their Service Department?

Finding the right dealership with a salesperson you trust means little if the mechanic working in the service department is a ham-fisted fool.

This is more of an issue when buying a new bike under warranty than it is when buying a used bike. With a used motorcycle, if you get a good deal, you can always take it to a mechanic you trust somewhere else. When you buy new, you may be forced to go back to the same dealership for warranty work; many shops balk at covering warranty work on motorcycles bought at other dealerships.

An unskilled mechanic actually wrecked the top end on one of my bikes once. This was at a shop where I'd developed a relationship with one of the salespeople, a decent fellow and a dedicated motorcyclist. I made the mistake of assuming that the personnel in the service department were as competent as my friend in sales.

I was leaving on a solo motorcycle trip to the Ozark Mountains in a couple of days, so I brought my motorcycle in for a complete tune-up. I wanted to make certain my bike was running well.

When I picked my bike up, it wouldn't idle. In fact, it never idled again. The mechanic, who I later learned had been hired because his father owned the shop, had over-tightened the valves, and before I left the parking lot, I'd bent a valve stem.

I was still somewhat of a novice and didn't know what had happened. I took the bike back to the service department, and even though they knew exactly what they had done, they blamed the problem on dirt in the carburetors. They kept the bike overnight to clean the carbs, but there was nothing they could do short of a valve job.

Shops like this usually develop reputations in the motorcycling community. Within two years of trashing my bike, this shop went out of business.

So how can you find out which shops offer reliable service? Wherever motorcyclists hang out, they talk about mechanical things. And they love to gossip. If you can find a coffee shop or bar where motorcyclists congregate, ask them about the reputation of a shop's service department. If several people agree on a shop to avoid, avoid it. If you have no local hangout, check with independent repair shops. These are often staffed by mechanics who cut their teeth in local dealerships and who usually know the scoop on other shops.

The Classified Ads

The other obvious place to hunt for a used bike is in the Classifieds section of a newspaper. I enjoy this form of shopping, because it puts me in direct contact with the local motorcycling community. When I go to look at bikes I found in classified ads, I meet all kinds of motorcyclists, from people who bought a bike on a whim years ago but never rode it much, to hardcore riders who are moving on to a different bike.

Shopping the classifieds requires you to bring even more knowledge to the transaction than buying from a dealership. The range of conditions you will find classified bikes in varies as widely as the personalities of the owners selling them. Even the most unscrupulous dealer fears lawsuits enough to make certain the wheels are correctly bolted on. (At least they usually do; I once tested a bike that handled so squirrelly, I stopped and discovered the dealer had mounted the wheel backward!)

You never know what to expect on a machine you found through the want ads. Pinch bolts may be missing from axles. Chains may be held together with baling wire. Seats may be attached with duct tape. Remember, your life depends on the condition of your machine, and any one of these conditions, as well as a host of other possible problems, could convert you into a grease spot on the pavement.

Many people will let you test ride a bike, but check it out carefully to make certain it's safe before taking it on the road. Later in this chapter, I'll show you what to look for when you examine a bike.

When buying a bike from a private party, obtaining a clear title is absolutely critical. As with buying from a dealer, make certain the information on the title matches the information on the bike. This is especially important on motorcycles with high theft rates, like Harley-Davidsons, but it's important with all bikes. A friend of mine once replaced the frame on his Suzuki after a crash without changing the title to reflect that change. One morning, he went out to the street to find his motorcycle had been carted off by the police. They wouldn't release the bike to him because of the irregular title. He ended up forfeiting the bike, because it would have cost him more to get it back than it was worth.

If you buy a motorcycle that turns out to be stolen, you will not only lose the bike, you may well end up in

Motorcycology
Another source of motorcycle ads are the newsprint magazines that contain nothing but photos of vehicles that are for sale. In many metropolitan areas, these magazines will either have large motorcycle sections or will be entirely devoted to recreational vehicles. While it's possible to find good buys through such magazines, more often than not, you'll find yourself chasing down overpriced bikes in much worse conditions than they appear in the photos. Still, these magazines are worth checking out. If nothing else, they're fun to read.

legal trouble for receiving stolen merchandise. Generally, this is only a problem when buying from private parties, but dealerships have sold stolen motorcycles, too. One clue that something may be less than above board is if the bike has a replacement title from another state.

Buying a motorcycle through the classifieds requires you to bring more to the table yourself, but it's often worth the effort. Private sellers don't have to build the overhead costs of running a dealership into the price, so the prices tend to be lower. Plus, you get to see a lot of cool bikes and meet a lot of cool people.

I read the classified motorcycle ads every day, even though I'm usually not in the market to buy a bike. I find it's a good way to keep up on the motorcycle market, as well as the motorcycling community. I like to see who's selling what, and how much they're asking. Sometimes, I find even more information than I expected. My all-time favorite ad, written by a guy selling his Harley Electra Glide, ended with the following phrase: "She caught me cheating, and now it's the big D for me: make offer."

Bulletin Boards

If you are lucky enough to have a local hangout for motorcyclists, chances are there's a bulletin board there, with ads and snapshots of bikes pinned on three deep. (If you don't have such a place, you will probably find a similar bulletin board at the shop of an independent mechanic.)

These bulletin boards contain some of the best deals available. Usually, the seller knows what he has and what it's worth, and is offering the bike at a fair price.

My all-time best motorcycle buy came off of one such board, a Suzuki GS650G. I went to look at the bike, not expecting to buy it because I only had $500 to spend, and the bike appeared to be in pristine condition—which it was (and still is).

The young man selling it was asking $800—a fair price, given the condition of the bike. When I told him I only had $500, he was ready to take it on the spot. I told him the bike was worth more and to think it over and call me the next day if he still wanted to sell it.

The next day he called, and I found myself the proud owner of what turned out to be one of the most reliable and rugged motorcycles I've ever owned.

Motorcycle Clubs

Motorcycle clubs are another rich source of used motorcycles. Members of clubs tend to buy and sell a lot of motorcycles. They trade bikes the way some kids trade baseball cards and comic books.

Again, check with other motorcyclists at local hangouts and shops to find out what kind of clubs operate in your community. I'll discuss clubs at greater length in Chapter 19, "Join the Club: Motorcycle Clubs," but for now, I want to point out the advantages of clubs when shopping for a motorcycle.

Members of motorcycle clubs tend to be long-time motorcyclists, people who love to talk about bikes. You can learn a great deal about every subject in this book from these people (I have), but they are an especially valuable resource when it comes to buying motor-cycles.

The bikes these folks sell tend to gravitate toward the higher end of the price scale, usually with good cause. The following is a list of reasons a motorcycle bought from a club member will likely be worth the money:

➤ Club members' bikes are usually in excellent condition. They take pride in their equipment, partly because they know their fellow members will judge them by the quality of their bikes, and partly because they bond with their machines even more closely than a "normal" motorcyclist (if there is such a thing) does. They treat their bikes like members of the family.

➤ People in clubs have enough motorcycle savvy to buy bikes that are worth some-thing, motorcycles with decent resale value.

➤ They know the value of their machines and usually won't ask more than they're worth, if for no other reason than that other club members will doubt their intelli-gence, should they get greedy.

➤ Motorcycle clubs are an especially tight subcommunity within the general motorcy-cling community. If one club member ripped off another club member, he or she would be ostracized from the group.

Garages

An astounding number of perfectly good motorcycles rest in people's garages. As pointed out in Chapter 2, "A Brief History of Bikes," Japanese manufacturers sold shiploads of motorcycles in the 1960s and 1970s. A lot of these bikes eventually found their way to corners of garages, where they've sat unlicensed for years.

Finding bikes this way can be problematic. For starters, if you snoop around in people's garages, you could find yourself in trouble with the law for breaking and entering. The best way to find out about these lost treasures is through word of mouth, which in itself presents a problem: These bikes aren't at the forefront of their owners' consciousness. Owners don't spend much time thinking about these machines and probably spend even less time talking about them.

If you do see a bike sitting in someone's garage, the trick is to figure out (a) whose garage it is, and (b) how to tell the owner you're interested in the bike without letting him or her know you regularly peep through people's open garage doors.

Once you've cleared that hurdle, the trick is to negotiate a price. Most likely, such owners have no idea what the real value of their bikes are, so you never know how much they

Steer Clear
Even if you get a good price on a garage bike, it might not be worth the trouble. Sitting idle causes problems, such as dried up seals: When rubber seals in the engine and suspension sit without fluids for an extended time, they dry up and crack, causing leaks and a host of other problems. Make certain a bike has been stored properly and that most of the fluids stay inside the engine.

will ask for them. The owner could throw out a number that is ridiculously low or high, or else guess something in the ballpark of reality.

If it's low, I go for it without regret. The owner has no use for the bike, other than as a place to store stuff on: I consider it my duty to liberate the neglected machine and make it a productive member of the motorcycling community. And I don't worry that I'm ripping the owners off. Obviously, they don't need the money, or they would have sold the bike long ago.

If the number is ridiculously high, my advice is to walk away. The owner believes that price to be the bike's true value, and if you try to barter, the person will probably be insulted.

What to Look For

Buying a used motorcycle seems something of a crap shoot to the uninitiated. Judging a dependable bike from a pile of junk may appear difficult to the first-time buyer, but a couple of basic motorcycle characteristics make it easier than you might think.

First, motorcycles have nothing to hide. If a frame has been repaired, you will see welds or cracks in the paint. If the bike leaks fluids, those fluids will ooze out before your eyes.

Second, there's just not that much to a motorcycle. Compared to cars, they are relatively simple devices.

Further simplifying the buying process is the fact that what you need to check is limited to just a few basic items; luckily, you won't need to worry about all the parts of a motorcycle covered in Chapter 5, "Anatomy of a Motorcycle" (at least on Japanese bikes—European and American machines present a few more challenges).

The things to look for when buying can be broken down into two broad categories: *condition* and *completeness*.

Critical: Condition

You need to ascertain the mechanical and cosmetic condition of a motorcycle before you make an offer.

Judging a bikes' cosmetic condition is easy: Just ask yourself how it looks. By looking at the bodywork and such items as mirrors, turn signals, and mufflers, examining those items for scratches, dents, and other deformities, you can usually tell if a bike is in good shape. Pay particular attention to the outside edges of those items, the edges likely to contact pavement in even the most minor tipover.

Usually you will find some evidence of a tipover, even if it's just microscopic scratches. Finding a machine that hasn't fallen over at least once is rare. If the scratches are so minor they are difficult to see, you needn't worry. Often, they can be minimized with some chrome polish and some elbow grease. (Be aware, however, that a dealer will also find these scratches should you someday decide to trade the bike in.)

Even if you find more major evidence of a low-speed spill, that shouldn't dissuade you from buying the bike; Just reflect the costs of cosmetic restoration in your offer. Often, the owner will have already taken such things into consideration when setting a price.

When purchasing European or American motorcycles, there are a few other things to watch for. Cosmetically, Harleys will more often than not be immaculate, but you need to check things such as the belt-drive system (discussed in Chapter 5). Fraying or missing teeth indicate future problems, problems that are expensive to correct.

The level of finish on European bikes tends to be lower than that of Japanese motorcycles, and corrosion can be a problem. This is especially true of Italian bikes, but it can even be a problem on BMWs. For example, BMW doesn't apply a clear finish to exposed aluminum on items such as the fork legs. While this finish tends to yellow with exposure to sunlight, giving the forks on older Japanese motorcycles a dingy appearance, it protects the metal from corrosion. This corrosion becomes more pronounced in coastal areas, because of the salt in sea air. It's also a problem for machines used during the winter, because of the salt placed on roads in snowy climes.

The outside condition of a bike can help give clues to the condition of internal parts. If a bike looks good and runs well (if it starts easily when both cold and hot, if it idles smoothly without making horrible noises, and accelerates adequately for a bike of its size), the odds are it's OK inside. The owner has more than likely lavished as much care on the motorcycle's internals as he or she has on the bike's appearance.

I once went shopping for a Harley-Davidson with a friend of mine who was looking for an Electra Glide. At one dealership, we found two of them. Both bikes were the same model year, both were similarly equipped, and both had around 57,000 miles on them. The price on each bike was identical. One bike was black, the other a hideous dusty-rose color. My friend was partial to black motorcycles.

Unfortunately, the black one was in much worse shape, cosmetically. It had spent much of its life sitting outside in the elements, judging by the corrosion on the engine and other aluminum parts. This was a red flag to me: If the previous owner had taken such abysmal care of the outside of the bike, what sort of care had he given the inside?

> **Motorcycology**
> Some motorcycles have built-in odd noises. Suzuki's two-valve GS series, for example, has a cam-chain guide that allows the chain to slap while idling at low speeds. This causes no damage whatsoever, but the mechanical knocking sound has caused many unnecessary top-end rebuilds because owners didn't know about the defect and thought something was wrong.

Motorcycology

If you have a high degree of mechanical skill, as well as access to tools and a decent workshop, rebuilding bikes that have been crashed can be an inexpensive way to get a decent motorcycle. But be forewarned: This is not an undertaking for mechanical novices.

I advised my friend to buy the rose-colored bike, if he was determined to buy either. But he bought the black one with the pitted aluminum.

The bike was nothing but trouble, right from the start. He'd had it less than a week when the clutch went out and left him stranded on the freeway. The next week, the drive belt went out. After we fixed that, he started having trouble with the carburetor. We took it apart and discovered that someone had tried to repair it using what looked like rubber cement.

My friend had that bike for several years, and he never did get it to run right, even after he overhauled the engine. He spent so much money fixing the thing, he could have painted the rose-colored bike several times over.

Completeness

Along with the condition of a bike, make certain that all the pieces are there. Items such as missing side covers or other body panels can cost as much as a cheap motorcycle.

Check a motorcycle to make certain it has the following items:

➤ Side covers. These are the plastic covers that cover components located behind the engine, under the seat. These can often break and come off the motorcycle, and are very expensive (and in some cases impossible) to replace.

➤ Emblems and insignias. These are often glued or screwed to the tank or sidecover, and are also difficult to find for older motorcycles.

➤ If a bike has an aftermarket fairing, make certain all the original lighting and turn-signal brackets and components come with the bike. Should you decide to restore the motorcycle to its original condition, you'll need these pieces, and on some bikes, they can cost as much as the motorcycle itself.

➤ Fenders. This will probably only be an issue if someone has tried to build a chopper out of a motorcycle. Generally, such bikes make poor candidates for restoration, and should be avoided.

Costs for individual parts, especially on Japanese motorcycles, run high, partly because of the Japanese manufacturers' practice of custom designing nearly every part on each individual model. On the other hand, Harley-Davidson, and to a lesser extent the European manufacturers, tend to use many of the same parts on various models. Only minor tweaks, such as different wheels and fenders, differentiate one Harley model from the next. This enables them to spread development costs across the entire line.

Be especially concerned with completeness when buying an older motorcycle. You may find items like side covers and seat covers unavailable for an older bike. These parts usually can be found with a little leg work. (I will discuss alternative parts sources, such as salvage yards, in Chapter 17, "Rx: Repair.") Just because a bike is not complete is no reason to reject it outright: Just reflect the potential cost of replacing parts in your offer.

What's It Worth?

You've found the bike of your dreams, it's mechanically and cosmetically perfect, and you already have visions of yourself roaming the highways on the beast. Now you have to figure out how much the bike is worth.

There's not much to negotiating the price of a new bike. Your best bet is to call every dealer within reasonable driving distance (remember, you will probably have to return to that dealer for warranty work) and find out what each one is charging for the model you're interested in. (Appendix A lists the current manufacturer's price for most of the popular models on the market.) Once you have the best price, you might want to go to the nearest dealer you trust and give them an opportunity to match it. Even if they can't match it exactly, if they can even come close, it might be worth a few extra dollars to buy from someone you trust, someone who is located nearby.

When shopping for a new motorcycle, you can save a lot of money by remaining flexible about which make and model to buy. Say you've decided to purchase a mid-sized cruiser, like Kawasaki's Vulcan 800 Classic. While searching for such a bike, you find a decade-old Honda 800 Shadow in mint condition at one-third the price of the Kawasaki. While the Kawasaki is a fine motorcycle, the Shadow is capable of providing every bit as much enjoyment, and with its shaft drive and hydraulically-adjusted valves, the Honda will save you hundreds of dollars per year in maintenance costs over the Kawasaki. You can pocket the money saved and use it to finance a cross-country motorcycle trip.

You can also save a lot of money by watching for carryover models. While shopping for the best deal on a Honda 750 Shadow, you might run across a brand-new last year's model Kawasaki 800 Vulcan for $1,500 less. In this case, maintenance costs will be roughly equal, since both bikes have manually-adjusted valves and chain drives, so if you keep an open mind, that will be an extra $1,500 in your pocket.

Buying a used bike is where the process most diverges from buying a car. Because motorcycle prices can fluctuate widely from region to region, depending on how large a market an area has, accurate price guides are difficult to compile.

> **Motorcycology**
> A guide I have found especially useful is *AMA Official Motorcycle Value Guide*, which is published three times a year. An annual subscription costs $30, and individual copies can be purchased for $12.95 by calling CPI, Ltd., the publishers of the guide, at 800/972-5312.

Further complicating the creation of useful price guides is the wide variation in the condition of each motorcycle. One seller's Yamaha 1100 Special can be in mint condition at 60,000 miles, while the next guy's can be a hunk of junk at 10,000 miles.

When deciding how much a bike is worth, a guidebook's value assessment is only part of the equation. In addition to things such as condition and completeness, you have to look at routine wear and tear. Keeping a motorcycle in tip-top running condition is an expensive proposition. A bike with a fresh tune-up is definitely worth more than a bike needing a tune-up.

Another item that increases a bike's value is fresh tires. You should be able to tell by looking whether the tires have low miles: Check the depth of the tread at the edges of the tire compared to the depth of the tread at the center. A good pair of quality tires can run you well over $300, with mounting and balancing, so factor that into your price determination.

Steer Clear

Before upping your offer because the seller assures you that a bike has had a recent tune-up, make sure he or she can provide documented proof the tune-up has been performed.

On the other hand, new tires of low quality actually detract from the value of a bike, at least in my personal equation. If a bike has a pair of bargain-brand tires, I have to either make the decision to drive on tires I consider unsafe, or toss out a nearly new set of tires and spend $300 on another pair. If a bike is wearing a pair of budget-brand tires, I automatically deduct $250 from my offer.

It's a good idea to speak with as many other owners of a certain model as you can before making a purchase (here again, belonging to a club can be beneficial). Also, check any service bulletins that may have been issued to your dealer on a certain model before buying that model.

These rough guidelines may help, but in the end, it's just going to be you and the seller. The entire process may boil down to how badly you want to buy the bike or how much the owner wants to sell it. One thing I can guarantee: If you buy the motorcycle that's right for you, one or two years from now, as you're riding down the road enjoying your machine, you will not be thinking, "Damn, I paid too much for this thing."

Making the Deal

Now comes the most crucial (and most nerve-wracking) part of the entire process: negotiating the deal. You've decided what the motorcycle is worth to you, and the seller knows what the bike is worth to him or her. Now the two of you have to see if those figures jibe.

For me, negotiating the price of a motorcycle is not the same as negotiating the price of anything else. People have more of an emotional attachment to motorcycles than they do to other goods: You're buying someone's passion. Whereas I have no moral qualms telling someone they're insane if they think a car or a radio is worth a ridiculous sum of money, I'll politely decline purchasing a motorcycle if the owner has an unrealistic opinion of its value. Its emotional value to that person may be such that the bike actually is worth the price to the owner (but not to me).

In such situations, you'll have to use your own judgment of the seller. If he or she seems reasonable, bring out the source you're using to arrive at your price and explain that their price is a bit steep. If the seller seems like a lunatic, extricate yourself from the situation as quickly as possible.

On the other hand, if the price is in the ballpark, I'll haggle until I get it in my acceptable window. If I can't, I'll usually give up (unless I really want the bike). There are a lot of motorcycles out there, and it's a buyer's market.

In the end, this is a decision only you can make. I've provided you with the basics, but when you're face to face with the seller, trying to make a decision that will affect your life for years to come, you have to be the final judge.

The Least You Need to Know

➤ The quality of a dealership and of its service department is almost as important as the quality of the motorcycle itself.

➤ Clubs are a great source of motorcycles and information about motorcycles.

➤ Before taking a motorcycle out for a test ride, inspect it as if your life depends on it, because it does.

➤ Be flexible when choosing a motorcycle.

Insider Tips on Buying a Bike

In Chapter 7, I told you how to buy your first bike. Now let me give you a few hints on other costs and responsiblities associated with buying a motorcycle, like maintaining, financing, and insuring that bike, as well as advice on trading bikes and some more tips on getting the best prices.

The purchase price of a motorcycle is just the tip of the iceberg when it comes to expenses you'll incur owning a bike. Maintenance will be a huge expense, but I'm going to give you some hints on how to minimize that expense.

A smart shopper can also minimize the costs of financing and insuring bike. I'm going to show you some ways to save money when you finance and insure a bike. I'm also going to offer some tips on trading in a bike, should you ever decide to do so.

Minimizing Maintenance Costs

Your choice of a bike can determine how much maintenance you'll need to do. Sometimes engineers design motorcycles with certain high-maintenance features to increase the performance of a bike, but more often than not, features that make a motorcycle easier (and cheaper) to maintain are excluded just to save production costs.

If you're after extremely high performance, you'll have to accept the fact that you'll have to spend more money on maintenance, but if you're willing to accept a slightly lower level of performance, there are features you can look for and riding habits you can practice that will help you keep maintenance costs down.

Three elements in particular will affect your maintenance costs: the shaft drive, the centerstand, and the valves. (See Chapters 16 and 17 for a description of these parts.)

Getting Shafted

Select a bike with a shaft drive. As you'll see in Chapters 16 and 17, chain maintenance is the most frequent procedure you'll need to perform on your bike. It's also the dirtiest.

Sporty bikes will usually have a chain, since chains tend to disrupt handling less than shafts. If you want such a bike, you'll usually have to accept a chain as part of the package. But there has been a trend in recent years to use chains on types of bikes that, by nature, aren't the best in handling, such as mid-sized cruisers. This is purely a cost-cutting measure on the part of the manufacturers.

If you want to buy a mid-sized Japanese cruiser, my advice is to get an older, used one, since these usually have shaft drives.

Another option is to select a bike with a belt-drive system. These can be a good compromise between the handling benefits of a chain and the maintenance benefits of a shaft. Belt-drive systems, like the one used by Harley-Davidson, require less maintenance than chains, but more than shafts. The main drawback of Harley's belt-drive system is that fixing one can be an expensive proposition.

Getting Centered: The Benefits of a Centerstand

Make certain your bike comes equipped with a centerstand. Until recently, all Japanese bike came with centerstands—it was one of the things that set them apart from Harley-Davidsons, which have never been equipped with modern centerstands.

In the 1980s, Japanese manufacturers began excluding centerstands from ultra-high-performance sportbikes, because the designs of the exhaust systems used in those bikes prohibited the mounting of centerstands, and also because centerstands hindered cornering clearance.

But in the past few years, they've also begun excluding them from bikes that already have limited cornering clearance, like cruisers. This is another cost-cutting measure. Combine lack of a centerstand with a chain drive, and I guarantee you will create new expletives while maintaining your bike.

Hydraulically Adjusted Valves

One of the costliest aspects of maintaining a motorcycle is adjusting the amount the valves move up and down.

This is a critical (and often neglected) part of motorcycle maintenance, because if the valve doesn't move down far enough during the combustion cycle, it can get bent and destroy the valve train. If the valve moves down too far, it can hit the top of the piston, destroying the entire top end.

It is also an expensive part of motorcycle maintenance. On most modern motorcycles, valve adjustment is too complex a job for an inexperienced mechanic to tackle alone. Most riders take their bikes into shops to have the procedure performed.

If the motorcycle has any body work which the mechanic has to remove to gain access to the valves, or if the motorcycle is constructed in a way that requires the mechanic to go to heroic lengths to gain access to the valves, the mechanic will also have to spend even more time adjusting the valves.

And to a mechanic, time is money. Shops often charge $50 per hour for a mechanic's time. On a multi-cylinder bike with body work, a mechanic can take several hours to adjusted the valves. Valve adjustments seldom cost less then $100, and on certain complex machines, can run as high as $250. Remember, this is a procedure you'll have to have performed at least once every year (even more, if you ride a lot).

But there is a way to avoid this expensive bit of maintenance. Back in the early 1980s, Honda introduced several motorcycle models that had overhead-cam engines with hydraulically adjusted valves. Suzuki and Kawasaki followed suit, introducing cruisers with similar systems. All new Harleys come with hydraulically adjusted valves.

While such systems slightly limited the performance of the motorcycles using them, they also completely eliminated the costs associated with valve adjustments. And for most motorcyclists, the performance limitations of hydraulically operated valves were academic, coming into play only at extremely high rpms. In the real world, motorcyclists seldom ride at such extreme speeds.

Cycle Babble
The out-the-door price is the amount you'll actually pay for a bike, factoring in all hidden costs like taxes, licenses, and other fees.

• If at all possible, select a bike with maintenance-free, hydraulically adjusted valves. This will decrease performance a bit, but that will only be an issue on bikes that demand ultra-high performance. On cruisers and standards, the difference won't be noticeable, and you'll save hundreds of dollars each year on maintenance costs.

Getting the Best Deal

To get the best deal on a bike, you're best off dealing directly with a sales manager. As I said in Chapter 7, call all the dealerships within the distance you are willing to drive (both to buy the bike and get it serviced), and have the sales manager quote you an *out-the-door price*. This will be the amount you'll actually pay and will include all hidden costs, like taxes, licenses, and other fees.

If the manager beats around the bush and won't give you a straight out-the-door price, he or she could be planning to stick you with some hidden costs. This may give you some insight into how the dealer will handle any warrantee work or other issues that might come up later, so you might want to shop elsewhere if the dealer is evasive.

You might already know that you'll find the best buys on bikes in the off season—in the fall and winter. What you might not know is that you'll find the very best buys on the last Saturday of a month, because at that time, dealers are anxious to meet their monthly sales quotas.

To Your Credit: Financing

Most people don't have the cash on hand to buy a new motorcycle, so many people are forced to finance bikes. The interest paid in finance charges can represent a significant amount of the overall cost of owning a motorcycle, so before you even go looking for a bike, you should arrange the lowest-priced financing you can find.

First, call at least three banks to get the following information:

➤ The interest rates for unsecured personal loans with payments spread out over both a 36-month period and a 48-month period.

➤ The same information about a loan if it is secured by the title to your bike.

➤ The monthly payment for a $10,000 loan in each instance.

You use the amount of $10,000 so that you can calculate your payments based on the amount you borrow. For example, if a bank quotes you a monthly payment of $320 for an unsecured, 36-month loan of $10,000, you can divide $320 by 10, and you'll know that you're being charged $32 a month for every $1,000 you borrow. If you borrow $4,000 to buy a Kawasaki 500 Ninja, just multiply 32 by 4 to learn what your monthly payments will be.

Getting Insured

Most states will require you to at least have liability insurance before you can operate a vehicle on public roads. If you finance your bike and use its title as security, you will need to have full coverage.

Full coverage isn't a bad idea anyway if your bike is worth a significant amount of money. But full-coverage insurance on a bike is expensive, especially if you live in a major metropolitan area. But there are some things you can do to minimize your expenses.

As I said in Chapter 4, "Choosing the Right Bike," most companies base insurance rates on several factors, such as the type of bike, the size of its engine, and the amount of expensive body work on the bike. They also take your driving record into account.

There's nothing you can do about your driving history (you can't change the past), but you can minimize your insurance costs by choosing a bike that is under 600cc and has minimal bodywork. The list of new bikes under 600cc without plastic fairings is short:

ATK 350 Enduro (548cc)

ATK 605 Enduro (598cc)

Honda VLX Shadow (583cc)

Kawasaki KLR250 (249cc)

Kawasaki Vulcan 500 LTD (498cc)

KTM 400R/XCe (398cc)

Suzuki DR200SE (199cc)

Suzuki DR350SE (348cc)

Suzuki GS500E (487cc)

Yamaha TW196 (346cc)

Yamaha Virago 250 (249cc)

Yamaha Virago 535 (535cc)

Yamaha XT225 (223cc)

Yamaha XT350 (346cc)

The list of used bikes that meet this criteria isn't much longer. In addition to used models of the bikes in the preceding list, it includes a few more choices:

Honda CB650SC/CB700SC Nighthawk

Honda FT500/VT500 Ascot

Honda VF500C V30 Magna

Honda VT500/VT600/VT700 Shadow

Honda XL350R/XL500R/XL600R

Kawasaki EN450 454 LTD/EN500 Vulcan 500

Kawasaki KLR600

Kawasaki KZ550/KZ550 LTD/KZ550 Spectre

Kawasaki ZL600 Eliminator

Kawasaki ZR550 Zephyr

Suzuki GS550E/L

Suzuki GSF400 Bandit

Yamaha XJ550 Seca/Maxim (although some Secas came with a small bikini fairing)

Yamaha XT550/XT600

Yamaha YX600 Radian

All these bikes will work as a first bike. Some will work better than others, and some will be better buys than others (see Appendix A, "Biker's Buying Guide to New Bikes," and B, "Biker's Buying Guide to Used Bikes," for lists of which are best first bikes and which are best buys). All will be relatively inexpensive to insure, especially the older, less expensive models.

Another trick for getting lower rates on your full-coverage insurance is to get a policy with a large deductible. Purchasing a policy with a $500 deductible instead of a $250 deductible means that you'll pay the first $500 to repair the bike if something happens to it. This might seem like a lot of money to shell out in case of an accident, but it won't take you long to save that much on your premiums.

Besides, if you do file a claim, almost every company will raise your rates an exorbitant amount (probably by as much as you'll spend just to fix the bike yourself if you have a higher deductible). If you do make a claim, most of the time, you will pay for it one way or another. Usually, it costs less to fix it yourself in the long run.

Trading Bikes

If your first bike is not what you had hoped, or if you're ready to move up to a different bike, you may face the decision of whether or not to trade.

Usually, you will get more money selling your bike straight out. In a couple of cases, I've made more by trading a bike, but the vast majority of times I've traded, I've lost money. In both cases where I came out ahead, I had an unusual motorcycle—one the dealer already had a buyer lined up for. If I had been able to find such a buyer on my own, I would have made more money than I did when I traded.

In most cases, it has cost me money to trade rather than to sell the bikes myself. Usually, I have traded just because I was busy with work and didn't have time to show the bikes. I knew I was losing money, but it would have cost me as much money to take the time to sell the bike myself as it cost me to trade.

The only advantage of trading is convenience. When trading bikes, convenience is usually expensive. You will almost always get more money selling your old bike yourself, and you will always get a better price if you buy your new bike without a trade.

You will have to decide whether to trade bikes or sell your old one yourself, and you'll have to make that decision based on your own situation.

The Least You Need to Know

➤ You'll save a lot of money over time by choosing a low-maintenance motorcycle.

➤ Make certain you know the out-the-door price before buying a bike.

➤ Interest can be a significant part of the overall cost of buying a bike, so shop around.

➤ In the long run, you can save a lot of money on insurance by having a policy with a fairly high deductible.

Chapter 9

Getting the Gear

In This Chapter

➤ The facts and myths of helmet use

➤ Which type of helmet provides the most protection

➤ Essential protective gear

➤ Gear that will help you beat the elements

➤ Where to find the best deals on accessories

We who define ourselves as motorcyclists tend to forget that, at their very core, motorcycles are toys. While we certainly use them for practical transportation, we primarily use them for fun. And part of the fun of owning a toy is buying accessories for it. Would Barbie be so popular if you couldn't change her outfits?

Fortunately, motorcyclists can choose from a variety of accessories and gear that even Barbie would envy. And not all of that gear is just for fashion or fun; a large part of it serves practical purposes. While some items I'll discuss in this chapter are optional, others are absolutely essential.

Helmets: Home Is Where Your Head Is

Topping your list of essential items should be your helmet.

The issue of helmet use causes more debate than any other issue in motorcycling, which is insane: It's like arguing for or against smallpox vaccinations during the nineteenth century.

Make no mistake about it: Not wearing a helmet is stupid. According to a long-term study conducted by Professor Harry Hurt for the University of Southern California's Head Protection Research Laboratory, you're five times more likely to suffer a serious head injury if you have an accident while not wearing a helmet than you are if you crash while wearing one. Every study ever conducted backs up Hurt's findings.

Given the overwhelming evidence supporting the effectiveness of helmets, you'd think everyone wears one, but you'd be wrong. Stand on any street corner in a state without helmet laws, and you'll see as many bare heads as you will see helmeted heads. People go to extreme lengths to justify their choice to not wear a helmet, but none of their justifications hold up in the face of all the available research. The arguments that helmets break necks, block vision, impair hearing, and cause overheating have been proven myths by every study ever conducted.

I believe most people who don't wear helmets make their decision based on peer pressure. Otherwise reasonable, intelligent adults seem more afraid of facing the ridicule of their comrades than they are of living out the rest of their lives as produce. I actually had a man at the annual motorcycle rally in Sturgis tell me he always wore a helmet but wasn't wearing one during the rally because his friends weren't wearing theirs. I was a rebel, I told him, and I wore mine anyway.

I was once in his position. I rode for over a decade without a helmet, mainly because when I was young, I hung out with hardcore Harley bikers, and they would have thought I was some kind of wimp had I worn a helmet.

When I was 25, I took a job working as an orderly in a rehabilitation hospital, in the head-and-spine-injury unit. One patient I worked with was a victim of a motorcycle crash. He didn't break a single bone in his accident, and had he been wearing a helmet, he would have walked away with nothing but his pride injured. But he wasn't wearing one, and he hit his head on a rock.

While his body was perfectly healthy, the patient couldn't remember where he was from one minute to the next. One of my jobs was to lead him to the cafeteria every day, because he forgot its location from one meal to the next.

That spring, my wife and I both bought motorcycle helmets, and I haven't ridden without one since.

Besides protecting your head, a good-fitting helmet actually makes riding more comfortable. Helmets reduce road noise, keep the wind blast out of your face, and keep bugs and other debris out of your eyes.

How Helmets Are Made

Helmets help keep the contents of your head on the inside rather than the outside by using four basic components in their construction:

➤ **The outer shell**   The outside of a helmet, usually constructed of fiberglass or injection-molded plastic, disperses energy from an impact across a broad area of the helmet before that energy reaches your head.

➤ **The impact-absorbing lining**   This area inside the outer shell, usually made of a dense layer of expanded polystyrene, absorbs most of the shock caused by an impact.

➤ **The comfort padding**   This innermost layer of soft foam and cloth conforms to your head and is primarily responsible for how comfortable the helmet is.

➤ **The retention system**   This consists of the strap connected to the bottom of the helmet that goes under your chin and holds the helmet on.

Helmets come in a variety of styles, from small, bowl-shaped half-helmets that protect your brain stem and not much else, to sleek fully-enclosed helmets that protect everything above your neck. In between are the three-quarter, or open-face helmets, which cover most of your head but leave your face unprotected. These give better protection than half helmets, but should your face contact the pavement at speed, an open-face helmet will provide you with a one-way ticket on the ugly train. Neither half helmets nor open-face helmets offer the comfort full-face helmets provide by shielding the wearer from the elements.

A top-line helmet like this Arai Quantum/e Cadalora Replica can cost as much as two cheap helmets, but it's worth it. Remember, there's a reason why cheap helmets are cheap. (Photo courtesy the manufacturer)

Whichever type of helmet you choose, the important thing is to choose a helmet. It is the single most crucial piece of motorcycle gear.

Choosing the Right Helmet

Helmets come in a variety of styles and prices. You can get a full-face helmet for under $100, while high-end helmets can run over $500.

Why do some helmets cost more than others? There are a variety of reasons. Paint schemes add to the price of a helmet; expect to pay more for a helmet with fancy graphics than for a solid-color helmet. (If the paint scheme replicates the helmet of a top racer, expect to pay more yet.) Some expensive helmets are more comfortable than cheaper helmets, while others are not.

Some helmets cost more because they use more expensive material in their outer shells. This may contribute to comfort by making the helmet lighter, but it doesn't make the helmet any safer.

Safety First

All helmets have to meet minimum safety standards set by the Department of Transportation (DOT). Two other organizations, the American National Standards Institute (ANSI) and the Snell Memorial Foundation, also certify helmets. A Snell certification is something I look for on a helmet. Snell won't certify a half or open-face helmet, as DOT will, and it also has more exacting standards for the retention system than DOT.

Steer Clear

If you choose a half helmet, be certain you are getting one approved by DOT. Lately, unscrupulous dealers have been placing DOT stickers (stickers applied to the helmet listing the helmet as DOT approved) on unsafe novelty helmets. Genuine DOT-approved helmets also have a label permanently attached to the inside of the helmet displaying DOT information, like the date of manufacture. Make sure you're getting the real thing.

Getting a Good Fit

When you get used to wearing a helmet, you will not feel comfortable riding without one. Of course, that assumes that you've picked a helmet that fits you well. A helmet that is too loose might flop around while you're riding, obstructing your vision, and a helmet that is too tight will live up to the worst predictions of the anti-helmet crowd.

If all heads were the same shape, choosing a helmet would be simple: You'd just match your helmet size to your hat size. Unfortunately, helmets have to conform to your entire head rather than just a ring around your forehead.

A helmet should feel fairly snug on your head to prevent it from sliding around and possibly obscuring your vision or falling off in an accident. It may feel too tight when you first put it on. When in place, a properly-fitting helmet should not slide around on your head. At the same time, you need to watch for *pressure points*—places where the helmet pushes uncomfortably against your head.

When you try on a helmet, wear it around the store for a bit, and when you take it off, note any soreness or red spots. Wearing a helmet that exerts pressure on your head can turn into a brutal form of torture after an extended period; improperly-fitted helmets have permanently turned many riders against helmet use. If the helmet you are trying on touches pressure points, try on a larger size or a different brand or model.

In Style: What to Wear

Although we can do a lot to make motorcycle riding safer, the fact remains that motorcycles tend to fall over more often than cars. Think about your soft skin hitting the hard pavement, and you start to see why we wear special clothing when we ride.

The following list describes the bare-minimum amount of protective gear you need to wear when riding:

➤ Over-the-ankle leather boots

➤ Leather, full-fingered gloves

➤ Long pants

➤ A riding jacket

This list defines the absolute minimal amount of clothing you can wear to ride safely, especially concerning the last two items (pants and jacket). You may have seen people riding in shorts, tennis shoes, and nothing else. My advice is to not become attached to these people, because should they survive even the most minor spill, they will not emerge from the experience as people you'd want to look at on a regular basis.

Denim actually provides a fair amount of abrasion resistance and should be considered the lowest acceptable standard for protective pants and jackets, but many riders prefer the safety (and style) of a purpose-designed riding suit. These suits, usually constructed of leather or special synthetic materials, like Kevlar and Cordura nylon, offer superior abrasion resistance and often have built-in armor to protect vital areas of a rider's body.

Steer Clear

Because of the difficulty involved in selecting a properly-fitting helmet, I strongly advise you to purchase your first one from a store where you can try on different models and sizes. While you can often save money by purchasing accessories through mail-order companies, you won't be saving any money if you can't wear the helmet you order from a magazine ad because it doesn't fit.

Steer Clear

Denim actually provides better abrasion resistance than fashion-weight leather, which is used in the construction of most leather garments available from sources that don't specialize in motorcycle gear. Make certain that your riding gear is constructed of competition-weight leather (leather that is at least 1.3 millimeter thick): Leave the fashion-weight stuff to the supermodels and biker wannabes.

Looking Good in Leather

Competition-weight leather (leather that is at least 1.3 millimeter thick) provides the best crash protection of any material, period. That's why it's the material of choice for racing suits. I can guarantee you (from personal experience) that buying a new jacket is much less painful than *road rash*, which is what riders call the abrasions from a crash.

Not all that long ago, a motorcyclist had one choice when it came to protective gear: the traditional leather biker jacket, like Marlon Brando wore in *The Wild One*. This lack of choice had its advantages: Back then, you knew who rode a bike and who didn't.

Once, a motorcyclist looking for a protective jacket had just one choice: The black leather biker jacket. (Photo ©1998 Darwin Holstrom)

The variety of styles and colors now available for leather riding gear probably has a lot to do with the increasing popularity of leather in the fashion world. No longer are motorcyclists forced to choose between Marlon Brando's biker jacket or nothing at all. Today's jackets and complete riding suits are available in as many styles and colors as are motorcycles themselves. And traditional black leather riding gear is now available in shapes and styles to complement every body type.

Synthetic Riding Suits: Ties Optional

While leather is still the optimum material for crash protection, an increasing number of riders choose synthetic riding suits. The advantages of leather are most apparent at extremely high speeds (which is why racers choose leather), but at speeds under triple-digit velocities, synthetic suits provide all the protection you are likely to need.

Aerostich's Darien Gore-Tex®–lined jacket and pants, which feature body armor in critical places, combine safety and outstanding protection from the elements. (Photo ©1998 Darwin Holmstrom)

These suits have certain advantages over leather. Most of them are machine washable, unlike leather, which must be sent to a cleaner. And many of them are waterproof or water-resistant, eliminating the need for special rain gear. Plus, these synthetic suits can easily be worn over regular clothing, a tremendous advantage for people who use their motorcycles to commute to work. Most synthetic suits are constructed with removable liners, allowing the rider to use them over a broad range of weather conditions. In hot weather, riders can wear light clothing beneath their suits, and as the temperatures drop, riders can put in the liners and wear extra layers of clothing. Aerostich even offers an electric liner for its Darien jacket.

Gloves: How Much Blood Can You Lose Through the Palm of Your Hand?

Many riders—even those mentioned earlier, who wear nothing but a pair of shorts and some sandals—wear a pair of gloves when they are riding, if for no other reason than for comfort.

Always wear a sturdy pair of leather gloves, preferably a pair with gauntlets that extend over your wrists. A good pair of gloves designed specifically for motorcycle use will have extra leather on the palms, knuckles, and fingers. This provides additional protection against abrasion in case of an accident.

Riders who like to consider themselves tough often wear fingerless gloves. While these will provide some palm protection in the event of a crash, they really offer very little hand protection. Plus, while you are riding, the wind stretches out the finger openings, and bugs can get blown in. Getting stung by a bee on the palm of your hand can make your ride home a painful and dangerous experience. Full-fingered leather gloves prevent this.

In fact, bees are one major reason to wear protective gear. They are a major part of the riding experience; sooner or later, you will get stung. Wearing gloves is one of the most effective ways you can avoid bee stings. I especially like gloves with large gauntlets that go well past the sleeve opening on my jacket; this keeps the little buggers from flying up my jacket sleeve and stinging my arm.

> **Motorcycology**
> Aerodesign's Aerostich Riderwear led the revolution in synthetic riding gear, and its riding suits, jackets, and pants still set the industry standard. But there is another reason to purchase Aerostich riding gear: it's cool. Wearing an Aerostich Roadcrafter suit or Darien jacket and pants into any motorcycle hangout will automatically mark you as one of motorcycling's elite troops.

A good pair of riding gloves will provide both comfort and protection. (Photo ©1998 Darwin Holmstrom)

Motorcycle Moments

One of the bloodiest accidents I've ever seen involved a rider who went down at over 70 miles per hour without gloves. He had a helmet on and wasn't seriously injured, except that he completely peeled off the skin from the palms of his hands. He lost over one pint of blood through just the wounds on his hands.

Fancy Footwear

Even choosing footwear for riding requires you to think. You need to wear a pair of over-the-ankle leather boots to protect your ankles from being burned by the exhaust pipes and from stones and other debris. You also need to take other factors into account when selecting a pair of boots.

On a motorcycle, your feet are an important part of your motorcycle's chassis: They are what hold up the motorcycle when you are at rest. In effect, when you aren't moving, the soles of your shoes are like an extra set of tires. Because of this, you'll want to wear a pair of boots with grippy soles. While fashionable cowboy boots provide adequate ankle protection, their leather soles are far too slippery for them to be safe riding shoes. If you wear cowboy boots, make certain they are work-style cowboy boots with grippy rubber soles. That holds true for any style of boot you choose.

I prefer a pull-on boot over a lace-up boot, and not just because they take less time to put on. I worry about laces coming loose and getting caught in moving parts.

Motorcyclists seem to develop unnatural attachments to their boots, perhaps because they are such an integral part of riding. I have a couple of pairs of riding boots that I've elevated to the status of pets.

My favorite boots are a pair of Harley-Davidson lineman-style boots I've had since college. These are the big, up-to-the-knee black leather boots that scare people when you walk into the room wearing them. I've ridden through thousands of miles of rain and snow in them, I've even crashed in them, and they still have the original pair of soles.

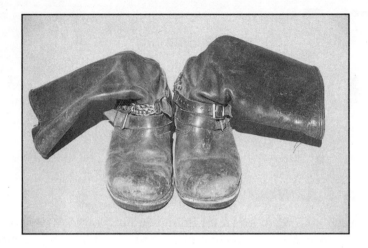

A good pair of boots, like the author's Harley-Davidson lineman's boots, will outlast several motorcycles. (Photo ©1998 Darwin Holmstrom)

Extreme Riding Gear

Nothing surpasses the pleasure of seeing the world on a motorcycle, because on a bike, you are right there, in the thick of it. That means you get to smell the freshly cut hay alongside the road you're riding down. The morning sun recharges you, just as it recharges the flora.

Motorcycology
When selecting a rain suit, choose as brightly-colored a suit as possible. Visibility is especially important when it comes to gear you will wear in low-visibility situations, like the rain. Do not buy a black rain suit. Face it, you're not going to look cool while riding a motorcycle in the rain, regardless of how tough your rain suit looks. Since being cool is out of the question, you might as well be safe.

The downside of all this nature worship is that you will experience the world in its entirety, and you must take the bad with the good. That means being prepared for any kind of weather.

Rain Gear

Ride long enough, and your rain suit will become as much of a part of your everyday riding gear as your helmet: You won't leave home without it. A good rain suit can turn a miserable, wet ride into a tolerable or even fun one.

Rain suits are either one- or two-piece suits, made of *polyvinyl chloride* (PVC) or nylon. I prefer the one-piece suits, since rain can seep in between the pants and the jacket on a two-piece suit.

PVC provides better rain protection than most nylon suits, but because it is so sticky to the touch, it can be difficult to get on and off. To get around this, the best PVC suits have a nylon mesh lining that slides against your leather riding gear. Look for a suit that has such lining in both the upper and lower portions.

In my experience, the best rain gear is a waterproof riding suit, like the Aerostich Darien jacket and pants, which are made of Gore-Tex Cordura material. With these, you don't have to bother putting a rain suit on when foul weather approaches and taking it off when it passes. Even the best rain suits are a hassle to put on by the side of the road on a windy day, and when they get wet, they can be real buggers to get off over leather.

As backward as it may seem, I've encountered a lot of resistance to rain gear. This strikes me as so odd. I know from long years of experience that few things in this world are as miserable as spending an entire day in drenched leather.

You can get a bare-bones two-piece rain suit for well under $50. Expect to spend over $100 for a top-quality one-piece suit.

Motorcycology
Think of rain gear as insurance against rain. If you need it, you'll be glad you have it, and if you don't need it, then you'll be glad anyway, because you had nice weather for your ride.

Ride long enough and your rainsuit will become part of your everyday riding gear: You won't leave home without it. (Photo ©1998 Darwin Holmstrom)

Freezing to Death: Beating the Cold

Motorcyclists tend to get cold more often than they get hot. Even on a relatively mild day, say 65 degrees Fahrenheit, the windchill on a motorcycle traveling at 65 miles per hour can approach freezing. *Hypothermia* (a condition where your body temperature drops to dangerously low levels) is a very real danger on a bike. As I said earlier, in cold weather, a synthetic motorcycle suit can be a real lifesaver, but even those who can't afford such a suit can throw together the proper gear for riding on a cool day.

Thermal underwear is a given if you plan to ride when it's cool. On a bike without fairing, I wear thermal underwear (tops and bottoms) whenever the temperature dips below 70 degrees Fahrenheit.

On really cold days, I wear jeans and a turtleneck sweater over my thermal underwear. I like to wear a sweatshirt over that, along with either chaps or riding pants. When the temperatures get too cold, the summer leather riding suits usually go into hibernation.

Even if you can't afford a Darien jacket with electric liner, you can still benefit from electrically-heated clothing on a budget. Aerostich, as well as several other companies, makes electrically-heated vests you can wear under your jacket. These vests can keep you toasty on even the coldest ride. On super-cold days, I've worn an electric vest under my rain gear, even though it wasn't raining. The vest warmed up the entire inside of the suit and kept me as warm as if I'd been driving a car.

Keeping your hands warm can go a long way toward keeping your whole body warm. Several companies offer electrically heated handgrip kits, and BMW offers them as an option on its bikes. You can also purchase something called *Hippo Hands*, sheaths that attach to your handlebars and surround your controls. These devices may look odd, but they provide exceptional protection against the elements.

Motorcycology
The only drawback of thermal underwear is that it tends to be bulky under your clothes. If this is a problem, another option is to wear silk long underwear. While this doesn't provide the warmth of thermal underwear, it still keeps you warm, without the added bulk.

Motorcycology
I've found that a one-piece pair of thermal underwear (a *union suit*) is preferable to the traditional two-piece set. When you dress in bulky layers, your clothes tend to ride up, creating a gap of bare skin between the top and bottom pieces of a two-piece suit. You can avoid this with a union suit.

For the ultimate in cold weather gear, Aerostich makes this electric liner that zips into its Darien jacket. (Photo © 1998 Darwin Holmstrom)

Baked, Boiled, or Fried: Beating the Heat

All motorcyclists have to deal with the heat. Riding all day under the hot sun takes a lot out of your body. You can become dangerously dehydrated and even suffer heat stroke. At the very least, you may become tired, and your judgment and riding skills will suffer.

When riding in the heat, always remember to drink lots of fluids to prevent dehydration. Many people don't wear a jacket on hot days, but this actually can contribute to dehydration, since the air rushing over your skin evaporates your bodily fluids. You should wear at least a light jacket. A variety of leather makers, like Vanson, market lightweight, ventilated leather summer riding jackets. These help you keep cool and still provide excellent abrasion protection.

Lightweight, ventilated jackets, like this Vanson SRXV, provide outstanding protection and keep you cool on hot days. This jacket uses Vanson's PROperf competition-weight leather (the same material used in racing suits) with double thickness in the elbows, shoulders, and waistband. (Photo ©1998 Darwin Holmstrom)

Vanson leather motorcycle jackets are also compatible with Vanson's Body Armor, which protects the elbow and forearm area, as well as the shoulders and spinal column. Hopefully you'll never need such protection, but if you do, you'll be glad it's there. (Photo ©1998 Darwin Holmstrom)

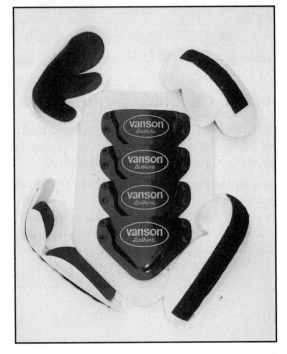

Again, synthetic riding suits make excellent hot-weather riding gear. You can remove the lining from most of these and just use the outer shell, which still retains all the armor and protective qualities. The suits themselves have many zippered vents, allowing you to control airflow. Aerostich recommends wearing long pants and a long-sleeved shirt under its suits, since theoretically its Cordura can melt under extremely high temperatures, but in all its years of manufacturing suits (and examining and repairing suits that have been through crashes), they have yet to find one case of this happening. While I can't condone this practice, your risks would probably be minimal if you chose to wear just shorts and a T-shirt under your Aerostich suit on an extremely hot day. You would still have far more abrasion protection than someone riding in jeans and a light jacket.

Accessories: All the Extras

A good part of the fun of owning a motorcycle is getting all the accessories that go along with it. Motorcyclists may try to convince you otherwise, but they lie. They love modifying their bikes and collecting gadgets.

A huge array of accessories is available for every type of bike and every type of biker, from cruiser windshields to travel trailers to global positioning units (computers that use satellites to tell you where you are) and bike-to-bike communicators. Some are mere novelties, things mainly used to amuse your friends when you stop for a cup of coffee. Other accessories come closer to necessities.

On the more frivolous side are the purely cosmetic items, things that serve no purpose except to alter a bike's looks.

Most accessories available today are usually harmless. That wasn't always true, especially during the chopper craze of the 1960s and 1970s. Some of the popular accessories of the day, like high *sissy bar* backrests and high handlebars, could induce high-speed wobbles in a bike's handling. Some accessories, like extended forks and aftermarket frames with steep rakes, actually made a motorcycle downright dangerous to ride.

Today's accessories can still have unintended side effects. I recently bought a Yamaha Venture, an ultimate-behemoth type touring bike, on which the previous owner had installed a pair of chrome covers over the vents in the side panel. While he probably found these covers attractive, they trapped heat in the engine compartment and made the bike run hot, so I removed them.

Cycle Babble
Such a simple addition as a **sissy bar**—the backrest put behind the passenger's portion of the saddle—can make a bike behave in a frightening manner at high speeds.

Motorcycology
If you choose to mount a windshield to your bike, select one that you can see over without the top of the windshield cutting across your line of vision. The airflow over a well-designed windshield will go over your face, directing wind, bugs, and debris to the top of your helmet. Plexiglas windshields aren't of high enough quality, optically, to provide an undistorted view of the road if you look directly through them. This is especially problematic at night.

The owner had also installed a strange set of 1950s-era taillights around the licenseplate frame. At first, I didn't care for the way these *Elvis lights*, as I call them, looked, but after a while, they grew on me, so I kept them. Besides, anything that makes you more visible to traffic is a functional accessory.

Windshields

On the closer-to-necessity side are windshields. While a bike with a sporty, forward-leaning riding position can get by without a windshield because the rider is naturally braced against the wind, on more laid-back bikes (like cruisers), an effective windshield can make the difference between a comfortable ride and a trip to the chiropractor.

A quality windshield, like this Street Shield from National Cycle, can make any motorcycle a more comfortable place to spend time. (Photo © 1998 Darwin Holmstrom)

Saddlebags

Saddlebags are probably the most useful accessory you can add to your bike, turning it from a pretty plaything into a practical form of transportation. Hard bags, which are more or less suitcases mounted to the bike, are the most useful, since they offer better weather protection, plus most of them can be locked. Unfortunately, few motorcycles offer them as options (although the number is growing). You can purchase them from aftermarket manufacturers, like GIVI, for many bikes. These tend to be expensive, but if you can afford a set, it is money well-spent.

You'll probably end up buying a pair of soft saddlebags that you mount over your seat. These are usually made of vinyl, leather, or nylon.

Saddlebags change a motorcycle from a toy into a practical form of transportation. Chase Harper's ET 4000 Saddlebags provide all the carrying capacity you'll need. (Photo ©1998 Darwin Holmstrom)

Tankbags

Tankbags also add much to a motorcycle's usefulness. These are similar to soft saddlebags, usually constructed of nylon, but they mount on top of the fuel tank. These can be mounted by adjustable straps, or by using magnetic mounts which consist of strong magnets in the base of the bags that stick to the tank. Of course, this requires that your tank be constructed of metal; such a system won't work on plastic tanks or tank covers.

Tankbags are great for traveling, not only because they offer extra storage, but because most of them also have a clear map pocket on top. If you've ever tried to unfold a map and read it at the side of a road on a windy day, you'll appreciate this feature.

The major drawback of using a tankbag is that the straps can scratch the paint on your gas tank. In general, tankbags don't do your paint any favors.

Once you've become accustomed to the convenience of a tankbag, like this 1150 expandable tankbag from Chase Harper, you'll use the bag every time you ride. (Photo ©1998 Darwin Holmstrom)

Steer Clear
Be careful of what you pack in a tankbag. I once crashed, and my motorcycle did a cartwheel, ejecting me from the saddle. In my tankbag, I had a metal toolkit. When I went off the bike, I landed with the tankbag under my chest. I was uninjured, except for several broken ribs from the tankbag containing the toolkit. Moral of the story? Never carry anything in your tankbag you wouldn't want to use for a pillow.

The variety of accessories available could fill its own book, and since they reflect an owner's individual taste, only you can decide which ones are right for your bike.

Where to Buy Accessories

Where you buy those accessories is up to you, too. You can buy your gear from a local dealer, or you can buy from one of several mail-order firms selling just about every accessory available, usually at discount prices. Both methods have drawbacks, and both have benefits.

When you buy from a local dealer, you see what you're getting: You can try on a helmet or a garment, or see if a windshield fits your bike without obstructing your view. And if you do buy something that won't fit you or your bike (although the chances of that happening are slim since the staff can help you select the correct item in the first place), you can always bring it back. Another advantage of buying local is that you get the item right away and don't have to wait for it to be shipped.

On the other hand, the mail-order places usually have a much wider variety of items than any local shop could afford to carry. Plus, they usually sell those items for less than the shops. The drawbacks are you don't get to check the fit of the items before purchasing them, and returning them can also be a hassle.

One other drawback of buying from a mail-order company is that you won't be supporting your local shops. A lot of smaller shops operate on a slim profit margin, and it wouldn't take much to put many of them out of business. When you buy from some company in a distant location, you could help put your local dealer out of business. This might not seem like it would concern you in any practical way, but it does. Should an emergency arise, and you need to repair your bike right now, that local dealer is awfully nice to have.

For a comprehensive list of companies that provide motorcycle accesssories, see Appendix D, "Resources."

Motorcycology
Often, the price difference between buying local and ordering from a discount company is not all that great, especially after figuring in shipping-and-handling charges. Chances are, your local dealer can come reasonably close to those prices, if given the chance.

The Least You Need to Know

➤ Although some states allow you to choose whether or not you wear a helmet, if you have a functioning brain, there is no real choice.

➤ Wear competition-weight leather to protect your body from the elements and in case of a crash.

➤ Not wearing gloves can turn a minor mishap into a visit to the emergency room.

➤ Rain suits can take the misery out of rain.

➤ While mail-order companies may offer a wide range of motorcycle accessories, your local dealer can actually help you choose the right accessories and avoid the need to return items.

Part 3
On the Road

Starting up your bike and hitting the road: This is what motorcycling is all about. All the rest of the motorcycling experience pales when compared to actually riding.

Riding is fun, but it's also serious business, with grave consequences should you make a mistake. Because of the serious nature of riding, you need to be prepared.

In this section of the book, I'll cover a variety of survival strategies for the street, as well as the basics of how to ride. I'll also discuss hazards you might encounter and what to do in case of an emergency. So get your helmet and riding gear and make sure your bike is ready to roll, because we're going riding.

Chapter 10

Preparing to Hit the Road

In This Chapter

➤ How to get in the right frame of mind for riding

➤ Understanding the licensing procedure

➤ How the Motorcycle Safety Foundation can help you learn to ride

➤ What switches and levers do

➤ Mastering the pre-ride inspection

You're just about ready to hit the road, but first you need to learn how to ride. You need to learn what the controls on a bike do, and how you make them do that. You'll need to learn how to prepare your motorcycle for the road, and you'll also need to prepare yourself.

Before you can even ride a bike, you have to get an instructional permit. After you learn to ride, you'll want to get your motorcycle endorsement. Not only will this keep you out of trouble with the law, it will also statistically lower your chances of getting killed on your bike.

If you haven't ridden before, you'll need to start from scratch. The things you learned when you learned to drive a car don't apply to motorcycles.

Every day you ride, you will encounter unexpected challenges, such as all kinds of crazed car drivers. In any encounter between a car and a motorcycle, the car has the advantage.

You'll have enough uncontrollable events to worry about while you're riding. You don't need to worry about things you can control, like the condition of your motorcycle. That's why you'll need to inspect certain components on your bike each time you ride.

And you'll also need to examine your own head before each ride. There's no room on a bike for a distracted or angry rider. If you are not totally in the moment, totally aware of where you are and what you are doing, you can endanger yourself.

In this chapter, I'll explain what you need to do to get your permit and motorcycle endorsement. I'll also show you how to use the controls on your bike, how to prepare your bike for each ride, and how to mentally prepare for each ride.

Getting in Your Right Mind: Mental Motorcycling

Riding a bike requires your undivided attention. If you preoccupy yourself thinking about the meeting you're late for while you commute to work on your bike, you might never make that meeting at all.

Steer Clear
Nothing gets your mind less right for riding than messing it up with alcohol or other drugs. Just one beer can upset your balance in ways you can't perceive but that can have fatal consequences. According to the Motorcycle Safety Foundation, 50 percent of all people killed on motorcycles had alcohol in their blood, but of that 50 percent, two-thirds had only had one or two drinks prior to their accidents.

Before you head out onto the public roads, you have to make sure your mind is right. As Strother Martin (the overseer in the film *Cool Hand Luke*) might have said, motorcyclists whose minds ain't right get to spend the rest of eternity in the box.

You need to clear your mind of distractions before you get on your bike. Do whatever it takes to get your mind right (including going to the bathroom—you'd be surprised at how your concentration can suffer when you've got a full bladder).

Another great distraction is anger at other drivers. Anger on the road is dangerous; it will cloud your judgment, and you need that to make the split-second decisions required to survive in traffic. You need to remain calm and collected in every situation, regardless of whether you are right or wrong. While you may have the right of way, the person in the car has your life in his or her hands. Don't start vehicular arguments with someone who can hurt you simply by turning a steering wheel. Instead, calmly remove yourself from such situations. Get as far away from the offending vehicle as possible.

Getting Licensed

As of 1994 (the most recent complete information I could find), every state except Alabama requires riders to obtain a special endorsement on their driver's license before operating a motorcycle. While this may seem like just another hoop to jump through, these states are doing you a favor. According to the Motorcycle Safety Foundation, unlicensed riders account for the majority of accident victims; by getting a license, you vastly increase your odds of not becoming a statistic. Licensing programs help get a safer, more knowledgeable population of motorcyclists out on the street.

Motorcycle tests, both written and riding, have improved a great deal since I first got my license back in the early 1980s. I'd have to say my first experience with the licensing procedure was useless. Whoever compiled the test obviously had no motorcycle experience, and the questions had no relevance to the knowledge needed to survive on a motorcycle.

I had a pleasant surprise when I retook the written test in the early 1990s; it actually asked useful questions. You had to know things about real-world motorcycling to pass.

Each state has a different written test with different questions. The most-useful tests are those devised in conjunction with the Motorcycle Safety Foundation. To obtain a study guide for your state's test, call your local Department of Motor Vehicles.

Getting Your Learner's Permit

The first step in getting licensed is to get your permit, which you receive upon successfully completing the written part of your test. The purpose of the permit is to allow you to get out and practice in the real world before taking your test. You should get your permit even before you actually learn to ride so that you can legally practice your riding.

In most states, getting your permit will allow you to ride during daylight hours, without a passenger. Most states have extra requirements for permitted riders, like not allowing them to ride after dark or allowing them to ride on limited-access highways only. You more than likely will be required to wear a helmet if you just have a permit—but that shouldn't matter to you, since after reading Chapter 9, you want to wear your helmet all the time anyway.

Getting Your Endorsement

You'll get your endorsement, the notation on your driver's license officially designating you as a motorcyclist, after you complete the riding portion of your test. For this, you'll be required to demonstrate your riding skills on either a closed course or on public streets.

When I took my test, I just rode around a city block, did a U-turn in the street without putting my foot down, and basically didn't kill myself. A tester watched from the sidewalk, and when I returned, he gave me my license, along with a speech informing me of the reasons why I should become an organ donor. This portion of the test has improved somewhat since then, but it still teaches you very little about the skills you'll need to survive on the mean streets. To gain those, your best bet is to take a Motorcycle Safety Foundation RiderCourse.

The Motorcycle Safety Foundation

A nationwide, not-for-profit organization established in March 1973, the Motorcycle Safety Foundation (MSF) works to make motorcycling a safer activity and has developed programs recognized around the world for their excellence and effectiveness. The MSF does the following:

➤ It works to make high-quality rider-training programs, designed for both new and experienced riders, available to as wide a population as possible.

➤ It works with state and national governments and organizations to promote motorcycle safety and to help adopt effective motorcycle-operator licensing practices.

➤ It collects data and information on motorcycle safety and works to get that information out to the public.

There is nothing you can do to better prepare yourself for the challenges of motorcycling than take an MSF RiderCourse. That applies to experienced riders as well as novices. The MSF has worked to make such courses available across the entire United States. Even if you have to drive a few miles to reach the RiderCourse nearest you, you can find no better use of your time if you're serious about motorcycling. To find the RiderCourse nearest you, call the Motorcycle Safety Foundation at 800/447-4700.

> **Motorcycology**
> Another advantage of completing an MSF RiderCourse is that many insurance companies give you a break on your premiums if you successfully complete the course. It is the single best thing you can do to ensure that you have a long and healthy career as a motorcyclist.

In addition to possibly saving your butt somewhere down the line, taking an MSF RiderCourse has immediate practical value. Over 20 states will grant you your motorcycle endorsement upon successfully completing a RiderCourse, saving you the trouble of going to a busy Department of Motor Vehicles office and taking a test. Even if the state still makes you take the test, many states give you extra credit for completing an approved RiderCourse.

Control Freaks: How to Ride a Motorcycle

On a motorcycle, you control the machine with your body, leaning into curves rather than steering the bike, which is why motorcycling provides you with a freedom no other form of transportation can. But controlling a bike requires more than just throwing your weight around. To be able to ride a bike, you need to orchestrate a complex series of actions between both your hands and your feet, all performed simultaneously, in perfect synchronicity.

Primary Controls

You'll use six major controls to operate just about every motorcycle made since World War II (with the exception of a couple of oddball bikes that use automatic transmissions). The location of these controls has been standardized on all motorcycles manufactured after the mid-1970s (although the location of the shifter and rear brake may be reversed on certain European and American motorcycles manufactured before that time). The following figures illustrate the standard places where you'll find controls on all but a few rare, collectible motorcycles.

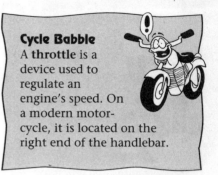

Cycle Babble
A **throttle** is a device used to regulate an engine's speed. On a modern motorcycle, it is located on the right end of the handlebar.

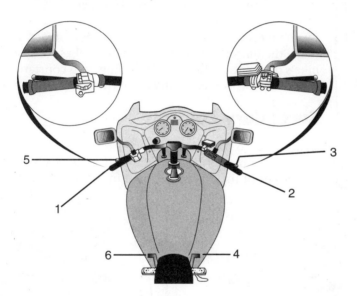

The six primary controls you'll use to ride your bike.

1. The **handlebars** are the levers attached to the top of the fork that you use to control the bike's direction. (Note that I didn't say *steer* the bike: Remember, at anything higher than parking-lot speeds, you *countersteer* the bike, using the handlebars to lever the bike over, not steer it.)

2. The **throttle** is a twist grip located on the right end of the handlebar. This controls your speed. You twist the grip toward you to increase the amount of fuel getting into the engine, thus increasing your velocity. All properly functioning, modern throttles have springs that automatically return them to the closed position.

Cycle Babble
The **front brake lever**, a lever mounted to the right side of the handlebar, in front of the throttle, controls the front brake. The **rear brake lever**, a lever near the right footpeg, controls the rear brake, and on some models with linked braking systems, the front brake. The **clutch lever**, located on the left end of the handlebar (the mirror image of the front brake lever), controls the clutch, and is used to aid in shifting gears. The **shift lever**, located near the left foot peg, moves the shifting forks in the transmission, which in turn shift the transmission's gears.

3. The **front brake lever** is the lever mounted to the right side of the handlebar, in front of the throttle, that controls the front brake.

4. The **rear brake lever** is the lever near the right footpeg that controls the rear brake, and (on some models with linked braking system) the front brake.

5. The **clutch lever** is located on the left end of the handlebar (the mirror image of the front brake lever). It controls the clutch and is used to help shift gears.

6. The **shift lever** is located near the left footpeg. It moves the shifting forks in the transmission, which in turn shift the transmission's gears.

By using these controls with your hands and feet, you can make the motorcycle stop and go, as well as control the bike's direction. While you are riding, you constantly use these controls—often, using all of them at the same time.

Secondary Controls

In addition to the six primary controls, you'll need to use a variety of other controls to ride a bike effectively. The most important of these are illustrated in the following figure.

The secondary controls you'll use to ride your bike.

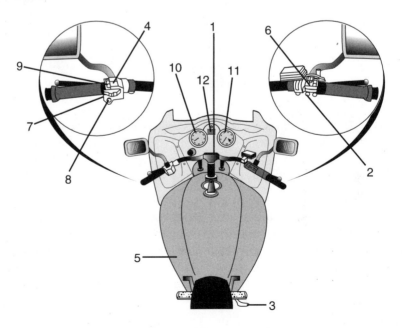

1. The **ignition switch** is similar to the ignition switch in cars, except it usually locks the fork as a theft deterrent, it operates a parking light, and it is separate from the starter; you don't turn the key to start a bike, like you do a car.

2. The **electric-starter button** is on the right end of the handlebar near the throttle. Nearly every motorcycle made today comes with an electric starter, which you operate by pressing this button.

3. The **kick-start lever** is an oddity on most bikes made today, except for some smaller dual sports and strictly off-road bikes, but you may encounter it on certain used bikes. It's usually located near the right footpeg (although it's located on the left side on certain European bikes). To work this device, you need to kick the lever in a downward motion with your leg.

4. The **choke or enrichment circuit** is a lever or a knob that is located in various positions but is usually found on the handlebars; you use it to help start your bike. This used to be a fairly straightforward system, but it has become more complex with the advent of fuel-injection systems and onboard computer technology.

> **Cycle Babble**
> The **ignition switch** on a motorcycle is similar to the ignition switch found in a car—it turns the ignition system on and off—but it also operates a parking light, and it is separate from the starter—you don't turn the key to start a bike, like you do a car. Rather, you use the **electric-starter button**, a button found on the right end of the handlebar, near the throttle, that operates the electric starter (an electrical device that starts the engine). To start bikes without electric starters, you'll need to use the **kick-start lever**, usually located near the right footpeg (although it's located on the left side on certain European bikes), which you operate by kicking in a downward motion with your leg.

5. The **fuel petcock** is a valve that controls the flow of fuel from the gas tank to the induction system; it usually has positions for On, Off, Reserve, and Prime. Prime is used only after the engine has not been run for an extended period of time; it fills the float bowels with fuel prior to starting the engine.

6. The **engine cut-off switch** (or kill switch) turns off the engine. If you can't start your bike, the first thing you should check is whether the kill switch is in the Off position.

7. All street-legal motorcycles manufactured in the past 25 years are equipped with **turn signals**.

   Unlike cars, many bikes don't have a self-canceling feature built into their turn-signal switches: On most modern bikes, you operate the turn signals by pushing the switch toward the direction in which you want to turn, then push it straight in to cancel the turn signal.

Motorcycology
Fuel petcocks are much less important on modern bikes than on older bikes; many modern bikes with fuel pumps don't even use traditional petcocks. Even on those that do have one, you'll seldom need to bother with it. On older bikes, you'll need to turn this switch off each time you park the bike and remember to turn in on when you restart it. The one big advantage of petcocks is their Reserve feature, which saves a small amount of fuel in the bottom of the tank, in case you run out.

Cycle Babble
A **speedometer** is a gauge that informs you how fast you're going. A **tachometer** is a gauge that indicates the number of revolutions your engine is turning each minute. **Indicator lights** (idiot lights) on a motorcycle are primarily the same as the indicator lights on your car, with the exception of a neutral indicator light, which is usually green and shows when the transmission is in neutral.

8. Your **horn** can save your life, so don't be timid about using it. You operate most horns by pushing a button located next to the turn-signal switch.

9. The **headlight dimmer switch** switches the headlight between high- and low-beam modes. On most modern bikes, you can't turn the lights off, so this switch just changes beams.

10. The **speedometer** indicates your speed.

11. The **tachometer** indicates the number of revolutions your engine is turning each minute.

12. The **indicator lights** (sometimes known as *idiot lights*) are primarily the same as the indicator lights on your car, with the exception of a neutral indicator light (usually green) that indicates when the transmission is in neutral.

Although these are all peripheral system controls used to augment riding, rather than directly to ride the bike, you will need to use most, if not all of them, every time you ride.

The Pre-Ride Inspection

Motorcycles require more upkeep than cars. This has always been the case, and it is still a fact of motorcycling life, even with the technological advances you learned about in earlier chapters. The consequences of a systems failure on a bike are much more severe than they are if something goes wrong with your car. Take a blown tire, for example. When a tire blows on your car, you can have difficulty controlling it. When the same thing happens on a bike, the danger level increases exponentially.

The best way to avoid a catastrophic failure is to inspect your motorcycle on a regular basis. Some items need to be checked more often than others; some should be checked each time you go out for a ride.

The Motorcycle Safety Foundation uses the *T-CLOCK method* to help remember what to check during the pre-ride inspection:

T	Tires and wheels
C	Controls
L	Lights and electrics
O	Oils and fluids
C	Chassis and chain
K	Kickstand

Motorcycology
You'll use your idiot lights more on a bike than you do on a car, especially the neutral light and the turn-signal indicator. Since most bikes don't have self-canceling turn signals, it's easy to forget that they're on.

This method is useful, but I'm going to present a simpler one, because I've found that by making the pre-ride inspection too complicated, you encourage riders to ignore the whole thing completely.

I try to check all the items on the T-CLOCK list fairly regularly, but to be honest, I don't check them all every time I ride. A lot depends on the bike I'm riding; for example, if I know that a bike doesn't use oil, I might only check the oil once a week. If the bike is an oil burner, I might check it in the morning, then check it a couple more times as the day progresses.

I've found that the cables and other controls on modern bikes seem to need less attention than those on older bikes; I might go a couple of weeks without attending to my cables and controls, depending on the conditions I've been riding under. As for chains, I prefer shaft-driven bikes, so I can eliminate that messy procedure entirely. I do check for loose bolts in the chassis and make certain the spring is attached to the kickstand each time I ride. The two things I consider absolutely essential to check before each ride are the tires and lights.

Checking the Tires

I check the air pressure in my tires each morning before I start my bike. I keep an air-pressure gauge in my jacket pocket, and I check the tires when they are cold (when the air inside them warms up, which it does very quickly while you ride, the pressure reads higher). Not only is riding with the proper air pressure in your tires safer, it makes your tires last longer. Check your owner's manual to find the proper air-pressure level for your motorcycle.

Whenever I check my air pressure, I also look over the tires themselves to check their wear, and also to look for any abnormalities, like bulges, damage to the carcass, and cracking in the sidewalls, as well as to make certain I haven't picked up a nail or a chunk of glass. I will not ride on a tire I have any questions about.

Keep a tire gauge in your jacket or on your bike so you can check the air pressure each morning.

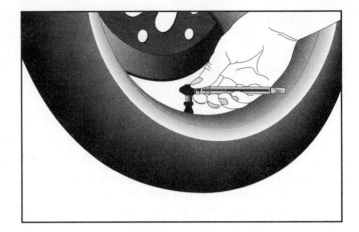

The best way to avoid a blowout is to keep a close eye on your tires, changing them as soon as they wear down to an unacceptable level, and to make certain they are free of debris, like nails or other objects that could puncture the tire.

At the same time I check the tires, I make certain the bolts holding the axles in place are tight. Probably the one thing worse than having a flat tire would be having a tire fall off completely.

Motorcycle Moments

A friend of mine once lost the front tire on his Harley chopper while we were riding to a rally together, because his axle bolts vibrated loose. He went end over end, landing in a ditch about 50 feet from his bike. Although he wasn't wearing a helmet, he seemed to be unhurt, except for a few cuts and bruises. We loaded his bike into a friend's truck and continued to the rally. My friend appeared to be none the worse for wear and tear, but later we learned he'd suffered a severe concussion, and to this day he doesn't remember a thing about that rally.

Looking at Lights

Your lighting system is fairly simple to overlook, but it can get you into a lot of trouble.

If your brake lights aren't working, you can end up with a Chevrolet enema before you even get out of town. Bikes stop more quickly than most cars, and car drivers, by and large, don't give themselves enough room to stop when they're following you. Brake lights are not much protection to keep tailgaters from embedding themselves into your nether regions, but they are all you have (at least until someone designs an anti-tailgating device that uses a 70mm cannon mounted on your saddlebag).

Motorcycle headlights and tail lights seem to fail more frequently than their automotive counterparts, probably because of increased vibration. Since most motorcycles only have one headlight, if it burns out, you will be up the creek when the sun goes down. It's a good idea to check both the high beam and low beam of your headlight when you check your tail light and brake light.

This might seem like a lot of preparation before you can ride, and it is, but the consequences of being unprepared on a bike are just too great.

Learn the controls of your motorcycle. Memorize them and test yourself on them. In an emergency situation, your life can depend on your split-second reactions. You can't afford to lose any time in reacting because you had to think about where a control was: That microsecond can cost you your life.

And internalize the habit of giving your bike a pre-ride inspection. You might feel tempted to skip it when you're late for work or trying to get to a movie on time, but the possible consequences of some sort of failure of your motorcycle could be so severe that you might never see a movie or be able to work again. Take a few minutes to check over your machine before you take your life in your hands. Those minutes may add years to your life.

Motorcycology
Motorcycle headlights usually have two elements: one for high beam and one for low beam. Only one element burns out at a time in a properly-functioning system, so you should still have a low-beam element if your high-beam element burns out, and vice versa. However, be warned that the remaining element will burn out soon after the first, leaving you in the dark. It's a good idea to always pack both a spare headlight bulb and tail-lamp bulb in your gear.

The Least You Need to Know

➤ Unlicensed riders account for a majority of all motorcycle fatalities.

➤ There is no better way to learn to ride than taking a RiderCourse from the Motorcycle Safety Foundation.

➤ The controls on a bike are completely different from the controls on a car.

➤ You'll need to use both your hands and both your feet, often all at the same time, to ride a motorcycle.

➤ Because the consequences of equipment failure on a bike are so much greater than on a car, you need to take a few minutes before each ride to inspect certain key components.

Chapter 11

Learning to Ride

In This Chapter

➤ How to control your bike

➤ The basic skills you need to start and stop a motorcycle

➤ Applying the brakes or throttle

➤ How to turn and change lanes

You're finally ready to hit the road. Everything you've learned so far has been to help prepare you for this moment. For some of you, what comes next will seem natural, and much of what I discuss may seem obvious. Others will find mastering your motorcycle a bit more challenging.

Those of you who have less difficulty need to assimilate this information as much as those who struggle—perhaps even more so. While your instincts will help you under-stand the dynamics involved in piloting a motorcycle, they won't provide you with all the skills you need to survive the brutal streets you are about to enter. Your natural abilities may even make you a bit lazy, and you'll quickly develop bad habits if left to your own devices.

I've found that people who have to put more thought into learning to ride a bike eventu-ally become safer motorcyclists than those who ride instinctively. Having to think about all the things they need to do seems to make them mentally more involved in riding, thus helping them develop safe habits from the beginning.

In this chapter, I'm going to provide you with the basic skills you need to ride a motor-cycle. In Chapter 12, I'll go into more advanced techniques. You should read both chapters before venturing out on the public roads.

Steering Clear

Some people seem to intuitively understand how to operate a motorcycle, while others need to consciously learn to do so. Neither group makes inherently better or worse motorcyclists. The latter group simply has to put a bit more mental energy into learning to ride.

I belong to the first group. When I was about eight years old, my neighbor got a minibike and let me and my brother ride it. I had no problem, and instinctively countersteered. My brother didn't do so well. His brain told him to turn the handlebars to the right if he wanted to go right, which on the surface, makes sense. In reality, a motorcycle doesn't work that way. He turned the bars to the right, the minibike veered left, he ended up in some hedges, and my neighbor's mother refused to let us ride the minibike again.

Unlike a car, a motorcycle can't turn if it doesn't lean. You steer a bike by making it lean, rather than turning the wheel. You do this by *countersteering*, or turning the handlebars in the opposite direction in which you want to turn. While your brain may try to convince you otherwise and force you to rely on the instincts used to drive a car, your brain is wrong. The laws of physics will prevail over your brain's common sense every single time.

When you turn the handlebar toward the right, the wheel will move toward the right—so far, common sense and physics are in complete agreement. But the rest of the motorcycle obeys other laws of physics and wants to keep moving in a straight line. This causes the entire motorcycle to roll on its center of gravity, forcing the motorcycle to lean to the left.

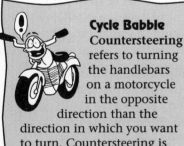

Cycle Babble
Countersteering refers to turning the handlebars on a motorcycle in the opposite direction than the direction in which you want to turn. Countersteering is the only way to get a motor-cycle to change directions at speeds of over 5 miles per hour.

When the motorcycle leans far enough over (the lean angle necessary to initiate a turn varies with speed—the faster you are going, the more you'll have to lean), the angle between the contact patch of the tire (the area of the tire touching the pavement) actually points in the opposite direction from which you initially turned the handlebars. This is true at any speeds over about 5 miles per hour.

The point is, you must countersteer a motorcycle, or turn it in the opposite direction in which you want to go, to control its direction. If you don't, you will end up like my brother on that minibike, except you probably won't be lucky enough to have a big shrub to land in.

Now that I've hammered that point into your head, it's time to crank up your bike's engine and go riding.

Parking-Lot Practice

Before you begin learning to ride, you need to find a safe place to practice, like an empty parking lot, where there are no other vehicles. Practice basic starting, turning, and stopping procedures until you are comfortable with your ability to start, turn, and stop before venturing out into traffic. Just mastering the basics of riding a motorcycle will prove challenging enough; you don't need to compound these challenges by adding the risks posed by other drivers. Or better yet, take a Motorcycle Safety Foundation RiderCourse, where you'll learn these skills in a controlled environment under the guidance of a trained instructor (see Chapter 10, "Preparing to Hit the Road," for details).

Starting the Beast

Even just getting on a bike requires a little knowledge. For starters, you always mount a motorcycle from the left side, because the kickstand is located on that side, so it will be leaning in that direction (provided it is not on the *centerstand*, a stand that supports the motorcycle in an upright position). Hold both handgrips on the handlebar to prevent the bike from moving, and swing your leg over the seat. When you're standing securely over the bike, straighten it with the handlebars. After you've comfortably balanced the bike, rest your weight on the seat.

Never forget to raise the kickstand when you get on a bike, since the protruding stand can jam into the pavement while you are riding and cause you to lose control of the bike and crash. To do this, use your left heel to kick the kickstand into the up position after you have balanced the bike.

If the bike is resting on its centerstand, cover the front brake lever with your right hand (rest it in position, so you can stop the bike once it starts to roll), and gently rock the bike forward, causing it to roll off the stand. When it is down off the centerstand, the centerstand will spring into the up position—as soon as this happens, stop the bike from rolling by applying the front brake. Once you're down, it's a good idea to check to make certain that the kickstand is in the up position— sometimes riders initially park the bike using the kickstand, then place it on the centerstand, forgetting to raise the kickstand.

The starting procedure varies with each motorcycle. For example, if you have an older motorcycle (anything manufactured prior to the late 1970s), you'll probably

Cycle Babble
A **centerstand** is a supporting stand located just in front of a motorcycle's rear wheel that secures the bike in an upright position.

Motorcycology
As silly as this may sound, don't forget to keep your feet planted on the ground whenever your motorcycle is stopped. Many people have actually fallen over while parked because they put their feet on the pegs before they were moving, or more commonly, forgot to put their feet down when they stopped.

have to turn on the fuel petcock before starting the bike (see Chapter 10). Otherwise, the bike won't start, or else it will start, then immediately die from lack of fuel. Most modern bikes have vacuum-operated petcocks that open as soon as the starter button is pushed and close when the engine is shut down.

Start Your Ignition

The next step is to turn the ignition switch on and make certain the kill switch is not in the Off position. Even the most experienced motorcyclist sometimes bumps the kill switch into the Off position, then wears his or her battery down trying to start the beast. You can save yourself a lot of grief by getting into the habit of automatically turning the switch to the On position each time you turn the ignition switch on.

The ignition switch is usually located on the dash, up near the instrument panel, but a recent trend is to locate the switch in some odd position under the seat or fuel tank, (where the switches were located on motorcycles manufactured prior to about 1970). This retro touch, which emulates the switch location on some Harley-Davidson models, appears on many of the newer cruiser-type motorcycles currently being manufactured in Japan.

Next, make certain your transmission is in neutral. Accidentally hitting the starter button while the bike is in gear can be a good way to fall over in your driveway, which is one of the worst ways to start out your ride. This is why the neutral light is so important on a motorcycle, but you can't always trust the light. On some bikes, the neutral light may light up when the gearshift lever is in a certain position, even if it hasn't completely disengaged the gears in the transmission.

Rock the bike back and forth to make certain you are in neutral—if you are in gear, you won't be able to move the bike more than a small distance before the rear wheel locks up and refuses to turn. If this happens, gently move the shift lever up or down until you can roll the motorcycle freely. If you have a bike that gives you a false neutral reading, you may have transmission or clutch problems.

After you've switched on the ignition, you'll more than likely need to set your choke, especially if the engine is cold. How much choke you have to use varies from bike to bike. This is almost a mystical procedure, and you'll need to use every one of your senses to learn the exact combination of choke and throttle needed. You'll need to listen to the engine turning over, feel it catch and begin to fire, smell the exhaust to see if you are giving it too much throttle and flooding the carburetors, watch the tachometer once the engine starts, and adjust the choke accordingly. A properly running motorcycle with perfectly-adjusted controls usually needs very little throttle to start when cold, although it may need a bit more when warm. Unfortunately, we seldom achieve absolute perfection in tuning our engines, causing the procedure to vary widely.

Now, pull in the clutch lever. Even though you've shifted to neutral, the light is shining brightly, and you've checked to make certain the transmission is in neutral, you can never be too careful on a motorcycle.

Here the procedure for starting a bike with an electric starter differs from starting one with a kick starter. On electrically-starting bikes, you start the engine with the press of a button. With the clutch lever pulled in, push the starter button, and the bike should fire up. It will make a brief grinding sound as the starter spins the flywheel in the engine, then when the engine fires (when the fuel charges in the cylinders begin to burn), you will hear the internal-combustion process taking place. When you hear this, release the starter button immediately.

If the engine does not fire immediately, don't hold the button down for an extended period of time, since this will drain the battery, burn out the starter, and cause other damage. Usually, if the engine doesn't fire immediately, the problem will be something as simple as your forgetting to turn on the fuel petcock or accidentally bumping the kill switch to the Off position.

> **Motorcycology**
> Different manufacturers use a variety of safety devices to ensure that you don't start a bike while it is in gear, like starters that only operate when the clutch lever is pulled in or when the transmission is in neutral. Unfortunately, there is no standard, agreed-upon procedure.

Kick-Starting Your Bike

Kick-starting is pretty much the same, except instead of just pushing a button, you'll need to use the kick-starting lever.

First, fold out the footpeg on the lever. If the lever is located on the right side of the bike (as it will be on all but a few oddball European bikes), lean the bike slightly to the left to give your hands more leverage against the force of your kick. (This supports the bike during the starting procedure.)

Quickly and forcefully kick the lever downward. The inertia of the engine will want to make the lever slam back up again on many bikes, slapping it against your shin or ankle with tremendous force if your foot slips off the peg, so make certain that you have a firm footing on the peg before kicking. Repeat this procedure until the bike starts. You'll soon understand the appeal of electric starters.

If all this sounds like a lot of bother, just be glad you're riding a modern bike—this procedure is simple compared to starting an old Triumph Thunderbird or Harley XLCH Sportster (probably the most difficult-to-start bike in history).

Taking Off—The Friction Zone

Taking off on a motorcycle is a lot like taking off in a car with a manually-shifted transmission, except that the controls are reversed (you operate the throttle, clutch, and front brake with your hands and operate the shifter with your foot), and you have to balance a bike and take off at the same time.

You let the clutch lever out to transmit power from the engine to the rear wheel on a bike just as you do in a car. The Motorcycle Safety Foundation describes the area in the clutch lever's travel where power first begins to transmit to the rear tire as the *friction zone*, a description I find useful. To find the friction zone, first pull the clutch lever in toward the handgrip, then shift the gear lever down into first gear.

Although the friction zone varies slightly from bike to bike, depending on such factors as clutch wear and adjustment, it falls near the end of a clutch lever's travel on a properly functioning bike.

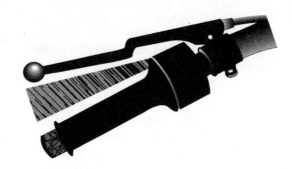

Now, with both feet on the ground, slowly ease the clutch lever out until you hear the engine begin to slow down. As the engine slows, the bike begins to move forward—you're in the friction zone.

Motorcycology
All motorcycles now sold in the United States use a standard shifting pattern, described as *one-down, four up* (or five or three up, depending on the number of gears). This means you push the lever down to engage first gear and up to engage the remaining gears, with neutral found between first and second gears. This may vary on older American and European motorcycles.

To continue through the friction zone, you have to apply the throttle to give the engine enough fuel, or the bike will stall. But if you give it too much fuel, you'll spin out of control and crash, which as I said, is a horrible way to begin any ride. And if you let the clutch out too fast, you'll either stall or spin out of control. It's a delicate operation, one that will become second nature to you soon enough, but one that requires some practice for now. When you start the bike for the first time, practice getting the engine into the friction zone a few times before riding, easing out the clutch lever until you find the friction zone, then pulling it back in.

When you feel you are ready to ride, ease out the clutch, giving the engine just enough gas not to stall. If you feel the engine about to stall, pull the clutch lever back in. And if you're accelerating too fast, ease up on the throttle. If you feel any loss of control, pull the clutch lever back in and gently apply the brakes.

Stopping What You've Started

I've noticed one common mistake people tend to make when they teach others how to ride—they show their students how to start without showing them how to stop. You'll see these people running around parking lots, chasing their students, shrieking, "Pull in the clutch! Pull in the clutch!" It's easy to forget that stopping is as important as starting, and for the beginner, it can be nearly as difficult a skill to master.

To stop, you'll need to use both your hands and both your feet at the same time. In one motion, you pull in the clutch lever with your left hand and squeeze the front brake lever with your right, while shifting down to first gear with your left foot and pressing down on the rear brake pedal with your right. Remember, when stopping, it's almost as important to keep the clutch disengaged as it is to use the brakes.

Using the brakes on a bike is much more challenging than using the brakes on a car. For starters, you'll have to use both your right hand and your right foot to brake, rather than just using your right foot as in a car. Plus, riding a two-wheeled vehicle introduces all kinds of weird chassis dynamics into the situation. I'll discuss these dynamics at greater length in Chapter 12, "Rules of the Road."

Your front brake is the most important of the two brakes. An average motorcycle relies on the front brake for 70–80 percent of its stopping power. Bikes with a more rearward weight distribution, like cruisers, rely more heavily on their rear brakes than sportbikes, but even on a cruiser, it is your front brake that does most of the work when you're stopping.

You don't want to squeeze the brakes too hard, or you'll lock up your tires and skid, especially the rear tire, which locks up more easily than the front tire. According to the California Highway Patrol, a rider locking up his or her rear brake is a factor in the majority of crashes. If your rear tire starts to skid, there's a good chance you'll either *lay the bike down* (slide down on the road and crash) or *high-side the bike* (start to slide in one direction, then flip over in the other direction). When you high-side the bike, you flip it by releasing the brake while skidding and allowing the tire to regain traction, jerking the motorcycle in the opposite direction.

Motorcycology
As silly as it is, the myth that you'll flip and go over the handlebars if you use the front brake persists among certain groups of motorcyclists (usually the same folks who don't wear helmets). The front brake provides 70 percent or more of your stopping power and should be considered your primary brake. Some bikes even have linked-brake systems to force riders to use their front brakes.

Cycle Babble
There are two basic types of motorcycle crashes: **laying the bike down**, which is when you slide down on one side of the bike, and **high-siding**, which happens when you start to slide in one direction, then flip over in the opposite direction.

141

Braking Practice

Locking up your brakes is a very dangerous situation. To help avoid it, practice stopping quickly in the parking lot, being careful not to lock up the tires. Only after you are comfortable with your ability to feel what the tires are doing through the brake lever and brake pedal should you venture out on public roads.

Even after you master braking, you need to constantly practice emergency stops. Go to an abandoned parking lot and practice stopping as hard as you can. First, practice stopping using just the front brake. At the slightest hint of the front tire locking up, release the front brake. If you lock up the front tire, you more than likely will fall down. Once you know the limits of your front brake and can instinctively apply it forcefully and quickly, begin adding a small amount of rear brake at the same time as you apply the front brake. Remember, the front brake does most of the work, and the rear brake locks the tire up much easier than the front, so you won't apply nearly as much pressure to the rear brake as you do to the front.

Parking the Bike

Once your bike is stopped, extend the kickstand to the down position, then gently lean the bike to the left until it rests securely on the stand. If your bike has one, it's a good idea to park the bike on its centerstand, since this provides a more secure perch than the kickstand.

If you've ever watched someone struggle to put a bike on its centerstand, you've probably watched him or her do it wrong. There's usually a trick to putting most bikes on their centerstands without throwing your back out:

1. First, stand beside the bike, facing it from the left side, and grasp both handlebar grips.

2. When you have a firm grip on the bike, take your right foot and lower the centerstand until you feel both its feet resting securely on the floor.

3. Then, balance the bike by the handlebars so that it rests perfectly upright.

4. Next, move one hand down and grasp the motorcycle frame under the rider's portion of the saddle (this gives you more leverage). Many motorcycles, like Honda's ST1100, have retractable handles to grasp when raising the bike onto its centerstand. Make certain that you have a good bite on the centerstand *tang*, the part sticking out that you place just in front of the heel of your boot, before raising the bike, since you'll be using your leg to lift the bike!

5. Lock the centerstand tang against your heel, so your boot does not slide. Once everything is secure, push down and backward on the tang with your leg while

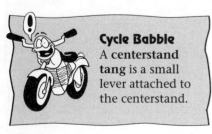

Cycle Babble
A centerstand **tang** is a small lever attached to the centerstand.

rolling the bike backward with your arms. A well-balanced bike should roll right back up on its centerstand.

Some bikes require more strength than others to lift on their centerstands, but if you do it right, you should be able to raise any bike up on the centerstand by yourself.

Make certain you have a firm grip on the centerstand tang with your boot before lifting the bike up on its centerstand. (Photo ©1998 Darwin Holmstrom)

Shifting Gears

As with any manual transmission, you'll need to shift your motorcycle's gears as engine speeds increase and decrease. Shifting up allows you to ride faster, and shifting down allows you to ride slower.

You shift up when your RPMs increase to a certain point—upshift too late, and you'll rev your engine excessively; upshift too early, and you'll *lug* your engine (*lugging* refers to the chugging sound an engine makes when it is in danger of stalling). The idea is to keep the engine in its *powerband* (the RPM range in which the engine generates most of its power).

Cycle Babble
The **powerband** refers to a certain RPM (revolutions per minute that an engine's crankshaft is spinning) range where an engine makes most of its power. Powerbands vary from bike to bike, depending on each bike's state of tune. Except for certain high-strung sportbikes, most inline four-cylinder engines make enough power for most riding situations between 5,000 and 7,000 RPMs. **Lugging your engine** means letting the RPMs fall below the engine's powerband.

Cycle Babble
Failing to engage gears is called finding a **false neutral**, because although the transmission is not in neutral, it behaves as though it is.

You want to keep the engine in its powerband for safety reasons as well as mechanical and performance reasons. Technically, when an engine is in its powerband, it is operating at its peak efficiency, which is good for the mechanical components in the engine and allows the motorcycle to accelerate quickly. If the engine is not in its powerband because it is running at too many RPMs, it causes excessive wear on its mechanical parts; if it is not in the powerband because of too few RPMs, it can cause *detonations* in the cylinders (tiny explosions that damage components), buildup of unburned hydrocarbons, and lack of power.

It's the lack of power that poses a safety problem. In the real world, you will encounter situations where you'll need to accelerate quickly to avoid an accident. If you don't have the engine in its powerband, you'll need to waste precious split seconds downshifting, and a split second can mean the difference between a near miss and a tragic accident.

To shift up, roll off the throttle at the same time as you squeeze in the clutch lever. When the throttle is fully closed and the clutch is disengaged, move the shift lever up with your toe in a firm, smooth movement until the lever stops. If you hesitate during the shift, you might not get it into the next gear. This is called *finding a false neutral* and can be potentially dangerous. When you have engaged the next gear (you can hear this happen and feel it with your foot), ease the clutch lever back out and slowly roll the throttle back up to speed.

You downshift as you decrease your speed. You need to do this with the same finesse as you upshift, because by down-shifting when the engine is revving too high, you can lock up your rear tire, just as if you had applied too much brake, causing you to lose control and crash.

To downshift, roll off the throttle and squeeze the clutch. Firmly press down on the shift lever, then apply a small amount of throttle as you ease out the clutch lever. When coming to a complete stop, you may shift all the way down to neutral without releasing the clutch, but again, you'll want to do this gradually. Many motorcycle transmissions can be damaged by shifting to a lower gear at too high a speed, even if the clutch lever is pulled in. This is especially problematic on older bikes or bikes with worn clutches.

Throttle Control

When I get into more advanced riding techniques in Chapter 12, I'll discuss things like chassis dynamics and throttle control in more detail, but even when you're first starting out in a deserted parking lot, smooth use of the throttle can make the difference between successfully learning to ride and a trip to the emergency room.

Depending on the drive system used (shaft versus belt or chain—see Chapter 5, "Anatomy of a Motorcycle"), motorcycles react differently to throttle input. The rear ends of shaft-driven bikes tend to move up when the throttle is applied, while chain-driven bikes tend to squat down a bit under acceleration. Either way, you're going to encounter some moving around back there when you ride. Jerky use of the throttle exacerbates whatever tendency a bike has to move around under acceleration, while smooth throttle use minimizes these effects.

And the more power a bike has, the more the rear end tends to jerk around under acceleration. That is one of the main reasons why smaller, less powerful bikes are easier to learn to ride—they jerk around less when you apply the throttle.

But even a smaller bike is going to have more than enough power to get you into serious trouble if you get ham-fisted with the throttle. Make certain you can accelerate and decelerate smoothly before venturing into traffic.

Motorcycology
You can slow your progress by carefully downshifting, a process called *engine braking*. To do this, you shift down one gear at a time, releasing the clutch after each downshift. But be careful not to do this too aggressively, or you can lock up the rear wheel and lose control. This is an especially useful technique when navigating mountain roads, helping you keep your brakes cooler so they remain near their peak efficiency.

Taking Turns

As I mentioned, you countersteer a bike, a process you'll just have to practice and learn. But turning a bike involves more than just countersteering. Because motorcyclists are less visible to other motorists while riding a bike, and because our potential for injury in an accident is so much greater, we need to take extra care when changing directions or changing lanes.

The first thing to remember is to reduce your speed before turning. Motorcycles are less stable than cars and are not able to corner as quickly. Also, braking upsets a motorcycle's chassis more than a car's, causing all sorts of strange dynamics. These antics can be especially dangerous while leaning over in a corner, so brake and reduce your speed before entering a curve.

Before turning or changing lanes, you should check your mirrors and glance over to visually ascertain that the lane you want to occupy is clear. Never rely just on your mirrors, which on most bikes give you a better view of your elbows and shoulders than they do of the traffic behind you. On the other hand, you shouldn't look completely over your shoulder to make certain the lane is clear, since this takes too much attention away from the traffic in front of you. There is a fine line between looking too long behind you and insufficiently checking to make certain your lane is clear, but you will have to straddle that line every time you ride. Making certain a lane is clear every time you change lanes is a great way to avoid having an accident.

When you are certain the coast is clear and are ready to turn, apply your turning signal well in advance to let other drivers know what you intend to do. Then lean the motorcycle into the turn by applying slight pressure to the inside of the handlebar in the direction you want to turn. As I discussed earlier, this causes the motorcycle to lean in the direction you want to turn. The faster you are moving, the more you'll have to lean the motorcycle to negotiate the turn. At normal highway speeds, you should lean with the bike. When negotiating tight turns that require you to ride more slowly, just lean the motorcycle while you remain in an upright position.

Once you have settled into a turn (I'll discuss the lines you follow through a corner in Chapter 12), roll on the throttle to maintain a steady speed or accelerate slightly. This helps keep the bike stable through the turn. Rapid acceleration or deceleration in a corner can cause you to lose control of the bike.

Taking the Test

When you have mastered these basic skills and feel confident in your ability, take your test and get your motorcycle endorsement as soon as possible. This will allow you more freedom as a motorcyclist, as well as save you from potential legal hassles. Getting a license also lowers your odds of getting hurt on your bike. To find out what is required for you to obtain your motorcycle endorsement, contact your local Department of Motor Vehicles.

The Least You Need to Know

➤ Countersteering is the only way to turn a motorcycle traveling at speeds higher than about 5 miles per hour.

➤ Before going out into traffic, find a deserted parking lot or some other place you can practice the basic skills of riding.

➤ The front brake provides 70–80 percent of a motorcycle's stopping power—use it.

➤ Practice being able to stop as quickly as possible without locking the tire up; most accidents involve the locking up of the rear tire under emergency braking.

➤ Smoothness is the key to successful throttle and brake use.

➤ Always look to make certain a lane is clear before turning or changing lanes—don't trust your mirror.

Rules of the Road

You've practiced riding your bike until the procedures discussed in Chapter 11 are instinctive. Now that you have the hang of riding and have received your motorcycle endorsement, you're ready to venture out on public roads. You're about to move up to a higher level of fun, but you're also about to move up to a higher level of risk.

The key to surviving on your motorcycle is awareness. You need to be aware of what you are doing, you need to be aware of what other drivers are doing, and you need to try to make other drivers aware of what you are doing. Much of it boils down to visibility. Visibility and awareness apply to every situation you may encounter, from riding on the freeway to negotiating a busy intersection in a city to riding down a deserted country road. By being aware and making yourself visible, you are trying to accomplish two things:

1. You are trying to avoid potentially dangerous situations. The best way to survive an accident is not to get into one in the first place.

2. You are trying to give yourself time to react to an unexpected situation as quickly as possible. Being aware shortens your reaction time in an emergency, and every fraction of a second available to react in a potentially dangerous situation dramatically increases your chances of avoiding an accident.

In this chapter, I'll show you different strategies to help you be more aware of what's going on around you, and I'll show you ways to make yourself more visible to other drivers. I'll also show you how to avoid potentially dangerous situations and ways to use other vehicles to your advantage. And I'll explain how to ride through a corner in a way that both makes you more visible to other traffic and also lets you see traffic as early as possible.

Driving in the USA

When riding a motorcycle, the safest attitude to adopt is to view every driver as unfit to be behind the wheel of a motor vehicle. Do this, and you'll be prepared for anything that might happen on the road.

Always treat other drivers like they don't know what they're doing. Many of them are too busy to notice something as small as a motorcycle. The number-one thing car drivers who hit motorcyclists tell police officers is, "I didn't see the motorcycle."

Unfortunately, you can't control other drivers' habits. But you can control your own.

Be Aware

Always be conscious of what's going on around you. You need to focus on what's ahead of you, because that is the direction in which a dangerous situation will most likely arise, but you also need to be aware of what's going on in your periphery and what's going on behind you.

In a study published at the University of Southern California (the Hurt Report, 1981), researchers studied 900 motorcycle accidents and identified the directions from which cars most often struck motorcyclists in collisions at intersections. According to the study, 77 percent of the collisions occurred from the front of the motorcycle, with nearly half (43.4 percent) occurring from the rider's front and left.

If the region around a motorcyclist were illustrated as the face of a clock, the area a rider needs to most focus on is the area from 10 o'clock to 2 o'clock, especially watching the area between 11 and 12.

That doesn't mean you can ignore all other areas. Just because a scant 5.5 percent of accidents occur in a motorcyclist's 5- to 7-o'clock range doesn't mean he or she can ignore that area. Percentages mean nothing if another driver creams you from the rear.

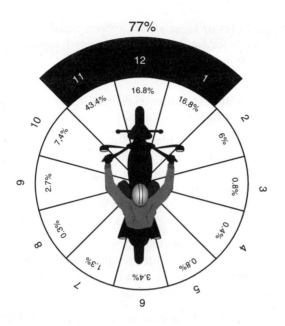

77%

This diagram shows the direction in which most motorcycle crashes occur. As you can see, 77 percent of a motorcyclist's danger comes from the front of a motorcycle, and 43.4 percent comes from the front and left.

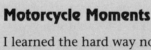

Motorcycle Moments

I learned the hard way not to play the percentages on a bike. My worst accident to date happened when I hit a deer that darted out from the weeds just about in my 9-o'clock range, which according to the Hurt report, has less than a 3 percent chance of happening. The statistical improbability of such an accident didn't make the experience any less painful.

Active Scanning

To be aware while you are riding, you need to constantly provide your brain with input. Since your surroundings constantly change while you ride, you need to continuously update the information you transmit to your brain.

Since your eyes are your primary brain-input device, you acquire the vast majority of the information you need to survive by seeing. But to survive on a motorcycle requires a very active form of seeing. You need to actively scan your surroundings while you ride.

While keeping the area in front of you foremost in your mind, you need to constantly scan all other areas around you for possible danger. Don't let your eyes fixate on any one object for more than a fraction of a second. Scan all aspects of your surroundings, and don't just focus on other traffic. Watch the condition of the road surface. Stay alert for

Motorcycology

A good way to become aware of potentially dangerous situations when you ride is to play the *What If?* game. While you ride and scan your surroundings, think about those elements that could quickly turn dangerous. Imagine what would happen if a piece of the sheet metal on the flat-bed truck up ahead came loose and flew off the truck. What would you do? Do you have enough space to maneuver out of the way in a hurry? And what if the driver of that slow-moving car in the oncoming lane suddenly decided to make a left turn into a driveway right in front of you? Are you prepared? Imagining such situations is good preparation, because sooner or later, they will happen.

potholes or loose gravel, which can be as slippery as ice. Watch for traffic entering the road, especially at intersections. Remember that driveways, parking lots, and crossings are intersections, too.

And watch for animals or pedestrians. If you hit a pedestrian or an animal on your motorcycle, you're both in trouble.

Make certain to include the rearview mirror in your scanning, but also turn your head slightly to check your blind spots, especially when turning, changing lanes, or stopping. Remember not to turn your head any farther than you have to in order to make certain your lane is clear so that you don't lose focus on the action in front of you.

To aid the scanning process, you can develop some techniques for using your eyes that help you constantly monitor the most dangerous area in front of you but also let you scan your entire surroundings:

➤ Focus on your intended path. Since you are moving rapidly through your surroundings, you need to concentrate on an area about 12 to 14 seconds ahead of your bike, since that will give you enough time to react to an emergency situation.

➤ Keep your eyes up, since that will aim your vision ahead, where the greatest danger resides.

You need to constantly scan your surroundings for potentially dangerous situations. That car in the oncoming lane making a left turn in front of you is most likely to kill you in this scenario, but any of the other elements in this picture could end your motorcycling career, too—from that woman on the sidewalk to that oil spot in the lane ahead of you.

➤ Move your eyes around, forcing them to move frequently and not become fixated on any one thing. This will widen your field of perception.

➤ Learn to recognize potentially dangerous situations. A vague movement out of the corner of your eye may be a deer preparing to leap in front of your bike or a car backing out of a hidden driveway. That shadow on the road ahead may be oil, fresh tar, or some other slippery surface that could cause you to lose traction and crash.

➤ Constantly monitor your rear-view mirrors. The region in front of your bike is the area you should primarily concern yourself with, but you constantly need to be aware of your entire surroundings, especially the area behind you.

Make awareness a required condition for riding a motorcycle; like your helmet, don't leave home without it. This is the surest way to have a long, healthy motorcycling career. As you get into the habit of being aware, you'll also find your automobile-driving skills will improve.

Avoiding Blind Spots

When a car driver sayshe didn't see a motorcyclist, he's probably telling the truth. Motorcycles are much smaller than other vehicles and are harder too see. Often, other drivers don't see a bike simply because they don't expect to see a bike. Or else the bike was hidden in the blind spot of the driver's car.

Motorcycle Moments

When I was a teenager living on my dad's farm, I was about to enter the highway at an unmarked intersection while driving a small truck with large mirrors, but I heard something odd, so I stopped. Just as I stopped, a motorcycle went zooming by. We had both been approaching the intersection at an angle that caused the motorcycle to remain hidden behind my mirror the entire time.

It was dumb luck that saved that motorcyclist's life. I learned a lesson that day that has probably saved my own life more than once—never assume that the other driver can see you.

To avoid riding in other drivers' blind spots, you need to know where those blind spots are. There's a simple experiment you can try to help you get an idea of just how little you can actually see from inside a car. The next time you see a motorcycle while you are driving your car, watch to see when the motorcycle is in one of your many blind spots.

If you haven't tried this, you'll be amazed at how often the bike is completely blocked from your view. Remember where your blind spots in a car are, and avoid riding in those positions when you are on your bike.

Jockeying for Position: Lane Positioning

You need to monitor the road ahead for debris that can cause you to lose traction and crash, and you especially need to watch for oncoming traffic turning left in front of you— the number-one hazard a motorcyclist will encounter at an intersection. You can count on at least one car making a left turn in front of you every single time you ride your bike in a congested area. I'll discuss this scenario more specifically in the next chapter, but for now the important thing for you to understand is that you need to be aware of other vehicles so that you can react as quickly as possible to any situation.

Motorcycology

One thing to keep in mind when scanning your surroundings and looking ahead is that your motorcycle goes where your eyes go. This is called *target fixation*. If you spot an object or some debris on the road, don't look at it. If you look at it, you will hit it, because your bike will follow your eyes. Once you've detected something you want to avoid, look at where you want to go instead of at that object. A good way to practice this is to identify a spot on a road and make a conscious effort to avoid it.

Your mind needs to be up there, ahead of the bike, processing every small bit of information available. The faster you ride, the farther ahead you'll need to look. You can maximize your forward visibility by properly positioning yourself in your lane of traffic.

Keep Your Forward View Clear

Always place your bike in a position that gives you the best view of what is ahead of you. You can see best when there is no traffic in front of you blocking your view. If at all possible, you should choose a lane in which there are no cars in front of you. If traffic is too heavy and no clear lanes are available, stay to the right or the left of the lane so that you can see past the vehicles in front of you.

Avoid riding in the center of the lane, because that's usually the slipperiest part of the road. Car engines, transmissions, and radiators are located between the car's wheels, and most of the slippery goop that cars drip on the highway comes from these parts and lands splat on the center of the lane. Your best traction, and your best view of the road ahead, is from the tire tracks in a lane, so ride there.

Make certain that you don't follow any vehicle too closely. Stay back far enough so that you'll see any debris, such as a rock or chunk of a tire, far enough in advance so that you can avoid it.

Motorcycle Moments

Following cars too closely is the surest way to end up hitting an object on the road. When I was 19 years old, some girls in a car waved and smiled at me as they passed my motorcycle on a four-lane highway. I sped my motorcycle up to get closer to them. Just as I got close enough to see the smiles on the girls' faces, they drove over a rock. There was no way for me to avoid the rock, so I relied on my motocross experience and wheelied over the rock. Which worked, but I was so shaken, I forgot all about the girls. Instead, I was disappointed with myself for getting into such a stupid situation. My dirtbike experience saved my hide, but if I hadn't been following the car too closely, I would have missed the rock entirely.

Tricks and Trucks

The worst position you can place your motorcycle in is behind a truck. Trucks (or large vans, sport-utility vehicles, and buses) completely block your forward vision and cause a variety of other problems as well. Because of their poor aerodynamics, trucks disrupt the air in ways that mess with your bike. The turbulent air coming off the back of a truck can move your motorcycle all over the road. Not only do trucks leave a rough wake in the air behind them, but they also leave a lot of debris. Trucks are usually filled with stuff, which often gets blown out of the back or leaks out on the road. Many of you have probably had to replace a windshield on a car because a stone flew out of a truck and hit your car. Imagine what that stone could do to your face.

Other things fall out of trucks besides rocks. Many trucks haul petroleum products or other chemicals. This can be nasty if it gets on you or your bike. I've been sprayed with stuff that has peeled off several layers of my skin. Trucks and motorcycles do not mix. As a general rule, you should just stay away from trucks entirely.

Because of the turbulent air surrounding a truck, passing one is a dangerous and difficult procedure, but there will be times, especially on multilane highways, when passing a truck will be your safest course of action. The worst thing you can do when passing a truck is to tense up and try to fight the turbulent air. Instead relax, learn what to expect, and let the turbulence work for you.

When you pass through the initial turbulent air coming off the back of the truck, a steady stream of air will either try to pull you toward the truck or push you away from it. (This depends on the direction of the wind. If the wind is coming from the side of the truck opposite your motorcycle, it will create a vacuum alongside the truck, pulling you toward it. If the wind is from your side of the truck, it will bounce off the truck and blow you away from the truck.)

Just relax and lean the bike toward the truck if the wind is trying to push you away, or lean the bike away from the truck if a vacuum is trying to pull you toward the truck. You want to do this smoothly, leaning your bike just enough to make it go straight down the road. As you get toward the front of the truck, you will encounter a blast of wind coming off the front of the truck, perhaps the most intense turbulence of the entire passing experience. You'll need to lean into this wind to keep going straight as you pass in front of the truck.

Use Other Traffic as Protection

After you become familiar with traffic patterns and get into the habit of automatically positioning your bike in the area that affords you the best visibility, you can begin to use other traffic as a shield. On multilane highways, you can position yourself so other drivers going in your direction block you from being struck by left-turning drivers in the oncoming lane. This is a skill that requires you to instantly read and assess a situation, and no two situations will be exactly the same, but if you master it, you will be able to move through crowded streets much more safely.

To do this effectively sometimes requires you to ride a bit aggressively to keep up with traffic. Sometimes, riding a bit aggressively can be a good defensive strategy. Some studies indicate that riders who go just a bit faster than traffic have statistically better odds of avoiding an accident than motorcyclists who ride at the same speed as other drivers or ride slower than traffic. My own experience backs up these studies. By moving slightly faster than other vehicles, I seem to have less trouble with drivers menacing me from behind, allowing me to concentrate more on what's going on ahead of me.

This does not mean that if you go out and ride as fast as your motorcycle will go you will be safer than if you travel at the speed limit. The key words here are *slightly faster* than traffic. And if you ride beyond your ability, you are not doing yourself or anyone else any favors. If you are uncomfortable riding faster than traffic, you should not do so.

Be Seen

Part of your job as a motorcyclist is to make yourself visible. It helps to wear brightly-colored clothing and helmets and to wear vests or riding suits that incorporate reflective material. This will make you more visible, especially in low-light conditions.

Use the high beam on your headlight during the daytime, when you won't blind oncoming traffic. In some states, it may be legal to mount a modulator on your headlight so that it pulses during daylight hours. Some studies indicate that such devices may be effective.

You should signal your intention to turn or change lanes early, giving other drivers time to notice you and prepare for you to move. Once you've determined that the lane you want to enter is clear, activate your turning signal and check your mirrors to see if the vehicles behind you slow down to let you turn. I sometimes accentuate my turn signal with a hand signal, just to get the attention of the driver behind me. Unfortunately, most drivers don't have a clue what hand signals mean, but at least it helps to alert them that I'm there. If the driver in the car is still coming at you full speed after you've signaled, you may want to speed up and wait until the next turn. Always remember to cancel your turn signal, especially in a situation like this.

Another trick to get the attention of other drivers is to tap your brake pedal (or lever) just enough to activate your brake light. Sometimes the flashing of your brake light can wake car drivers from whatever stupor they are in. And use your horn if you have to, but don't rely on it. The horns on most motorcycles are only slightly louder than the rubber-bulb horns on some bicycles.

Sometimes a quick zigzag on your part may get a driver's attention, but it may also confuse him, so be careful about trying this technique. Even if you think you have a car driver's attention, don't assume that you do. You may think you made eye contact with a driver, but maybe he still doesn't notice you. Do what you can to make yourself more visible, but always act as if you are invisible.

Steer Clear
Never trust the turning signals of other vehicles. Often, other drivers will drive down the road for miles with their turn signals flashing for no good reason, but usually they just turn whenever the mood strikes them with no warning whatsoever.

The Three Rs: Riding, Reading, and Reacting

Learn to read traffic while you are riding your motorcycle. After a while, certain clues will alert you to potentially dangerous situations. For example, when you are riding down a street lined with parked cars, you should watch for people getting out of a parked car and opening their door in front of you. Even worse, they could pull their car away from its parking spot and into your lane.

You can almost count on at least one driver doing something stupid in certain situations. For example, when you pull up in a lane alongside a line of cars stuck behind someone making a left-hand turn, expect at least one of them to pull into your lane, right in front of you, to get around the turning vehicle. When you see this situation, slow down to give yourself time to react, move over to the far-right side of your lane to give yourself room to escape, and get ready, because it's going to happen.

Steer Clear
When riding alongside parked cars, you not only need to watch for potentially dangerous situations concerning the cars—you need to monitor the entire situation. You need to watch the people getting into and out of the cars and to watch for whatever manner of danger lurks on the other side of the cars, where you can't see. Expect anything—dogs, basketballs, children—to come darting out from between the cars.

Identify Hazards

To read potentially dangerous situations, you need to learn to identify the types of hazards you are most likely to encounter. These hazards can be divided into three main groups:

1. Cars, trucks, and other vehicles. Other traffic has the most potential to do you bodily harm while you're riding a bike, and every driver on the road has the potential to be your executioner. Never trust any of them, but learn to identify those most likely to try to take you out.

2. Pedestrians and animals. Although slower moving than vehicles, pedestrians and animals are more unpredictable because they can change direction much more quickly, and their movements don't follow the usual patterns of traffic.

3. Stationary objects. These can be anything from a piece of junk on the road to potholes, signposts, trees, guardrails, or anything else. These won't cut you off like other vehicles or dart in front of you like an animal, but they do limit where you can move to avoid a dangerous situation.

Steer Clear
One stationary object posing a potential danger at an intersection that you might not have considered before is the paint on the road, which can be quite slippery. This includes the bars marking the crosswalk, the directional arrows, and words such as "Stop Ahead" that are painted in the lane. Never stop on the paint, and make certain that you put your feet down on unpainted pavement when you stop.

The most dangerous places to ride are intersections, partly because they often contain all of the hazards mentioned here. Any place where other traffic may cross your path poses a potentially dangerous situation.

Watch the Front Tires

Watching the front tires of a car will give you some clue about what that car will do next. The front tire of a car has to turn before the car turns. When I'm riding in heavy traffic, I constantly monitor the front tires of cars around me. Seeing the front tire turn will give you an extra split second to react in an emergency situation.

Watching the front tire can alert you to a left-turning driver about to cross your path. If someone in an oncoming lane slows down, be aware of what his front tire is doing and prepare to react accordingly. Even if you're not in an intersection, the person could be preparing to turn in front of you to enter a driveway or a parking lot, or even just to make an illegal U-turn. It can happen anywhere, and often does. Watch for people who appear to be pulling into a parking space and then do a U-turn right in front of you.

Learning to read traffic helps a great deal, but it does not make you invulnerable. You could become the world's foremost traffic-reading expert and still be taken by surprise.

Always expect the unexpected. Look both ways, even when crossing a one-way street, because fools can come from anywhere, and the world is filled with fools.

The Safety Zone

When you are on a bike, your fenders are your own flesh and blood, and you don't want to challenge thousands of pounds of metal with them. Because of your vulnerability, you want to keep as much free space around your motorcycle as possible. I've already discussed not getting boxed in, not following traffic too closely, and trying to ride in lanes with no traffic in front of you, but there's more you can do to increase the safety zone around you and your bike.

When you're riding, always try to find a spot in traffic that provides you with the most room possible. Sometimes that will mean moving over into a safer lane. Always try to be in the lane that gives you the most free space to ride in.

How you change lanes can increase your margin of safety. Make certain that you don't change lanes while you are in another driver's blind spot. And make certain that a driver from the lane on the other side of the one you intend to occupy doesn't have the same intention. If the people right next to you have a hard time seeing you, imagine how hard it is for the person two lanes over.

Do whatever you have to in order to get out of a situation where another motorist is following you too closely. Unfortunately, you'll have to rely on evasive actions, like changing lanes or speeding up, to extricate yourself from this very dangerous situation.

Again, never follow other vehicles too closely. At the very least, give yourself two seconds of space between you and the car ahead of you. This will give you the minimum space you'll need to swerve, brake, or perform a combination of both actions if an emergency situation arises.

Poor road conditions will increase the space you'll need to have in order to stop. If there is oil, gravel, wet leaves, or any other debris on the road, that will increase your stopping distance, too. Factor the condition of the road into the equation and allow extra space between you and the vehicle in front of you.

Following too closely can get you killed even when doing something that seems relatively safe, like pulling into a parking lot. The person in front of you may suddenly stop or slow way down as he or she enters the parking lot, leaving you stuck and unable to get out of the way of oncoming traffic.

Motorcycology
While riding in any kind of high-risk area (which describes most places you'll ride), always cover your front brake with at least a couple of fingers—that is, ride with at least two fingers resting on your front-brake lever. Also, make certain that your foot is in position to use the rear-brake pedal. Having your hand and foot in position to stop will give you an extra fraction of a second to stop.

You even need to be aware of your safety zone in the parking lot itself. Parking lots are especially dangerous places, since people are looking for parking spaces and not watching where they are going.

It's difficult to discuss all the dangerous situations you may encounter without sounding like an alarmist or giving you a negative view of the sport of motorcycling, but it's not as bad as it sounds. Practice the procedures I've outlined in this chapter, and soon they'll be as much a part of your routine as countersteering and shifting gears. You always need to remain conscious of these dangerous situations, since that is the best way to avoid them, but as you practice and internalize these procedures, you'll become more at ease with your ability to cope with any situation that comes your way.

The Least You Need to Know

➤ Awareness is the key to surviving on a motorcycle. Always be aware of your surroundings, and actively scan your surroundings at all times.

➤ Do everything in your power to make yourself visible to other drivers, but never assume that they see you. Avoid riding in other drivers' blind spots.

➤ Stay as far away from trucks as possible.

➤ Don't let yourself get boxed in by other traffic—always leave yourself room to get out of a dangerous situation. Keep as much free space around you and your motorcycle as possible.

➤ Use other traffic to shield you from left-turning drivers.

Chapter 13

Street Survivors: Steering Through Sticky Situations

In This Chapter

➤ Riding safely through intersections

➤ Techniques for freeway riding

➤ Controlling your motorcycle in corners

➤ The importance of remaining calm

In Chapter 12, I stressed the need for awareness and how important it is for you to constantly scan your surroundings so that you can identify potentially dangerous situations. Now it's time for you to learn more about those dangers and how to deal with them. In this chapter, I'm going to explain how to ride in specific situations.

The problem with discussing specific situations is that every situation differs. For every bit of advice I provide in this chapter, I can think of possible situations where that advice doesn't apply. I'm going to provide you with generally-accepted procedures for dealing with certain situations, but when you're by yourself out on the road, you're going to have to make your own decisions based on your own observations in a given situation. Keep in mind the principles in this chapter as general templates, but in the end, rely on the information you gather through your own diligent observations to ultimately guide your actions.

Intersection Encounters

As I said in Chapter 12, the most dangerous situation you'll encounter on a bike is a driver turning left in front of you, and most often that happens in some sort of intersection, making intersections the most dangerous places to ride.

You can do much to minimize that danger by following certain procedures when approaching and passing through an intersection.

When you ride through any intersection—that is, any area where traffic can possibly cross your lane of traffic, always consider the following:

➤ Slow down. This puts you in control of the situation. It gives you more time to scan the intersection for potential dangers. The earlier you can detect a dangerous situation, the quicker you can react to avoid it. Slowing by just 10 miles per hour reduces your necessary stopping distance by almost half.

➤ Cover your front brake when riding through an intersection. This reduces your reaction time.

➤ Position your bike away from other cars. This gives you room to maneuver out of the way if an errant car jockey fails to see you and moves toward you.

➤ Watch the front tires of other vehicles. I discussed this in Chapter 12, but it's doubly important at an intersection. An oncoming vehicle with its tires turned toward your lane can pull in front of you nearly half a second quicker than can a vehicle with its wheels pointing straight ahead. In this situation, half a second is literally worth a lifetime.

➤ Make absolutely certain an intersection is clear of other traffic before you proceed. Watch for drivers stopped in other lanes waiting to turn—they may not see you and turn in front of you. Slow down enough to allow yourself room to stop.

Memorize the above rules, internalize them, and make them part of your riding techniques. By doing this, you'll significantly reduce your chances of getting in an accident.

Types of Intersections

When riding, consider any area where something might cross your path an intersection. This includes the usual places, like crossings and where two roads meet, but it includes a lot of places you might not consider to be intersections.

For example, turnouts are intersections. Turnouts are often located at scenic points, and people pulling into and out of them tend to pay more attention to the scenery than to traffic. This applies to any spot where people congregate alongside a road, like a beach, a bridge people fish off of, or a park-and-ride parking lot (parking lots along roads where commuters leave their cars and get on buses). Always slow down when passing such a place, and move away from the side of the road the turnout is located on, giving yourself more room to maneuver.

The most dangerous intersections are the intricate ones, where several roads converge at once. Traffic doesn't follow usual patterns at such intersections, and vehicles enter the road at unexpected angles. Often there will be *frontage roads* (roads running parallel to main roads) merging at such intersections, too, further confusing everybody. When riding through these intersections, slow down even more than you normally do, because you have more activity to monitor.

Moving Through Intersections

When passing through an intersection while you're following a vehicle that blocks your view, like a bus, watch for left-turning vehicles that are unable to see you behind the bus. Again, leave plenty of space between you and the vehicle in front of you so that you have room to get out of the way. And position yourself in the part of the lane that allows you to see and be seen.

> **Steer Clear**
> In some ways, alleys are similar to intersections, because you have to watch for traffic crossing your path in an alley. Alleys are filled with blind driveways, and people often back their cars out without looking. Even a diligent driver who looks before backing up might not be able to see you because of some obstruction, like a fence or a trash dumpster. And kids and animals like to hang out in alleys, too. Slow down when you ride through an alley, and watch for kids, dogs, cats, and cars.

When you are following large vehicles in traffic, you may not be able to decide where to position your bike. If you can see oncoming vehicles clearly, it's best to ride on the far-right side of the lane, positioning yourself as far away as possible from a left-turning driver. But if you're following a bus or a truck, you may be better off riding in the far left part of the lane, where they can best see you, and where you can scan for possible left-turning drivers.

Stopping at an Intersection

When approaching an intersection where you need to stop, pay extra attention to the vehicles behind you. Be especially careful when stopping on a yellow light, in case the driver behind you thinks yellow means *put the accelerator to the floor and drive like crazy*.

Because of the danger of drivers rear-ending you at intersections, you need to scan for a possible escape route whenever you approach an intersection. Always position yourself toward one edge of the lane or the other to provide the quickest escape route, should you need one. Choose the side of the lane that gives you the most free space to maneuver out of the way, which will usually be the side of the lane farthest away from oncoming traffic.

When you stop behind a vehicle, don't pull up close behind it. If you do so, you'll block yourself in. You won't have room to move out of the way if the vehicle in front backs up, and you won't have room to get around the vehicle in front if the vehicle behind you doesn't stop. Always leave enough room between you and the vehicle in front of you so that you can move around it in an emergency situation.

Motorcycle Moments

Once, while riding a borrowed ultimate-behemoth-type touring bike, I slightly misjudged the distance I needed to stop at an intersection; I didn't misjudge it enough to hit the vehicle in front of me, but I did stop too close to it, boxing myself in. The car behind my bike stopped close behind me. As I waited for the light to change, I heard the screeching of tires behind me, followed by a loud crash. Someone had rear-ended one of the cars behind me. All I could do was hang on and hope I wasn't about to become the most injured domino in a line of dominoes. I was lucky—the accident didn't make its way to me. And I was stupid. If I had been creamed at that intersection, it would have been my fault as much as anyone's.

Leaving yourself enough room to maneuver is important any time you have to stop, whether or not you're at an intersection. Even on the freeway, expect trouble from behind, and monitor the traffic behind you. If you see a vehicle behind you that's not stopping, look for a clear spot and rapidly accelerate toward it.

To do this, your bike will have to be ready to go. When you sit at an intersection, or anytime you have to stop when there is traffic around, keep your bike in first gear, with the clutch lever pulled in. That way, if you need to get out of someone's way in a hurry, you won't have to waste time putting the bike in gear.

When you stop at an intersection, look for the best traction for putting your feet down. Avoid putting your feet down on any damp, shiny, or dark spot. The spot may be oil, antifreeze, or diesel, which is the most slippery fluid you'll encounter. (Some people refer to diesel on the road as *black ice*.)

Also be careful not to put your feet down on any painted lines or marks in an intersection. Painted spots will be slippery, and just a small slip of your foot when you are stopping can cause you to wipe out. And remember, if you fall down because of something slippery on the road, there's a pretty good chance that whoever is following you will also hit the slippery stuff and possibly lose traction, too.

The safest part of the lane to put your foot down in is the tire track. As I said in Chapter 12, the slippery goop that drips off cars builds up in the center of the lane. When you put your foot down, place it at the edge of the tire track farthest away from the center of the lane.

Leaving an Intersection

When leaving an intersection, the number-one thing to remember is not to proceed until you're absolutely certain that the path is clear.

When the light turns green, wait until things settle before entering the intersection.

When starting through an intersection from a standing stop, it is especially important not to trust eye contact as a means of determining if another driver has seen you. Even if another driver sees you, he or she might not register your motorcycle as traffic.

Turning in Intersections

The same rules that apply to passing through an intersection apply to turning at an intersection. Make certain that all lanes are clear before making a turn.

Often, other traffic will block your view at an intersection, especially if a turning lane is present. If you find your view blocked, slowly ease ahead until you can see past the offending vehicle. Remember, when you do this, your tire will enter traffic before your view clears, so be extra cautious. Lean forward and stretch your neck ahead as far as is comfortable, being careful to remain stable and in control of the bike, to see around the vehicle blocking your view. This will help make certain you don't roll your bike out in front of an oncoming vehicle when you ease ahead to clear your view.

When making a turn at an intersection, be extra careful when trucks are present. Trucks with long trailers make wide turns, and they often need more than one lane to negotiate a turn in an intersection. If you pull up beside a truck, thinking the truck is going straight, and the truck turns in your direction, you could be trapped.

You may be able to power ahead and get out of the situation, but then you run the risk of being struck by an oncoming vehicle hidden from your view by the truck. If you're lucky, there will be a shoulder instead of a curb at the side of the road, allowing you space to get away from the trailer.

Your best course of action is to not get in such a situation in the first place. Avoid squeezing between a truck and something else at all costs, even if it means not entering a turning lane and having to use a different route.

Steer Clear
Realize that some people consider the first part of a red light just an extension of the yellow. I've almost been taken out by drivers who continue through intersections when they have a red light. The only way to protect yourself from red-light runners is to slow down when you ride through an intersection. Always make certain the path is clear before entering an intersection, even if you have the right of way.

Slippery when wet

Drivers turning left in front of you are the number one hazard you will encounter on a bike.

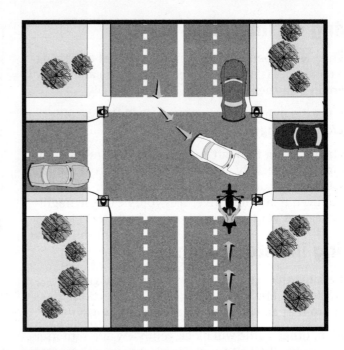

Avoiding Dangerous Intersections

Some intersections are death traps for motorcyclists. You will encounter intersections with electromagnetic stoplight sensors (which trigger a change in the traffic light by detecting large masses of metal over them) that can't detect an object as small as your motorcycle. At such intersections, you can find yourself faced with the choice of running a red light or waiting until a car pulls up behind you, neither of which is an acceptable option.

Other intersections may have too many obstructions—like signs, lightposts, and buildings—for you to make certain all lanes are clear before you enter them.

If you know of an intersection like this, one that makes you uncomfortable, avoid it if at all possible. Even if you have to ride a few extra miles, if you can select a safer route, your chances of arriving are improved by avoiding dangerous intersections.

Motorcycology

If you stop at an intersection with an electromagnetic sensor, the placement of your motorcycle can determine whether the sensor will recognize your bike. Electromagnetic sensors are usually located under the pavement toward the end of a lane. You can often see them by looking for a cut in the pavement, usually square-shaped, that extends from nearly one side of the lane to the other. The sensor itself is located beneath this cut, and if you stop your motorcycle directly over the part of the cut that runs parallel with your lane, you can trigger the light to change.

Freeway Riding

Although it might not seem likely, limited-access multilane freeways are statistically much safer than city streets and highways with intersections. There are two reasons for this:

1. Traffic moves in only one direction on freeways.

2. Freeways remove your number-one hazard: vehicles in oncoming lanes turning left in front of you.

But riding on a freeway presents a new set of challenges. Traffic moves faster on freeways, meaning that things happen faster. You have to look even farther ahead on a freeway to give yourself more time to react to an emergency. The faster traffic moves, the farther ahead you need to look.

On a freeway, you have to be careful not to ride too fast. Motorcycles can cut through freeway traffic more quickly than cars, making it easier to speed on a bike. But riding much faster than traffic puts you at risk, because if you're riding too fast, you won't be able to react if a car moves into your lane.

And even though you don't have intersections on a freeway, you have on ramps and off ramps, both of which create challenges for a motorcyclist.

On ramps are especially tricky on a bike. These often consist of tight turns, forcing you to lean hard to turn your motorcycle. This in itself wouldn't be that problematic, but on ramps usually have extra-slippery surfaces, forcing you to negotiate the ramp more slowly than you would in a car. The cars, of course, won't slow down for you, and will tailgate you or even try to pass you.

Having to negotiate the curve on an on ramp is the first challenge; the second challenge is to adjust your speed once you have negotiated the curve so that you can enter traffic safely. This is where a motorcycle's capability to accelerate quickly comes into play.

As you round the curve of an on ramp, monitor the traffic in the lane you will merge in and locate a safe

Steer Clear

Watch for cars trying to pass you when you are negotiating an on ramp. This may seem insane, but some drivers actually do it. The combination of slippery surface and tight curve will limit your speed on an on ramp, but that won't matter to some car jockeys. If a driver does try to pass you on an on ramp, all you can do is move over and let the driver by.

Motorcycology

When you ride as far away from on and off ramps as possible, this places you in what is usually the fastest lane of traffic. This can be the safest lane to ride in, since you only have to worry about traffic moving on one side of your motorcycle. But it can also be a more dangerous lane, if traffic is moving so fast that you don't have enough time to react if someone moves into your lane. Like everything else, the key here is awareness of your surroundings. Take into account such factors as the amount of traffic and how fast traffic is moving when selecting the safest lane.

165

space to enter that lane. Once you have finished negotiating the curve and the motor-cycle is upright, accelerate toward the safe spot you've identified, adjusting your speed so that you can safely merge with traffic.

When passing an on ramp where other traffic is merging onto the freeway, move over to a lane as far away from the on ramp as possible. Drivers merging into your lane may not see your motorcycle and may mistake the space you're occupying as a free spot to enter traffic. And other drivers in your lane may be watching the merging traffic and not see you. If they move over to let the merging traffic enter, they may hit you.

This is also a problem at off ramps. If you are driving in the lane closest to the off ramp, you risk getting cut off by a driver who doesn't see you and thinks he or she has a clear shot at the off ramp.

Slow down as you approach an off ramp. As with an on ramp, your safest location is as far away from the ramp as possible.

Watch for drivers who don't see you as they cut across traffic to get on an off ramp.

Changing Lanes

Because traffic moves so quickly on a freeway, changing lanes requires extra caution on your part, especially on freeways with more than two lanes of traffic. On such multiple-lane freeways, not only do you need to check to make certain the lane is clear before you enter it, but you need to check to see if someone from another lane is moving into the free spot you have identified.

The speed of traffic also makes the vehicles behind you more of a threat when changing lanes on a freeway. You always need to let the vehicles behind you know what you intend to do. Once you have made certain that a lane is clear, slow down and use your turning signal early. Do everything possible to communicate your intentions to other drivers. Watch to make certain the car behind you is slowing down.

And remember not to trust that the other driver sees you, just because he or she slows down. Even if the other driver sees you slow down, he or she might not see your turning signal, since motorcycle turning signals aren't very bright and can be hard for other drivers to see, especially in bright sunlight. Before you change lanes, make certain the driver behind you isn't planning to change lanes, too.

Steer Clear

Getting cut off by the vehicle behind you while you change lanes on a freeway illustrates the importance of avoiding tailgaters. When other vehicles follow you too closely, carefully get out of their way and let them pass. Remember to signal early and make definite moves so that the driver behind you is aware of what you are doing.

Make certain that the vehicle beside you doesn't attempt to change lanes at the same time you do.

As I said in Chapter 12, when you change lanes, don't do so in other drivers' blind spots. This is another situation where the speed of your motorcycle comes in handy. You can use that speed to accelerate out of other drivers' blind spots, moving into a position where they can see you.

Always make sure you're riding in the correct gear for a given speed. To accelerate quickly, you need to keep your revs in the powerband. Remember, your motorcycle was designed to operate most efficiently at certain RPMs; when you ride with your tachometer in the most efficient rev zone, you can instantly accelerate if you need to.

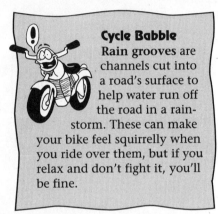

Cycle Babble
Rain grooves are channels cut into a road's surface to help water run off the road in a rainstorm. These can make your bike feel squirrelly when you ride over them, but if you relax and don't fight it, you'll be fine.

Rain Grooves

Some roads have grooves cut into their surface to facilitate the removal of water in a rainstorm. These rain grooves are especially common on freeways. They can cause your bike to feel unstable—a disconcerting experience, even for expert motorcyclists. But don't worry; even though your bike may feel like it is moving all over the place, it is a relatively harmless situation. That is, unless you panic.

When you hit rain grooves, the best thing to do is relax your grip on the bars and just ride it out. If you tense up and try to fight it, your bike will only move around more.

Splitting Lanes

In some states, it is legal for a motorcycle to ride between lanes of traffic. This is known as *splitting lanes*. Doing this when traffic is moving at normal speed is, of course, insane—a form of suicide. When traffic is moving normally, remain in your normal lane of traffic.

Lane splitting is not a task for a beginning rider. But for an experienced motorcyclist, splitting lanes when traffic is moving very slowly or is stopped can be as safe or safer than just sitting there, if for no other reason than it gets you out of traffic more quickly and reduces the amount of time you're exposed to danger.

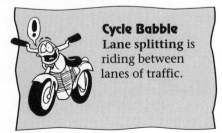

Cycle Babble
Lane splitting is riding between lanes of traffic.

Some general rules help make lane splitting safer:

➤ Only ride about 10 or 15 miles per hour faster than traffic is moving. If traffic is moving at 15 mph, then ride no faster than 25 or 30 mph between lanes. If traffic is stopped, keep your speed under 15 mph. If you ride any faster, you won't have time to react if someone pulls out in front of you.

➤ If traffic slows, don't immediately hop between lanes and start lane splitting. Traffic may be slowing for just a moment and will speed up again. Make certain that traffic is slowing or stopping before lane splitting.

➤ Watch for other motorcyclists who might be lane splitting before pulling between the lanes. If traffic is stopping, the odds are some other motorcyclist has the same idea that you do. Focus primarily on what's in front of you, but always be aware of what's behind you.

➤ Watch for people changing lanes. If you see an open spot in traffic, you can almost count on someone crossing from another lane to take that spot. It's best to try to keep a car on either side of you, which will block other vehicles from crossing your lane.

➤ If freeway traffic is stopped, or moving very slowly, it's best to move over to the fastest (farthest left) lane before lane splitting. This decreases your odds of encountering merging traffic or drivers making sudden lane changes.

➤ When traffic stops, watch for people opening their car doors. It happens more often than you might think.

Riding in the Twisties

While motorcycles are more maneuverable than cars, they can't go around corners as quickly. It's a simple matter of *traction*—four big tires grip the road better than two small ones.

But motorcycles can corner as quickly as you need them to if you ride them correctly.

Traction: A Sticky Matter

The reason four car tires grip the road better than two small tires is because when you have larger tires, and more of them, more rubber touches the road.

A variety of factors contribute to your bike's traction. The material your tire is made of plays a role. Softer, stickier rubber grips better than harder rubber. Tire temperature affects traction, too, since the colder the tire, the harder the rubber. A tire that has been heated up through use has more gripping power than a cold

Cycle Babble
Traction refers to a tire's capability to grip the road; it's the potential for friction between your tire and the road's surface.

Steer Clear
Motorcycle tires are designed to operate at a certain temperature; they need to heat up a bit before they provide proper traction. Professional racers keep their tires in warming machines prior to going out on the track, but even then, they wait until they have heated up their tires before they get on the throttle. You probably won't require racing levels of adhesion from your tires, but applying too much throttle in a curve before your tires are warm is a quick way to crash.

Cycle Babble
The **contact patch** of your tire is the area of your tire that actually contacts the road while you ride.

tire. The shape and depth of your tread contribute to traction. The surface of the road also plays a role.

When cornering, the *contact patch* of your tire is critical to traction. The contact patch is the part of the tire that actually touches the road.

The relatively small amount of rubber in the contact patch is the main reason motorcycle tires can't corner as well as cars. Plus, unlike cars, motorcycles lean when they turn. As your motorcycle leans, the contact patch of its tires decreases, meaning that you have less traction available in a turn.

To further complicate matters, when you accelerate, decelerate, or brake, you upset the chassis of your motorcycle, causing it to move around. This causes the amount of pressure on your tires to vary, which in turn causes the size of your contact patch to vary.

Gravity Is Your Friend

I've made taking a curve on a motorcycle sound like going on a ride at a carnival, and there are similarities, but on a bike, you're in control. By practicing proper cornering techniques, you can actually make all this commotion work for you instead of against you.

Motorcycology
Smooth throttle control is one of the primary reasons for choosing a smaller, less powerful motorcycle for your first bike. The more power available when you twist the throttle, the harder it will be for you to develop smooth throttle control. Bikes that have abrupt throttle response, a characteristic of bikes with narrow power bands, are more difficult to control, while bikes with a broader power band deliver smoother, more controllable power.

Get your braking done before you turn. Apply the brakes when the motorcycle is upright, before you lean over to turn. If you brake when you're leaning over, you're much more likely to skid than you are if you brake when the motorcycle is upright. Remember, when you're leaning over, you have less traction available.

Because of that lack of traction, you must use the throttle smoothly in a corner. Maintaining a steady engine speed keeps your bike settled in a curve, while jerky use of the throttle upsets your bike. The smoother you are with your throttle, the more control you have over your bike.

Don't accelerate or shift during a corner, since this will upset your chassis. Wait until you've finished the turn and your bike is once again upright to accelerate. As you develop your technique and become more proficient at taking curves, you will be able to apply power slightly earlier as you exit a corner. When you do this, you make the motorcycle's dynamics work for you, because when you accelerate, you place more weight on the rear of the motorcycle, thus increasing your traction. As you become more familiar with your bike's reactions to throttle input, you can use that increased traction as you exit a corner.

Dangerous Debris

You always need to scan the surface of the road for debris, like leaves, sand, fluids, and gravel buildup, but the situation in which these conditions will most often lead to a crash is when you encounter them in a curve. These materials tend to accumulate on the outside edge of a curve, so pay close attention to that part of the road when scanning a corner.

If there is debris on a curve, slow down to give yourself time to maneuver around the debris. If you are unable to avoid the debris, don't panic and hit the brakes, since that will make you more likely to lose traction and crash than if you maintain a steady speed through the corner. If you've slowed down to a safe speed before entering the corner, you should be all right.

If you are going too fast and need to slow down in a corner, stand the bike up for a brief moment, brake, then immediately lean back into the curve. If you do this for more than a split second, you will run off the road, which sort of defeats your purpose.

> **Steer Clear**
> Approach areas where shade covers the road with extra caution, especially in the morning, when shaded areas can be slippery from dew or frost. You may not be able to see debris like sand or oil in a shaded area. When you are unsure of the condition of the road, slow down.

Don't Panic

If you find yourself going into a curve too fast on dry pavement, don't panic. Just lean harder into the curve. The more you lean, the sharper you turn. You need to trust the capability of your tires. Although motorcycles have less traction than cars, they have more traction than you might imagine. Just watch a Grand Prix racer go through a curve leaned over so far that it looks like he's riding sideways. That should give you an idea of just how much traction a motorcycle can have.

Leaning harder actually slows you down. By leaning harder, you can scrub off excess speed with your tires. The most important thing is to keep a cool head. Unless you are going at a ridiculous speed, if you don't panic, you should be able to make just about any corner.

Your safest bet is to make certain you're not going too fast when you enter the corner in the first place. If you're in doubt, slow down even more. You can get in a lot less trouble by going too slow through a corner than you can by going too fast. If you're riding within your abilities, you should be able to stop a bike at any time, as well as maneuver around any obstacle, whether you are going straight or around a corner.

Cornering Lines

The path you take through a corner plays an important role in both safety and speed (the safest line through a curve is also the fastest). By selecting the right route, you increase your visibility and make yourself more obvious to oncoming traffic.

The most important thing is to stay in your lane. One of the leading causes of fatalities among people who treat public highways like racetracks—hotshots who ride at unsafe speeds on twisting public roads—is straying over the center line and getting hit by oncoming traffic.

When going around a corner, treat your lane like it's the only part of the road that exists. The oncoming lane might as well be a cliff or a solid wall of rock, because under no circumstance can you ride there when going around a curve.

When approaching a corner, move to the outside of the lane before entering the turn. This lets you see farther around the corner, and it also makes you visible to oncoming traffic earlier. When you enter the corner, turn hard, moving away from oncoming traffic as you negotiate the curve. Racers take this line through a curve because it is the fastest way to do so, but you do it on the street because it affords you the best visibility of oncoming traffic and any hazards that might be on the road ahead.

The Least You Need to Know

➤ Slowing down when going through an intersection or taking a turn puts you in control of the situation.

➤ When stopping at an intersection, always leave enough room between you and the vehicle in front of you to allow you to maneuver around it in an emergency.

➤ Never enter an intersection until you are absolutely certain that all lanes of traffic are clear.

➤ Riding too fast on a freeway puts you at risk, because it decreases the time you have available to react if another vehicle moves into your lane.

➤ Never cross over into the oncoming lane of traffic while negotiating a curve.

Chapter 14

Staying Alive: Special Situations and Emergencies

In the previous four chapters, I've explained procedures for riding in normal conditions, but you will encounter special situations that require you to modify your normal riding procedures.

In this chapter, I'm going to explain the techniques required to ride in these situations, and I'm also going to discuss how to handle emergencies. Regardless of how well you master safe riding techniques, sooner or later, you will be faced with an emergency situation. Like anything in life, some things are out of your control. There's always that one deer running out from behind a shrub just feet in front of your bike, or that one drunk driver who happens to fall asleep at the wheel and veer into your lane. If you go down, it may not be your fault, but you will be the one who feels the pain.

But even if the worst happens, even if you do go down, there are things you can do to minimize your risk. Racers frequently go down at 150 miles per hour and walk away from the accident. In this chapter, I will also discuss techniques that can reduce your risk of injury if you do go down.

Riders on the Storm

Riding in the rain challenges your riding skills, because on wet pavement, you have even less traction available than you normally do. Because of this, you can't:

Motorcycology
Some motorcycle gloves have chamois strips on the backs of the fingers that you can use to wipe the rain from your visor. It may be a good idea to buy such a pair.

➤ Lean as hard. As I said in Chapter 13, leaning decreases the size of the contact patch of your tire, which in turn decreases your available traction.

➤ Stop as quickly. You need to use your brakes with caution in the rain.

➤ See (or be seen by other drivers) as well. The rain is especially problematic for a motorcyclist, because you have no windshield wipers on a bike. The rain covering your visor, goggles, or windshield can only be removed by you or the wind.

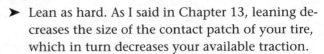

Motorcycology
You should always wear bright, reflective clothing when riding a motorcycle, but because of the reduced visibility during a rainstorm, brightly colored rain gear is crucial. Not only is visibility decreased during a rainstorm, but when it's raining, other drivers are even more unlikely to be watching for motorcycles than they normally are. You need to do everything you can to help other drivers see you.

Even though it is more challenging, riding in the rain can be relatively safe, provided you use extra caution. The most important thing to do is slow down. The combination of decreased traction and decreased visibility drastically reduces your acceptable margin of error in the rain.

Smoothness is even more important on wet pavement than on dry pavement. Jerky steering or throttle input that you wouldn't normally notice on dry pavement can cause you to lose traction and crash in the rain.

You also need to take extra care to ride in the tire tracks in the rain, because the oil embedded in the center of the lane rises to the surface during a rainstorm, especially just after the rain starts. This goop always limits traction, but just after rain begins to fall, the stuff is especially slippery. Plus, you can't see it as well, since the pavement is covered with water.

You might not notice a worn tire in dry conditions, but when the road gets wet, a bald tire becomes extra deadly. Part of the reason tires have grooves cut into them is to help move water away from under the tire's contact patch. These grooves are too shallow on worn tires to allow the water to move, causing the tire to *hydroplane*—that is, to float above the surface of the water. As you might guess, a tire that hydroplanes is an extremely low-traction situation. This is one of the primary reasons you should always make certain your tires are in good condition.

Night Rider

Reduced visibility is your primary challenge when riding at night. And at night, there are even more dangers you need to see than during the day, since many animals roam around at night. Plus, a higher percentage of other drivers are drunk at night than during the day. This is especially true on the weekends.

One of my closest calls involved a suicidal raccoon in the middle of the night. I was giving a girl a ride and showing off a bit, when a raccoon trundled out in front of my bike. I was going much too fast to stop or even swerve around the animal, so relying on my dirtbike experience, I gave the bike extra throttle, aimed the bike straight at the raccoon, and pulled back on my handlebars. I wheelied over the poor critter, became airborne, then landed perfectly, without upsetting the chassis. Even though I handled the situation effectively, my riding partner was not too impressed. She never rode with me again.

After I reached the point of no return, I did some things right in that situation, but if I'd been practicing proper night-riding techniques, I wouldn't have gotten into the situation in the first place. Here's what I did wrong:

1. I rode too fast. When riding at night, always slow down.

2. I rode out of my headlights. The lights on a motorcycle only illuminate a small part of the road, making obstacles and debris invisible. If you can't see a hazard, you can't avoid it. When you do see an obstacle, you have much less time to avoid it than you do during daylight hours. Adjust your speed so that you are able to stop or swerve as soon as you spot any potentially dangerous situation.

> **Motorcycology**
> Sometimes an animal's eyes will shine in your headlights like a glass reflector. Seeing such "reflectors" alongside the road should serve as a warning to you that an animal is present. Slow down upon seeing the slightest twinkle, and monitor the edges of the road with added diligence. Remember that many animals, like deer, travel in groups, so if you see one, there are probably more in the immediate area.

Motorcycle headlights are improving, but they still don't illuminate the road like the headlights on a car. Adding additional driving lights can help increase your field of vision.

To get the maximum visibility from your headlight, you need to make certain that it's properly adjusted. The high beam should touch the road at its maximum range, yet the low beam should be below the eye level of approaching motorists. The procedure for adjusting the headlight varies from bike to bike. Consult your owner's manual to find the procedure for your particular bike.

When riding at night, learn to read the headlights of the car in front of you. You may be able to follow another vehicle (remembering to allow even more space between you and that vehicle than you do during daylight hours) and use its headlights to help increase your field of vision. If the headlights of the vehicle ahead bounce, you can expect a bump in the road. If the vehicle swerves, the driver may be trying to avoid something, like an animal.

Two for the Road

Part of the fun of motorcycling is sharing it with another person (or riding *two up*). Bringing a passenger along can make the experience of riding more rewarding, but it also requires extra care on your part.

Adding a passenger changes the weight distribution on your bike, which in turn changes the handling dynamics. The bike will turn differently with a passenger on board and will need more distance to stop. You can compensate for this somewhat by adjusting your suspension and increasing the air pressure of your tires. Suspension adjustments vary from bike to bike, but most modern motorcycles at least have a preload adjustment on the rear shocks that you can adjust to a firmer setting for carrying a passenger. Again, consult your owner's manual for the exact procedure for your bike.

Motorcycology
Always go over the rules with your passenger before riding. The other person may not be aware of things that seem obvious to you. Once, I gave a ride to a stranded motorist on the back of a sport-touring bike. I helped the young man put my spare helmet on and gave him an extra pair of gloves I had in my saddlebag, then took him to the nearest gas station for help. I thought I'd done a good job preparing the kid, but after I dropped him off, my wife, who followed on her motorcycle, said he'd ridden the entire way with his feet sticking out in the air—I'd forgotten to tell him to put his feet on the footpegs.

Before riding with a passenger, go over some rules of the road with him or her. Explain the following concepts:

➤ The passenger should not get on the bike until you have it off the stand and secure in an upright position.

➤ The passenger should hold onto you by the waist or hips while riding. Some riders may prefer to grasp the passenger's hand rail (on bikes so equipped), but I always feel more secure when the passenger grasps my waist or hips.

➤ The passenger should keep his or her feet on the footpegs at all times, even while the bike is stopped.

➤ The passenger should keep his or her feet away from all hot parts, especially the exhaust pipes.

➤ The passenger must sit behind you on the passenger portion of the seat. If there is no passenger seat, there should be no passenger. And never seat a child on the gas tank in front of you. Also, the maximum capacity of a bike is two people. Never attempt to give a ride to more than one person.

While giving someone a ride, have him or her relax and lean with you, or else remain upright. Whatever they do, they shouldn't stiffen up and lean away from a turn. This greatly reduces your ability to negotiate a corner.

Above all, don't try to impress your passenger with your riding ability. I once came upon an accident scene where a kid and his date wiped out in a corner on their way to a frat-house formal. The young man had tried to negotiate a curve too fast. Both victims wore evening party clothing instead of protective gear, and neither had a helmet. The bike was totaled, but neither the rider nor the passenger was seriously hurt. They were a mess, though, with their expensive clothes shredded to bits, and both had numerous cuts and bruises. He was embarrassed, and she was furious. Being a passenger on a motorcycle is exciting enough, and nothing will impress your passenger more than a safe, smooth ride.

> **Cycle Babble**
> A **constant-radius** turn is a turn with a steady, non-changing arc. In a **decreasing-radius** corner, the arc gets sharper as you progress through the curve, while in an **increasing-radius** corner, the arc becomes less sharp.

Oddball Corners

In Chapter 13, I discussed cornering techniques. These techniques apply to normal turns with a *constant radius* (the curve follows a constant arc). Sometimes, the shape of a curve can change in mid-corner, forcing you to alter your technique.

A change in the shape of a road can take you by surprise, forcing you to change direction in mid-corner. Like everything else in motorcycling, the key to dealing with these situations is awareness. If you are riding on an unfamiliar road, slow down and expect anything. What looks like a smooth, fast corner upon entry may be a sneaky decreasing-radius curve that will cause you to run off the road.

Increasing-Radius Curves

An *increasing-radius* curve is a curve that gets less sharp as it progresses. In a way, these corners are less dangerous than a normal corner, but they may require you to alter your course in mid-curve. If you are prepared, you can use the extra room you will have in an increasing-radius curve as bonus safe space.

If you're prepared, you can pass through an increasing-radius curve more safely than you can a constant-radius curve.

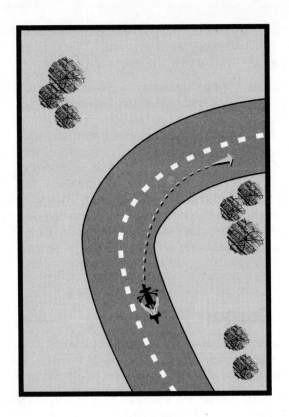

Decreasing-Radius Curves

The most challenging type of corner you will encounter is the *decreasing-radius* curve—a curve that gets sharper as you progress through it, forcing you to turn more sharply as you go. And as I told you in Chapter 13, you don't want to make sudden movements in a corner. Your best bet is to always expect a decreasing-radius corner; always be prepared to lean a bit more to successfully negotiate a turn. If the radius of the corner does not decrease, that just means you'll have more room to maneuver. If it does decrease, you'll be ready.

Multiple Curves

The technique for riding through a single curve may not be the best technique for riding through multiple curves. By starting in the part of the lane away from the direction you are turning, as you do on a single curve, you may find it difficult to negotiate the second curve. When you get to a snaky section of road like this, first slow down more than you would for a single curve. Then position yourself in the first curve so that you'll be best able to negotiate the following curves.

Riding through multiple curves will test your ability to countersteer your bike. To successfully negotiate such curves will require you to get physical with your machine. You'll need to be able to go from leaning hard in one direction to leaning hard in another direction in an instant.

When riding on an unfamiliar road, always expect a curve to get sharper as you progress, and be prepared to lean harder to complete the turn.

Crowned Roads

Some roads are shaped with a pronounced peak in the middle to facilitate water runoff. These roads change the angle of your tires' contact patches, limiting your lean angle, causing your bike to steer differently. When you are riding on irregularly-shaped pavement, slow down.

Group Riding

Motorcyclists tend to be social creatures, and as such, tend to ride in groups. For many people, riding with friends is the most enjoyable aspect of motorcycling. Sometimes it's fun to ride in a large group of bikes just to see the looks on people's faces as you ride by. You may be accountants or lawyers or paramedics, but when you pull into a gas station with a large group of motorcycles, some people act like the Hell's Angels just came to town, which in a twisted way, is kind of fun.

Going out for a ride with your friends can be a blast, but it will require extra effort on your part to do it safely. You'll be riding with people whose riding skills vary, along with their temperaments.

Group Riding Techniques

When riding in a group, you can ride in one of three formations:

1. Staggered formation. In this formation, the motorcycles line up on both sides of the lane, with one bike on the left side, the next bike on the right side, the following bike back on the left side, and so on, with each bike maintaining a two-second interval between the next bike. This formation keeps the group close together while maintaining the maximum amount of safe space around each bike.

2. Single-file formation. When you are out riding with your friends on a winding road, you will all need to use your entire lane to safely negotiate each corner. On such roads, ride in a single-file formation. Remember not to follow each other too closely, or if one person goes down, he or she might take down other riders, too.

Steer Clear
When riding with other people, let your ability determine your speed—not theirs. I've got a friend, a motorcycle-safety instructor, who can ride circles around me, regardless of what kind of bike either of us is riding. When we go out, I just let him go and catch up with him later. If I try to keep up, I'll go down. I've seen it happen to other riders.

3. Side-by-side formation. When bikes ride side-by-side, they reduce the amount of safe space between each bike, so this type of formation should be discouraged. Sometimes, an escort may require you to ride in such a formation to make the group as compact as possible, but otherwise, avoid riding two-motorcycles abreast.

Sure, They're Your Buddies, but Can You Trust Them with Your Life?

When riding with your friends, watch out for group mentality taking over. This is when everyone tries to outride everyone else. Many otherwise-sane riders crash when group mentality takes over.

When riding in a group, ride for yourself and no one else. Be aware of who you're riding with, where they are, and how fast they're going. Above all, don't ride above your own ability. It's a lot more embarrassing to go down in front of your friends than it is to arrive a few seconds later than they do.

SOS: Emergency Situations

Nobody is perfect. Ride long enough, and you will go down, regardless of how careful you are, how diligent you are, or how skilled you are. Even if you always ride within your ability, not everything is under your control.

The types of emergency situations you can encounter are infinite, but they can be classified into two general categories: losing traction, and hitting something or having something hit you.

Losing Traction

The most common and usually least consequential emergency you will encounter is losing traction and falling down.

Remember, don't panic. If you remain calm and use smooth throttle control, you can often regain control after you have lost traction. If your back tire starts to slide, don't drop the throttle. When you suddenly quit supplying power to the back tire, it violently regains traction, jerking your motorcycle in the opposite direction. Your best bet is to ride the slide through.

If it's too late, and you know you're going down, just relax, let go of the bike, and ride it out. If you're wearing your protective gear—and you should *always* be wearing your gear—chances are you're going to be OK. Try to slide on your back. Keep your arms and legs stretched out, and try not to let them dig into the ground, which can cause you to flip through the air. Stay relaxed. Stay low to the ground, and try to move away from the motorcycle. Don't stand up until you're sure you've stopped.

Hitting or Being Hit

If you strike a small object, it is possible to prevent yourself from crashing by following the proper technique.

If you find yourself in the position of being unable to avoid a small object or piece of debris, don't slam on the front brake. This will cause your motorcycle to pitch forward, forcing your front tire into the object rather than over it. It will also cause your front tire to lock up, and if ever you needed traction from your front tire, now is the time.

Motorcycology
Many motorcyclists learn how to crash by riding dirtbikes. You are much more likely to wipe out on the rough surfaces found off-road than you are on smooth pavement, so dirtbikers crash much more often than streetbikers. Learning how to react in a crash is probably the most important off-road skill that transfers to the street.

Try to hit the object as straight on as possible. Apply a bit of throttle to take some weight off the front tire, and as you strike the object, pull back on the handlebars. If you remain calm, you can ride over the object without crashing.

Being struck by another vehicle is probably the most serious type of accident you can have, followed by you striking another vehicle. Both situations are extremely dangerous, but if you strike another vehicle, at least you have a split second to react. When you are struck by another vehicle, you usually don't know what hit you.

The only way to deal with such situations is to avoid them—remember to be aware of your complete surroundings, and above all, ride at a speed slow enough to allow you time to react.

What to Do After an Emergency

Motorcycology
Always carry a first-aid kit on your bike. A first-aid kit is something you hope to never need, but if you do, you'll be glad you have it. At the very least, your first-aid kit should have bandages, tape, something for bee stings, and some form of antibiotic ointment. In an emergency situation, a cellular phone can be the most critical piece of first-aid equipment you can carry.

If you do have a crash, you need to remain calm. If you are still on the road, you need to move off the road, if at all possible. No matter how badly you're hurt, you will be hurt worse if you stay in traffic.

Once you're out of harm's way, you need to take stock of your injuries, particularly to your spine. Check to see if you can move your fingers. Don't move any more than necessary until you're absolutely certain you haven't damaged your spine. Above all, don't remove your helmet until you have made certain that you have no spinal damage, since that can cause even worse damage. Even if you have damaged your spine, you may be OK and suffer no paralysis if you don't further damage your spinal column.

If you are able to walk away from a crash, you can treat it like an automobile accident; exchange insurance information if other drivers are involved and remove your motorcycle from the roadway, if it is safe to do so. If there is any chance of spinal injury, all you can do is wait for help.

How to Raise a Fallen Bike

Once you've determined you're all right, you need to turn your attention to your fallen bike. If you're lucky, it will be safe to ride. But be careful, because incorrectly raising even a small bike can injure your back. You've just survived a wipeout; wouldn't it be embarrassing to injure yourself when you pick up your bike?

If possible, find someone to help you lift the bike. If you have to lift it by yourself, there are procedures to help prevent you from injuring your back.

When picking up your bike, use leverage to avoid straining your back. If the bike has *case guards* (metal tubes mounted around the engine to protect the engine cases in a crash), grab the handlebars and roll the bike toward you on the case guards, using the bike's momentum to get it upright. Bend your knees and use your legs, not your back, to lift the machine upright.

If the bike doesn't have case guards, grasp the lower side of the handlebar (the side under the bike), turn the front wheel toward you, grasp some solid part of the frame, and work your knee under the seat. Then, use your legs to lift the bike. You might want to extend your side stand, in case you get the bike upright and it falls over in the opposite direction.

Don't smoke anywhere near the fallen bike, since gas will most likely have dripped out. There may also be battery acid that has dripped out. This can burn holes in your riding gear and even your skin, as well as corrode metal parts on your bike. You'll want to check the level of the fluid in your battery after a fall.

Once you've gotten the bike upright, check for other damage, too. Brake, clutch, and shift levers can get bent or broken in a fall. Riding a bike with a broken clutch or brake lever is difficult and dangerous. You may be in a situation where you have to ride away from your crash site with a broken or bent lever, but replace it as soon as possible.

Also check your wheels and tires after a crash. Make certain that a fender or chain guard isn't rubbing on your tire. Make certain that your handlebars are firmly attached to your fork. If your handlebars break loose, you're going to crash again.

In the majority of all emergency situations, the only thing that will be hurt is your pride. Swallow it and count your blessings. Once you have calmed down, reconstruct the events leading up to your crash. Chances are, in retrospect, you will remember ways you could have avoided the accident entirely. Remember these things the next time you ride, and you will greatly decrease your odds of ever crashing again.

The Least You Need to Know

➤ The area between the tire tracks on a highway lane is at its most slippery just after rain begins.

➤ Don't ride out of your headlights at night.

➤ You need more room to stop when riding with a passenger.

➤ The safest method of group riding is usually in a staggered formation.

➤ The most important thing to do in an emergency situation is to not panic.

Chapter 15

Doing It in the Dirt: Riding Off-Road

In This Chapter

➤ Using off-road skills to improve your on-road performance

➤ Riding up and down hills

➤ Advanced techniques for riding over ledges and obstacles

➤ Riding on a variety of surfaces

Many motorcyclists, myself included, started out riding off-road. We got our first dirtbikes when we were children and pretty much taught ourselves to ride.

Learning to ride off-road has some advantages. When you ride off-road, you remove the number-one hazard you'll face on public highways and streets—other drivers. And the dirt is more forgiving than the pavement, should you fall down.

Which you will do more often off-road, simply because you'll be riding over more rugged terrain than the relatively flat surfaces covering most roads. There are a lot more rocks, ruts, holes, and trees in a forest than on your average city street.

Quite a few road racers practice riding off-road during their off seasons. They claim that riding off-road hones their skills and makes them better racers. Off-road riding is a fun way for all of us to sharpen our riding skills, whether we race or not.

Riding off-road demands different skills from you as a rider. You need to develop your ability to read surface conditions to a much higher level than you would by just riding on the street, because you are going to encounter a much wider range of conditions. And because of the power and torque available from off-road bikes, combined with the low-traction surfaces you'll encounter, you need to be even smoother with your throttle than on a streetbike. You'll need to learn to use your throttle to help you clear obstacles, and in some situations, steer your motorcycle.

You'll need to learn how to sit on a dirtbike, how to distribute your weight, and the proper posture needed to control the machine. In this chapter, I'm going to give you a brief description of the challenges you'll encounter off-road and show you how to adapt to those challenges.

Form Is Function: Posture

Balance is extremely important to successful dirt riding, and to achieve good balance, you need to practice good posture. Because dirtbikes are so light, you use your body movement to steer them more than you do on a streetbike. In the dirt, you need to get physical with your motorcycle.

Your posture, combined with proper throttle control, will make the difference between successfully climbing a hill and crashing and burning. And the proper posture for going up a hill isn't the same as the proper posture for going down.

Generally, you want to keep your weight centered over the motorcycle. To accomplish this, you'll use one technique when going uphill and another when going downhill.

Going Uphill

Climbing a hill on a motorcycle can be one of the most fun aspects of off-road riding, but it can also be one of the most dangerous. You need to use some common sense when deciding whether or not to climb a hill. You may not have the skill needed to climb some hills. Even if you do, your motorcycle might not be able to make it.

Make certain that you know what is on the other side of a hill before you climb it. If you are riding up a hill that you can't see over, slow down until you can see what's on the other side.

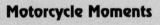

Motorcycle Moments

When I was growing up, my friends and I loved to climb hills on our dirtbikes. One friend could ride up hills the rest of us could never get over—he had a natural talent for hill climbing. Unfortunately, he was a bit short on common sense and often went riding over hills before he knew what was on the other side. Once, while I was following him through unfamiliar territory, he climbed a hill, but I went around it, preferring to see what was on the other side before attempting the climb. I rounded the hill just in time to see him and his motorcycle plunge into a 25-foot ravine. He was unhurt, but his motorcycle was toast.

The problem with slowing down to see what's on the other side of a hill is that you need your momentum to carry you to the top. On a steep hill, if you lose momentum, you lose the battle. If you're unfamiliar with the terrain you're riding in, take some time to explore your surroundings, check out the hills (and what's on the other side of those hills) before attempting to climb them.

When approaching a hill, keep both feet firmly on the pegs. Shift into low gear and accelerate before ascending the hill. If the hill isn't too challenging, you can remain seated. Just shift your weight forward by sliding forward on the seat. If the hill is steep, stand up on the footpegs and lean as far forward as you can while still remaining in control of the bike. The more weight you can put over the front wheel, the less your chance of flipping over backward, which is exactly what you don't want to do.

When going over a steep hill, move as far back as possible to place as much weight over the rear wheel as you can.

If the hill is too steep and your bike begins to stall, you'll have to downshift if you can. Shift smoothly and quickly, being smooth on the throttle to avoid doing a wheelie and flipping over backward.

If you don't have enough power to make it, but you're still moving ahead and have enough space to turn around, you can turn around and ride back down. If you stop, or if you can't continue and don't have enough room to turn around, you have a problem. If you have good enough footing to maneuver the bike once you've stopped, apply the front brake and remain stopped until you are stable.

If you don't have a solid footing, you're going to fall down. Usually this will only hurt your pride, but if you're on an extremely steep hill, you and your bike may fall back down the hill. If this happens, all you can do is try to get out of the way of the falling bike, then chastise yourself for being foolish enough to try a hill so far beyond your ability.

Steer Clear
Getting stuck on the side of a steep hill with your bike is both dangerous and hard physical work. Wrestling a bike around while trying not to fall down a hill is usually enough to make most sane people think twice the next time they're tempted to climb a hill that is too steep.

If you've managed to avoid falling, and you're sitting there squeezing the front brake, wondering what to do next, you can use gravity to help get you turned around. Turn your wheel toward whichever direction is most clear behind you, then gently ease off the front brake—not enough to get yourself rolling, but just enough to slowly move to the side. Keep the bike leaning toward the top of the hill, since the upward side is the only side on which you'll have a firm footing. Lean away from the top, and you're going down the hill the hard way. When you're sideways, ease ahead and turn down the hill, following the trail you took up.

If you've fallen, follow this same procedure, except remain off the bike, standing on the downside of the machine as you turn it around. Remember to use the hand brake as you maneuver the bike, or you could run yourself over.

Going Downhill

You might not think so, but descending a hill can be as challenging as climbing a hill. In fact, if you don't know what you are doing, you can wipe out even more spectacularly going downhill.

Steer Clear
Gravity can be your friend when going downhill, but it also makes wipeouts happen more quickly and more violently. When you fall down while climbing a hill, it seems to happen in slow motion, because your momentum is carrying you up, away from the ground. When your bike pitches you off while going downhill, it happens pretty quickly, since your momentum is already carrying you down, toward the ground.

Point the motorcycle directly at a hill before descending. The more straight on you are when going down, the less your chances of wiping out. Slide your butt back on the seat as far as you can, while still maintaining a firm grip on the handlebars, to transfer weight to the rear. Shift into low gear, and don't give the engine any gas as you go down. Let the engine assist in your braking. Use the rear brake liberally, but be careful about locking up the tire. Be very cautious when using the front brake, especially in low-traction situations. When going downhill, your front end will want to dig into the ground. Using your front brake will increase this tendency and can send you flying over your handlebars.

Ledges and Embankments

As your hill-climbing skills improve, you may want to seek out more challenging terrain. Riding up and down sharp ledges and embankments can provide those challenges, but you really need to use your head here. There is a fine line between a ledge and a cliff, and if you purposely go plunging off a cliff, chances are you won't get much sympathy while you recuperate in the intensive-care ward.

Use the same basic technique for climbing ledges and embankments that you use to climb other hills, only more of it. You'll need to shift your weight farther forward, apply more throttle, and gain more momentum. Again, be aware of what is at the top of the embankment. If you successfully climb the embankment, you're going to be going at a pretty good clip as you crest the top. As you get over the top, let off the throttle, and prepare to deal with what you find at the top.

When going down a short, steep hill, you may need to give the bike a little gas as your front tire goes over the edge to keep the bike from getting hung up on the ledge. Otherwise, follow the normal downhill procedure.

Things That Go Bump in the Road

Even on the worst paved road you can find, you won't encounter obstacles like stumps, logs, boulders, and roots. When riding off-road, these obstacles are part of the package, and you'll need to know how to deal with them. If you hit such obstacles when you are unprepared, they can deflect your front tire, causing you to crash.

To avoid these obstacles, concentrate on the trail ahead of you, scanning for objects in your path. Adjust your speed for conditions. If you are riding through dense foliage, slow down until you can effectively determine what's ahead of you.

Motorcycle Moments

My friend had a habit of going up hills without knowing what was on the other side—also had a tendency to ride too fast for conditions. He was a gifted rider but didn't have the common sense of a goose, and I'd often round a bend on a trail to find him extricating himself and his bike from a shrub or a tree because he had hit an obstacle he hadn't seen. He was a faster rider than I was, but more often than not, I arrived before he did.

Even if you avoid hitting an obstacle with your bike, if you don't maintain a proper riding position, you can hit it with your toes or feet, especially on a narrow trail. To avoid this, ride with the balls of your feet on the footpegs so that your toes don't hang below your motorcycle's frame. This prevents you from catching your toes on obstacles, which more often than not will lead to a bunch of broken bones in your feet. And having to ride 20 or 30 miles to the nearest emergency room with a bunch of broken bones in your feet is no fun. You'll have to trust me on that.

If you hit an obstacle that deflects your bike, resist the urge to stick your leg out. This will upset your center of gravity, making you more likely to go down, and it also creates the risk of knee injury. As bad as breaking a bunch of bones in your foot sounds, it's actually a pleasant experience compared to a knee injury. Rather than sticking your foot out, keep your feet on the pegs and shift your weight around to correct your bike's course.

Riding over an obstacle is a maneuver best left only to an experienced rider. It requires precise throttle control, along with the ability to bring the front wheel up in the air at will. This is known as *doing a wheelie* and normally is not acceptable motorcycling behavior. But when riding off-road, being able to do a wheelie can spare you many painful crashes.

If you have to ride over an obstacle, approach it as directly as possible, trying to hit it straight on (at a 90-degree angle). As your front wheel is about to strike the obstacle, apply some throttle to unload the front wheel and pull back on the handlebars, being careful not to give the bike too much gas so that you don't flip over backward. You are now doing a wheelie, with your back tire rapidly approaching the obstacle. If the obstacle is reasonably small, close the throttle before the rear wheel hits it. This will bring your front end down, and you can drive over the obstacle with your back wheel.

Make certain that you know what you are doing before attempting to ride over an obstacle.

If the obstacle is too large for your back wheel to go over without your bike getting hung up, you shouldn't be attempting to go over it in the first place. If you're in the middle of the attempt when you realize you're in trouble, that observation won't help you much. At the exact moment your rear tire catches the obstacle, apply a bit more throttle. This should launch you over the obstacle. To do this, you should be experienced at jumping and be able to land on your back wheel, which is, theoretically, what should happen. Either that, or you will fly into the brush. As I said, this is a procedure best left to an expert rider. Before attempting it, you should know your bike and your riding techniques so well that the entire procedure comes to you naturally.

Surface Conditions

The defining characteristic of a road—even a lousy, decomposing road—is a relatively level surface. The surfaces found off-road vary as much as the flora and fauna, but they can be broken down into three general categories:

➤ Sand

➤ Water and mud

➤ Rocks

The one thing these surfaces have in common is that they're all low-traction situations. Learning to cope with low-traction riding can greatly improve your street-riding skills. When you lose traction on the street, your greatest danger comes when you suddenly regain traction, because this violently pitches your motorcycle in the opposite direction. You need to learn to ride a slide out using smooth throttle control rather than abruptly releasing the throttle when you slide, which will cause you to regain traction too quickly.

Because the dirt is more forgiving (you won't regain traction so abruptly when you release the throttle), you can practice sliding off-road without as much danger of *high-siding* (crashing) the bike. Sliding on the pavement will always require a more delicate use of the throttle, and your off-road skills won't translate directly to the street, but at least you'll know how to slide and control the bike in a slide. This knowledge can save your life in an emergency.

While the three categories of off-road surfaces all have low traction in common, each will require a slightly different riding technique.

Motorcycology
Learning to ride under the low-traction conditions encountered off-road is the most important skill you can transfer to street riding. Learning how a motorcycle reacts in low-traction conditions and to control a motorcycle in such conditions can be invaluable information on the street. But remember one important difference: On pavement, when your bike regains traction after losing traction, it does so much more violently and quickly than it does when riding off-road.

Sliding Through Sand

When riding in sand, the front end of your bike will feel as if it is moving through a thick fluid. You'll never quite feel like your front end is planted, yet the snaky movements it makes won't be as abrupt as in rocks, water, or mud.

The key to riding in sand is to remain relaxed. Keep your feet on the pegs and your head up, your eyes focused ahead. Your bike will move around (*undulate* might be a better description), but this is normal.

Throughout this book, I've always told you to slow down when encountering a potentially dangerous situation, but that advice doesn't apply to riding in sand. Here, you'll want to speed up, going fast enough for your tires to rise to the top of the sand. When riding on sand, you want to re-create the condition of hydroplaning on water, as discussed in Chapter 14. There, you wanted to avoid hydroplaning. Here, it's a good thing. If you slow down in the sand, your bike will plow in, which could cause your front wheel to jackknife or veer to one side.

When turning in sand, you have to be especially careful to keep your front end from jackknifing. You need to get as much weight as possible off the front tire. Shift your weight to the rear of the bike, and apply the throttle to unload some weight from the front end. When you master the technique, you'll find you use your throttle to slide the rear end around to turn in sand more than you actually steer the bike. You can consider this an extreme form of countersteering.

A general tip to keep in mind when riding in sand is that you should accelerate sooner and brake later than you would when riding on surfaces that provide better traction. The drag created by pushing your wheels through sand means it takes your bike longer to accelerate and less time to slow down than when you're riding on higher-traction surfaces.

Steer Clear

If you encounter a *low-water bridge* on a paved road (a place where the road descends into a creek or river), follow the procedures outlined here, and be extra cautious. If the water is moving quickly, it may actually pull your wheels downstream. You must remain calm when this happens. Keep your weight centered, so neither the front nor the rear wheel washes out from under you, and proceed at a slow but steady pace, keeping your eyes focused on the road ahead, where it rises out of the water.

Wheeling in Water

Riding in water and mud will provide you with skills that translate directly to street riding, since you may encounter such conditions on-road as well as off-road.

Surfaces under water are especially slick. This applies to riding over low-water crossings on public roads as well as riding through streams and swamps. If there is debris present, like fallen leaves or pine needles, the surfaces become even more slippery. Again, this is true of the water on a road as well as the water encountered while riding off-road.

When riding through water, ride slowly, and be prepared for whatever your front tire may encounter, since you won't be able to visually scan submerged surfaces. I've stressed the importance of using smooth throttle and brake control in all situations, but no other situation requires you to accelerate and brake more smoothly than riding in water.

When riding through water, you should

➤ Beware of surface irregularities, like rocks and holes, that are hidden by the water.

➤ Learn to read different water surfaces. You can get some idea about how deep the water is by the way it moves. If you see shallow ripples, the water is probably being disturbed by the surface underneath, meaning that it is not too deep. If the water is slow-moving and calm, it is probably deeper.

➤ Maintain your momentum, and focus on the opposite bank or where the road emerges from the water at a low-water crossing.

➤ Keep speeds relatively low. In addition to minimizing the damage if you fall down, this keeps water from splashing up onto your engine.

After riding through water, your brakes may be wet and ineffective. Dry them by applying light braking pressure while riding until they return to normal power.

If you have submerged your bike's engine, you'll want to change your oil as soon as possible.

Water and mud go together, since where there's water, there's mud, and where there's mud, there's water, but riding in mud requires you to modify your technique a bit. The biggest difference is that when riding in mud, you'll usually encounter ruts. When you do, stay relaxed and let your tires follow the ruts. Don't fight the front wheel or try to turn out of a rut. It is a fight the rut will win. Again, I know this from first-hand experience. Look ahead to where you want to go rather than down at the rut.

If you're riding through heavy mud and your bike begins to bog down, don't open the throttle abruptly. Doing so will only cause your tire to dig down deeper, getting you even more stuck in the mud. You wouldn't believe how heavy a 300-pound motorcycle can feel when it is stuck in the mud. Your best bet is to apply gas gradually, trying to keep your forward momentum.

Motorcycology
In over 20 years of riding, nothing has caused me to crash more often than ruts. Ruts that have been hidden in tall grass are the worst, since you can't see them, but trying to turn out of a rut I could see has to rank as the second most common cause of the crashes I've had. These usually have been quite spectacular, often of the end-over-end variety. Moral of the story? Don't fight a rut.

Riding in Rocks

Riding in rocks differs from riding in mud or sand in many ways. The most important difference is that sand and mud are by nature very soft, while rocks tend to be very hard.

Like water, you'll encounter surfaces composed of many small rocks on a streetbike. Often, you'll find such surfaces on a long driveway or at a construction sight. I won't kid you: Encountering such surfaces on a huge streetbike stinks.

The technique for riding on a surface composed of small rocks is similar to riding on sand: Maintain a steady speed, using smooth throttle and brake control. It differs in that you don't need to go as fast. Your tires won't plow in quite as deeply as in sand. You must still maintain a steady pace, but it just doesn't have to be as quick a pace.

Another difference between small rocks and sand is that the movements of your front end caused by the rocks will be jerkier and less fluid than the undulation caused by the sand. Again, your best way of dealing with this is to remain relaxed and ride at a moderate, steady pace. If you tense up and grip the handlebars too tightly, the front-end movements caused by the rocks will increase in intensity.

Many riders go their entire lives without venturing off pavement. By doing so, they miss one of the most enjoyable aspects of motorcycling. If it is at all possible, I recommend that you pick up an inexpensive trailbike in addition to your streetbike and hit the trails every chance you get. You won't regret it.

The Least You Need to Know

➤ Proper posture is crucial for maintaining control of your bike off-road.

➤ The skills learned by riding off-road transfer to riding on-road indirectly, not directly. The increased traction on-road will require some modification of off-road emergency techniques.

➤ Riding off-road teaches you important techniques for dealing with low-traction situations.

➤ Don't exceed your abilities off-road.

Part 4
Living with a Motorcycle

In Part 1, I told you just how far motorcycle technology has advanced in the past few decades. Today's motorcycle requires a fraction of the effort needed to keep a pre-1960 model running.

But motorcycles still need more maintenance than any modern car. There are still routine procedures you'll need to perform, not just to keep your bike in top condition, but to ensure your own safety. You can't afford an equipment failure on a bike.

By buying the simplest bike that meets your needs, performing routine maintenance, and not running the bike into the ground, you can get the most out of your motorcycle.

Chapter 16

Zen and the Art of Motorcycle Maintenance

In This Chapter

➤ Tools you need to maintain your bike

➤ Spotting potentially dangerous tire and brake problems

➤ Changing oil and why you need to do it

➤ Maintaining your chain

People either love performing maintenance on their motorcycles or they hate it. In his book *Zen and The Art of Motorcycle Maintenance*, Robert M. Pirsig writes that the reason some people hate motorcycle maintenance is because it is part of the "inhuman language" of technology. "Anything to do with valves and shafts and wrenches is a part of that dehumanized world," he writes. Pirsig is from the other group, the tinkerers and fiddlers who think nothing of tearing apart their engines and adjusting their valves. He finds working on his bike a form of therapy, a communion with something greater than himself. "The Buddha, the Godhead, resides quite as comfortably in the circuits of a digital computer or the gears of a cycle transmission as he does at the top of a mountain or in the petals of a flower," he writes.

I'm firmly in the anti-technologists' camp on this one. It's not because I'm against technology. It's just that I'm not very good at mechanics.

Still, I perform most of my own maintenance. Financial realities dictate that I do my own work. And I've always managed to keep my bikes running. If I can do it, you can do it. Whether you are a mechanical savant like Pirsig or a ham-fisted fool like me, with a little practice, a little patience, a little knowledge, and of course, some tools, you can do most of the things required to keep your bike on the road. In this chapter, I'll tell you how.

This chapter deals with routine maintenance, while Chapter 17 deals with repairing your bike if it breaks down. Many of the procedures used in routine maintenance are the same as those used to repair your bike. So use the two chapters together.

Tools of the Trade

Unless you own a Harley-Davidson, your bike will most likely come with a toolkit. This may be located under the seat, behind a side-cover panel, or in a special compartment somewhere.

Most Harleys don't come with standard toolkits. Although BMW equips its bikes with high-quality toolkits, standard toolkits are usually of poor quality and are best left for emergency situations. When you do maintenance at home, you'll want to equip yourself with a decent set of tools. At the very least, you'll want to have these tools:

➤ Air-pressure gauge. Buy a gauge of good quality, and keep it clean so that it provides you with an accurate reading.

➤ A wrench set. Buy the highest-quality set of wrenches you can possibly afford— cheap ones will bend and break. The most versatile wrenches are combination spanner wrenches. These have an open-ended spanner at one end and a box-end (fully-enclosed) spanner at the other. Harleys use SAE standard fasteners (the type of fasteners used by most American manufacturing firms, measured in inches, rather than millimeters), so get a standard set of wrenches if you buy a Harley. All other bikes use metric fasteners.

➤ An Allen wrench set. Many fasteners on motorcycles use Allen-head bolts instead of traditional hex-head bolts. This means the bolts are turned by an Allen wrench—a wrench you insert in the center of the bolt instead of around the edges. As with regular wrenches, get a standard set for a Harley and a metric set for everything else.

Motorcycology
The tips of screw-drivers are called *blades*, and like knife blades, they get dull and rounded off over time. When that happens, you're likely to strip screws. When the tips of your screwdrivers get dull, replace them.

➤ Screwdrivers. You will need both standard (flat-tipped) and Phillips (X-shaped tips) screwdrivers in a variety of sizes. As with all your tools, you will find that your work goes much better if you buy high-quality screwdrivers.

➤ A ratchet and a set of sockets. These will become your most used tools, so get the best set you can afford. For motorcycles, get a set with a 3/8-inch drive ratchet, with as many different-size sockets as you can. Again, Harley takes standard, everything else takes metric.

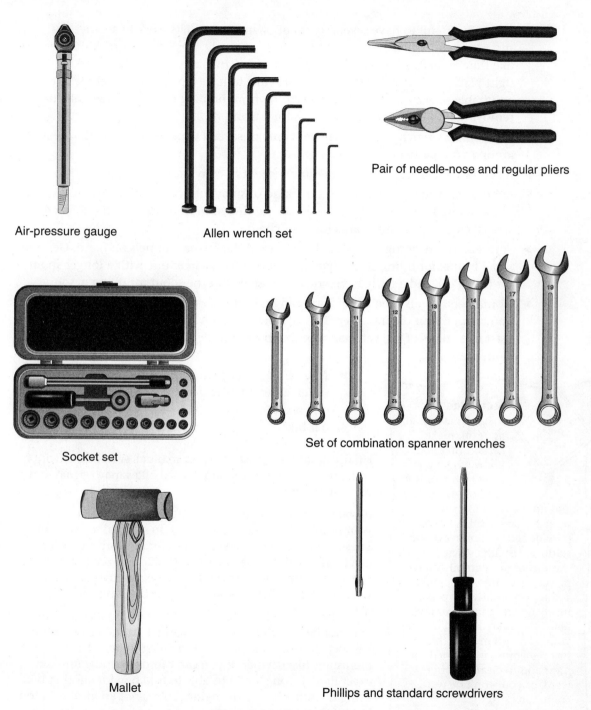

Air-pressure gauge

Allen wrench set

Pair of needle-nose and regular pliers

Socket set

Set of combination spanner wrenches

Mallet

Phillips and standard screwdrivers

A good set of quality tools will make motorcycle maintenance easier and less frustrating.

➤ Pliers. It's useful to have several types of pliers. Basic pliers work in a variety of situations, but you'll also need to get a pair of needle-nose pliers—the kind that look like they're made from a hummingbird's beak. These are useful when working in tight places and with small objects. I also like to have a pair of channel-lock or adjustable pliers. I use these for everything from holding odd-size, large bolts to removing oil filters when my filter wrench won't fit.

➤ An oil-filter wrench. These wrenches come in several varieties. Get one that best fits around your particular oil filter.

➤ A soft-faced mallet. You will sometimes need it to convince an obstinate part to move.

➤ Lubricants. You'll need to have some kind of spray lubricant, like WD-40, on hand to loosen up tight bolts. If you have a chain-driven motorcycle, you'll also need special cleaners and lubricants for your chain.

➤ Funnels. You're going to need at least a few different-size funnels on hand. Get one small funnel for filling electrolyte in your battery, a larger one with a longer spout for filling oil, and a fairly large one with a screen in the spout for filling gasoline.

➤ Containers. You'll need to get a gas can and some sort of pan to catch oil in when you change your oil and filter. This container should be large enough to hold at least five quarts of oil, yet shallow enough to fit under your bike when it is on its centerstand.

Steer Clear
When you change your oil, make certain that you know where you can dispose of the used oil. It's illegal and unsafe to dump the oil or spread it on a road. Some areas provide certified oil-recycling stations. Usually, service stations or drive-in oil-change places have large waste-oil storage capabilities. If you ask nicely down at the local Kwiki Lube, they may let you dump your waste oil in with theirs. Just remember not to make a mess and to clean up afterward, or you won't be welcome back.

➤ A stool. More than one weekend mechanic has suffered debilitating nerve damage from squatting in one position for too long while working on his or her bike.

Finally, you'll also want a repair manual. A new bike will come with an owner's manual; used bikes may or may not come with one.

If you're serious about performing your own maintenance, your best bet is to buy an actual shop manual for your bike. These manuals, designed as guides for authorized dealer mechanics, will be specific to your bike and tell you the best way to perform each procedure. These manuals are expensive, but they will save you money in the long run.

If you buy a used bike that is no longer in production, you may not be able to find a shop manual. In such cases, your best bet is to buy one of the aftermarket manuals from publishers like Clymer. If you can't find a manual for your exact model, you should be able to find one for another bike using the same family of engine. This is not an ideal solution, but it is better than nothing.

Keeping the Shiny Side Up: Supporting the Bike

Before doing any work on your bike, make certain it's securely positioned. If your bike has a centerstand, use it for procedures that don't require you to remove any heavy parts from the bike, like changing oil and tightening the chain.

If you need to remove heavy parts, like wheels and tires, you'll need to find another method of supporting the bike, because when you remove the parts, you'll change the weight distribution of the bike, upsetting the balance on the centerstand. You'll also need to use an alternative method of supporting the bike if it's not equipped with a centerstand.

I use a variety of materials to support my bikes, depending on the bike. I've created stable stands by using cinderblocks with two-by-fours as buffers to keep from damaging the parts under my bike. The key is to make certain that your blocking is stable.

Some companies sell special motorcycle lifts. While these are expensive, a good lift is your safest, most secure method of supporting your bike while you work on it. Some companies sell rear-end stands that prop a bike up by the swingarm, which are fairly affordable.

Oil: Your Bike's Blood

Oil serves three purposes in your bike's engine:

1. Oil reduces friction and wear, making all internal parts move more smoothly and efficiently.

2. Oil dissipates heat. It carries heat away from the moving parts of an engine as it flows over them. On some bikes, oil is sprayed on the hottest parts of an engine, like the underside of the piston domes, to enhance heat dissipation. Such engines are referred to as *air and oil cooled*.

3. Oil cleans the inside of your engine. The inside of your engine is filled with metal parts that rub together at tremendous speeds, causing microscopic particles of metal to shear off. Your oil removes these particles and traps them in your oil filter.

Steer Clear

If your bike has a fairing that extends around the bottom of the engine, remove this before placing your bike on any kind of support, since the plastic isn't strong enough to support the bike and will break under the machine's weight.

Two-stroke engines use oil differently than four-stroke engines (see Chapter 6, "Start Your Engines"). In a two-stroke, the oil enters the engine with the fuel charge and is burned up and eliminated with the exhaust, causing the characteristic blue smoke coming from a stroker's exhaust pipe. This is why the EPA isn't very fond of strokers.

Four strokes recirculate their oil, using either a *dry-sump* system, in which the oil is stored in an external container, or a *wet-sump* system, in which the oil is contained in the engine's crankcase. Except for Harleys and some dual sports, most bikes use wet-sump systems.

Cycle Babble
In a wet-sump **system**, oil is stored in the engine's crankcase. In a **dry-sump system**, oil is stored in an external tank.

Motorcycology
When checking oil, your bike should be in an upright position (unless otherwise stated in the owner's manual). On bikes without center-stands, this means you need two people: one to support the bike and the other to check the oil.

Another thing to keep in mind is that most bikes require you to simply rest the cap in the hole to get an accurate reading on the dipstick, rather than requiring that you screw the cap down. Your owner's manual will tell you which method to use.

Checking the Oil Level

On a two stroke, you'll need to check the oil level every day, since two strokes are designed to burn oil. On a modern, properly-running four stroke, though, you only need to check the oil level two or three times a week. If you have a bike that uses lots of oil, check more often.

On two strokes and dry-sump four strokes, you'll check the oil level in the external tank, usually located either beneath the seat or within the frame itself (although on some late-model Harleys, the tank is down by the transmission). On a wet-sump four stroke, you'll check the oil level at the bottom of the engine. In all cases, you'll either check by inserting a *dipstick* (a flat blade connected to the filler cap) into the oil tank, or you'll simply look into a *sight glass* (a window into the tank). The sight-glass method is much easier and less messy.

If the oil level gets down near the add mark, fill the tank back up to the full mark, but be careful. It usually takes much less oil than you might imagine to fill the tank to the full mark, and overfilling your tank can cause as many problems as running it too low. Pour in a small amount, then recheck the level. Keep doing this until you reach the full mark.

Changin' Oil

The single most important thing you can do to ensure a long engine life for your motorcycle is to perform regular oil changes. As you ride your bike, two things happen to your oil:

1. The molecules in the oil break apart, causing the oil to lose its lubricating properties.
2. The oil gets contaminated with the microscopic particles that wear away from the parts inside your engine, causing the oil to become more abrasive.

Organic oil (lubricants distilled from organic crude oil) starts to seriously break down after only 1,000 miles. Synthetic oil (lubricants created using synthetic, or man-made, materials) takes a bit longer to break down. All oil becomes contaminated by 2,000 miles. I change organic oil in a bike every 1,000 miles. When I use synthetic oil, I change it every 2,000 miles. By following this procedure, I can easily get over 100,000 miles on a bike without any engine problems.

Manufacturers will recommend up to 7,000 miles between oil changes, but I would never wait that long.

Engine oil comes in different grades (marked with a complex code, such as 10w30, that designates weight and viscosity) with different additives. Most motorcycle manufacturers recommend motorcycle-specific oil in a certain grade, often 10w30 on liquid-cooled bikes and 10w40 on air-cooled bikes. Using motorcycle-specific oil in the recommended grade is not a bad practice, but I prefer to use slightly heavier oil, especially in warm weather or if I'm going to ride hard. On a liquid-cooled bike, I normally use 10w40, switching to something heavier, like 20w50, in extreme conditions.

Here's how to change your oil:

1. Drain the oil. Locate the drain plug, which is somewhere on the bottom of the engine on wet-sump systems (the location varies with dry sumps), and place your pan-shaped container under the plug. When you remove the plug (usually, a hex-head bolt), the oil will come out with some force, so take that into account when placing the pan.

2. Remove the filter. Change the filter every time you change the oil. There are two types of filters—the *canister* type, which has a replaceable filter element located in a canister attached to the engine, and the *spin-on* type, which spins on and off like an automotive oil filter.

   When removing a canister-type filter, be extremely careful not to strip the screws holding the canister on, and thoroughly clean the area around the canister before removal. There will be a spring and some metal washers inside the canister to hold the filter in place. Note their location for when you install the new filter, and after you remove the old filter, wipe out the inside of the canister with a clean rag. Be careful not to lose the spring or the washers.

Motorcycology

Recent friction-modifying additives used in some automotive oils may seriously damage your bike, so you should probably use motorcycle-specific oil. I use an automotive synthetic oil (Mobil 1), which so far has not incorporated the offending additives. It's much less expensive than motorcycle-specific oil and performs well. However, if Mobil begins putting friction-modifying additives in Mobil 1, I'll switch to a motorcycle-specific oil.

Steer Clear

Drain the oil when the engine is hot, since then the oil will be more viscous and will drain completely. This creates a challenge, since the oil will be scalding hot, as will the engine and other components. Be especially careful to avoid the exhaust pipes, which can cause serious burns.

203

A spin-on oil filter is much more convenient to change than the canister-type filter.

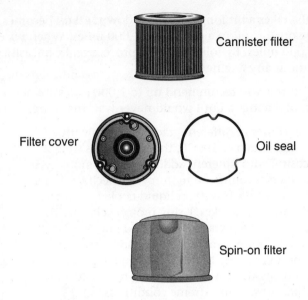

Cannister filter

Filter cover

Oil seal

Spin-on filter

3. Clean and replace the drain plug when the engine is done draining. Most drain plugs have a magnetic tip to collect metal shavings from inside the engine. Thoroughly clean the tip before replacing the plug. Some drain plugs have a metallic washer to enhance the plug's seal. Make certain that you don't lose this washer when removing the plug. Also make certain that the surface of the engine is clean before replacing the plug.

4. Replace the filter. With a spin-on filter, smear oil around the rubber seal attached to the new filter before mounting it to create an oil-tight seal between the filter and engine.

   A canister-type filter will come with a rubber seal for the canister. Make certain to use a new rubber seal with each change. When you have the seal in place, smear it with clean oil, making sure you don't get any foreign material on the rubber, before replacing the canister. Mount the new filter inside the canister, making certain to assemble the spring and washers correctly. And when retightening the bolts, be extra careful not to strip any threads. Because of the spring holding the filter in place within the canister, it is easy to get the canister slightly askew when mounting it, which could lead to thread misalignment. If you encounter the slightest resistance when replacing the bolts, make certain that everything is aligned before proceeding.

5. Refill the oil. Fill the oil to the full mark, then restart your engine to pump oil into your filter. Be extra careful when doing this, and don't rev the throttle any more than is necessary, because your engine will not be properly lubricated upon startup. Let the engine idle for a minute or two, and then shut it off and recheck your oil level. The oil level will have gone down because of the oil pumped into the filter. Refill it to the full mark.

After you have changed the oil, keep a close watch on the oil level, and visually check for leaks around the drain plug and filter. The most likely source for an oil leak is around the filter in a canister-type unit. If you get even a small particle of dust between the rubber seal and the engine, you might notice an oil drip from the canister. This will only get worse. If this happens, you need to get a new rubber seal and do the whole thing over again.

Air Filters: Clearing the Sinuses

Air filters prevent dust and dirt from getting sucked into your engine, but over time they become plugged up with all that dust and dirt. When this happens, your bike doesn't get enough air to properly mix the fuel charge entering your engine, leading to poor performance and increased gas consumption. Air filters are made of paper or foam. Foam filters must be soaked in a special oil. They're located in a bike's *air box*, a chamber connected to the carburetors. When a filter becomes clogged, you have to replace it (if it is a paper type) or clean it (if it is made of foam).

First, you need to remove the filter. On modern bikes, the air box is usually located under the gas tank or under the seat. See your owner's manual for the removal procedure, since it varies with each model of bike.

Next, replace a paper filter or clean a foam filter. To clean a foam filter, soak it in a nonflammable cleaning solvent, then gently squeeze it to remove excess dirt. Apply fresh oil, squeezing off any excess oil, and replace the filter.

Motorcycology

Replacing a stock, paper air filter with a quality aftermarket filter can noticeably improve your bike's performance, but it can also cause some problems. To meet EPA emissions requirements, many bikes have carburetors that mix more air into the fuel charge than they should. This lessens emissions, but it decreases performance and causes the engine to run hotter than it should. By using an aftermarket filter, you increase the airflow even more. This can raise engine temperatures to dangerous levels, especially on an air-cooled bike. Because of this, it might be a good idea to have a qualified mechanic rejet (insert new parts that increase the flow of gasoline) your carburetors if you use an aftermarket air filter.

Batteries: An Electrifying Experience

Batteries are one area where motorcycle technology hasn't kept pace with automotive technology. Bike batteries still need frequent attention. You should check the level of the electrolyte in your battery at least every week or two.

Just locating the battery might be a problem. Batteries used to be located under a bike's seat, but now you can find them anywhere, from up by the headlight to back by the swingarm. Consult your manual.

Once you've found the battery, check the electrolyte level by looking at the side of the battery. The battery case will be made of translucent plastic, allowing you to see the level of the fluid inside. If the level is slightly low, you can add distilled water. If the level is extremely low, you'll need to get some battery acid, which is nasty, dangerous stuff. Be certain not to get it on your body or clothing, and don't breathe the fumes.

Several things can cause extremely low electrolyte levels. Your battery may have cracked or in some way come apart and is leaking, in which case you'll need to replace it immediately. Or you may have tipped the bike over or leaned it far enough for the electrolyte to drip out the overflow tube at the top of the battery. Or your charging system may be malfunctioning, overcharging your battery and evaporating the fluid. If you suspect charging-system problems and you're not a skilled mechanic, it's probably time to take the bike in for professional help.

Keeping Cool

Today, most bikes use some sort of supplemental cooling system. Some bikes spray cooling oil from the engine's sump on internal hot spots. Other bikes use a liquid-cooling system similar to that found in most cars. The liquid-cooling system is the most common on today's streetbikes and requires some maintenance on your part.

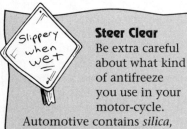

Steer Clear

Be extra careful about what kind of antifreeze you use in your motor-cycle. Automotive contains *silica*, an abrasive designed to keep the cooling system polished inside. This abrasive can damage a motorcycle's water pump, leading to engine failure and expensive repairs.

At least once a week, you should check your coolant level. Usually, you do this by checking your overflow tank, a white plastic tank located in a position remote from the radiator. When you do this, you should also give your radiator hoses a visual inspection, looking for cracks and leaks. If you need to fill coolant, use a mixture of motorcycle-specific antifreeze and water, as recommended in your owner's manual. Every couple of years, you should replace the coolant.

Chain Maintenance

If you have a chain-driven motorcycle, maintaining your chain will become your most frequently performed chore.

You'll need to adjust the tension of the chain, clean it, and lubricate it on a weekly basis (more often, if you put a lot of miles on your bike).

Checking the Tension

To check the tension, grasp the chain on the underside of the swingarm, about halfway between the front and rear chain sprockets, and move the chain up and down. Check several spots on the chain by rolling the bike ahead and rechecking the tension. If the chain moves up and down more than about an inch, it needs to be tightened. If the amount the chain moves varies from spot to spot, the chain may have a tight spot. If the tight spot is severe enough, you may need to replace the chain. I'll tell you how to do that in Chapter 17.

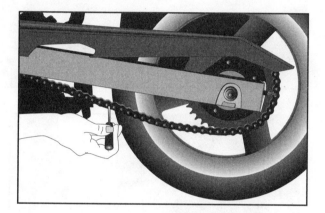

Check the tension along the chain's lower run, about halfway between the front and rear sprockets.

Adjusting the Chain

To adjust the chain, place the bike on the centerstand, or rest it on its side stand if you have no centerstand, and recheck the chain's tension. On the centerstand, your chain's tension may vary from when you first checked it, because the distance between the sprockets may differ slightly. On the centerstand, the swingarm hangs lower than when the bike is resting on the wheels, arcing the rear sprocket closer to the front and making the chain feel looser. Take this difference into account when adjusting the chain—if you adjust the chain to its proper tension on the centerstand, it may become too tight when off the centerstand, and a too-tight chain can break and shoot off your bike like a missile.

Loosen the axle nuts. You will have to remove a security pin on most bikes when undoing the axle nuts. Once the axle nuts are loose, you can adjust the chain. You do this by adjusting bolts on the end of the swingarm on either side of the wheel. Usually, there will be hex-head nuts on each bolt—an inner nut to move the axle, and an outer nut to lock the other in place when finished. Loosen up the outer nut, then carefully adjust the inner nut, moving the nut on one side of the wheel a small amount, then moving the other nut an equal amount.

When you have tightened your chain by the desired amount, tighten down the outside nuts. Retighten the axle bolts, and insert a new security pin. When you adjust axle bolts, make certain that you adjust the bolts on either side of the wheel evenly, or you will cause your back wheel to become misaligned with your front wheel.

Loosen but don't remove the axle bolt.

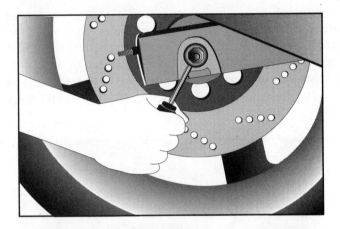

Make certain to adjust the bolts on each side of the wheel the exact same amount. Don't overtighten the chain.

The procedure for adjusting your chain varies from bike to bike, but most bikes use some form of this method. Some bikes have a bolt on the back of the swingarm, with the locking nut between the bolt and the swingarm. A few bikes, especially modern sportbikes with single-sided swingarms, use an eccentric cam on the axles to adjust chain tension. See your owner's manual for the procedure for adjusting these types of chains.

Cleaning and Lubricating Your Chain

To get the most use out of a chain, you'll need to keep it clean and lubricated. Most bikes now use longer-lasting *O-ring* chains (chains with internal lubricant kept in place by rubber seals), but these still need surface lubrication. The problem with O-ring chains is that many substances degrade rubber O-rings, including common lubricants and cleaning solvents. Use only cleaners and lubricants approved for use on O-ring chains.

To clean a chain, place an O-ring–approved cleaner on a soft brush, and use that to clean the grime off the chain. When you get all the crud off, wipe the chain dry before applying fresh lubricant. This is a messy, dirty, frustrating job, but it greatly increases chain life, and chains and sprockets are extremely expensive.

To lubricate your chain, aim the spray from the can of lubricant at the inside of the chain while rotating the wheel to evenly coat the chain. Like all motorcycle maintenance, this is infinitely easier if you have a centerstand. Clean off excess lubricant from the wheels and tires.

Motorcycle drive chains now last much longer than they did just a few years ago, but they also cost a lot more than they used to. And they still wear out. Add in the cost of replacing drive sprockets (which are usually replaced at the same time as the chain), and you're looking at spending $200.

You can minimize wear on your chain by not beating on your bike. The harder you accelerate, the more you stretch your chain.

Shaft Maintenance

Although shaft drive systems require much less maintenance than chain drives, you will need to change the oil in the pinion assembly on the back wheel once or twice a year. This is a simple process. Drain the old oil by removing the drain plug at the bottom of the housing, replace the plug, and refill the housing back to the recommended level by removing a plug at the top of the housing and pouring the gear oil in there. Gear oil is extremely heavy oil (usually 80 weight) that you can buy at nearly all motorcycle dealerships. To check the oil level, remove the filler plug and visually check the level.

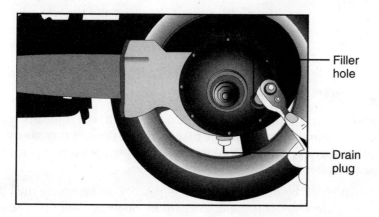

Filler hole

Drain plug

Filling oil in rear-wheel pinion-assembly a couple times a year is far easier than cleaning, lubing, and adjusting your chain each week.

Cleaning Up

Some of us clean our bikes obsessively, while others prefer to let the grime accumulate, but sooner or later, even the grubbiest motorcycle needs a bath. Even if you like your bike grubby, it's a good idea to clean your bike once in a while, if for no other reason than that cleaning allows you to inspect the bike thoroughly, checking for fluid leaks, loose bolts, and other problems.

Don't use pressure washers on your bike, because many delicate parts are more exposed on a motorcycle than on a car. A pressure washer can force dirt and grime between seals, causing bearing failures and other problems. Instead, get a large bucket of warm, soapy water, a sponge, a soft brush, a chamois, and a bunch of soft towels and rags, and wash your bike by hand. It's not that hard if you follow the proper procedure:

1. Degrease the bike. Apply degreaser to the grimiest parts of the bike, like the engine, wheels, and swingarm, with a soft brush. A hard brush may scratch painted surfaces.

2. Wash the bike with soap and water. Wash the bike from top to bottom with the sponge, making certain that you wash off all the degreaser. Use a small brush (like a toothbrush) to get in those hard-to-reach places. Wipe the bike dry with the chamois cloth.

Steer Clear
When washing your bike, use a special, low-salt detergent. Normal household detergents have a high alkali content and can cause erosion.

3. Polish the bike. Use chrome polish on chromed metal surfaces (but not chromed plastic surfaces, since the polish may melt the plastic). Every so often, use a light polish to buff out the paint, but don't use this every time you wash, since it takes off a thin layer of paint with every use.

4. When you are done, apply a hard wax to the painted bodywork and buff it out until it shines. This is especially important after polishing the paint, since the polish softens the paint and the wax protects it. Apply a light coat of lubricant, like WD-40, to unpainted metal surfaces to prevent erosion.

On Ice: Storing Your Bike

Winter storage is the worst part of owning a bike. It's not difficult, but it means you won't be able to ride until spring. First, clean the bike so that it doesn't corrode over the winter. Make certain that the bike is dry before storing it. Empty the oil and place fresh oil in the engine (you don't need to worry about the oil filter).

Drain the carburetor float bowls by turning off the fuel petcock and running the bike until the engine dies. You can also drain the float bowls by opening their drain screws, which are located at the bottom of each carb's float bowl, but be careful not to let gas drip onto hot surfaces. Then, remove the battery and store it in a warm place. Fill the fuel tank to the very top; this prevents corrosion from forming on the inner surfaces of the gas tank. Add a fuel-stabilizing additive to the tank, and you're ready for winter.

In the spring, you'll need to replace the battery, refill the float bowls by turning the fuel petcock to the "prime" position, and again drain the oil and add fresh oil. If you've done everything right, your bike should start right up.

The Least You Need to Know

➤ Buy quality tools—it's less expensive in the long run than buying cheap tools.

➤ Before working on your bike, make certain it's properly supported so that it doesn't fall on you.

➤ Don't use automotive antifreeze in a motorcycle.

➤ Overtightening your chain can cause as many problems as not tightening it at all.

➤ Clean your bike regularly and store it carefully.

Chapter 17

Rx: Repair

In This Chapter

➤ Should you take your bike in or fix it yourself?

➤ Saving money by removing your own wheels

➤ Fixing potentially dangerous brake problems

➤ Replacing your chain and sprocket

In this chapter, I'm going to tell you about more in-depth repair procedures than I went over in Chapter 16. I'm going to explain how to perform the most common repairs you will encounter, like changing tires, replacing brake pads, bleeding brake lines, and replacing chains and sprockets. On most bikes, the procedures generally follow those I outline here. There will be minor differences, which is why you'll also need a repair manual. For more specific repairs, you're going to have to rely solely on your repair manual.

If you can master working on your own bike, you will attain new levels of freedom and autonomy. And you'll save a pile of money. But mastering these procedures will take much time and effort on your part. You'll need to invest in the proper tools. You'll need patience.

Take It In or Do It Yourself?

Should you take your bike in to have someone else work on it, or should you do the work yourself?

Motorcycology

As you read through this chapter, remember that properly supporting your bike is even more important when performing the repairs in this chapter than it was when performing the maintenance procedures in Chapter 16.

A lot of that decision depends on whether you can find a shop you trust. (As I mentioned in Chapter 7, "Buying Your First Bike," you should have done your research on this before you bought your bike.) A good, trustworthy shop will have trained mechanics who have the right tools for every situation. But a bad shop can bung your bike up worse than you could yourself, then charge you a lot of money for it.

If you learn to do the work yourself, you'll never be at the mercy of some shop's schedule for getting your bike fixed. And you'll develop skills that could prove valuable in an emergency. But you'll also have to buy a lot of expensive equipment.

There are benefits to both methods of repair, and ultimately, you'll be the only person who can decide which method is best for you.

Where the Rubber Meets the Road: Tires

Tires are one of the items you need to inspect each time you ride. Look over your tires each morning, checking for cracks, cuts, irregular swelling, and objects like rocks or nails embedded in the tread. Check tire wear—a tire that looks OK one morning can be noticeably worn the next, especially if you've been riding hard or the air temperature has been high (tires wear faster when the pavement is hot).

Worn tires impair your bike's handling, especially in the rain, and are much more likely to suffer catastrophic failure than newer tires. Your tires may have wear bars that appear as the tires age, but chances are, your tires' performance and safety will have begun to deteriorate long before the wear bars appear.

Get in the habit of checking the air pressure in your tires each morning. A sudden loss of air indicates a potentially serious problem. Minor fluctuations in air pressure are normal and are often caused by changes in the air temperature. If your air pressure is a little low, inflate the tire until it reaches the pressure recommended in your owner's manual. If it is drastically low, examine the tread for a hidden nail or some other object that may have punctured the tire.

If a tire is punctured, repair is possible. You can patch a tube or put a plug in a tubeless tire, but I don't recommend either maneuver, except as a way to get your bike to a repair shop. The consequences of a blowout are too great. Replacing a tire or an inner tube is much cheaper than months of painful rehab therapy.

Removing the Rear Wheel

If you need a tire replaced, you should let a repair shop with the proper equipment do the job. That equipment is too specialized and too expensive for most amateur mechanics to have in their own shops, and the consequences of incorrectly mounting a tire are too great. But when you need to change a tire, you can save a lot of money by removing the wheels yourself and bringing the wheel assembly into a shop.

The method for removing motorcycle wheels differs with each bike, depending on the method of securing the axle, the drive system, and the brake systems. Some bikes require the disassembly of suspension components or bodywork. The method described here is for a chain-driven motorcycle with disc brakes. Consult your repair manual for specific details.

> **Motorcycology**
> When removing the axle, make certain that you are passing the axle through the swingarm in the right direction. Many axles have a big end on one side and a securing bolt on the other. If the axle won't move in the direction you are tapping, or if it stops moving abruptly, make certain that you're not trying to push it through the swingarm in the wrong direction.

1. First, remove the axle. To do this, remove the split keys securing the axle nuts in place, then undo the nuts. Some axles may have additional pinch bolts securing them in place that aren't obvious upon first inspection of the assembly. Make certain that you have loosened or removed all bolts holding the axle in place, then gently tap the axle through the swingarm with a soft-faced mallet.

Be gentle when tapping the axle through the swingarm. If it takes more than a light tap, chances are something is not properly loosened up.

2. Once you have the axle past one side of the swingarm, it should move freely through the wheel. A couple of things may hinder its progress. If the chain is too tight, it may pull the wheel forward, causing the axle to bind. If this is the case, loosen the axle adjustment bolts, being careful to adjust the bolts on both sides an equal amount. If the wheel falls down a bit after you move the axle through one

side of the swingarm, it will also cause the axle to bind. You may have to support the wheel with your knee while removing the axle to prevent this.

Some bikes will require you to unhook the rear shocks from the swingarm, allowing the swingarm to drop low enough for the axle bolt to clear the exhaust pipes. In extreme cases, you may have to remove the exhaust pipes entirely.

3. Next, remove the wheel. Remove the spacers between the wheel and the swingarm, making notes of their location. (To help remember their locations for reassembly, I lay them out on a rag, along with the axle, in the exact order they go on the bike.) Push the wheel forward and unhook the chain when there is enough slack. Move the chain away from the wheel. You may want to remove the chain guard to allow you to move the chain free of the wheel.

You may have to remove some items to get the tire to clear the swingarm.

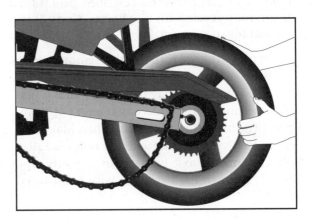

On shaft-driven bikes, wheel removal is usually easier than on chain-driven bikes. The main difference is that you pull the wheel away from the pinion housing to unhook it from the drive system rather than pushing it forward and removing the chain.

You may have to undo the brake caliper to make room to remove the wheel. If you have to do so, hold the caliper while you remove the wheel, then make certain it is securely supported until reassembly. Don't let the caliper hang by its hose.

4. After you have had the tire changed and the wheel balanced, reassemble by reversing the process. Don't forget to install a new split key to lock the axle bolt in place. Make certain that everything is properly assembled before riding, and stop to check all the bolts frequently the first few times you go riding.

Steer Clear
Never ride hard just after you have mounted new tires. New tires are slippery for the first few dozen miles, so ride with extra caution while breaking them in. At first, they may have less traction than the ones you just replaced.

Removing the Front Wheel

Removing the front wheel is similar to removing the rear wheel, except it's a bit easier, because you don't have a drive system to deal with or a swingarm to work around. You may have to remove a speedometer cable, though.

Since you won't have to work around a swingarm or drive system, the front wheel is easier to remove than the rear wheel on most bikes.

To remove the wheel, first unhook the speedometer cable, if necessary. Then remove the axle. On many bikes, the easiest way to do this is to undo the end caps at the bottom of the fork, allowing the axle along with the entire wheel-tire assembly to drop out the bottom. If it works that way, simply roll the tire ahead, remove the axle bolts, and pull the axle out. Other bikes require you to remove the axle bolts and push the axle through the wheel to remove the assembly, much as I discussed doing with the rear wheel. Either way, note the location of any spacers between the wheel and the fork.

You may have to remove the brake calipers to remove the front wheel. If so, make certain that you don't let them hang by their hoses.

To reassemble, just reverse the procedure.

Tires can prove to be major wallet drainers. Motorcycle tires cost much more than their automotive counterparts, running as high as $300 apiece for premium sport radials. And they won't last nearly as long as a car tire. A person who logs a lot of miles can easily expect to run through at least one set of tires per year.

A Screeching Halt: Brakes

In all my years of riding, I've only seen two people get killed in motorcycle accidents, both on a race track. One of them was killed when his front brake lever came off. This illustrates just how important your brakes are. If even the least complicated part of the system fails, it could cost you your life.

Cycle Babble
Many bikes use a combination of **disc brakes** on the front and **drum brakes** on the rear. You will find this combination especially common on cruisers. Disc brakes use stationary calipers that squeeze pads against discs that rotate with the wheel, while drum brakes use horseshoe-shaped brake shoes that expand against the inner surface of the wheel hub.

There are two kinds of brakes—*disc brakes* and *drum brakes*. Most modern bikes use disc brakes in front. Many also use disc brakes in back, but some still use drum rear brakes. Disc brakes slow your motorcycle by squeezing pistons inside a caliper, which is attached to your frame or fork and doesn't rotate, against a disc attached to your wheel, slowing both the disc and the wheel it is attached to. Drum brakes work by expanding the brake shoes—stationary, horseshoe-shaped devices inside your wheel hub—against the inner surface of the hub, which is part of the rotating wheel.

With disc brakes, you will need to periodically change the *brake pads*—metal-backed fiber pads located at the ends of the pistons in the calipers. These pads are the surfaces that actually contact the brake disc, and they wear down over time.

With drum brakes, you will need to replace the shoes as they wear down.

Checking Brake Pads

The procedure for checking pad wear varies according to the design of the caliper. Some designs allow you to simply look between the caliper and the disc, but many designs have a cover on top of the caliper that can be pried off with a screwdriver. This gives you a clear view of the pads. Some designs require you to remove the caliper entirely to inspect the pads.

If the brake-pad material is wearing thin, it is time to replace the pads. Sometimes, the material will change in texture over time, especially if the pads have been subjected to extreme heat or some contaminant. If you notice a decrease in your brakes' performance, you should replace the pads, even if they appear to have enough material on them.

On many calipers, you can inspect the pads by popping a cover off the top of the caliper with a screwdriver.

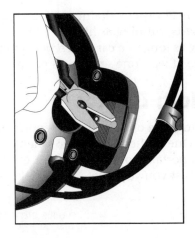

Replacing Brake Pads

Again, the procedure for replacing brake pads varies from caliper to caliper, so the instructions presented here are just a general guide.

On some caliper designs, the correct procedure doesn't require you to remove the brake calipers. Others will require you to do so. This is usually accomplished by removing the two bolts holding the caliper to the caliper carrier.

The pads are held in place by pins that pass through the caliper body. The pins are retained by some sort of clip or by a split key. First remove the clip or key, being careful not to lose any pieces, since they don't come with the new pads. When you are unfamiliar with the procedure, it helps to take notes on the order in which you remove parts.

Remove the pads with a pair of pliers, and insert the new pads. Since your new pads will be thicker than the old, worn pads, you may have to ease the piston back into the caliper. This should require little force. If you need to use something to push the piston back in the caliper, use something soft, like a wooden stick, instead of a metal object, like a screwdriver, since the metal can damage seals and the surface of the piston.

> **Steer Clear**
> When the caliper is removed from the disc, or when you remove the pads from the caliper, do not squeeze the brake lever. Also be careful not to contaminate the caliper or pad with brake fluid, oil, or dirt, since this can cause your brakes to malfunction.

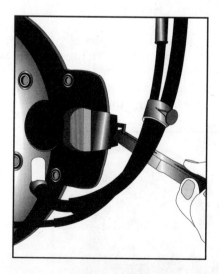

Because the old pads were worn, you may have to move pistons back in their calipers when replacing brake pads.

While the pads are out, check the pistons' dust seals for any tears.

After you have inserted the pads, simply reverse this procedure, referring to your notes for the correct order of assembly. If your brake uses clips to retain the pad pins, you can reuse

Motorcycology
A certain amount of grooving in the disc surface is natural, but if it becomes too grooved, braking performance can diminish. The only repair for a grooved disc on a bike is replacement—an expensive proposition. To extend disc life, I go over discs with rough sandpaper each time I replace brake pads, being careful to wipe off all debris from the sanding before I replace the calipers.

Steer Clear
The springs holding the brake shoes in place are strong, so be careful not to pinch your fingers when removing and replacing shoes.

Two strong springs hold the brake shoes in place.

those. If you have a split key retaining the pins, use new split keys instead of reusing the old ones.

When you check your brake pads, you should also check your *discs* (these are the metal rotors the caliper presses the pads against). If you replace your pads before they become too worn, your discs should last a long time, but if your pads wear down too far, they can damage the discs. You can check your disc by looking at it and feeling its surface for irregularities.

Checking Shoes

The only way to check the brake shoes is to remove the wheel from the bike, which I explained earlier in this chapter. After you remove the wheel, pull the back plate from the brake drum. This should be so loose that it will fall off on its own if you tip the wheel upside down, but don't do that, since the fall could damage the brakes.

It's difficult to judge the wear of the brake shoes by visual inspection, since you really don't know what they are supposed to look like, so rely on your manual to provide you with information on acceptable shoe-wear limits.

Replacing Shoes

The brake shoes are held in place by strong springs as well as clips on some designs. Remove the clip, and squeeze the brakes together to release the tension on the springs. Remove the springs and lift the shoes out. Install the new brake shoes by reversing the procedure.

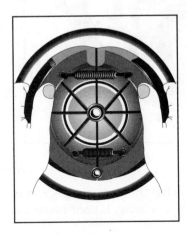

Brake-Lever Adjustment

Many bikes come with adjustable brake and clutch levers, items that both improve comfort and safety, because they allow you to react more quickly in an emergency. You adjust the handlebar levers by rotating a numbered dial located where the lever pivots.

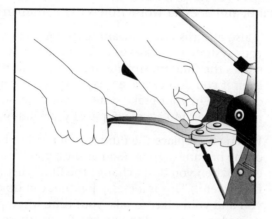

Adjusting your brake levers can decrease your reaction time in an emergency, saving your life.

The pedal angle on your foot brake is also adjustable, and finding the proper angle can make a huge difference in your reaction time. On drum rear brakes, the angle is adjusted by a *movable stop*—a bolt located near the rear of the pedal. This bolt usually has a lock nut similar to that used on the rear-axle adjusting bolt. On disc rear brakes, the adjusting bolt will be part of the lever connecting the brake pedal to the master cylinder, and it works in much the same way as a drum brake lever adjuster.

On drum brakes, you will have an adjustment for free play located on the lever that actuates the brake shoes. You will need to tighten the nut on the end of the connecting rod as the brake shoes and other components wear. Be careful not to overtighten the free play, or the bike may accidentally activate the brake when bouncing on a bump. You need to keep enough free play to allow the bike to move up and down on its suspension without activating the brake.

Motorcycology
The distance between the rear wheel and the engine varies slightly as the bike moves up and down on its suspension. The rear-wheel assembly is *unsprung*—that is, it does not move with the suspension. This is why you need to leave some free play in components connected to both the rear wheel and the frame or engine, like the rear drum brake lever and the drive chain.

A Bloody Mess: Bleeding the Brake Lines

Disc brakes operate by moving hydraulic fluid from the *master cylinder*—the reservoir to which the brake lever is connected—and the calipers. The fluid, which comes in several varieties that can't be intermixed (the variety your bike needs is stamped on its master-cylinder reservoir cover), is one of the nastiest substances you will ever encounter. It melts plastic, disintegrates paint, and does far worse things to the human body.

Steer Clear
Never use brake fluid from a container that has been opened—it may contain fluid absorbed from the atmosphere. Always use a fresh container. And make certain that you're using the correct type for your brake system. The cover of your master cylinder will be marked DOT 3, DOT 4, DOT 5, or DOT 5.1, referring to the type of fluid needed. Use only that type of fluid.

It also absorbs water, meaning that if you have a leak in your system, you have to fix it immediately, since water makes the fluid mushy and decreases your braking power. Even if you don't have a leak, atmospheric moisture will condense in your brake system over time, so you'll need to replace the fluid every couple of years, anyway.

When you replace the fluid, you'll need to bleed the air out of the braking system. (Sometimes, you'll need to do this even when you don't change the fluid, just to get air out of the system.) This is a messy job that can do damage to both you and your bike, so take your time when performing this procedure. To bleed the brakes, follow these steps:

1. Remove the reservoir cap at the top of your master cylinder by unscrewing the screws holding it in. This cap has a rubber diaphragm underneath it. Remove this to expose the fluid. You may want to wrap a cloth around the bottom of the master cylinder to capture leaked fluid before it reaches any painted metal or plastic parts.

When removing the brake master-cylinder cover, be careful not to get any brake fluid on your bike or yourself.

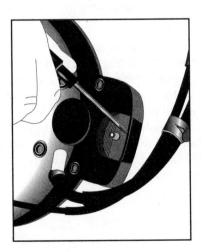

2. Fill the reservoir with fluid. Use only fluid from a sealed container (old cans of fluid absorb water from the atmosphere), and only use the fluid your braking system was designed for. Be careful not to spill, since the fluid will destroy all bike parts it touches. Then replace the diaphragm.

3. Bleed the brakes. There will be an odd-looking nipple on your caliper. Put one end of a clear plastic tube over the nipple, and put the other end of the tube in a jar with some hydraulic fluid inside. Loosen the nipple one turn, and squeeze the brake lever gently, causing fluid to flow through the tube. Tighten the nipple and release the lever. If you see bubbles in the tube, repeat the process until they disappear. Refill the reservoir and refit the rubber diaphragm prior to squeezing the brake lever. Repeat this procedure for each caliper.

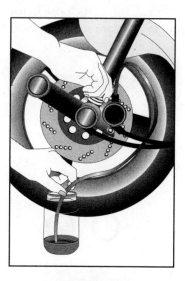

You'll need to have a length of clear plastic tubing on hand to bleed your brakes without making a mess.

Chain and Sprocket Replacement

As mentioned in Chapter 16, modern O-ring chains last much longer than the roller chains used in the past, but they also cost much more to replace. Proper maintenance—keeping the chain clean, well-lubricated, and properly adjusted—can increase the life of your chain, but sooner or later you'll need to replace it. And when you do, you'll need to replace the sprockets to which the chain is connected.

Chains have a *repair link*—a link in the chain that can be disassembled for chain repair—or they are of the continuous-loop variety. Replacing a continuous-loop chain requires special tools and is best left to a professional. The procedure here applies to chains with split repair links:

1. Clean the chain and sprocket area. This is the dirtiest, grimiest, and slipperiest area on your bike. Cleaning the area will make your job much easier.

2. Remove anything that blocks access to your sprockets. You will have to remove the rear wheel and the casing covering the front sprocket. You may also have to remove your chain guard and other items.

3. Disassemble the chain's repair link. Using your pliers, squeeze the spring clip off of its pins. Then you can remove the side plate and push the link out the other side. You can now remove the chain.

4. Remove the sprockets. The bolts holding the sprockets on will be tight and difficult to remove. It might be easier to loosen the bolts on the rear sprocket when the wheel is still mounted on the bike. To do this, have someone hold the rear brake and help stabilize the bike, and break the bolts loose before removing the wheel. Once the bolts holding the sprockets on are removed, you should be able to lift off the sprockets.

The instructions for assembling your chain's split repair link will be provided with the chain.

It may be easier to break the bolts on the rear sprocket loose before removing the rear wheel.

5. Replace the sprockets and tighten down the bolts, then remount the rear tire.

6. Put on the new chain. The new chain will be shorter than the old one, so you'll need to adjust your rear axle accordingly, remembering to turn the bolts on either side of the wheel evenly to maintain wheel alignment. Place a newspaper under the chain so that it doesn't get dirty if you drop it, then feed the chain over the rear sprocket, along the top of the swingarm, then over the front sprocket. This will allow you to connect the chain on the bottom of the swingarm, where you'll have more room to work.

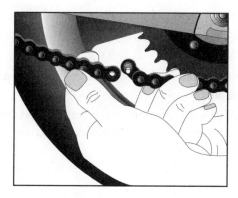

You'll need to adjust the axle bolts to connect the chain, since the new chain will be shorter than the old, stretched one. Make certain to move both adjusting bolts the same distance to retain wheel alignment.

7. Assemble the split link with the rubber O-rings. (The chain's manufacturer will include instructions for doing this with the chain.) Then insert the split link through the two ends of the chain, connecting the chain. Place an O-ring over each exposed pin, put the side plate over the pins, and push the retaining clip over the pins, making certain that the closed end of the clip faces toward the chain's

Steer Clear
Make certain that you place the round end of the split link's retaining clip in the direction the chain travels, with the split end facing away from the direction in which the chain travels. If the split end is facing the direction in which the chain moves, road debris could wedge between the clip, causing it to come loose and leading to the loss of your chain.

direction of travel. This means that the closed end will be facing the rear sprocket if you're working on the part of the chain that lies under the swingarm.

8. Adjust the chain to the proper tension as described in Chapter 16, then make certain all bolts are tight. The chain will probably stretch quite a bit when it is new, so check the tension more frequently than you normally would.

As you perform these procedures, you will get a better idea of your mechanical abilities. You may find that you have a knack for doing your own repair. If so, cautiously branch out, performing more and more of your own repairs.

Even if you can afford to have someone else do all this work, if you learn to perform your own maintenance and repair, you'll derive more satisfaction from the motorcycle ownership experience.

The Least You Need to Know

➤ Check your tire pressure every morning.

➤ New tires are slippery and need some time to be broken in properly before they provide all their potential traction.

➤ Always use the brake fluid your brake system was designed to use, and only use brake fluid from a sealed container.

➤ When replacing the split link in a drive chain, make certain that the round, unsplit end of the retainer clip points in the direction in which the chain moves.

Chapter 18

Creative Customizing and Collecting

In This Chapter

➤ Why customize your bike?

➤ Types of custom motorcycles

➤ Setting goals for customizing your bike

➤ What to look for when collecting motorcycles

In 1885, Gottlieb Daimler cobbled together the Einspur, the first gasoline-powered, purpose-built motorcycle. The vehicle was just a testbed for his engine, and as soon as he had a motor strong enough to power a four-wheeled vehicle, he abandoned his Einspur. History is a bit unclear about what happened to the vehicle after that. My guess is that it fell into the hands of the first motorcycle enthusiast, who promptly customized the thing.

Motorcyclists have been customizing their machines since the beginning of the sport. Whether we ride a run-of-the-mill Universal Japanese Motorcycle (UJM) or a priceless collectible bike, we can't resist personalizing our machines.

Motorcyclists also like to collect motorcycles. People collect bikes for different reasons. Some collect bikes as investments, although the value of such investments has not been proven. Most of us collect bikes just because we like them. (Motorcycles seem to follow you home, sometimes.)

In this chapter, I'm going to help you decide whether or not you should customize your bike and how to get started. I'm also going to explain the basics of collecting bikes. I'll offer advice on which bikes may be good investments, but mostly, I'm going to try to help you find motorcycles that make you happy. Ask any serious collector, and he or she will tell you that's what it's all about.

Why Customize?

Originally, people modified their motorcycles to improve them in some way. In the early years of the sport, for example, many motorcyclists added a windshield, some saddlebags, or perhaps a sidecar to their bikes.

Cycle Babble
The custom bikes American riders built after World War II were called **bobbers** because owners cut off, or "bobbed," much of the bodywork.

After World War II, customization in the United States focused on improving performance. Young American men and women had been exposed to lightweight, high-performance European motorcycles during the war. When they came home, the old U.S. bikes just didn't cut it. Most motorcycle riders had to figure out alternative methods to get higher performance out of their bikes.

How'd they do it? They simply lightened their bikes. They unbolted every non-essential part they could unbolt or torch. This became the pattern for customization in this country, and to this day, the *bobbers*, as the original chopped customs were called, still set the pattern for U.S.-style custom bikes.

As the performance levels of stock motorcycles climbed, it became less necessary to customize a bike to attain more speed. But people now customize for other reasons, too.

Cycle Babble
The term **ape hangers** was coined at the height of the custom-bike movement to describe tall handlebars that forced the rider to reach skyward to grasp the controls, making the rider adopt an ape-like posture. Harley-Davidson recently copyrighted this term, but it has been around since at least the 1960s.

Some people customize for style. Modifications like lowering a bike's suspension, altering its steering geometry, and adding *ape-hanger* (tall) handlebars—the modifications that have come to define the term *custom* for many people—actually detract from a bike's performance, but scores of people do these things to their bikes anyway. (Many of the radically-customized motorcycles you see in bike shows are actually unridable.)

But there's an alternate movement in the realm of motorcycle customization. Many people still modify their bikes to increase their usefulness. People add aftermarket suspension components to improve a bike's handling. They mount windshields, more comfortable seats, and hard luggage to make a motorcycle a better long-distance tourer. They add aftermarket air filters and rejet their carburetors, not only to make their bikes faster, but to make them more efficient. In a way, customization has come full circle.

Comparing Customs

Ask a typical American to describe a custom bike, and he or she will most likely describe the radical chopper-type bike. Such bikes account for the largest segment of customization in the United States, but elsewhere in the world, other types of customs have been more prevalent. In the past few years, some of the other styles of customs have been gaining in popularity in the United States, especially the cafe racers and streetfighters that have long been popular in Europe.

Choppers

Choppers define American motorcycle style. The original bobbers were American hot rods, stripped-down Harleys, and Indians built for speed. As other, faster motorcycles became available, custom Harleys evolved from the bobbers of the 1940s into the choppers of the 1960s. By then, chopper style had become carved in stone: extended forks; high handlebars; a low, fat tire on the back; a tall, skinny tire up front; and a tall backrest or sissy bar.

Steer Clear

I don't recommend building a chopper-type custom. Such bikes tend to be so foul-handling, they are unsafe on the road. Riding a motorcycle is challenging enough on a bike you can steer. If you want to own such a machine, I recommend buying one from an established customizer who knows what he or she is doing when building the bike.

Slippery when wet

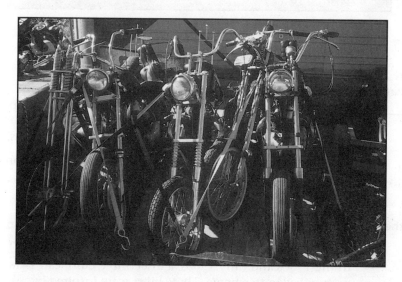

While typical choppers with extended forks looked pretty groovy, the bikes handled so poorly that they were unsafe to ride. (Photo © 1998 Darwin Holstrom)

In the 1970s and 1980s, choppers evolved into low riders, becoming longer and lower. Now low-rider–type customs are more common than traditional choppers, although the original chopper-type customs have been making a comeback in the past few years.

The original bobbers were either Harleys or Indians. When the British began exporting large numbers of bikes to the United States in the 1950s, these, too, became popular bikes to chop. Initially, customizers also chopped Japanese bikes, but by the early 1980s, Harleys once again ruled the custom-bike market in the United States. But due to the difficulty of obtaining new Harleys, along with their soaring prices, Japanese bikes have begun to regain popularity in the custom scene. You can now buy aftermarket customizing parts for a variety of Japanese cruisers.

Harley-Davidsons have long been the motorcycles of choice for customizing projects, but in recent years, Japanese bikes, like this Honda Shadow, have become more popular among customizers. (Photo © 1998 Darwin Holstrom)

Cafe Racers

While Americans were busy chopping their Harleys, the Europeans took a different approach to customization. For many post-war Europeans, motorcycles were the only form of transportation to which they had access. In Europe, motorcycles were (and still are) used more frequently as practical transportation than they are in the United States.

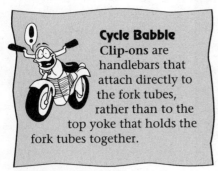

Cycle Babble
Clip-ons are handlebars that attach directly to the fork tubes, rather than to the top yoke that holds the fork tubes together.

Thus, customization tended to be more heavily focused on practical improvements. That, combined with the more liberal attitude toward driving fast in many European countries, meant that Europeans were more interested in building faster, better-handling customs than they were in adding higher ape-hanger handlebars and taller sissy bars.

In the 1950s and early 1960s, a discernible European style of custom began to emerge. These bikes were inspired by

European racing motorcycles. Owners moved their footpegs toward the rear and lowered their handlebars, often using handlebars that clipped directly on the fork legs (*clip-on handlebars*). This placed the rider in a crouched, forward-leaning position. Some owners adapted small fairings to their bikes to mimic the fairings used by racers.

Cafe racers, like this Rickman-framed Honda 750 from the mid-1970s, have long been popular in Europe and are gaining popularity in the United States as well. (Photo © 1998 Darwin Holstrom)

These bikes became known as *cafe racers*, supposedly because their owners hung out in cafes and raced each other from cafe to cafe. Such bikes have always had a cult following in the United States, a following that continues to grow over time. There are probably more cafe racers in the United States right now than at any time in history. In some cities, like Minneapolis and San Francisco, the popularity of cafe racers rivals that of custom Harleys.

Although when taken to the extreme, cafe racers can be as uncomfortable to ride as choppers, when modified correctly, cafe racers handle much better than choppers. Another benefit of building a cafe racer instead of building a chopper is that it's much cheaper. To build a respectable chopper, you'll either need to start with a Harley-Davidson or with one of the big Japanese cruisers—an expensive proposition, either way.

You can do a very nice cafe chop on just about any older Japanese motorcycle—bikes you can pick up for less money than you'd spend on tax and a license for a big new cruiser.

> **Cycle Babble**
> **Cafe racers** are motorcycles modified to resemble racing motorcycles from the 1950s and '60s. They are called "cafe racers" because their owners supposedly raced from cafe to cafe in London, where the bikes first appeared in the 1960s. Converting a stock motorcycle into a cafe racer is known as doing a **cafe chop** on a bike.

Streetfighters

While Yankees progressed from choppers to low riders, in Europe, cafe bikes evolved into *streetfighters*: stripped-down, hopped-up road warriors of the type the original post-war customizers in this country might have devised if they had had access to modern technology.

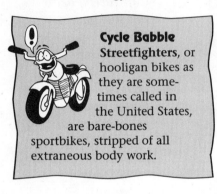

Cycle Babble
Streetfighters, or hooligan bikes as they are sometimes called in the United States, are bare-bones sportbikes, stripped of all extraneous body work.

Streetfighters are all function. They have no bodywork, no fancy paint, and no chrome. They owe their very existence to practicality.

As sportbikes became more and more complex, they also became more expensive to buy and more expensive to repair after minor crashes. Insurance companies began writing off perfectly functional sportbikes rather than replacing expensive plastic pieces.

European motorcyclists, with war-bred practicality, started rescuing those damaged bikes, but instead of replacing expensive body parts, they just trashed all the plastic. Like American customizers in the 1940s, they chopped off all the extraneous parts, replacing only what was needed, like the headlight. In fact, they often bolted on a couple of headlights. When the whole thing was ready, they applied a coat of flat-black paint (to protect the surfaces of the exposed metal, not for any cosmetic reasons), then went out and rode the wheels of these streetfighters.

These bikes proved so popular that the manufacturers got in the act. A variety of companies began marketing sporting bikes without any bodywork, but no one got the streetfighter look down as well as Triumph. The latest Speed Triple T509 embodies the streetfighter look.

Triumph nailed the streetfighter look with its latest Speed Triple T509. (Photo courtesy Motorcyclist™ *magazine)*

So You Want to Customize Your Bike...

If you are interested in customizing your bike, you need to ask yourself a few questions:

1. What do I want from my bike? Do I want to improve some functional aspect, like comfort or handling? Do I want to improve my bike's performance? Do I just want to change my bike's appearance? What you want from your bike will guide you when deciding what changes to make.

2. What compromises am I willing to make to get what I want? A motorcycle represents a series of compromises made by the designers and engineers who created it. They made those compromises for a reason. Altering one aspect of your bike can cause unintended consequences in some other aspect. Honestly assess what you are willing to sacrifice before making any changes.

3. How much am I willing to spend? There are many small, inexpensive alterations you can make to your bike that will improve its comfort, handling, appearance, and performance. But making major alterations usually costs a lot, and there's no guarantee you'll achieve your desired results. Before embarking on a major modification of your motorcycle, make certain that you know what you want, that your intended modification will achieve that goal, and that the results will be worth what they'll cost you.

Only after you've answered these questions should you make any major modifications to your bike.

By nature, customizing is a personal process. Only you know what you want and need from your bike. Part of your task as a new motorcyclist will be to learn as much as possible about your bike. As you become more familiar with your machine, you'll have a better idea of how to modify it to suit you.

I recommend starting out small. Identify an aspect of your bike you'd like to improve, like comfort. Perhaps you can add a windshield or a better seat. Make incremental changes when possible. That will help you avoid making serious mistakes that will be difficult (and expensive) to correct.

Discussing various methods for modifying your bike will fill a book in itself. Fortunately, there are many fine books available on the subject. You can order most of these from Whitehorse Press or Motorbooks International (see Appendix C).

Steer Clear
Don't make drastic modifications to your bike until you are certain of your goals. Making a radical alteration that turns out to make the bike less appealing can be an expensive misstep.

Slippery when wet

Classic, Collectible, or Just Old? Collecting Motorcycles

Ride long enough, and you'll notice something about motorcycles: No one can own just one. Becoming a motorcycle collector is an insidious process. It starts when you buy a better bike but can't quite bring yourself to sell your trusty old one. Then you'll decide to explore a different aspect of riding, like off-road riding or touring, so you'll buy a bike suited for that purpose. But you still won't be able to part with the other two. Then you'll run across a pristine example of a classic bike you've always wanted, and you'll just happen to have enough money to buy it, so...

By this time, you're too far gone to turn back. Like it or not, you're a collector. But it could be worse. Peter Egan, who writes for *Cycle World* magazine, once wrote that everyone needs at least four motorcycles: one for touring, one for sport riding, one for riding off-road, and one classic bike to keep it all in perspective. So go ahead and indulge yourself. Motorcycles have gotten much more expensive in the past 15 years, but they are still cheap compared to cars. And they take up less space. You can park up to six bikes in the space of one car, with some careful packing.

Collector's Choice

In the late 1980s and early 1990s, some investors decided British motorcycles were going to rapidly appreciate in value, and overnight, the price of Triumphs, Nortons, and BSAs skyrocketed. Many of the people buying these bikes were not motorcyclists: They were investors out to get rich.

Steer Clear
Don't collect motorcycles because you think you'll make money. You won't. Even if you pick a winner, you'll be lucky to recoup the money you spend on upkeep and maintenance. If you want to get rich, try the stock market. If you want to collect motorcycles, collect bikes you like.

Some people got rich off of the entire debacle, but for the most part, it wasn't the investors—it was the people who sold the motorcycles at inflated prices. The Brit-bike boom lasted a few years, and then prices declined. British bikes still cost more than they used to, even when their prices are adjusted for inflation and appreciation, but they're back down to somewhat reasonable levels.

The lesson to be learned from all this is that you shouldn't buy a bike solely as a financial investment. It's a risky proposition at best. Even if you get lucky and buy a bike that does increase in value, it probably won't increase enough to cover the expenses you incur while you own it.

If you're interested in a particular type or brand of bike, you can look for a particular model or year that may someday be worth more than other models or years, but that is a secondary consideration. When deciding what to collect, your first concern should be collecting bikes you like.

What Do You Like?

Before you start collecting bikes, ask yourself what you like. Do you like classic Japanese bikes? Do you like the brutal efficiency of BMWs? How about the fluid style of Italian sportbikes? Or the simple elegance of British bikes? Perhaps you like classic American motorcycles. Whatever your style, your individual preferences are of key importance when you begin collecting bikes.

What's Your Mechanical Skill Level?

How much time and energy are you willing to devote to the upkeep of your bikes? An American or British bike will require a lot more work to keep running than a Japanese bike or a BMW. Italian bikes will fall somewhere in between. Know your abilities before you start buying bikes with maintenance requirements that you are unprepared to deal with.

What's Your Budget?

You also need to ask yourself how much you're willing to spend. With the exception of Japanese bikes, any of the motorcycles mentioned in this chapter will take a serious bite out of your bank account. You can still pick up a decent British bike or a BMW for under $4,000, but if your taste runs toward Italian or American bikes, you'd better have considerably more cash available.

You can still find nice, older Japanese bikes for fairly low prices, though. The prices of a few early models, like Honda's Benley Super Sport 125, have shot through the roof, but you can still pick up a very nice mid-1970s CB 750 for under $1,500, and you can find clean examples of other Japanese bikes for a lot less than that. Few of these bikes will ever have any serious investment value, but they're fun to ride, easy to maintain, and make great projects for cafe chops.

Few Japanese motorcycles have joined the ranks of true classics. Those that have, like this Honda Benley Super Sport 125, will run you well into the five-figure price range. (Photo © 1998 Darwin Holstrom)

235

What Constitutes a Classic?

Classifying a bike as a classic is an almost mystical process. To be a true classic, a bike needs to have just the right combination of rarity, competence, and charisma to tickle collectors right in their reptilian stems.

Some bikes are firmly established as classics. No one questions the status of bikes like Moto Guzzi's V7 Sport, Ducati's Round Case 750SS, Mike Hailwood Replicas, Harley's Knuckleheads and Panheads, Indian's Chiefs and Fours, any Brough or Vincent, BMW's R60s, Ariel's Square Fours, Norton's Commandos, or BSA's Gold Stars. But to get one of these bikes, be prepared to shell out some serious cash. And be prepared to wait, because there are only a handful of these bikes on U.S. soil, and most of those are owned by collectors who have little interest in selling them.

If you decide you can't live without a true classic, like this Vincent Rapide (left) or Ariel Square Four, you better have access to some serious cash. (Photo © 1998 Darwin Holstrom)

If you decide to fork over the big bucks to buy a classic, make certain that you're getting the real thing. For example, earlier Triumph Bonnevilles are much sought after by collectors, while collectors tend to show little interest in the later models with dry-sump oil reservoirs in their frames. And if you invest your life savings in a Round Case Ducati SS, make certain that you're getting the real thing, since other Ducati models can be converted into convincing SS replicas.

One way to tell a true Round Case Ducati 750SS from a fake is to check the frame. Most SS models didn't have provisions for mounting a centerstand, and on most fakes, the mounting lugs will have been ground off. But some very early race bikes did have some mounting lugs, and these are the most collectible of all Ducatis. Compounding this confusion is the historically shoddy record keeping of the Ducati factory. Given the complexity involved, your best bet is to hire a recognized expert to authenticate the bike, like Phil Schilling. Such a service won't come cheap, but if you have enough money to purchase this particular bike, you can certainly afford to authenticate your investment.

How can you tell if a bike is for real? Read all you can about a particular bike before buying one. If a bike's really a classic, there will be a plethora of books about it. Appendix C, "Resources," lists the names and addresses of a couple of publishers who specialize in motorcycle books. Call and get their catalogs, and you'll find books on every classic bike made.

Steer Clear
When shopping for a classic bike, make certain you're getting the real thing. Buying a fake can be one of the most expensive mistakes you'll ever make.

If you're interested in collecting classic bikes, get in touch with your local antique motorcycle club. Members of such organizations can provide you with more knowledge about classic motorcycles than any other source. And these people love motorcycles. You'll find no shortage of advice, and you may even be able to find someone who can help you locate the exact bike you're looking for.

Future Classics?

Given the scarcity and cost of true classics, collecting might seem out of most people's reach. And it can be a real gamble. Your odds of losing money are much greater than your odds of making money. That's why I recommend only buying bikes you like and bikes you will use.

That doesn't mean you can't have a lot of fun, and possibly even make some money someday. There are useful bikes that qualify as great buys right now that might become classics sometime in the future.

Say, for example, that after you've become a proficient rider, you decide to buy a hard-core sportbike. You can buy any of the Japanese sportbikes.

Or, for about the same price as a 600cc Japanese Sportbike, you can buy a used Ducati 900SS. The 600s might be a bit faster than the Ducati, but the Ducati is faster than you'll ever be able to ride on public roads. And it's easier to ride fast than most 600s. In other words, it's more sportbike than you'll ever be able to use in the real world. It will require more maintenance, and you'll need to know a mechanic skilled in adjusting its valve gear, but down the road, it may be worth the bother.

Hang on to the Ducati for 10 or 20 years, and then compare its value to the value of a 20-year-old Japanese 600. The 600 will be worth less than a steaming bowl of jack, while the Ducati will be worth what you paid for it, provided you've taken good care of it. And if that particular model appreciates, as some people speculate it might, you could come out ahead. (If you factor in your maintenance costs and inflation, you still would have done better to invest in the stock market, but a Ducati is much more fun to ride than a few thousand shares of Archer Daniels Midland.)

If you're trying to decide between getting this Ducati 900SS FE or buying a top-shelf Japanese sportbike, you may want to ask yourself which will likely be worth more money 10 years from now. (Photo courtesy Motorcyclist™ magazine)

There are other bikes that, by nature of their rarity or oddity, may someday become collectible—bikes like Yamaha's GTS, a sport-tourer with an automotive-style front suspension instead of traditional forks, and Honda's six-cylinder CBX. But if you buy one of these, do so because you want the bike. That way, you'll have more fun, and you won't be disappointed if you don't make a fortune.

The Least You Need to Know

➤ Some modifications can make a motorcycle dangerous to ride.

➤ Get to know your bike and what you want from it before modifying it.

➤ If you want to get rich, invest in the stock market, not in classic motorcycles.

➤ When shopping for a classic, make certain you're getting the real thing.

Part 5
The Motorcycling Community

So far, I've concentrated on you and your motorcycle. From a safety perspective, that's the most important part of riding, since when you're out on the road, you're all you have to depend on.

But there's much more to motorcycling than just solitary riding. You have now become part of an extended family: the motorcycle community. In this part, I'll tell you about different aspects of that community and what it has to offer you.

Join the Club: Motorcycle Clubs

Motorcycles and motorcycling fascinated me for as long as I can remember. When I was six years old, I was already figuring out a way to get a motorcycle for myself. Not long after I finally got my first bike, I discovered an aspect of motorcycling I hadn't even considered before: the motorcycling community. I started to hang out with other kids who had motorcycles, and we began riding together.

The main benefit of joining a motorcycle club is camaraderie. Motorcyclists often feel out of place around nonmotorcyclists, the odd gearhead in the crowd. Motorcycle clubs provide social outlets for motorcyclists, a place we can get together with our own kind and talk about riding and bikes without having to worry about boring each other. A club is a nexus where the motorcycling community comes together.

Steer Clear
I have personal experience with some of the clubs listed in this chapter, while others I've just heard of or read about. Not all clubs will have your best interests at heart. Some groups may be more interested in collecting dues than offering anything of value to members. I haven't run across any that fit that description (all the groups I have experience with have been worthwhile), but like anything else in motorcycling, use your head when joining a club.

Whatever your interests, you'll find a motorcycle club with members who share those interests. In this chapter, I'll discuss different types of clubs. I'll also tell you what these organizations have to offer you.

How Motorcycle Clubs Were Born

A lot of the disaffected young people returning to America from World War II—people unable or unwilling to assimilate into mainstream American society—banded together to form the infamous outlaw motorcycle clubs. One such club, the Booze Fighters, became the model for Johnny's Black Rebels Motorcycle Club in the film *The Wild One*. Another of the post-war outlaw motorcycle clubs to gain some notoriety was the Hell's Angels.

The Japanese invasion led to another development in the motorcycle club scene. With all those nice people out riding around on their Hondas, it was only natural that some would form clubs. Which they did, by the thousands. Today, you'll find clubs devoted to every make of bike ever built, from ATK to Zundap, along with hundreds of clubs for specific models.

Today, there's a motorcycle club for just about every segment of society. You'll find motorcycle clubs for members of different ethnic groups, motorcycle clubs for computer geeks, and motorcycle clubs for gay and lesbian riders. Along with the traditional outlaw motorcycle clubs, you'll find law-abiding clubs for police officers and fire fighters. There are clubs for recovering alcoholics and clubs for people who like to get falling-down drunk.

Structured clubs allow motorcyclists to pool resources and achieve things individual bikers could not. In the early years of motorcycling, clubs often centered around competition. Racing clubs were able to maintain racetracks and organize events much more efficiently than individual motorcyclists. That's still the case today, and race-promoting organizations tend to maintain club-like atmospheres.

Types of Clubs

Categorizing clubs is as difficult as categorizing human beings, always a tricky and dangerous endeavor. When you divide people into groups, you end up placing people in the wrong category as often as you place them in the correct category. At best, that's confusing; at worst, it can be hazardous to your health. Placing members of the Bandidos Motorcycle Club into the same category as the Hell's Angels Motorcycle Club might seem logical to an outsider, but certain humorless members of the two groups might not find it amusing. With that in mind, I'll attempt to describe the general categories of motorcycle clubs. (Note that you'll find contact information for many of the clubs mentioned in this chapter in Appendix C, "Resources.")

Off-Road and Trail-Riding Clubs

A major challenge faced by off-road riders is finding a place to ride. Very little land remains open to trail riders. Off-road and trail-riding clubs often maintain trail systems for members. Even those clubs that don't maintain their own trail systems will be able to help you find public or private land where you can ride. Off-road clubs usually conduct organized rides for members and often organize competitive events.

Off-road clubs exist in most areas of the country. For example, Panhandle Trail Riders Association (PANTRA) maintains a trail network that extends from Washington State to Montana, with trails across the Idaho panhandle for members to use.

Other off-road clubs focus on organizing competitive events. Without clubs like the Polka Dots Motorcycle Club, for example, which puts on three races each year near Sacramento, California, few off-road events would take place.

Off-road clubs may have higher dues than some other types of clubs, but maintaining trails is an expensive business. If you like to ride off-road, membership dues in a good club can be the least expensive way to gain access to a good trail system.

Racing and Sportbike Clubs

Sportbike clubs are similar to off-road clubs in function. They organize sport tours for members and, for some clubs, arrange access to regional racetracks. Sportbike clubs tend to be less labor-intensive than off-road clubs, because their rides usually take place on public roads, so there are no trails to maintain. The only way many riders can afford access to a closed-course racetrack where they can practice high-performance riding is through a club that arranges the rental of track time.

Motorcycology
Make certain that you have mastered your riding skills before joining a club dedicated to sport riding. Such clubs tend to place a premium on safe riding and have little tolerance for motorcyclists who ride beyond their skills. Club members are experienced riders who don't appreciate some poorly-skilled hotshot endangering their lives.

Antique-Motorcycle Clubs

If you collect and restore antique motorcycles, you'll find membership in one of the many antique-motorcycle clubs around the country essential. When restoring a bike, you can search for years for just the right carburetor you need to get your bike running or for the exact fender or tail lamp for your specific model and year. By using the extensive network of experts found in antique-bike clubs, you can make that process considerably easier. And if you can't locate a part through contacts made in an antique-bike club, club members can probably help you find someone who can make the part for you.

Many antique clubs are organized under the umbrella of the Antique Motorcycle Club of America (A.M.C.A.), a not-for-profit organization founded in 1954. Worldwide membership in the A.M.C.A. is now more than 7,500, many of whom attend A.M.C.A. national meets held around the country each year. The club also publishes its own magazine, which comes out four times annually.

Woody Carson, national director of the Antique Motorcycle Club of America, and his one-of-a-kind 1925 Indian Prince LX2. (Photo ©1998 Darwin Holstrom)

Make- or Model-Specific Clubs

Many clubs were formed by fans of a particular brand or model of motorcycle. Some of these clubs, like the Norton Owners Club, are organized around a brand or model of motorcycle no longer produced and could be classified as antique clubs as easily as make-specific clubs. Other make-specific clubs, like the Harley Owners Group (HOG), tend to have a heavy ratio of people who own new bikes in their ranks. New bikes need less technical support than older bikes, so clubs like HOG serve more as social outlets than as practical sources of parts and information.

HOG, a factory-sponsored club with 300 affiliates worldwide and nearly 1 million members, is one of the best-known motorcycle clubs in the world. HOG has helped fuel Harley's spectacular comeback as much as technological improvements to the bikes themselves. HOG helped Harley-Davidson foster a tight-knit community among its customers that in turn helped foster customer loyalty that borders on fanaticism.

Cycle Babble

Older, air-cooled BMW Boxer twins are called **Air-heads**, while newer, air-and-oil-cooled Beemers are called **Oilheads**. There are motorcycle clubs organized by and devoted to the interests of owners of Airheads and Oilheads.

BMW owners form another tightly knit community of riders. And these folks take their riding seriously. Many Beemer owners put tens of thousands of miles on their bikes every year, and often rack up over 100,000 miles on their machines. Some owners have been known to put 200,000 miles, 300,000 miles, or even more on a single motorcycle. Serious motorcyclists like this deserve a serious club, and the BMW Motorcycle Owners of America (BMWMOA) is indeed a serious organization, putting on some of the finest rallies in North America and producing a monthly magazine that rivals any motorcycle journal you'll find on the newsstands.

Often, clubs devoted to a single popular model will emerge, like the Shadow Riders Club USA, a club for fans of Honda's Shadow cruisers. Sometimes, clubs will organize around a particular type of engine used by a company, like the Airheads Beemer Club, a club for owners of BMW motorcycles powered by air-cooled Boxer motors. This group was organized in response to the increasing complexity and cost that accompanied BMW's recent technological advances.

Then there are make-specific clubs that could just as easily be categorized as sport-riding clubs, organizations like the Crazed Ducati Riders of Massachusetts. Some might argue that there is no difference between a Ducati rider and a sport rider. (Some might also argue that Crazed Ducati Riders is redundant, but that's another story.)

The most useful make- or model-specific clubs are clubs devoted to *orphan bikes*—rare bikes that are no longer in production. Such clubs can be invaluable sources of parts and technical information.

A group that fits this category is the Turbo Motorcycle International Owners Association (TMIOA). The TMIOA was originally started in 1987 for owners of Honda's CX Turbo motorcycles, but in December 1988, it broadened its focus to include coverage of all the factory turbo-charged motorcycles. Turbo bikes were built by all the Japanese manufacturers in the early 1980s, but to some degree, they all suffered from mechanical problems and never became popular. Now these bikes are sought after by collectors, but parts availability is a serious problem, especially given the history of mechanical troubles in such bikes. Clubs devoted to turbo bikes can save a turbo owner a lot of time and money when it comes to keeping his or her bike on the road.

Cycle Babble
Orphan bikes are rare bikes that are no longer in production. Finding parts and accessories for such bikes can prove difficult.

Touring Clubs

Joining a touring club is a great way to get travel tips and advice from motorcyclists who have actually been there (regardless of where "there" is). You'll learn things from members of touring clubs you won't learn anywhere else, like where to find good restaurants and hotels, how to find the best roads, the locations of speed traps, and roads to avoid.

Sometimes, touring-oriented clubs will center around a particular model of touring bike, like Honda's Gold Wing or Yamaha's Venture. One such group, the Gold Wing Road Riders Association (GWRRA), is the world's largest club devoted to a single model of motorcycle. GWRRA members organize some of the most extravagant club gatherings in the United States.

Motorcycology

When getting traveling advice from another rider who belongs to a touring-oriented club, take that rider's riding habits and personality into account when deciding whether or not to act on that advice. Some touring riders might consider a ride down the Alaska Highway a nice weekend jaunt.

Locale-Specific Clubs

Often, clubs will form with no common denominator other than location. Motorcyclists just want to get together with other people from their area who ride, regardless of what they ride or how they ride. Such clubs can provide you with information on riding in an area you won't find anywhere else, an especially valuable service for new riders. The WetLeather motorcycle club, for example, exists so members can get together and discuss the challenges faced by motorcyclists in the Pacific Northwest.

Female Motorcyclist Clubs

Women have been riding motorcycles as long as men, although never in as great numbers. And women have had their own motorcycle clubs almost as long as men. Organizations like the Motor Maids have long been a part of the motorcycling scene.

But in recent years, the number of women who ride has grown, and now more women ride their own motorcycles than ever before. As more women enter the sport, the number of women's motorcycle clubs has grown, as have the variety of women's clubs.

Motorcycology

Many of the clubs for riders of a certain age won't exclude you if you are too young to join. They may accept you into the group, although not as a full member. It may be worth the effort for you to find such a group, since older riders generally have more experience and can teach newer riders a great deal.

One of the largest women's groups is Women On Wheels (WOW). When WOW was founded in 1982, women who rode their own bikes were still exceptions, oddities in the motorcycling community. WOW provided an outlet for these women, a place where they could get together with other female riders. Today, there are WOW chapters all across the United States.

In the past few years, more specialized women's motorcycling clubs have emerged, too, like the Ebony Queens Motorcycle Club, a club for black women.

Age-Specific Clubs

A trend that has gained momentum as the baby boomers age is the rise of age-specific clubs, organizations composed of motorcyclists who have reached a certain age. For example, the Retreads Motorcycle Club consists of riders who are at least 40 years old.

A group of Retreads kicking back at a local watering hole after a long ride. (Photo ©1998 Darwin Holstrom)

Lately, a few clubs composed of riders under a certain age have sprouted. In Oregon, for example, there's an organization called the Mudrats, a club for people 15 years old and younger who like to ride dirtbikes and all-terrain vehicles.

Spiritually Oriented Clubs

During the past 20 years, Christian motorcycling clubs have multiplied prolifically. The Christian Motorcyclists Association (CMA), one of the largest of these organizations, can be found at rallies and events around the United States.

Christian motorcyclist groups do a great deal to promote a positive image of motorcycling to the general public. If you are so inclined, joining such a club would be an ideal way to combine your spirituality and passion for motorcycling.

Christians aren't the only group to combine their spiritual beliefs with motorcycling. There are Taoist and Buddhist motorcycle clubs, and there are pagan motorcycle clubs. There is even one group, the Bavarian Illuminati Motorcycle Club, that quotes the western mystic Aleister Crowley in its club bylaws. The club has very little of what could be called structure, but members do receive a suggested reading list that includes *The Illuminatus! Trilogy*, by Robert Anton Wilson, and *Heart of Darkness*, by Joseph Conrad, as well as an eclectic collection of books on motorcycling and mysticism.

Activity-Oriented Clubs

A variety of clubs combine other interests with motorcycling. Sometimes, these clubs combine motorcycle-related interests. If you're interested in motorcycling and camping, for example, you can join the International Brotherhood of Motorcycle Campers, a group dedicated to riders who camp out rather than stay in motels when they tour on their motorcycles.

Other clubs combine motorcycling with unrelated interests, like the Motorcycling Amateur Radio Club (MARC), composed of motorcyclists who are also Ham-radio operators.

Motorcycle Moments

A man who lived in the town where I attended college once mounted a small refrigerator on the back of his motorcycle and rode the bike like that for an entire summer. Years later, I met the guy and asked him about the fridge. It turned out he was a member of the Motorcycling Amateur Radio Club, and he mounted his Ham radio in the fridge to protect it from the elements. He gave up that system because the weight disrupted his motorcycle's handling, and now he tows his radio in a special trailer.

Motorcyclists who are unable to ride because of the weather and who have access to a computer can even join virtual motorcycle clubs, organizations like Cyber-Bikers On The Web. These are clubs for people who love to ride but also like to surf the Internet.

Socially Active Clubs

Many motorcycle groups form to support certain causes and hold poker runs and other events to raise funds for charity. One such group, Friends of Children with Cerebral Palsy, located in Regina, Saskatchewan (Canada), organizes an annual Ride for Dreams to raise money to help children with Cerebral Palsy.

Another club that raises a lot of money for a specific charity is the Women's Motorcyclist Foundation (WMF). In 1996, WMF organized the National Pony Express Tour, a 14,537-mile motorcycle relay around the perimeter of the United States, to raise awareness of breast cancer and to raise research funds for the Susan G. Koman Foundation in Dallas, Texas. Female motorcyclists who participated in the ride (and their supporters) raised $317,000. The WMF has organized another National Pony Express Tour for 1998, and there are plans to hold similar, smaller events around the country.

Profession-Related Clubs

Often, motorcyclists in certain professions form motorcycle clubs with other members of their profession. One of the most famous clubs of this type is the Blue Knights, a club composed of law-enforcement officials. Chapters of the Blue Knights are located in all 50 states, as well as 12 other countries.

Creative Clubs

People are getting more creative when forming motorcycle clubs. Often, these are just groups dedicated to having fun, like the Good Vibrations Cycle Riders, located in Florida. Good Vibrations holds no meetings, collects no dues, and has just one bylaw in its charter: Have fun.

Other groups solely devoted to having fun have also appeared around the country. The Hells Rice Burners Motorcycle Club from the Delaware area was formed for people who ride ratty old Japanese bikes. Ideally, members should pay no more than $25 when they buy their bikes. Little is known of the ominous Death's Head Motorcycle Club, located deep in Appalachia, except that members have a proclivity for body modification, such as piercing, tattooing, scarification (making shallow cuts in the skin), and branding.

There are clubs for curmudgeon motorcyclists, and there are clubs for vampires who ride, like the Santa Cruz Vampires Motorcycle and Scooter Club. There is even a club for riders who don't like to bathe. Biker Scum is an organization dedicated to the pursuit of happiness through riding and the neglect of personal hygiene. Believe it or not, this club is quite popular. Originally formed in central Texas, the club now has chapters in Pennsylvania; Virginia; California; Indiana; Ontario, Canada; and Okinawa, Japan, with chapters planned for Estonia and England.

One club that might be of interest to readers in the Costa Mesa, California area is EasyRiders, a club for new riders. EasyRiders pairs up new riders with more experienced riders for relaxed rides that are instructional as well as fun.

The American Motorcyclist Association

No single group plays a more influential role in motorcycling in the United States than the American Motorcyclist Association (AMA), a 220,000-member organization founded in 1924.

The world's largest motorsports sanctioning body, the AMA oversees more than 80 national-level racing events all over the United States. These events encompass the entire motorcycle-racing spectrum and include events as diverse as the Superbike races at Daytona, Supercross and Arenacross racing, dirt-track racing, and hill climbing. The

Motorcycology

There is no more effective way to protect your rights as a motorcyclist than to join the AMA. Write to

American Motorcyclists Association
33 Collegeview Road
Westerville, Ohio 43081-1484

You can call the AMA at 800/ AMA-JOIN (800/262-5646)

or e-mail it at

ama@ama-cycle.org

AMA's Member Activities Department coordinates thousands of amateur races across the country, with dozens of competition classes for everyone from grade-school kids to senior riders. Through its 1,200 chartered clubs, the AMA oversees more than 3,700 road-riding and competition events each year. If there's motorcycle racing taking place in the United States, the AMA is probably involved.

Perhaps even more important than its promotion of racing is the work of the AMA Government Relations Department, which works harder than any single organization to make riders aware of bad laws and antimotorcycling discrimination at the local, state, federal, and corporate level. You'll be amazed at some of the antimotorcycle legislation proposed at all levels of government, as well as the discrimination to be found in the workplace. Fortunately for all of us, during its 75 years of existence, the AMA has developed successful methods for dealing with discrimination against motorcyclists. Even if you join no other motorcycle organization, I highly recommend joining the AMA.

Finding a Club

One of the best ways to locate a club in your area is to contact the AMA and get a list of AMA-chartered clubs in your area.

If you know of a local place (such as a bar, cafe, or motorcycle shop) where motorcyclists hang out, you can ask the motorcyclists there if they know of any local clubs. The Internet is also a terrific resource for finding motorcycle clubs, especially some of the more off-the-wall organizations.

You can also check Appendix C for contact information for some of the national motorcycle groups that may be able to put you in touch with local groups in your area.

After you've found a club, look into it before joining. Attend a couple of meetings and visit with members. Perhaps you might even go for a ride with them. If you enjoy the time you spend with members, chances are you'll enjoy being a member.

Joining a club may not be a necessity for enjoying the sport of motorcycling (motorcycling is, in the end, a solitary activity), but it can greatly enhance the experience. The enthusiasm club members have for riding is infectious and can motivate you to explore new areas of the sport. And if you live in a climate where you can't ride for long periods of time each year, meeting with your motorcycle club can help you make it through the long winter months.

The Least You Need to Know

➤ Club memberships can be practical as well as fun.

➤ Clubs can be great sources of hard-to-locate parts and information.

➤ Many clubs do a great deal of work supporting nonmotorcycle-related causes, like breast-cancer research.

➤ Joining the AMA is the best way you can ensure the future of motorcycling.

Chapter 20

The Open Road: Touring and Rallies

In This Chapter

➤ Preparing your bike for a trip

➤ Planning your trip

➤ Packing gear on your bike safely

➤ Learning about motorcycle rallies around the country

Ever since I started riding motorcycles, I've felt a powerful desire to explore new places on a bike. As soon as I was old enough to get my motorcycle endorsement, I began taking serious motorcycle tours.

I enjoy all aspects of riding, from commuting to work to trail riding, but I enjoy touring on a bike most of all. I find nothing more thrilling than cresting a hill and seeing a new expanse of world open up before me. Whether I'm exploring the Sand Hill region of Nebraska, the High Desert in Southern California, the lush Ozark Mountains of Arkansas, or the wheat fields of Minnesota, I never get bored when I'm traveling on a bike.

In this chapter, I'm going to share some of the tips I've learned over the course of my trips with you.

I'm also going to talk a bit about where to go on your motorcycle (as well as where not to go). And, I'll discuss different motorcycle-related events you can attend, such as rallies.

Any Bike Is a Touring Bike

If you have a dependable motorcycle, you can travel on it. Ed Otto, a competitive long-distance rider, rode 11,000 miles on a Honda Helix scooter during the 1995 Iron Butt Rally, the most grueling long-distance motorcycle rally in the world.

Honda's Helix scooter might not be the ideal mount for 1,000-mile-a-day rides, but at a more relaxed pace, it can make a fine traveling companion. (Photo courtesy Vreeke and Associates)

Of course, some motorcycles make better tourers than others. Selecting a bike to tour on is an individual choice. It doesn't matter how well a motorcycle works for other riders—what matters is how well it works for you. How well does your motorcycle fit you physically? Is it comfortable on day-long rides? How well do its power-delivery characteristics suit your riding style?

You also need to feel comfortable with the reliability of your bike. You don't want to get stranded in the middle of some unfamiliar urban area or isolated mountain road on a bike. Before you decide to take a bike on an extended trip, you should know its mechanical condition. If you do travel on a bike that has a tendency to break down, you should be familiar enough with the bike's mechanics to perform some basic repair work on the side of the road.

> **Cycle Babble**
> The **Iron Butt Rally** is the most grueling long-distance motorcycle rally in the world. Participants ride around the perimeter of the United States, often including side trips that take them hundreds, even thousands, of miles out of their way. To finish the rally requires that you ride at least 10,000 miles in 11 days. Top-10 finishers often ride 12,000 to 13,000 miles in that time.

Planning a Trip

I have a tendency to overplan trips, marking out each gas stop on my map, along with my estimated time of arrival. But some of my best motorcycle tours have been the least planned. I once went on a meandering two-week trip through Wyoming and Colorado with a friend who is perhaps the least-organized human being I've ever met.

Once I let go and gave control to a higher power (in this case, my buddy's disorganized ways), I had the most relaxing trip of my life. And I saw more of the country I rode through than I ever had before. I discovered that the most entertaining road is the road to nowhere.

Touring Range and Fuel Stops

But even on the road to nowhere, you have to prepare at least a minimum amount. Motorcycles have small gas tanks and can only travel a short distance between fuel stops, at least when compared to cars. You need to plan your trip so that you know you'll be able to find fuel when you need it.

Some bikes have more touring range than others, depending on the size of their fuel tanks and what kind of gas mileage they get. For example, a bike with a 4.7-gallon tank that gets 36 miles per gallon on average can travel 169.2 miles before you have to start walking, while a bike with a 3.7-gallon tank that gets 54 miles per gallon on average can go almost 200 miles before refueling.

Touring and sport-touring motorcycles generally have big fuel tanks, but sometimes they burn so much gas, you really don't have that great a range. Cruisers tend to have smaller tanks, but some cruisers, especially the V-twins, use less fuel, so they can travel nearly as far. Some bikes with exceptionally small tanks, like older Harley-Davidson Sportsters, can barely travel 100 miles before they start sucking air out of their tanks.

Not only is having to constantly refuel your bike time-consuming and annoying, it can be dangerous. There are many areas in the United States, especially in the West and Southwest, where you can easily ride 150 miles between gas stations. These are isolated areas, and if you were to run out of fuel in such a place, you would probably be eaten by buzzards before someone found you.

Motorcycology

If it's at all possible, don't overplan your trips. The best motorcycle tours are the kind where you don't have to be anywhere at any given time. This gives you time to stop and really experience the unusual things you encounter along the way.

Motorcycology

Learn to predict whether or not a town will have an open gas station by checking its population. State road maps always list the names of all the towns in the state, along with their populations. A town with a population of 500 or more should have a gas station, but the station may be closed in the evenings and on Sundays. To find an open gas station after hours or on a Sunday, you'll need to find a town with a population of 1,000 or higher. Make sure you plan your course accordingly.

Motorcycology
When traveling through isolated areas like the American West, it's better to err on the side of caution when planning your fuel stops. It's better to refuel too often than to not refuel often enough.

Even if you aren't going any place in particular, keep your bike's range in mind when deciding which roads to take.

Don't push your luck when it comes to refueling. If you are getting low on fuel and pass a gas station, refill your tank. If you decide to wait until the next town, you could find that town has no gas station.

Keep in mind that your fuel mileage can vary, depending on conditions. If you are riding fast or have a heavy load, you can count on running out of fuel sooner than if you are traveling more slowly or carrying a lighter load.

Preparing Your Bike

Throughout this book, I've tried to stress the importance of properly maintaining your motorcycle. When traveling long distances on a bike, this is especially important. If your bike were to break down in an isolated mountain pass, you could freeze to death before someone found you. Making certain your bike is in good shape prior to taking a trip serves an economic purpose as well. Having a breakdown far from home can be much more expensive than having your bike fall apart while commuting to work. When you break down in an isolated area, you don't have the luxury of shopping around for the best prices. You also don't have the luxury of finding a mechanic you trust.

Your best bet is to get your bike in as good shape as possible before taking a trip. Study the procedures in Chapters 16, "Zen and the Art of Motorcycle Maintenance," and 17, "Rx: Repair." Make certain that you perform all routine maintenance. Here's a checklist of procedures you should always perform before an extended trip:

➤ Change the oil.

➤ Top off the electrolyte in the battery.

➤ Check your coolant.

➤ Tighten every bolt on your bike.

➤ Replace leaky fork seals, as well as worn bearings and bushings in the frame.

➤ Replace worn shocks and fork springs.

➤ Pay close attention to your tires. If there is the slightest possibility that your tires will wear out on your trip, replace them before you go.

What to Bring?

No matter what I tell you, you will probably overestimate the amount of clothing and gear you'll need when you take your first motorcycle trip. But here are my suggestions for all you need for a safe, comfortable ride.

The Clothes Make the Motorcyclist

On my first extended trip, which I took about 15 years ago, I brought a couple of different jackets (for riding in a variety of weather conditions), along with five or six complete changes of clothing, including some dressy clothes in case I wanted to go out to eat or on a date.

Now I bring a couple of pairs of jeans, a couple of turtlenecks, a couple of sweat shirts, and a couple of T-shirts. I may bring three T-shirts if the weather is hot, or if I plan to be gone a week or more. And I bring pretty much every pair of underwear and socks I own. If I go out for a nice dinner, I wear my cleanest pair of jeans and the turtleneck with the fewest holes in it.

Your best bet is to travel light on a bike. Only bring clothing you'll wear. And you'll always seem to wear less than you bring. As you become a more experienced motorcycle traveler, you'll find that you bring less clothing on each successive trip.

Motorcycology
When packing for a motorcycle trip, pack light. A lighter load will tax your motorcycle less and not have such a pronounced effect on your bike's handling. Leave a little extra space for any souvenirs you might pick up.

Tools You'll Use

Although I pack less clothes for each successive trip, I find that my list of must-bring gear grows each year. Every time I've needed an item I didn't have, I've included that item on following trips.

I always bring a small selection of extra tools, even when I'm on a new bike. The toolkits that come with most bikes will do in a pinch, but I always like to have an extra set of combination spanner wrenches, a couple of pliers (needle-nose pliers and channel-lock pliers), a ratchet, and a small selection of sockets. I also include a cigarette lighter, a small selection of nuts and bolts (including some for connecting my battery cables to my battery), some electrical connectors, a roll of wire, and a couple of rolls of tape (friction and duct tape).

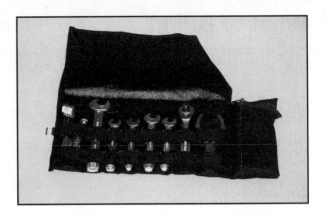

This tool pouch from Chase Harper provides an ideal way to pack your tools for a long motorcycle trip. (Photo ©1998 Darwin Holmstrom)

Safety First: First Aid

I also carry a first-aid kit with me. I make certain that kit includes:

➤ A selection of bandages, including gauze bandages

➤ Adhesive tape

➤ An antibiotic of some sort

➤ Something for bee stings

This is a list of the absolute minimum amount of items a first-aid kit should include. If you can pack a more complete kit, you should do so, even if you need to leave something else behind to make room for it.

For the Scenic Routes: Photographic Equipment

I'm a photographer and always bring my camera equipment when I travel, which presents some challenges on a bike. The greatest of these challenges is weather protection. If you have watertight hard luggage, this is not as much of an issue, but riders with soft luggage will have to come up with a way to keep the rain off their camera equipment. Before a trip on which I'll be using soft luggage, I buy a box of the most durable garbage bags I can get (the kind for bagging leaves seems to be the toughest), then double wrap my cameras in these bags.

When your camera is packed away in your luggage, it can take too long to reach it, so I have a fanny-pack–type camera bag. If you want to keep your camera ready to use when you ride, I highly recommend this type of bag.

Another option is to use small point-and-shoot cameras when you travel. You can keep these in your vest pockets or fairing pockets, where they'll stay dry and be ready when you need them.

If you pack your camera in your luggage, whether you have soft or hard luggage, be careful not to place it in a location where it will bounce around. Just the vibration from your bike can pound expensive cameras to pieces; if they bounce around in your trunk or against your shock absorbers while in your saddlebags, you could end up with very expensive paperweights instead of cameras.

Carrying your camera in a fanny pack, or carrying a point-and-shoot camera in your vest pocket, can eliminate much of this problem. If you transport your camera in your luggage, pack soft items, such as towels, clothing, or pillows, around it to absorb shocks and vibrations.

Motorcycology
Always buy a large box of heavy-duty garbage bags before going on a motorcycle trip. You'll be amazed at the uses you'll find for them. I place my clothes in them, then put the garbage bag in my saddlebags. Not only does this protect my clothes from getting wet, but it makes it easier to pack and unpack my saddlebags. I also wrap my sleeping bag in garbage bags. If you've ever had to spend a night in a wet sleeping bag, you'll see the value of this practice.

Protective Gear

I always wear a full-face helmet with a visor when traveling. Not only does a full-face helmet provide superior protection in an accident, it provides superior protection from the elements and superior comfort.

The most versatile piece of protective gear you can own is a waterproof riding suit like Aerostich's Darien jacket and pants (mentioned in Chapter 9, "Getting the Gear"). These suits eliminate the need for rain gear, freeing up a lot of luggage space, and they provide unmatched versatility. With all liners in place, such suits provide excellent cold-weather protection, yet with the liners removed and with all vents opened, they are the best hot-weather gear you can buy. This is especially important when traveling in high mountains, where temperatures can vary by 60 or 70 degrees in just a few miles.

Steer Clear
Make certain that your load is secure when packing a bike for a trip. If something falls off, it could get caught in your wheel or chain, causing you to lose traction and crash.

You Can Take It with You: Packing Your Bike

Once you've decided what to bring, you'll need to figure out how to bring it with you. Packing techniques are more important than you might think. If your gear falls off your bike, the best you can hope for is that you'll just lose a few items. A more likely outcome is that your gear will get caught in your wheels or chain, causing you to crash.

Luggage

To provide enough carrying capacity for touring, you'll need to have some sort of luggage. Most bikes will accept soft saddlebags and a tankbag; these items are the easiest and most economical way to provide extra carrying capacity on your bike.

Soft luggage, like this tankbag, tailpack, and saddlebags, all from Chase Harper, can convert just about any motorcycle into a tourer. (Photo ©1998 Darwin Holmstrom)

Steer Clear
When mounting soft luggage on your motorcycle, make certain that your luggage doesn't come into contact with your exhaust pipes, or you could lose your belongings in a fire.

Some bikes won't accept soft luggage because of the shape of their tail pieces or because their exhaust pipes ride too high. This is especially problematic on sportbikes. Some bikes won't accept tankbags, either, because of the shape of their gas tanks. If this is a problem on your bike, there are tailpacks that strap onto the rider's portion of your seat. If you can't mount soft luggage and you don't have a passenger seat on your bike, you'll need to carry all your belongings in a backpack or choose a different bike for traveling.

A few companies, like Givi, make hard luggage for many motorcycles. This luggage is expensive, and mounting it can prove quite a challenge, but the convenience of hard luggage makes it a worthwhile investment.

If soft luggage won't fit on your motorcycle, you can carry your gear in a tailpack, like this Supersport from Chase Harper. (Photo courtesy the manufacturer)

Hard luggage, like this Givi Wingrack system, can make a motorcycle significantly more useful. (Photo courtesy the manufacturer)

In addition to soft luggage and a tankbag, I strap a duffelbag to the passenger seat of my bike. This provides all the carrying capacity I've ever needed.

Camping

If you choose to camp rather than stay in motels when you travel, you can save a lot of money, but you also need to bring a lot of extra gear. The bulkiest items you'll need to pack are your tent and sleeping bag. But if you use your head when packing, you can use these items to help make your load more secure. I'll tell you how to pack your camping gear in the next section.

Loading Up

Before attempting to pack your bike, go to your nearest bike shop and buy at least four bungee nets. *Bungee nets* are stretchy webs made of nylon ropes with metal hooks that attach to your bike. They are the most wonderful devices ever invented for motorcycle touring, especially if you camp out.

Motorcycology

You should make certain that you have at least four *bungee nets* (stretchy webs made of nylon ropes) before packing your gear on your bike. These remarkable little devices are the most versatile means of securing a load on a motorcycle that I have ever found.

Use a pyramid design when packing a load on a bike—put the widest, stiffest pieces on the bottom, and put the narrower, spongier items toward the top. My own method is to lay my duffelbag crosswise on the passenger seat, so that the ends of the bag are resting on my saddlebags. Behind that, I lay my tent, also crosswise. I then place a bungee net over the two items, tightly securing it in the front and in the rear.

Then I lay my sleeping bag in the crotch created between the tent and the duffelbag. Often, a single bungee net won't go all the way around my sleeping bag and still solidly attach to the bike, so I'll secure the bungee net in the front of the load and stretch it as far over the sleeping bag as it will go. Then I'll hook the rear of the bungee net to the hooks of the bungee net holding the tent and duffelbag in place. If the top net won't reach the hooks of the bottom net, I'll hook it to a place on the bottom net where the nylon cord is doubled up. Next, I firmly attach another bungee net to a secure point behind the load and hook it to the front of the bungee net covering the sleeping bag, again trying to attach it to the hooks on the other net. The fourth bungee net is a spare, since they sometimes stretch or break.

Steer Clear

Check your loads frequently when traveling on a bike, including your soft luggage. The vibration from your bike can loosen hooks and straps. If you find a strap or a bungee hook that has worked its way loose, take the time to adjust it. The consequences of luggage flying loose can be deadly.

Different-size loads require variations on this theme. If you're traveling two up, you'll need more carrying capacity. Unless you are riding an ultimate-behemoth touring bike or you're pulling a trailer (neither of which I recommend until you're an experienced rider), you should probably consider not camping when traveling two up.

Using a luggage rack also requires you to alter your methods of packing. A luggage rack can increase your carrying capacity and provide you with more secure points to attach bungee nets, but make certain the rack is mounted securely, and make certain you don't overload the rack.

You may have to make adjustments to the method described here, but if you structure the load so that it is solid and securely attached to the bike, using a pyramid method to keep your center of gravity as low as possible, you should be fine. Check your load frequently (including the straps attaching your soft luggage to your bike), and if anything starts to loosen up, take the time to adjust and tighten it.

First, attach the widest and stiffest items at the base of your load. (Photo ©1998 Darwin Holmstrom)

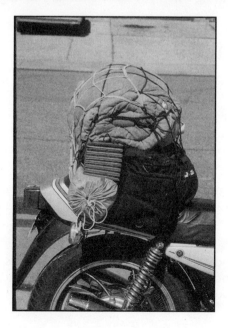

Next, attach narrower, softer items. (Photo ©1998 Darwin Holmstrom)

Pacing Yourself

Traveling on a motorcycle drains you physically much more than traveling in a car. It's important that you receive proper nutrition and rest when riding.

Unfortunately, fine dining isn't easy on the road. Road food is notoriously unhealthy and doesn't provide the kind of energy you need for touring. Try to eat as many carbohydrates as you can. Have pancakes for breakfast instead of an omelet. (And eat all your toast.) Have salads for dinner instead of steaks.

Most important, make certain that you drink enough water. If you just drink soda or coffee, the caffeine in those drinks actually depletes your body's supply of water. Get in the habit of buying a bottle of water each time you stop for gas instead of buying a can of soda. On-board water sytems are increasing in popularity. Aerostich Darien jackets even have a special pocket to hold Camelback water systems.

When riding long distances, exhaustion can creep up on you, diminishing your riding skills. You may not even be aware it is happening. This is especially problematic on hot days and can cause otherwise safe riders to make mistakes. As I've said repeatedly, you can't afford to make mistakes on a bike.

You need to be aware of your mental and physical condition. When you feel yourself getting tired, stop. Find a rest area and stretch your legs. Pull into a convenience store or gas station, buy some juice and a bag of peanuts, find a shady spot in the parking lot, and sit down for a bit. If you are out in the middle of nowhere, find a crossing or turnout where you can park your bike, then find a shady spot to lean against a tree, or lie down in the grass and watch some clouds go by. Take a nap if you feel like it. It may slow down your schedule, but if you continue riding when you're exhausted, you might never get where you're going at all.

Motorcycle Madness: Rallies

So now that your bike's all dressed up, you probably want some place to go. Just about any place makes a good destination for a motorcycle tour—a visit to friends, relatives, or just to nowhere in particular.

If you have no particular destination in mind, you might want to attend a motorcycle rally. Rallies make a logical destination for a bike trip. While the trip is its own reward on a bike tour, rallies are hard to beat as far as destinations go.

The types of rallies you'll find are almost as varied as the types of clubs I discussed in Chapter 19. There are rallies for cruiser fans, rallies for tourers, rallies for sportbike riders, and rallies for antique bikes. There are Norton rallies, Moto Guzzi rallies, Ducati rallies, and BMW rallies.

Whatever your interests, you can find a rally where you'll meet hundreds, or even thousands (in some cases, hundreds of thousands) of like-minded riders. Rallies are places you can go and revel in all aspects of motorcycle culture.

Major Rallies

Motorcycle rallies have distinct personalities. Some are mild-mannered and relaxed, while others are obnoxious and just plain rude. Most fall somewhere in between. The biggest, loudest, rudest rally of all is Bike Week at Daytona.

Bike Week: Daytona

Held during the first week of March each year in Daytona, Florida, Daytona Bike Week, which celebrated its 57th anniversary in 1998, is the wildest party in the United States.

Daytona began as a racing-oriented event, and racing still plays an important role in the rally. The American Historic Racing Motorcycle Association (AHRMA) helps sponsor and organize some of the best historic racing in the country at Daytona, along with a variety of antique-bike shows and contests.

Steer Clear
If you find events like a bikini pull offensive, you'll probably want to avoid Daytona Bike Week.

Antiques and classics aren't the only motorcycles raced at Daytona. You can catch dirt-track racing, Motocross racing, and drag racing, along with the Daytona 200 Superbike race, the rally's main event.

But it's the variety of other activities taking place that gives Daytona its unique character. All kinds of motorcycle-related events take place during Bike Week, like the American Motorcycle Institute's Brute Horsepower Shoot-Out Dyno contest, Spider's Show of World's Most Unusual Motorcycles, the Annual Alligator Road Tour, Side Car & Trike Day, the Classic & Modern Japanese Bike Rally, the European Bike Day & Show, flea markets, swap meets, and the Rat's Hole Custom Chopper Show.

The nonmotorcycling activities are what really make Daytona infamous. Many of these are not family-oriented activities. In addition to the ever-present live bands, free beer, and wet T-shirt contests, you'll be able to take in the Ugliest Old Lady contest, the Biggest Beer Belly contest, egg wrestling, the Slippery When Wet Oil Wrestling contest, his and hers tattoo contests, a celebrity bra auction, and Jesse the World Famous Human Bomb, who can blow himself up at least three times during the rally.

But Daytona is not all racing and debauchery. The American Diabetes Association sponsors a charity ride, the Real Ride For The Cure, and the American Red Cross holds a blood drive each year.

Daytona is not a destination for the easily offended, nor is it a place for anyone with a low tolerance for loud Harley-Davidsons. But if you're looking for an adventure on the wild side, you might want to check out Bike Week.

Sturgis Rally & Races

Sturgis is somewhat tamer than Daytona, generally attracting an older crowd, but calling it a family event is a bit of a stretch. Held the first full week of August each year in Sturgis, South Dakota, the Sturgis Rally & Races is a Midwestern version of Daytona Bike Week.

Like Daytona, racing was the original purpose for the gathering at Sturgis, but over the years, the spectacle of the rally began to eclipse the racing. There is still a lot of racing at Sturgis, sponsored by the AMA and the Jackpine Gypsies Motorcycle Club—everything from hill climbing to vintage racing to Grand National Dirt Track racing. That alone is worth attending the rally.

But also like Daytona, it's all the other events taking place that give Sturgis its character. Main Street during the rally becomes a sea of black leather and denim, swirling around the vendor booths lining the sidewalk.

Main Street in Sturgis, South Dakota becomes a sea of chrome, leather, and denim during the annual Rally & Races, held each August. (Photo ©1998 Darwin Holmstrom)

One of the best things about the rally at Sturgis is riding in the Black Hills of South Dakota. The roads in the Black Hills offer terrific riding any time of the year, but during Bike Week, you'll be sharing those roads almost exclusively with other motorcyclists.

Sturgis gained a reputation in the 1970s as a wild party spot for outlaw bikers, but the wild days are history. Like the motorcycling public in general, Sturgis is becoming more mature.

Americade

For people who prefer not to spend their vacations being part of the world's biggest freak shows, there are other, more mature rallies that dispense with the tattoo contests and bikini pulls. The largest of these is the Americade Motorcycle Rally.

Americade was first held in May 1983 and takes place the first week of June each year at Lake George, a resort community in upstate New York. By 1986, total attendance reached nearly 10,000 riders, making Americade the largest touring rally in the world. Approximately 40,000 riders attended the rally in 1997. Statistics collected by the folks running the rally show that the average attendees are likely to be married, 40 to 60 years old, and riding a touring motorcycle, although the rally attracts riders of all stripes, persuasions, and ages.

Other Rallies

As motorcycles become more popular, appealing to more diverse and ever larger numbers of riders, motorcycle rallies multiply and become more diverse.

Most motorcycle clubs (like those mentioned in Chapter 19) hold national rallies. Women on Wheels holds its International Ride-In each summer at various locations around the country. The Christian Motorcyclists Association holds several rallies each year. The International Retreads has a big get-together each summer, as do the Harley Owners Group, the BMW Motorcycle Owners Association of America, the Moto Guzzi National Owners Club, and just about every other group you can imagine.

The American Motorcyclist Association holds its Vintage Motorcycle Days (VMD) at the Mid-Ohio Sports Car Course in Lexington, Ohio each July, and this event provides some of the most spectacular vintage racing in the country.

One of the more entertaining events held each year is the Davis Rally, held in New Hampton, Iowa every September. This rally offers much the same experience as Americade, with a bit more elbow room: Only about 4,000 motorcyclists attend each year, rather than 40,000. Another small rally that provides big entertainment is the Sportbike Rally in Parry Sound, Ontario. This is a great place for Yanks to go and see Canadians' take on the sport.

One of the great things about all rallies is that you get to meet interesting people, many of whom you encounter again and again over the years. While the motorcycle community is growing, it's still a relatively small group, and sooner or later, you'll meet just about everybody, from Willie G. Davidson to Dennis Rodman. If you attend some rallies, you might even bump into me—I'll be the bald guy talking about motorcycles.

The Least You Need to Know

> ➤ Any dependable bike that you are comfortable riding can be a touring bike.

> ➤ While it's fun to be spontaneous when traveling on a bike, you should at least plan where you'll make your next fuel stop.

> ➤ Make certain that your bike is in top running condition before taking a trip, and don't take off on questionable tires.

> ➤ Sloppy packing on a motorcycle can lead to your gear falling off and getting caught in your wheels, causing you to crash.

> ➤ Attending rallies is a great way to meet other members of the motorcycling community.

Chapter 21

Speed Racer: Motorcycle Road Racing

In This Chapter

➤ The influence of racing on the sport of motorcycling

➤ The different types and classes of racing

➤ International Grand Prix racing and other racing events

➤ Why Grand National Dirt Track racing is considered the American form of racing

Motorcycle road racing is as old and varied as motorcycling itself. Given the historical importance of racing and the impact it has had on street riders, a surprising number of motorcyclists have not discovered how exciting racing can be for spectators and competitors alike.

Racing provides drama as intense as any work of fiction. Take the great American racer Kenny Roberts' first two International Championship Grand Prix seasons, for example. After defying all odds and becoming the first American to win a Grand Prix World Championship in his rookie season on the International Grand Prix circuit, Roberts broke his back during practice six weeks before the start of his second season.

It looked like the end of the line for the young racer, but fans were amazed to see Roberts back on the track by the second race of the year. The season that followed provided a tale as suspenseful as anything Hitchcock could have whipped up. The championship was not decided until the final race. Roberts' ultimate win after such a devastating accident has to rank as one of the all-time great triumphs in motorsports history.

That's an extreme example, but incredible displays of human spirit are everyday occurrences on the race track.

In this chapter, I'm going to give you an overview of some of the more popular forms of road racing. I'll tell you a bit of history about the sport and about the people and organizations that make racing possible.

A Brief History of Motorcycle Road Racing

Motorcycle competition has been around as long as motorcycles themselves. Whether that takes the form of two sportbike riders trying to see who's faster on a twisty road, or two Harley owners trying to see who can glue more chrome "Live to Ride, Ride to Live" badges to their machines, competition always has been and always will be a part of motorcycling.

While cosmetic competitions pose nothing more than aesthetic threats, it soon became apparent that racing motorcycles on public roads posed a hazard to both riders and nonriders alike. By the turn of the century, promoters and racers were already working to organize racing, whether that racing took place on racetracks (as it tended to do in the United States) or on closed sections of public roads (as it often did in Europe).

Fédération Internationale Motocycliste (FIM)

As motorcycle racing grew in popularity, the need for organization grew. This was especially true in Europe, where motorcycle racing became a matter of national pride among fans from competing countries. In 1904, the Fédération Internationale des Clubs Motocyclistes (FICM) was created to develop and oversee international motorcycle racing, as well as to promote motorcycling in general.

In 1949, the FICM became the Federation Internationale Motocycliste (FIM). Originally headquartered in England, FIM transferred to Switzerland in 1959.

The FIM is now the primary sanctioning body for world-championship motorcycle racing events, and it oversees both the International Grand Prix Championship series and the World Superbike series. The FIM also grants authorization for a variety of other types of motorcycle racing, including everything from Motocross to sidecar racing.

The American Motorcycle Association and Racing

Since its formation in 1924, the American Motorcyclist Association (AMA) has maintained a presence in almost all aspects of professional motorcycle racing in the United States, including road racing, Motocross, speedway, Enduro, and observed trials.

Since the early 1970s, the AMA has been the American affiliate of the FIM. The AMA participates in the FIM's management and rules-making processes, and has hosted many world championship motorcycle racing events. The AMA has also been heavily involved in amateur motorcycle racing. It runs the world's largest amateur motorcycle racing program.

Types of Racing

As I said in Chapter 3, "Street Squid or Dirt Donk? Types of Motorcycles," one bike served all purposes in the early years of the sport. You could buy a 500cc BSA Gold Star thumper, ride it to church on Sunday morning, make some quick alterations after church, and race it Sunday afternoon. And you could race it in any type of race you chose, whether it was a dirt-track race, an off-road scrambles, or an international Grand Prix event.

Those days are long gone. Every type of race bike is a highly specialized machine.

In modern professional road racing, bikes are generally divided into three main categories: Supersport, Superbike, and Grand Prix. Supersport motorcycles are based on street-legal production motorcycles, with only minor modifications permitted. Superbikes are also based on street-legal production motorcycles, although extensive modifications are allowed. Grand Prix motorcycles are pure racing bikes designed solely for racetrack use.

Motorcycology
Because Grand Prix bikes aren't based on production bikes, their designers aren't hampered in any way by designing around international pollution regulations. As a result, designers use two-stroke engines in their Grand Prix bikes almost without exception.

In the United States, dirt-track racing is also popular. This type of racing takes place on oval tracks with dirt surfaces. The bikes raced in dirt track racing are purpose-built racing bikes, like those used in Grand Prix racing, but they do bear some resemblance to street-going motorcycles.

Grand Prix Racing

If you want to get into Grand Prix racing, prepare to spend some bucks. The AMA runs Grand Prix series' for several displacement categories, but to get a competitive bike will cost you, and the larger the bike, the more it will cost. Leasing a Honda NSR500, the bike that has won most Grand Prix World Championships during the past decade, will cost you at least $1 million per season. Buying a top-of-the-line 500cc Honda NSR500V V-twin, perhaps the most potent race bike a non-factory-affiliated individual can buy, will set you back $100,000.

Racer Joey Dunlop crosses Ballaugh Bridge on a Honda NSR 500V during the Isle of Man TT. (Photo ©1998 Brian J. Nelson)

The smaller Grand Prix bikes are a bit more affordable, but they still cost more than all of but the most expensive streetbikes. The NSR500V's little brothers, the RS250R and the RS125R, cost $22,400 and $12,900, respectively. Thirteen grand may seem a bit steep for a 125cc motorcycle, but it's relatively cheap for a Grand Prix racer.

FIM World Championship Grand Prix Series

The World Championship Grand Prix series is the most prestigious motorcycle racing series in the world—the pinnacle of FIM racing. The bikes in the 500cc class are the highest-performing machines on the face of the planet. To get a ride on a 500cc Grand Prix bike requires years of dedication and superhuman riding skills. If you're good enough, dedicated enough, and lucky enough, you may get a spot on a Grand Prix team, but the vast majority of us mere mortals will have to settle with just watching the best of the best race them.

Unlike superbike and supersport racers, which are based on street-going motorcycles, 500cc Grand Prix race bikes have nothing at all in common with any motorcycle you can buy. These machines are purpose-built racers wholly unsuited for public consumption and are so challenging to ride that only a select few professional road racers are ever able to master them. That is why only the very best road racers ever make it to the 500cc World Championship Grand Prix level.

To get an idea of just how much these bikes differ from anything you can buy for the street, check out the specifications of Alex Criville's 1996 Honda NSR500 Grand Prix racer. The engine is a two-stroke water-cooled V-four, but the angle of the V is 112 degrees. That almost makes it a horizontally-opposed four, like the engine found in early versions of Honda's Gold Wing.

But this engine has about as much in common with the Gold Wing's motor as it does with the Briggs and Stratton powering your Weed Whacker. With its electronically-controlled variable exhaust port valve and Keihin flat-valve carburetors, this engine puts out well over 200 horse power. To put this into perspective, this 30-cubic-inch engine cranks out as much horse power as a 454-cubic-inch Chevrolet V-8.

Less than one in one million riders will ever get to ride one of these machines, so the closest most of us will come will be attending a Grand Prix race. Unfortunately, there hasn't been a U.S. Grand Prix for years. If you want to see these bikes in action, the closest Grand Prix races are in Brazil and Argentina.

AMA Grand Prix Motorcycle Racing

If you are unable to make it to Europe, Asia, or South America to see an International Championship Grand Prix race anytime soon, don't worry. The AMA sanctions several national Grand Prix series in the United States.

The AMA Grand Prix classes are Open Single (for single-cylinder bikes of any displacement), 650cc GP Twins, Open GP Twins (for twins of any displacement), 125cc Grand Prix, and 250cc Grand Prix.

Grand National Dirt Track: American Racing

In America, many early races were held on horse-racing tracks at county fairgrounds around the country.

After World War II, this type of racing began to take the form we know today, and in 1954, the AMA established the Grand National Dirt Track series. Today, that series is the oldest and most traditional racing program the AMA sanctions, and dirt-track racing has developed a personality that is distinctly American.

Although the series now consists only of dirt-track events, until 1986, several road-race nationals were included. As machines became more and more specialized, it became obvious that machines built for dirt-track racing were not suitable for use on paved courses, and machines built for paved courses certainly weren't suitable for use in the dirt, so in 1986, the AMA divided dirt track and road racing into two distinct AMA Championship series.

Over the years, a number of manufacturers have had success in the Grand National series, such as Triumph, BSA, Yamaha, and Honda, but it is in this environment where Harley-Davidsons are in their element, and Harleys have captured more Grand National Championships than any other make.

Dirt-track racers make this look easy, but if you've ever tried sliding a motorcycle sideways through a turn at 100 miles per hour on a rutted dirt road, you'll know it's anything but. (Photo ©1998 Darwin Holstrom)

The bikes, especially the Harleys, are raw machines. Everything is in front of you—big, air-cooled cylinders and huge clutches down where there should be a foot peg. These bikes have a mean, gut-wrenching beauty no other motorcycle possesses.

Anyone who rides those machines over 100 mph sideways on those surfaces has to have absolute faith in their abilities, along with no fear whatsoever. Seeing the superhuman feats dirt-track racers perform week after week out on racetracks across America will humble even the most arrogant street squid.

Production-Based Motorcycle Racing

By the early 1970s, it was clear that the escalating cost of racing motorcycles was going to make it increasingly more difficult for people to take up the sport. To try to keep racing affordable, clubs organized new series based on *production motorcycles*—motorcycles anyone could walk into a showroom and buy.

Such series proved popular with fans, and now some production-based series can cost nearly as much to get into as Grand Prix racing. Fortunately, new series are formed every year, many with rules specifically designed to keep costs down.

Superbike Racing

Superbike racing motorcycles are based on production streetbikes, but with extensive modifications, both to the powertrain and to the chassis. Because of this, superbike racing is much more expensive to get into than supersport racing.

Superbike racing is also one of the most popular forms of racing with fans. Although extensively modified and capable of near–Grand-Prix levels of performance, superbikes still look like the bikes you or I can buy. Because of that, fans identify with these bikes. Two Superbike series in particular, the AMA's Up-to-750 Class Superbike series and the FIM's World Superbike series, now rival World Championship Grand Prix racing in popularity.

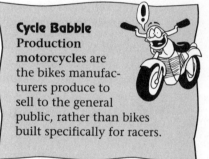

Cycle Babble
Production motorcycles are the bikes manufacturers produce to sell to the general public, rather than bikes built specifically for racers.

Motorcycle Moments

When I first started riding, I was more interested in dirtbikes than streetbikes. I might have remained a dirt rider had I not discovered superbike racing. In particular, I owe my interest in streetbikes to two men and one bike: Phil Schilling, Cook Neilson, and their "California Hot Rod," the highly-modified Ducati 750SS Neilson rode to victory in the 1977 Daytona Superbike race. Following the exploits of Neilson and Schilling and their Hot Rod, to my eye the most beautiful motorcycle of all time, motivated me to move from the dirt to the street.

World Superbike Racing (WSB)

Although the World Superbike Racing series has only been around since 1988, it has become one of the most prestigious international racing series in the world. The original idea was to provide the highest-quality four-stroke racing possible, while at the same time keeping the appearance of the racing bikes as close to the streetbikes they were based on as possible.

It worked. Motorcycle manufacturers realized the sales boost that success in such an international championship racing series would give them, and they gave the series their full support, either fielding factory teams, or giving full factory support to chosen independent teams.

Now World Superbike racing's popularity is edging into Grand Prix territory. Its star riders, people like Carl Fogarty, Troy Corser, Scott Russell, Doug Polen, Raymond Roche, and Fred Merkel, have become international motorcycle celebrities. Ducati's dominance in the series has restored that company's racing reputation, and in the process, its success on the showroom floor.

And unlike International Championship Grand Prix racing, you won't have to go to Brazil to see a race live. The U.S. round of the series is held each summer at the Laguna Seca racetrack in Monterey, California.

AMA Superbike Racing

Hot on the heels of FIM World Superbike racing in worldwide popularity is our very own AMA Superbike Racing series. It is, after all, the prototype for World Superbike racing, and many of the same people who race in WSB also race in the AMA Superbike series. As its popularity grows, so grows the money involved, and AMA Superbike has actually been attracting riders away from WSB in recent years.

AMA rules for superbikes allow factory racing equipment (motorcycles or parts designed specifically for racing motorcycles). Aftermarket and factory high-performance parts are allowed without limit. You can *overbore* your engine (drill out the cylinders to increase engine displacement) up to 4 percent over the maximum limit for each class. There are no limitations for tires.

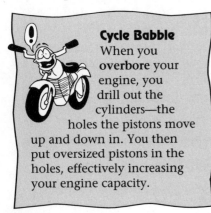

Cycle Babble
When you **overbore** your engine, you drill out the cylinders—the holes the pistons move up and down in. You then put oversized pistons in the holes, effectively increasing your engine capacity.

The AMA sanctions three classes of superbikes:

➤ Up to 450cc (open-displacement singles, twins up to 650cc, and Honda VF500 are also allowed)

➤ Up to 600cc (twins up to 750cc are also allowed)

➤ Up to 750cc (open-displacement twins and motorcycles prepared to AMA specifications for 750cc superbikes are also allowed)

Supersport Racing

Supersport class racing motorcycles are unmodified street motorcycles as delivered to the dealer from the manufacturer for use on public roads. In the United States, the AMA requires all supersport racers to comply with all applicable U.S. laws, with the exception of modifications made to improve safety. Limited-production motorcycles are not allowed in AMA Supersport classes.

For an AMA Supersport race bike, the following items must be completely stock, identical to the equipment on a bike you can walk into a dealership and buy:

> **Motorcycology**
> Because of the limited modifications allowed to the bikes, building a supersport racer is one of the least expensive ways to get into motorcycle road racing in the United States at the national level.

➤ Frame and swingarm assembly

➤ Front forks (aftermarket springs and air caps are allowed)

➤ Wheels

➤ Gasoline and oil tanks

➤ Fenders and side covers

➤ Brakes (racing-type brake pads and stock-sized aftermarket disc-brake rotors may be used)

➤ Stock carburetors, with the exception of internal jetting changes, which are allowed

➤ Seat

A few modifications are allowed. You can add a fork brace and steering damper, and you can replace suspension components to improve handling. Racing-only tires are not allowed, but to get around that, a variety of racing tires are now legal for street use. Airboxes and air-filter elements may be removed or replaced with aftermarket items. Original equipment fairings may be removed or replaced with replica fairings, as long as the aftermarket fairings are true copies of the original.

Overboring the engine up to one millimeter is allowed in each class, and aftermarket racing exhaust systems are allowed, but ignition systems must remain stock (although ignition timing may be adjusted or modified).

AMA Supersport Classes

The AMA divides supersport racing into a variety of classes, based on engine type and displacement:

➤ Up to 450cc (open-displacement singles, and twins up to 650cc are also allowed)

➤ Up to 600cc (twins up to 750cc are also allowed)

➤ Up to 750cc (open-displacement twins are also allowed)

➤ Open class, which consists of bikes over 750cc

Vintage Racing

Even more affordable than supersport racing is vintage racing, sponsored by organizations like the American Historic Racing Motorcycle Association (AHRMA). Because this type of racing is accessible for so many people, it becomes more popular every year, both with fans and with racers. Racers enjoy the chance to get out and race these classic machines, and fans love to watch the bikes in action. And the racing itself is as exciting as any modern series.

Motorcycology
Although vintage racing can be one of the least expensive ways to get into racing, many people think it is also one of the most entertaining forms. Often, people racing vintage bikes are former racers, people who have known and raced with one another for decades. Over that time, many close friendships have formed, and that bonding creates a positive and entertaining atmosphere at vintage racing events.

Such racing does present challenges for racing organizers. Consistent rules for the preparation of motorcycles for vintage racing are difficult to create and enforce. This means that organizers have to rely on the honor system.

Finding parts for older machines that are out of production can be a problem, forcing racers to use altered and non-standard parts. This makes it difficult for organizers to require the use of stock items, as they do in supersport racing.

Most vintage racing series use some variation of the following classes:

➤ Lightweight classic vintage (up to 250cc)

➤ Junior classic vintage (251cc to 350cc)

➤ Senior classic vintage (351cc to 500cc)

➤ 750cc formula vintage

➤ Lightweight classic superbike

➤ Open classic superbike

To be eligible for most forms of vintage racing, you'll need to start with road-racing or street-going motorcycles manufactured prior to 1968 (although there are usually exceptions for certain bikes).

There are a few restrictions on how you can build a vintage racer. You have to use carburetors that are consistent with the period during which the bike was manufactured, and you can't use modern, box-section swingarms. You can use modern treaded racing tires and rims, but they have to be in the original size.

If you want to race something a bit more modern, you can build a bike for the Classic Superbike class. Motorcycles manufactured between 1973 and 1985 are eligible for this

Many Harley-Davidson Knucklehead motorcycles, like this one owned by motorcycle collector Jerry Stageberg, fell victim to customizers and ended up becoming choppers. (Photo © 1998 Darwin Holmstrom)

This may look like a standard motorcycle compared to today's bikes, but back in 1963, this Triumph Bonneville represented the state of the art in sporting motorcycles. In the hands of a good rider, a strong-running Bonneville will still acquit itself well today. (Photo © 1998 Timothy Remus)

The late 1990s have seen the return of a dynamic European motorcycle industry. The latest company to get back into the motorcycle business in a big way is Italy's Laverda. Shown here is a 750 S Formula. (Photo courtesy the manufacturer)

The German firm Mz has resurrected a type of motorcycle many thought extinct: the sporting single. Mz Skorpions, like this top-of-the-line Replica, are some of the highest-performing thumpers ever sold to the public. (Photo courtesy the manufacturer)

Moto Guzzi's V10 Centauro Sport is nothing if not unique. Many riders feel no other motorcycle blends traditional styling and modern technology with the same flair as a Moto Guzzi. (Photo courtesy the manufacturer)

Retired motorcycle racers Jerry Stageberg (left) and Al Burke (right) look over Stageberg's Vincent Rapide. Vincent motorcycles are the Holy Grails for many motorcycle collectors and command top prices. (Photo © 1998 Darwin Holmstrom)

If you want to buy a true classic motorcycle, like this Ariel Square Four, owned by motorcycle collector Jerry Stageberg, you'll probably have to take out a second mortgage on your house. (Photo © 1998 Darwin Holmstrom)

The resurrected Triumph Motorcycles Limited let the world know it was serious about building sportbikes when it introduced its Daytona T569, a three-cylinder, fuel-injected machine that ranks among the world's finest motorcycles. (Photo courtesy the manufacturer)

Today Jerry Stageberg races "Ol' Dynamite," his antique Ariel Red Hunter, in vintage racing, but when he began racing this very bike in 1947, it was a state-of-the-art racing machine. (Photo courtesy Motorcyclist™ magazine)

The legendary 750SS is the motorcycle that cemented Ducati's status as the world's premiere sportbike manufacturer. (Photo courtesy Motorcyclist™ magazine)

*With the techno-
logically stunning
CBX, Honda asked
the question, "Is
the world ready for
a six-cylinder
sporting motor-
cycle?" The answer
was a resounding,
"No!" While the
silky smooth engine
made the CBX one
of the fastest
motorcycles built in
the 1970s, its
width hindered the
bikes handling, and
its complexity
made the machine
a nightmare to
maintain. (Photo
courtesy Vreeke and
Associates)*

Yamaha's brilliant YZF-R1 packs a 131.4 horsepower engine into a 448-pound motorcycle, creating the highest power-to-weight ratio of any production road-going vehicle ever built. You can scare yourself with one of these. (Photo courtesy Motorcyclist™ magazine)

With the all-conquering 1973 903 Z1, Kawasaki created the fastest production vehicle ever sold to the public. By today's standards, however, the mighty Z1 would be considered slow. (Photo courtesy the manufacturer)

Four-time World Grand Prix motorcycle champion Mick Doohan makes riding his Honda NSR500 at 200 mph look easy as he rounds a curve during the 1994 U.S. Grand Prix at Laguna Seca.(Photo © 1994 Rick Menapace)

Old Moto Guzzis never die—they just go vintage racing. (Photo © 1998 Brian J. Nelson)

Most motorcyclists agree that BMW built some of the finest, most elegant motorcycles in history. (Photo © 1998 Brian J. Nelson)

series, provided that they have air-cooled engines and twin-shock rear suspension. There are two classes in the series: the Lightweight Classic Superbike class (which includes bikes up to 550cc) and the Open Classic Superbike class (bikes up to 1100cc). This type of racing is the single most affordable way you can get into the sport, since often you can pick up examples of these bikes for around $500, and if you do a lot of the work yourself, you can have them ready to race for another $1,000.

Other Racing Series

In addition to the main national series, you can become involved in one of a dizzying array of other types of racing. I've only been able to include a few examples, but if you start looking, you will find a lot more.

AMA Pro Thunder Class

AMA's Pro Thunder Class Racing series is an attempt to do what the Superbike series was originally intended to do—make racing affordable by building racing bikes from existing streetbikes. This series is limited to bikes that aren't competitive in superbike and supersport racing—in other words, there are no four-cylinder machines allowed. The main qualifications for racing in the Pro Thunder class follow:

➤ Racers must be based on street motorcycles available in the North American market.

➤ Bikes can use single-cylinder engines of unlimited displacement.

➤ Four-stroke, liquid-cooled twins can range from 600cc to 850cc; this qualification excludes the Ducatis that have dominated superbike racing for much of the past decade.

➤ Air-cooled, four-stroke V-twins can range from 700cc to 1250cc.

➤ No desmodromic valve gear is allowed. This qualification will eliminate even the pedestrian Ducatis from competition, since every Ducati manufactured over the past couple of decades has used desmo valves.

➤ Three-cylinder bikes can range from 700cc to 900cc.

British-European-American Racing Series (BEARS)

Another interesting racing series is the British-European-American Racing series (BEARS). To compete in this series, a bike must have a 500cc-to-1300cc four-stroke engine (with the exception of bikes using Norton rotary engines, which are permitted), and both the engine and the frame must be of non-Japanese origin. To prevent the series from being dominated by Ducati superbikes, four-valve desmodromic engines are not permitted.

The Isle of Man Tourist Trophy (TT)

Although no longer a sanctioned Grand Prix race (the British Grand Prix moved to Silverstone in 1976 because the Isle of Man course was deemed too dangerous), the Isle of Man TT is arguably the world's most famous motorcycle road race. The Mountain Circuit, where the race has been held since 1911, is also one of the world's most dangerous race courses.

Back in the early years of motorsports, races were often held on public roads that were closed down for a race. England had a law against closing public roads for racing, so racing promoters worked with the government of the Isle of Man, a small hunk of land in the Irish Sea, to open a race course there. Automobile racing began at the Isle in 1904, and the first Tourist Trophy motorcycle race was held in 1907.

During the time the race has been held on the Mountain Circuit, a wicked-fast 37.7 route over public roads, speeds have risen a bit. In 1911, O. C. Godfrey won the Senior 500cc TT on an Indian, with an average speed of 47.63 mph. The current lap record, held by Carl Fogarty, is 123.61 mph, set in the 1992 Senior TT.

Except for being interrupted by a couple of world wars, first between 1914 and 1920, and again between 1939 and 1946, TT and races have been held every year at the Isle of Man. From 1949 until 1976, the Isle of Man Mountain Circuit was part of the International Grand Prix Motorcycle World Championships.

The Isle of Man TT is one of the last old-style races in the world, and as such, it is one of the world's deadliest races. Run on public roads rather than purpose-designed race courses, the Mountain Circuit lacks even the most minimal safety standards. There are no runoffs for riders to regain control on if they veer off course. Instead, the rider will likely end up in trees, against a stone wall, or in a fence, should he or she make the slightest mistake on the narrow, winding roads. Such obstacles prove much less forgiving than the hay bales lining most race courses. When averaged over the race's 90-odd-year history, at least a couple of riders are killed per year.

Motorcycology

The future of the annual TT races is anything but certain. The races are extremely popular, drawing huge crowds to the Isle each year. Fans enjoy watching the historic races, but nobody wants to see racers get killed. For years, various groups have tried to shut down the TT, and sooner of later they will succeed. My advice is that if you are at all interested in seeing racing history, get to the Isle of Man Tourist Trophy as soon as possible. You may not get another chance.

Drag Racing

I have to admit that I used to have a prejudice against drag racing. I thought it seemed crude and silly compared to motorcycle road racing. I couldn't have been more wrong, as I found out when I finally attended a motorcycle drag race.

The first motorcycle drag race I attended was an All Harley Drag Racing Association (AHDRA) event, and it forever changed my view of the sport. Watching the drag racers straddle their freaky-looking machines as they rocketed down the eighth-mile track at speeds of over 150 mph made me realize that drag racing requires every bit as much skill as road racing—it just requires different skills.

The noise, the smell of burning nitro, the sheer power of the drag-racing spectacle can only be compared to a religious epiphany or a Led Zeppelin concert. (Photo ©1998 Darwin Holstrom)

And the entertainment provided by drag racing at least equals that provided by other forms of racing. If you ever have an opportunity to see a motorcycle drag race, do so. You won't regret it.

I urge you to discover the excitement of motorcycle racing for yourself, either as a fan or as a racer. Attend any motorcycle racing event you can, whether it's a club supersport race, a vintage dirt-track race, or a hill climb. And when you find yourself unable to attend such events, call the publishers listed in Appendix C, "Resources," order some of the excellent books available on the subject, and read about racing.

The Least You Need to Know

➤ The AMA is the primary sanctioning body for motorcycle racing in the United States, and it is involved in nearly all organized racing in the United States.

➤ Motorcycles racing in the World Championship Grand Prix series are some of the most powerful machines on the face of the planet, producing around 400 horsepower per liter.

➤ Classic superbike racing is the least expensive way to get into motorcycle road racing.

➤ The Isle of Man TT is one of the oldest races in the world, providing fans with a view into the past.

Chapter 22

How to Become a Motorcycle Road Racer

In This Chapter

➤ Getting started in racing

➤ Getting your racing license

➤ Taking a racing course

➤ Preparing your bike for racing

I hope that many of you will become racing fans after reading Chapter 21, partly because I want more people to become interested in this exciting sport, but mostly because I want to share something that has brought me so much pleasure.

Some of you may want to become more than just racing fans; some of you may want to become racers. In this chapter, I'm going to tell you how you can become a motorcycle road racer. It's not as difficult as it might seem. While expensive, racing motorcycles is still much less expensive than automobile racing. It requires more training and skill than automobile racing, but here you're in luck. In recent years, several quality road racing schools have appeared—places where you can learn to race or just learn to be a better rider. And you can find racing classes in just about any region of the country.

How to Become a Racer

Racing is not as dangerous as it might seem. It's more dangerous than a lot of activities—crocheting, for example—but less dangerous than others. Many racers feel safer on the track than they do on the street, and statistically, they have a point. On a racetrack, the flow of traffic is controlled; everyone moves in the same direction, at roughly the same speed. And on a track, you eliminate your number-one traffic hazard: the left-turning driver.

Motorcycology

To be successful in motorcycle racing, you need to have good upper and lower body strength, and you need to be in good cardiovascular condition. The best riders work out on a regular basis and eat low-fat, high-carbohydrate diets.

Actually, by riding on a track with nothing but similar racing motorcycles, you eliminate the danger of car and truck drivers completely, a safety advantage you will learn to appreciate as soon as you begin riding on public highways. Racing a motorcycle is safer than you might think, and you can minimize what danger there is by proper preparation.

Vehicular Chess

Motorcycle road racing is a physical activity. You need to be able to wrestle your machine from a hard left turn to a hard right turn in a heartbeat. You need to be in fairly good physical condition. But racing is also a mental activity. A good racer not only rides fast, but he or she maneuvers for position on the track much like a master chess player controls the area of a chessboard.

Levels of Racing

One thing to keep in mind when you start racing is that you are not going to start at the top. Even if you have 100 grand to drop on a Honda NSR500V Grand Prix bike, that won't buy your way into the International Championship Grand Prix circuit. Without the skill, training, and experience to ride the bike, you'll be a danger to yourself and others.

But you wouldn't want to start out in such rarefied atmosphere even if you could. What fun would it be to go out and constantly get humiliated by the finest racers on the planet? That's why there are classes for almost any rider.

The Central Roadracing Association, the club that conducts road racing in Minnesota, has a couple of classes that are ideal for beginners: the Ultralightweight class and the Lightweight class, which are two of their most popular classes. The racing is a bit slower than it is in the Supersport or Superbike classes, but trust me: It's fast enough. Speeds of 90 to 100 miles per hour may sound slow to a spectator used to seeing the speeds of over 170 mph attained by some World Superbike racers, but when you're out there riding around the track, it seems pretty darn fast.

And getting into such classes is much less expensive. You can build a competitive racer for under $2,000 if you do much of the work on it yourself.

Besides low cost, part of the reason these categories are so popular with beginners and experienced racers alike is because the racing is much more competitive at these levels. When you get to national-level Superbike racing, a handful of racers with huge budgets and full factory support dominate the sport. At this level, everyone is more or less equal, and riding ability plays more of a role in succeeding than sophisticated equipment.

Club Racing

The most convenient way to get into road racing is to become involved in club racing. Although competing professionally at the national or international level can be prohibitively expensive, most areas around the United States have racing clubs that provide relatively affordable amateur racing. There are dozens of such clubs around the country, but I'm going to focus on two: American Federation of Motorcyclists (AFM), a California-based club that has been very influential in road racing across the country, and Central Roadracing Association (CRA), a Minnesota-based club, because that is the only racing organization with which I have personal experience.

Motorcycology
Most motorcycle road-racing clubs have categories and classes for just about every level of rider, from 17-year-old experts to 70-year-old novices. If you have the slightest desire to go racing, you can't use age or experience level as an excuse not to do so.

American Federation of Motorcyclists (AFM)

One example of a club that promotes roadracing is American Federation of Motorcyclists (AFM), a California-based organization that conducts seven to nine racing events each year at the Sears Point racetrack in Sonoma, California; the Thunderhill Park Raceway, near Willows, California; and the Buttonwillow Raceway Park, near Buttonwillow, California.

Central Roadracing Association (CRA)

Central Roadracing Association (CRA), located in Minnesota, conducts club racing at Brainerd International Raceway (BIR). CRA events are wildly popular with racing fans across the upper Midwest, with events attracting fans from as far away as Montana and Colorado. Without CRA, organized road racing would not exist in the region.

Racing Categories and Classes

Categories and classes may differ slightly from one racing organization to the next. You'll need to consult the rule books of the organization you are joining for specific details, but most more or less mirror the categories used by CRA.

CRA has three general motorcycle competition classes: Supersport, Superbike, and Grand Prix. In addition, it conducts races for a variety of amateur classes, generally divided according to engine displacement: Ultralightweight, Lightweight, Middleweight, Heavyweight, Unlimited, and Lightweight Sportsman Superbike.

➤ **Ultralightweight:** The smallest (and slowest) bikes run in this class, making it the best choice for a beginning racer, but it is also popular with racers right up to the expert level, because the racing is usually very competitive. This class is dominated by Suzuki's GS500E, but other popular motorcycles include Yamaha's RD350/RD400 series of two strokes, Kawasaki's Ninja 250, and single-cylinder motorcycles. They also have an Ultralightweight Grand Prix class in which Honda RS125s and Yamaha TZ125s compete.

➤ **Lightweight:** This popular class—in which motorcycles like Yamaha's FZR400, Kawasaki's EX500, and Honda's Hawk 650 compete—is also great for beginners. Although this class is dominated by more powerful motorcycles, a good rider on a Suzuki GS500 can be competitive in this class. Older, air-cooled 600cc motorcycles like Yamaha's FZ600 are also allowed. In the Lightweight Grand Prix class, early-model Honda RS250s and Yamaha TZ250s are allowed.

➤ **Middleweight:** The Middleweights, one of CRA's most popular classes, feature all current 600cc sportbikes, like Honda's CBR600F3, Kawasaki's ZX6R, Yamaha's YZF600, and Suzuki's GSX-R600. In 1997, CRA began allowing Triumph Speed Triples, Ducati 900SSs, and Harley-Davidson 1200 Sportsters to compete in this class. In the Middleweight Grand Prix class, current-model Honda RS250s and Yamaha TZ250s compete.

➤ **Heavyweight:** Popular 750cc sportbikes—like Suzuki's GSX-R750, Kawasaki's ZX7, and Yamaha's YZF750—compete in this class, along with Ducati's 851/888/916 series and the new Honda VTR1000s and Suzuki TL1000Ss.

➤ **Unlimited:** This expert-only class (novice racers are not allowed on motorcycles larger than heavyweight) has no displacement limits. Any motorcycle—from 600cc and 750cc sportbikes to Suzuki GSX-R1100s, Honda CBR900s, and Yamaha YZF1000s—can compete, as can any Grand Prix motorcycle (but so far, no rider has been able to scrape together $100,000 to buy one).

➤ **Lightweight Sportsman Superbike:** This is a class for older, lightweight motorcycles. Except for Yamaha's FZR400 and Honda's Hawk 650, just about any lightweight superbike is allowed.

➤ **Middleweight Sportsman Superbike:** This is also a class for older 600cc sportbikes like Honda's Hurricane 600, Suzuki's Katana 600, and Kawasaki's Ninja 600. Yamaha's FZR400 is also allowed. The Lightweight Sportsman and Middleweight Sportsman races are usually run together.

Licensing

All clubs require you to purchase a racing license, which usually costs between $45 and $125. Some clubs will accept the licenses of certain other clubs, while some organizations will require you to go through the entire process from scratch before you can race in their club.

The licensing requirements vary from organization to organization (again, you'll need to check the rule books of any organization you are thinking of joining).

> **Motorcycology**
> All road-racing clubs require you to obtain a racing license before you can race, and all require you to complete some form of rider course before getting a novice license.

Racing Schools

To go racing, you are required to attend some sort of new rider's course. You can attend these through the clubs themselves, or you can attend one of the courses offered by various high-performance riding schools.

High-Performance Riding Schools

Schools specifically for people who want to learn to race, or who just want to ride better, have appeared across the country in recent years, and many of these schools take their classes on the road, offering high-performance riding courses at racetracks around the county. Completing a course from an accepted riding school qualifies you for a novice license in most clubs. Even if you don't race, attending a course offered by one of the following schools raises your riding abilities to new heights and makes you a much safer rider.

California Superbike School (CSS)

Founded by Keith Code, former racer and trainer of such legendary racers as Eddie Lawson, Wayne Rainy, Doug Chandler, and John Kockinski, CSS is one of the oldest and most respected high-performance riding schools.

Begun in 1980, this school set the standard for what a high-performance riding school should be. Courses are now offered at three levels: Level 1 focuses on throttle control and cornering lines; level 2 focuses on overall awareness of your surroundings; and level 3 concentrates on things like the position of your body on the bike and the mental aspects of motorcycling.

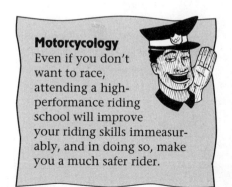

> **Motorcycology**
> Even if you don't want to race, attending a high-performance riding school will improve your riding skills immeasurably, and in doing so, make you a much safer rider.

Among instructor Keith Code's former pupils is racing champion John Kocinski, shown here aboard a Honda RC45 at the 1997 Laguna Seca World Superbike race. (Photo ©1998 Brian J. Nelson)

If you attend CSS, you will receive instruction from Mr. Code himself; in other words, you will learn to race from the man who trained some of the greatest racers in motorcycle history. The full course is offered for $525, or $315 if you provide your own bike. Whatever the cost, the price is still a bargain when you consider who your teacher will be.

Freddie Spencer's High-Performance Riding School

When I bought my first streetbike, Freddie "Fast Freddie" Spencer was the hottest motorcycle racer in the world. During a 30-year racing career (1966–1995), the man learned a thing or two about riding, and if you take this course, he'll share his secrets with you. Courses are offered at two levels: SR for street riders and SR Pro for those with racing aspirations. These courses are not cheap, costing $1,150 and $1,750, respectively, but for 30 years' worth of Fast Freddie's experience, it's well worth the price.

Motorcycology
While many racing clubs will still require you to attend their own racing class, many will give you a discount for attending a racing school like CLASS.

CLASS Safety School

Begun by three-time AMA Superbike champion and English expatriate Reg Pridmore way back in 1978, CLASS offers a couple of decades' worth of experience in training riders in the art of going fast safely. These one-day courses, offered at racetracks around the country, cost only between $275 to $295. It would be worth that much money just to hang out with Pridmore (by all accounts one of the nicest people ever to be involved in racing) and his son Jason for a day, but for your money, you will also receive invaluable riding skills.

Team Suzuki Endurance Advanced Riding School (TSEARS)

The Team Suzuki Endurance Advanced Riding School's chief instructor is another of my childhood racing idols: Dave Aldana, winner of the very first AMA National Superbike race. As a kid, I though Aldana's racing leathers, decorated in a skeleton motif, made him look like some sort of superhero on the track.

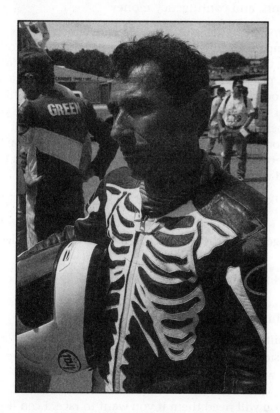

TSEARS head instructor and champion racer Dave Aldana in his famous "Skeleton Bones" racing leathers. (Photo ©1998 Brian J. Nelson)

Held in concert with actual racing events at various tracks around the country, these courses not only teach you to race, they also provide you with the intense atmosphere you will have to function in as a racer. Graduating from a TSEARS course will even earn you a novice racing license in a couple of national organizations.

Club Racing Classes

Most clubs offer their own racing classes that cost considerably less than the racing schools, but they still have a lot to offer both street riders and racers. The curriculum of such classes varies from club to club, but the courses offered by AFM and CRA are fairly representative examples.

AFM Race School

To help new racers get started, American Federation of Motorcyclists conducts the AFM Race School several times each year. This course is one of the most complete racing classes offered by a racing club. They try to make their courses fun, too, by holding races for new riders, complete with trophies, championship points, and contingency money.

Motorcycology
If you attend a racing class offered by a racing club like AFM, you need to provide your own motorcycle and racing gear.

Everyone has to pass the AFM Race School before they can compete, even if they have completed a professional course like CLASS, although AFM does give a $25 discount if you can prove that you've completed a course in an accepted school during the previous 12 months. AFM's philosophy is that while high-performance riding schools give you track experience, you'll still need to learn many minor details before competing in real races. You'll need to learn about safety flags and bike preparation, as well as what to expect and what to do when racing with other people.

You need to provide your own bike and gear for AFM's Race School. To participate, you must have the following:

➤ A set of one-piece or zip-together leathers in excellent condition (no holes, rips, or tears)

➤ An undamaged full-face helmet with a 1985 or 1990 Snell sticker inside that has not been damaged

➤ Boots at least eight inches high; gloves in excellent condition

➤ A back protector (either built into the leathers or separate) that consists of impact-resistant plastic on the outside and foam on the inside, and covers the spine from the shoulders to below the waist

These items are expensive, but you will need them if you want to race. Even if you don't race, such gear provides excellent protection on the street.

Preparing a Race Bike

As with just about everything in racing, the details of race-bike preparation vary from club to club, but most follow the requirements set forth by AFM fairly closely. You can race just about any bike in AFM, as long as it meets basic safety requirements and passes technical inspection, since AFM offers classes for bikes from 125cc to over 1000cc, and for bikes with little or no modifications to bikes built specifically for racing.

To prepare your bike for AFM racing, you'll need to remove some of the street equipment, like turn signals, mirrors, license plate and brackets, passenger footpegs, sidestand, and centerstand. Headlights and tail lights need be removed or taped over.

Cooling systems can't contain any antifreeze, since spilling that slippery substance on a track poses a serious safety hazard. You'll need to install three number plates: one on each side and one on the front. Some bikes have an area on the fairing or seat that is large and flat enough to hold a number sticker. Novice number plates are yellow with the assigned AFM number in black. As a safety precaution, certain bolts, nuts, and fasteners need to be safety wired or have locking devices.

The best way to learn how to set up your bike for racing is to obtain a rule book from the club you want to race with and study it. Then, go to a race to browse through the pits, look at the bikes, and talk to people about how they set up their own bikes. I've found racers to be some of the nicest, friendliest people I've ever met, and I think you'll find them very helpful to talk to when getting started in motorcycle racing.

> **Motorcycology**
> The best way to learn about preparing a bike for racing is to visit the pit area of a racetrack during a race and talk with the racers. Most will be more than happy to offer you advice.

Buying Your First Racing Bike

When buying your first racing bike, follow the recommendations I outlined for buying your first streetbike. Choose a motorcycle that will allow you to get the most racing time and fun for the least money. Select a bike that isn't so large that it intimidates you or hinders your ability to learn. Bikes like 250cc twins (such as Kawasaki's Ninja 250), most thumpers, and 500cc or 650cc twins are good choices for beginners.

An alternative to preparing a race bike yourself is to buy a motorcycle that has already been converted into a racer. One of the best places to find such a machine is from road-race–oriented want ads, like those found in the back of *Roadracing World* magazine. You can also find race bikes for sale in the pit areas of racetracks when races are being held.

Even if you have never considered becoming a motorcycle racer, you might want to give the idea some thought. The excitement generated on a racetrack is a peak motorcycling experience that can't be found anywhere else. And racing on a track is much safer than racing on public roads.

> **Motorcycology**
> Sometimes buying a bike that has already been built for racing is cheaper than preparing your own bike.

Attend a high-performance riding school and see if you are interested in becoming a racer. Even if you decide the sport is not for you, at the very least, you'll improve your riding ability immeasurably.

The Least You Need to Know

➤ Racing requires good mental and physical preparation on your part.

➤ There is a class of racing for riders of all ages and experience levels.

➤ All racing clubs require you to attend some sort of racing class and obtain a racing license.

➤ It can be cheaper to buy a race bike than it is to build one.

Biker's Buying Guide to New Bikes

Motorcyclist™ magazine runs an *Annual Buyer's Guide* in its March issue, which lists all street-legal motorcycles for sale for the following year, along with technical specifications, prices, and editors' comments. This guide alone makes subscribing to *Motorcyclist*™ worth the money. I've used its guide as a general template for this appendix, which lists all street-legal motorcycles for sale in the United States in 1998, but I've modified the guide to be more useful for a new rider.

My recommendations vary somewhat from those of *Motorcyclist*™, because I'm judging a bike using different criteria. The magazine publishes its guide for experienced motorcyclists, who look for different qualities in the machines than new riders would. My recommendations are geared more toward beginning riders, although experienced riders may also find them useful. I've evaluated each bike using the following criteria:

Ease of use   Learning to ride is difficult enough without choosing a difficult motorcycle to learn on. In evaluating the bikes in this guide, I've placed a premium on power characteristics (since you will find smooth throttle control to be easier on bikes with a broad, smooth powerband) and on ease of handling.

Note that ease of handling is not the same as outright handling prowess; when I discuss ease of handling, I'm talking about how maneuverable a bike is in the kind of situations in which you will ride. A bike might be the best-handling machine on the racetrack but be a real handful when you practice braking and swerving in the parking lot. Bikes that combine smooth power and easy handling earn my Best First Bike rating.

Versatility	Since you probably aren't going to go out and buy several bikes right off the bat, your first motorcycle should be well-rounded—capable of serving you in a variety of situations. It should also be a bike you can grow with, rather than a machine you'll want to ditch midway through your first season of riding.
Value	If you're anything like me, the money you have available to purchase a motorcycle is limited, and you need to get the most for your hard-earned dollars. I've listed 1998 prices, as reported in the 1998 *Motorcyclist*™ Buyer's Guide, following each model's name. Bikes that represent the best value for your money earn my Best Buy rating.
Ease of maintenance	Since I don't have an unlimited expense account to maintain my fleet of bikes, I perform most basic maintenance procedures myself and take ease of maintenance into account when I purchase a bike.
Fun	Since the primary purpose of motorcycling is to have fun, it would be foolish to select a bike based solely on its practicality. I've included Style under the category of Fun. I didn't feel it warranted its own category, because it relies so heavily on opinion, and my opinion of what looks stylish may vary from yours. If you like the way a bike looks, don't worry about what I or anyone else thinks about it.

I've marked motorcycles that are easy to learn on as Best First Bikes. Bikes that combine functionality and value are marked as Best Buys. Price weighs heavily in the Best Buys category, so a bike like BMW's F650ST, which earns a Best First Bike rating, doesn't get a Best Buy rating, simply because other bikes offer similar attributes at a much lower price.

Following the Buyer's Guide section, I've compiled a list of all the best first bikes, a list of the best buys, and a list of the bikes that are both best first bikes and best buys. I've organized this appendix alphabetically by manufacturer. I've grouped bikes together by type of bike within each section. For example, all of Harley's Softail series are together, as are its Sportsters.

American Dirt Bike

In spite of the name, American Dirt Bike sells street-legal dual sports, although you won't find one on any showroom floor. Each bike is built to the individual customer's specifications.

Avenger   ($7,500–$10,500)

There is no standard Avenger—each is a custom-built personal machine, with engine displacement ranging from 350cc to 635cc. The only common thread is that all are powered by four-stroke, single-cylinder engines.

ATK

This small American company primarily manufactures pure-dirt bikes but builds a couple of dual-purpose thumpers that are street legal.

605 Enduro   ($7,795)

One of the few big dual sports that will run away from any of the Japanese dual sports when the trail ends and turns to swamp. If that is worth an extra $2,000–$3,000 to you, you might want to consider this one.

350 Enduro   ($7,295)

The 350 Enduro might be the most dirt-worthy, dual-purpose bike you can buy, but it's also the most expensive 350 you can buy.

Bimota

This small Italian company made its reputation by buying engines from other companies and constructing high-performance motorcycles around those engines. Except for the Mantra, all Bimotas are extreme sporting machines with uncompromising riding positions. Bimota recently broke with tradition and produced its first in-house engine, the two-stroke V-twin powering the Vdue.

SB8R   ($22,850)

This bike stuffs the engine from the TL1000, Suzuki's 1000cc V-twin sportbike (which cranks out more horsepower than most cars), into a 400-pound bike. Definitely not a beginner's bike, but if you can afford the price, you're probably well-insured.

SB6R   ($21,250)

Similar to the SB8R, except this one uses a 1100cc Suzuki four-cylinder engine and weighs a few pounds more.

YB11 Superleggera   ($20,275)

If a motorcycle weighing about 400 pounds and armed with nearly 150 horsepower doesn't scare you, it should. Abandon hope, all new riders who go here.

Mantra   ($18,530)

This is the only Bimota that is anything other than a single-purpose race bike for the street. Powered by an air-and-oil-cooled Ducati 904cc V-twin, the Mantra makes good power where it's easiest to use—in the middle of the RPM range. If you like the styling and have the money, this might be the bike for you.

500 Vdue   ($20,775)

While this is the star of the Bimota line, don't get too excited about buying one: Bimota only imported 60 of these babies for 1998, and all were spoken for before they hit U.S. shores.

BMW

Ever since BMW built its first opposed twin-cylinder motorcycle just after World War I, it has maintained a well-deserved reputation as the crafter of some of the finest motorcycles ever made. It also earned a reputation for building conservative motorcycles thought by some to be unexciting. Whether or not that reputation was deserved in the past, it's certainly not deserved today. Modern BMWs use cutting-edge technology to produce some of the most exciting motorcycles available.

As is the case with BMW automobiles, BMW motorcycles are not cheap, but quality of this level seldom is. If you can afford to buy a BMW for your first motorcycle, and you wish to do so, I recommend that you go for it. Although most models are on the large side for a new rider, clever design and tractable engine response make these motorcycles much easier for a beginner to ride than other bikes of similar heft and engine displacement.

R1200C   ($12,990)

Beemer's boxer-powered entry into the cruiser market. There's nothing else that looks like this bike. Style is the main reason to buy this bike, since it costs more and is less functional than other BMWs. Should you be taken by the looks of this beast, you'll wind up with one of the best handling cruisers around, powered by a torquey engine capable of amusing you for years. Expect to drop an extra $1,300 for the antilock brake system (ABS)..

K1200RS   ($15,990)

BMW's interpretation of the venerable inline four engine differs from Japan's; BMW flopped the engine on its side and mounted it longitudinally (lengthwise), rather than transversely (crosswise) in the frame. The *big K-bikes*, as four-cylinder Beemers are called, have proven to be competent, reliable machines with easy-to-use engines, but they are too large for a new rider.

R1100RS ABS   ($14,880)

Beemer's boxer-powered sport tourer. Combine good handling, a torquey engine, manageable weight, and comfortable ergonomics, and you wind up with a bike that rocks. It's a bit excessive for a beginner but forgiving enough to do the job if you insist on starting out with a big bike.

R1100RT ABS   ($15,590)

This sport tourer may represent the best compromise between sportbike and tourer on the market. But it's not a beginner's bike. Even though it's a relatively light touring bike, it's still more motorcycle than most beginners will be comfortable with.

R1100GS ABS   ($13,550)

This big dual sport has one of my all-time favorite engines, a version of BMW's boxer engine tuned for more torque than other versions. Although lacking a bit in top speed, this bike wheelies better than any other 600-plus-pound motorcycle. If you're comfortable with this bike's bulk (and its price), you may be able to learn to ride on it, although I recommend starting out smaller.

R1100R   ($9,990) (Best First Bike)

Photo not available

This is the only big Beemer light enough to really be manageable for a new rider. With a windshield and some hard luggage,
this one makes an excellent touring bike. The *antilock brake
system* (ABS) adds $1,500 to the price tag.

F650ST   ($7,590) (Best First Bike)

This is one of the finest single-cylinder motorcycles ever made,
but also one of the most expensive. The *Funduro*, as it is called
in Europe, is a great beginner's bike, but if money is an issue,
you can get more for your dollars elsewhere.

Buell

Erik Buell, a former Harley-Davidson employee, began manufacturing his own line of
bikes using Sportster engines and was so successful that Harley recently bought Buell
Motorcycles.

S1 White Lightning   ($10,599)

Buell's engine-mounting system has tamed the brutal shaking
of the Sportster engine, allowing engineers to extract impressive
amounts of power from the old beast, but the seat on this
model, Buell's top-of-the-line sportbike, prevents it from being
anything but a hot rod suited for brief, around-town antics.

S1 Lightning   ($9,999)

A slightly detuned version of the White Lightning.

M2 Cyclone   ($9,399)

A more pedestrian version of the Lightning, with a seat that, while not exactly comfortable, isn't shaped like a medical instrument.

S3/S3T Thunderbolt   ($11,999–$12,799)

This bike is Buell's most well-rounded machine. The S3T is a sport-touring version, with a roomier riding position and hard luggage. Like all Buell's, a version of Harley's 1200 Sportster engine powers this bike. That engine makes this a fairly easy bike to learn on, if you can afford its steep price.

Ducati

Owning a Ducati requires more of a commitment than owning most other bikes, if for no other reason than their use of desmodromic valve-actuation systems. While all Ducatis are great sportbikes, if you choose to buy one, make certain that a mechanic skilled in the delicate art of tuning a desmo engine is available to you.

ST2   ($12,495)

Ducati's sport-touring bike—a fairly comfortable, great-handling bike with hard luggage—places more emphasis on the sport part of sport touring than do most of its peers.

900SS FE   ($10,995)

FE stands for *Final Edition*, indicating that this is the last iteration of Ducati's highly-regarded air-cooled 900cc sportbike.

916 ($16,495)

Ducati's street version of the motorcycle that dominated superbike racing throughout the 1990s is one of the most capable extreme sportbikes you can buy. This makes it totally unsuited for an inexperienced rider.

900SS CR ($8,295)

You can't get a 900cc Ducati for less money than this stripped-down version of the 900SS. For the $2,700 you save over the FE, you'll get cheaper suspension components, a small, half fairing instead of a full faring, and no carbon-fiber bodywork.

M900 Monster ($9,995)

The Monster has been difficult to categorize, because even though it lacks bodywork, it is neither a cruiser nor a standard. Instead, it is a hard-edged sportbike without bodywork. It is also quite popular.

M750 Monster ($7,695)

The smaller version of the Monster offers more power than most beginners can use, but of all Ducatis, it is probably the most manageable Ducati for a new rider.

748 ($13,495)

While the engine on this bike is smaller than the 916's motor, this bike is still much too powerful for a new rider. It certainly is pretty, though.

Harley-Davidson

Even though all Harleys use just two engines, the way those engines are used creates bikes with distinct personalities. You can place them in two broad categories: Harleys that are relatively smooth running and Harleys that vibrate like a giant electric sander.

The basic engine design of all Harleys ensures that they vibrate, but through clever engine-mounting systems on some models, Harley has isolated much of that vibration from the rider. On other models, The Motor Company simply bolts the engine to the frame and lets the vibrations rip.

All Sportsters and Softail models use the solid-mounting system, while all the touring models and models that use Harley's Dyna chassis isolate most of the vibes from the rider. If the bike has "Dyna," "Electra Glide," or "Road" in the title, it's smooth. If the bike has "Softail" or "Sportster" in the title, it vibrates.

Road Glide ($16,825)

With this unusual take on a traditional touring bike, Harley has attempted to recreate the style of some of the show bikes built by customizers like Arlen Ness.

Electra Glide Ultra Classic ($18,065)

Harley's top-of-the-line touring bike, this one comes with every electronic gizmo you can imagine as standard equipment.

Electra Glide Classic   ($15,775)

This may look just like the last Harley Elvis ever bought, the one sitting in the museum at Graceland, but it works a whole lot better on the road. Fuel injection will cost you an extra $245 on this model, but it's money well spent.

Electra Glide Standard   ($12,725) (Best Buy)

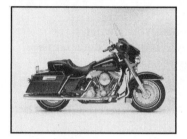

A touring bike for Harley lovers on a tight budget, this is essentially a stripped-down Electra Glide. For the $5,340 saved over the Ultra Classic, you forfeit a trunk, fairing lowers, some chrome, a sound system/CB radio, and cruise control, but you still get the same lump of a V-twin motor and all that Harley mystique.

Road King   ($14,725)

If the Electra Glide Classic looks just like Elvis' last Harley, the Road King looks just like his first. It may look like an antique, but the Road King uses the same vibration-isolating frame as the Electra Glide touring bikes.

Road King Classic   ($15,960)

With this bike, Harley took its Road King one step further, giving it leather-covered saddlebags, huge whitewall tires, and spoked wheels—none of which contribute in any functional way, but they sure look snazzy.

Dyna Wide Glide ($14,775)

If you want your chopper and want it rubber-mounted, too, this is your bike. This motorcycle has all the characteristics of a classic chopper (high, ape-hanger handlebars; a bobbed rear fender; a tall, skinny front wheel; and a feet-forward riding position), but it also uses Harley's latest-generation vibration-isolating frame.

Dyna Convertible ($14,100)

Harley calls this bike *Convertible,* because the owner can convert it from a touring bike to a cruiser by removing a detachable windshield and a pair of saddlebags.

Dyna Low Rider ($13,750)

Think of this bike as a Wide Glide with more conservative styling.

Dyna Super Glide ($10,865) (Best Buy)

Harley's lowest-priced big twin comes with few frills, but it is basically the same motorcycle as any other in the Dyna series and every bit as competent a motorcycle.

Heritage Softail Classic ($15,275)

This bike comes with every leather surface covered in studs for that maximum Elvis look. If you're not in any particular hurry, a smooth-running Heritage Classic makes a nice touring bike.

Heritage Springer ($17,145)

This bike does the Heritage Classic one better, adding to the Heritage retro formula a springer front end, a design Harley originally abandoned in 1949 on its big twins and the rest of the world abandoned years earlier. Harley's updated springer fork actually works pretty well.

Softail Custom ($14,125)

Think of this one as a Springer Softail with a hydraulic fork.

Springer Softail ($14,765)

This model uses Harley's springer-type fork but mounts it to a motorcycle with traditional chopper-type styling.

Fat Boy ($14,595)

This bike was not very popular when introduced in 1990, but when Arnold Schwarzenegger chose it as his mount for *Terminator 2: Judgment Day*, it suddenly became the Harley to have if you wanted people to think you were on Hollywood's A-list.

Sportster Sport ($8,395)

When Harley decided to try to put the concept of sport back into the Sportster line, it built this 1200cc (74-cubic-inch) hot-rod machine. With its top-of-the-line suspension components, this may be one of the best-handling Harleys ever built.

Sportster Custom ($8,670)

This is Harley's Sportster styled for the chopper crowd.

Sportster 1200 ($7,610)

Harley's generic version of the 1200 Sportster.

Sportster 883   **($5,245)**

Being Harley's price leader, this bike has fewer frills and extras than any other bike you can buy, but it's still a Harley. For a lot of people, that's enough.

Sportster 883 Hugger   **($5,945)**

By using suspension components with less travel, Harley got the seat height down to about knee level, making the bike rougher riding in return. For this, along with a couple of chrome doo-dads and a pair of buckhorn handlebars, you'll pay a $700 premium over a standard 883.

Honda

In his 1966 book, *The Hell's Angels: A Strange and Terrible Saga,* author Hunter S. Thompson writes of a recurring nightmare in which he is offered cheap Honda stock but passes it up. If that was a nightmare in 1966, it would be infinitely more of one today. Honda is the dominant force in the motorcycle industry. Harley may have a lock on the big cruiser market, but Honda dominates just about every other market segment. To understand why this is, you need look no further than Honda's bike lineup.

Gold Wing SE   **($17,399)**

Since its introduction in 1975, Honda's Gold Wing has defined touring motorcycles. Today's Gold Wings, with their 1500cc six-cylinder engines, are the best yet. The SE version has every amenity conceivable, yet in the hands of an experienced rider, it can run with bikes half its considerable size. Many people consider this bike the ultimate ultimate behemoth.

Gold Wing Aspencade   ($15,199)

This one's a bit less well-equipped than the SE version, but that's like saying one sumo wrestler is fatter than the next. So what? The Aspencade still has more features than any sane person would dare ask for.

PC800 Pacific Coast   ($8,600) (Best Buy)

Powered by an 800cc V-twin with shaft drive and hydraulically-adjusted valves, this bike is good for years of trouble-free service. Its unique trunk/saddlebags make it exceptionally useful. While this may be too much bike for a beginner, it's easier to ride than any other touring bike.

Valkyrie   ($12,799) (Best Buy)

This "Übercruiser" defies the laws of physics. The thing weighs over 700 pounds with a full tank of gas yet feels nimble out on the road. And when you open the throttle, it's like taking off in a jet plane. It also has some of the best brakes in the business. This one is definitely too much bike for a beginner, but it's one great cruiser.

Valkyrie Tourer   ($14,199)

This bike, with its hard saddlebags and big windshield, adds an extra bit of practicality to the Valkyrie formula.

CBR1100XX   ($11,499)

Not really a sportbike, but not a sport tourer, either, the only category this bike fits into is *fast*. In fact, it is one of the two fastest motorcycles ever sold to the public (the other is Kawasaki's ZX11). Either of these bikes is capable of an honest 175 miles per hour. If that sort of thing is important to you, these are your bikes.

ST1100   ($11,799)

Honda's big sport-touring bike is one of the finest sport tourers available, but it is not a bike for inexperienced riders. Expect to drop an extra $2,500 to get one with antilock brakes.

VFR800F Interceptor   ($9,499)

Although this is another experts-only-need-apply model, it is a remarkably versatile machine, with plenty of sporting potential, yet comfortable enough for everyday riding and sport touring. While this is a favorite among the sport-touring crowd, Honda continues to confound observers by not offering integrated hard saddlebags on this model.

CBR900RR   ($9,999)

Called the *Fireblade* in Europe, the 900RR is one of the most potent sportbikes on the face of the planet and is best suited to experienced riders.

CBR600F3 ($7,799)

One of the best-selling bikes in the world, the F3 is America's most popular 600cc motorcycle, both on and off the racetrack. While this, like the other 600cc bikes, may seem like a small motorcycle, it's an extremely potent machine, and if you get on one of these before you're ready, you can get yourself in deep trouble.

CBR600F3 Smokin' Joe's Edition ($8,199)

Identical to the normal F3, this version sports the same paint job as Miguel Duhammel's championship-winning race bike. In case you haven't guessed, Duhammel is sponsored by a cigarette company, and Smokin' Joe alludes to a certain carcinogen-huffing dromedary.

VT1100T Shadow Tourer ($10,999) (Best Buy)

The 1100 Shadow line uses two versions of one engine to power four different models. One version uses a staggered crankshaft to calm the shaking inherent in such a design, while the other version uses a single-pin crankshaft that makes the bike vibrate like a Harley. The Tourer uses the smoother engine, combined with hard luggage and a windshield for those of you with long-distance travel aspirations.

VT1100C1 Shadow Spirit ($8,599) (Best Buy)

This model combines the Tourer's smooth engine with chopperesque styling. It's also the best deal in the 1100 Shadow lineup. These are very reliable motorcycles.

VT1100C2 Shadow American Classic Edition　　　　($9,199)

This model uses the vibrating version of the 1100 V-twin engine. A very attractive cruiser, but down on power compared to the Spirit or Tourer versions.

VT1100C3 Shadow Aero　　　　($9,699)

A different styling treatment distinguishes this bike from the American Classic Edition.

VT750C Shadow American Classic Edition　　　　($6,299)
(Best Buy) (Best First Bike)

Photo not available

While the 750 Shadows are less expensive than their larger siblings and just as attractive, they require more routine maintenance because they have chain final drives and manually-adjusted valves. Despite the extra maintenance, they are still nice bikes. Any of the small Shadows make good bikes for a beginner.

VT750D Shadow American Classic Edition Deluxe　　　　($6,599)
(Best Buy) (Best First Bike)

The same as the regular 750 Shadow, with a few chrome bits and a fancy paint job thrown in.

VT600D Shadow VLX Deluxe (Best Buy) (Best First Bike) ($5,999)

The small Shadows are maneuverable and fairly comfortable bikes, with roomy riding positions. With a windshield and some saddlebags, you can even tour on them. The VLX is no exception.

VF750 Magna ($7,499)

Photo not available

This cruiser uses a V-four engine instead of the more common V-twin. While it doesn't have as much snort as a Valkyrie, this hot-rod bike will blow the chrome off any of the Shadows. It handles fairly well for a cruiser, too.

Although many new riders may be intimidated by its size, the broad V-four powerband makes this a fairly easy bike to learn on.

CB750 Nighthawk (Best Buy) (Best First Bike) ($5,799)

Even though this is a fairly large bike, it makes a great motorcycle for new riders. Its combination of balance, stability, and maneuverability makes it much easier to ride than most other 750cc bikes. And because it's a 750, you can ride it an entire lifetime without outgrowing it. Combine its grace with its low price and easy maintenance, and this bike may be one of the best values in motorcycling.

XR650L (Best Buy) (Best First Bike) ($5,499)

If you want a street-legal motorcycle that is capable of serious off-road riding, this is your bike.

Kawasaki

Back in the 1960s and 1970s, Kawasaki built a reputation as *the* performance company, first bringing its infamous three-cylinder two-stroke bikes to the United States, then dropping the Z-1 on us. Today, Kawasaki still builds some of the hottest sportbikes on the market, but it's rapidly earning a reputation as the source of the best deals in all of motorcycling.

Vulcan 1500 Classic   ($10,699) (Best Buy)

Kawasaki's entry into the big V-twin cruiser market may just be one of the best buys in cruiserdom. This is a big bike, too big for most beginners, but there's a lot to like about the Vulcan—like shaft drive, hydraulically-adjusted valves, the recent addition of a fifth gear to the transmission, and those all-important retro looks.

Vulcan 1500 Nomad   ($11,999) (Best Buy)

The $1,300 you'll spend by choosing the Nomad over the Classic will buy you a lot of nice stuff—like a windshield; hard, lockable luggage; cast wheels; tubeless tires; a stiffer frame; triple disc brakes; air-adjustable suspension; and more.

Vulcan 1500   ($8,699) (Best Buy)

This is basically the same bike Kawasaki introduced in the late 1980s. The styling of this bike has been criticized, but its low price and powerful engine keep customers coming back.

Vulcan 800 Classic ($6,999)
(Best Buy) (Best First Bike)

Kawasaki's 800 Vulcan series use a frame with hidden shocks, like Harley's Softail series and Honda's VLX, to give the bike that antique Hardtail look. These bikes don't have the snort of their bigger siblings, but they have more than enough power and make better beginners' bikes. The Classic has a more antique, retro look.

Vulcan 800 ($6,499)
(Best Buy) (Best First Bike)

The same basic bike as the Classic, but with chopperesque styling.

Vulcan 750 ($5,999)
(Best Buy) (Best First Bike)

Kawasaki introduced this one way back in the fall of 1984 as a 700 and has changed it little since then. Kawasaki went the high-tech route with the original Vulcan, but that proved an unpopular path, so the 750 has many features not found on newer mid-sized Vulcans, like hydraulically adjusted valves (four per cylinder) and shaft drive.

Vulcan 500 LTD ($4,999)
(Best Buy) (Best First Bike)

This bike has the distinction of being the only Vulcan that doesn't use a V-twin engine. Rather, it relies on a parallel twin appropriated from the 500 Ninja. Which is not a bad thing, since the little Ninja engine is a famous overachiever.

Voyager XII   ($12,399)

This bike represents Honda Gold Wing's last remaining competitor from Japan for the title of ultimate behemoth touring bike, but in actuality, the only area where this bike is competitive is in price. These are very nice touring bikes but are not in the same league as the Gold Wing.

Concours   ($7,999) (Best Buy)

This is a Kawasaki's entry into the sport-touring market, which is dominated by bikes like Honda's ST1100. This bike, introduced in 1986, set the standard for such bikes back then, but today it is overshadowed by newer bikes like the ST1100 and BMW's R1100RT. But at this price, and just a tick over half the price of the Beemer, who cares? This has to be the best buy in all of motorcycling.

Ninja ZX11   ($10,599)

Either the fastest or second-fastest motorcycle in the world, depending on which magazine you read. If you live in a world where law-enforcement officials let you drive at speeds nearing 200 mph, that's important. Otherwise, it's academic. The biggest Ninja is a nice bike, but it is definitely not for a beginner.

Ninja ZX9R   ($9,999)

Photo not available

While this one won't outrun the ZX11 on a straight road, it will show the bigger bike its tail on any twisty road. Because it is much lighter than the 11, the ZX9R makes a much better sportbike. Although the 9 will only hit a paltry 169 mph (compared to the 11's 175 mph), this is still way too much motorcycle for anyone but an experienced racer.

Ninja ZX7R   ($8,999)

This bike exists only for superbike racing, which it does well. Doug Chandler won the AMA Superbike series in 1996 and 1997 on one of these. But it's too uncompromising to make a functional streetbike. It's one of the most uncomfortable motorcycles you can buy. If you're looking for something resembling a practical motorcycle, look elsewhere.

Ninja ZX6R   ($7,999)

This bike's a bit more comfortable than the ZX7R, but its intended purpose is still racing; because of that, its usefulness in the real world suffers.

Ninja ZX6   ($6,999) (Best Buy)

The ZX6, predecessor to the ZXR, gives up a little performance to the latest repli-racers, but it makes up for it by being a surprisingly versatile streetbike. And what little performance it gives up is unusable by most mere mortals living in the real world, anyway. Even though this is a usable, all-around motorcycle, its abrupt throttle response makes it difficult for a beginner to master.

Ninja 500R   ($4,999)
(Best Buy) (Best First Bike)

This is one of the best beginner bikes on the market. Its forgiving 500cc parallel twin allows new riders to develop crucial skills, like smooth throttle application, yet packs enough power to keep you entertained for years. Its nimble chassis and light weight make the bike easy to learn on, yet in the hands of an experienced rider, it can run with the best bikes out there.

Ninja 250R
(Best Buy) (Best First Bike)

($2,999)

This is the most motorcycle you can buy for less than $3,000. Although this is only a 250, its high-tech liquid-cooled parallel twin has enough power for freeway riding.

KLR650
(Best Buy) (Best First Bike)

($4,799)

This bike is the beststreetbike of all the big thumper dual sports. You might not want to take it up a horse trail through the Rocky Mountains, but it works quite well on unpaved roads and even logging trails and fire roads. Plus, it costs $700 less than Honda's XR650L.

KLR250

($3,949)

While 250cc dual sports are fun and very easy to learn on, 250cc single-cylinder engines tend to lack the power for long-distance freeway riding. Unless you specifically want a dual sport, I recommend getting the Ninja 250R instead.

KTM

KTM is an Austrian company that specializes in off-road-only bikes. In recent years, it has branched into dual sports and streetbikes.

Duke

(Price not available)

If you have confidence in your self control, this 609cc thumper may make a decent learner's bike, but because it is so light and handles so well, it tends to bring out the worst behavior in many riders.

620 R/Xce   ($6,298)

KTM's dual sports make great dirtbikes, but you pay for that capability, both in dollars and in versatility—to create a machine with such high off-road capabilities, KTM engineers had to sacrifice some on-road ability.

400 R/Xce   ($6,598)

Photo not available

The 400's not as good a streetbike as the 620, but it's an even better dirtbike.

Laverda

The Italian company Laverda, on the verge of extinction for nearly a generation, recently began exporting motorcycles to the United States for the first time since Ronald Reagan's first term in office.

750S Formula   ($13,900)

The 748cc parallel twin powering this sportbike is thoroughly modern in every way, but so is this bike's price.

750S   ($11,800)

A milder version of the Formula.

668 Diamante   ($10,250)

This bike, with its air-and-oil-cooled engine, isn't quite as modern as the 750, but it costs a lot less.

668 Ghost   ($8,995)

This is Laverda's naked standard version of the Diamante. While it costs considerably less than any other Laverda, it still costs more than Ducati's M750 Monster, its closest competitor.

Moto Guzzi

Moto Guzzi, Italy's oldest motorcycle manufacturer, has a world-wide following that rivals Harley-Davidson's in customer loyalty. While Moto Guzzi doesn't import a bike into the United States that could be considered a beginner's bike, the torquey V-twin engine powering all of its motorcycles is easy to use.

Because of throttle stiffness on carbureted Guzzis, I would not recommend any older Moto Guzzi to a beginner. In recent years, however, Moto Guzzi has switched to fuel injection, which has eliminated much of this throttle stiffness.

V11EV California   ($11,690)

For a cruiser, the California is quite nimble and easy to ride. Past Guzzis have had archaic linked-brake systems that can distract a rider and tend to need frequent expensive repair, but many of the problems with these systems have been addressed on this latest California. While too large for a beginner, this is a fine motorcycle and easier to drive than most other large cruisers.

V10 Centuro   ($13,490)

The name is pronounced *Chentarro*. This is one of the most stunning motorcycles on the market, but it may be too quirky to be a practical all-around motorcycle, and it's definitely not a good bike for a beginner.

MZ

Prior to the fall of the Iron Curtain, East German manufacturer MZ was known for its sporting two strokes. Now it is making a name for itself by building Yamaha-powered sporting thumpers.

Skorpion Replica   ($10,500)

The 660cc engine in this limited-edition model, based on MZ's European race bikes, makes a bit more horsepower than other Skorpions, but you'll pay $1,650 a piece for those two ponies. This one is best left to the collectors.

Skorpion Sport Cup   ($7,195) (Best First Bike)

This great-handling, lightweight bike will work for a new rider, but it's more highly strung than most other thumpers, making it harder to master. Even so, it still makes a much better beginner's bike than any of the 600cc four-cylinder sportbikes.

Skorpion Traveler ($7,595) (Best First Bike)

Because of its low weight, MZ's interpretation of a sport tourer, with its 660cc thumper engine, is one of the few sport tourers a new rider won't find intimidating.

Skorpion Mastiff ($7,195) (Best First Bike)

This Skorpion might be named after a big, slobbering dog, but it looks like something else entirely. What that is, I'm not sure. It will work as a first motorcycle, if you like its looks.

Skorpion Baghira ($6,995) (Best First Bike)

Like all the Skorpions, MZ's entry in the big dual-sport thumper market would make a fine first bike, but be prepared to spend more than you would for a Japanese dual sport.

Silverstar Gespann ($7,995)

The Gespann includes a sidecar as standard equipment and is the only MZ to be powered by an engine other than Yamaha's 660cc single. This one uses a Rotax 494cc single. If you're looking for a thumper with a sidecar, your choice is pretty much limited to this rig.

Suzuki

In the late 1980s and early 1990s, Suzuki didn't have the best luck with its new motorcycles, producing a series of unsuccessful bikes like the GSX1100G standard, the RF series sportbikes, and the original GSX-R600 repli-racer, but things seem to be picking up for the company. Its latest lineup is the strongest Suzuki has had in over a decade.

VL1500 Intruder   ($9,899) (Best Buy)

This new bike was developed from Suzuki's VS1400 Intruder, introduced in 1987. That bike has proven reliable over the years, so this newest version should be no exception. And at less than $10,000, it's a bargain. Fortunately, it maintains the 1400's low-maintenance shaft drive.

VS1400 Intruder GLP   ($8,549) (Best Buy)

These big cruisers have been dependable, functional motorcycles over the years, but their long forks make them feel a bit floppy in corners. New riders may find this disconcerting.

VS800GL Intruder   ($6,549)
(Best Buy) (Best First Bike)

Unchanged since its introduction in 1986, the original Intruder's styling doesn't seem as fresh as it did back then, but it's still a pretty bike. It does suffer from the same floppiness as the 1400 version.

VZ800 Marauder
(Best Buy) (Best First Bike)

($6,099)

Photo not available

The $450 you save by buying the Marauder over the 800 Intruder will get you slightly better handling, but you'll sacrifice the shaft drive. Over the years, you will spend more than $450 on chains and sprockets for this one. I'd go with the Intruder.

LS650P Savage

($4,549)

The only thing Savage about this little single-cylinder cruiser is its name. It's an attractive bike, with a low-maintenance drive belt, but the engine is weak, even when compared to other thumpers. If I were in the market for this type of bike, I'd spend the extra $700 and buy a Sportster, just for its superior resale value.

GSF1200S Bandit

($7,199) (Best Buy)

The big Bandit is much too powerful to be a beginner's bike, but for an experienced rider, it may be the best all-around motor-cycle you can buy. It's relatively light; handles great; offers comfort; protects you from the elements with its fairing; and costs less than the latest 600s. You could commute to work on this bike, then throw on some luggage and take it from coast. It's probably closer to a do-everything motorcycle than any bike built.

GSX750F Katana

($7,199)

When Suzuki introduced its Katana series in 1988, they were cutting-edge sportbikes. But over the years, as sportbikes became more extreme, the Katanas seemed more like standard motorcycles. And they are good, comfortable, all-around bikes, although they may be a little intimidating for a beginner. The 750 would earn a best-buy rating, except for the fact that it costs as much as a big Bandit.

GSX600F Katana
(Best Buy) (Best First Bike)

($6,199)

You don't give up all that much when you choose the 600 over the 750 Katana, but you do save $1,000. I'm hesitant to recommend the 600 to a new rider, because while far from cutting edge, it is a powerful motorcycle capable of getting you into a lot of trouble. On the other hand, this is a very nice motorcycle—one you can both learn on and live with for a long time.

GSF600S Bandit
(Best Buy) (Best First Bike)

($5,699)

A smaller version of the 1200 Bandit, this bike still offers all the performance any sane person can use on a public road. Mechanically similar to the 600 Katana, the Bandit gives up a bit of handling to the Katana, along with a dab of weather protection, but it costs $500 less.

GS500E
(Best Buy) (Best First Bike)

($4,299)

This bike traces its roots back to the mid-1970s and Suzuki's first four-stroke motorcycle. It's a fun, inexpensive bike, similar to Kawasaki's 500 Ninja, but it's a bit underpowered compared to the Ninja. I believe most riders will outgrow the GS500 before they tire of the Ninja.

GSX-R1100

($10,499)

This bike really only exists for open-class racers and lunatics who ride on the street as if they were on a racetrack. It's too uncomfortable for everyday use and much too powerful for a beginner (and even most experienced riders). If you were ready for a bike like this, you wouldn't be reading this book.

TL1000R   ($9,499)

Suzuki's Ducati-challenging V-twin sportbike; the comments about the GSX-R1100 apply to the TL, and then some.

TL1000S   ($8,999)

Suzuki makes two distinct versions of its V-twin sportbike. Both use the same engine, with different frames. Neither is comfortable enough for real-world use, but the R is even more uncomfortable than the S. While they are both cutting-edge sportbikes, because of their abrupt power delivery, they both make about the worst first bikes conceivable.

GSX-R750   ($9,299)

This bike was built for the sole purpose of winning superbike races, and while it is more comfortable than the GSX-R1100, the riding position is still too extreme for most nonracetrack applications. In the right hands, this can be the fastest bike on the road, but only the most advanced riders (usually people with considerable racetrack experience) can get the optimum performance from this racetrack-oriented engine. It's not an easy bike to ride, even for experts.

GSX-R600   ($7,799)

A smaller version of the 750, the 600 was built to compete in supersport racing and is a poor choice for a beginner looking for a streetbike.

DR650SE   ($5,349)
(Best Buy) (Best First Bike)

This bike splits the difference between the dirt-worthiness of Honda's XR650L and the on-road capability of Kawasaki's KLR650. For many people, this is the ideal dual sport.

DR350SE   ($4,649)
(Best Buy) (Best First Bike)

Photo not available

The smaller DR is an easier bike to ride off-road, but for that, you'll give up a bit of on-road capability (you'll also save $700).

DR200SE   ($3,799)

Like Kawasaki's KLR 250, this is an easy bike to learn to ride on, but one you'll probably outgrow too soon.

Triumph

The Triumph motorcycle company selling bikes today is not the same as Triumph Cycle Ltd., established in England back in 1903. The last of the old Triumph motorcycles, descendants of Edward Turner's original Speed Twin, rolled off the assembly line in 1982. British investor John Bloor bought the name and applied it to a line of thoroughly-modern motorcycles he began selling in 1991. Unlike the troublesome Triumphs of old, these bikes are reliable, functional machines.

Trophy 1200 ($11,795)

Triumph's big Trophy has a rip-snorting four-cylinder engine, attractive bodywork, and excellent integrated luggage. It comes up a little short compared to other sport tourers only because it lacks a shaft final drive, a feature many long-distance riders place a premium on.

Trophy 900 ($10,795)

Although the 900 gives away 300cc and one cylinder (like most Triumphs, the engine is a three cylinder) to the 1200, most riders don't mind, because the 900 is also lighter and handles better than the bigger bike.

Sprint Executive ($8,995) (Best Buy)

This bike has a smaller fairing than the Trophy 900 but otherwise is very similar, right down to the excellent integrated hard luggage. While not the steal that Kawasaki's Concours is, the Executive offers more for your money than just about any other bike.

Sprint Sport ($8,695)

The same basic bike as the Executive, but without the hard luggage and with more power and a more sporting riding position.

Trident 900

($7,995) (Best Buy)

This is the naked version of the standard Triumph triple. All the 900 Triumph triples are a bit too heavy and a bit too powerful for a novice, but their smooth power and abundant torque make them easier to learn on than any other 900cc bikes.

Thunderbird Sport

($8,795) (Best Buy)

This is Triumph's hot-rod cruiser. It is one of the fastest, best-handling cruisers you can buy.

Thunderbird

($8,995)

This is Triumph's attempt to cash in on the nostalgia factor Harley has capitalized on so well. If you squint and look at it from the right angle, it looks a lot like the Thunderbird Marlon Brando rode in *The Wild One*.

Adventurer

($8,995)

This spinoff of the Thunderbird seems to be Triumph's answer to Harley's Wide Glide. Both the Adventurer and Thunderbird are fine all-around motorcycles. Choosing on over the other is simply a matter of personal preference.

T595 Daytona   ($10,695)

If the Adventurer is Triumph's answer to Harley's Wide Glide, then this is Triumph's answer to Ducati's 916, meaning it's a single-purpose, hard-edged sportbike.

T505 Speed Triple   ($9,995)

This is Triumph's new naked bike. Its riding position is too extreme to call it a standard, but it will probably make a better all-around bike than the Daytona. Unlike other models in Triumph's lineup, both the Daytona and Speed Triple use Triumph's latest generation of engines.

Tiger   ($9,995)

This is Triumph's entry in the leviathan dual-sport category. It's a bit too top-heavy to make a good beginner's bike, but the version of the 900cc triple used in the Tiger is the easiest of all versions to ride.

Ural   ($4,495 – $7,795)

Ural motorcycles came into existence during World War II, when the Russians smuggled five BMWs into Russia, dismantled them, then built copies. Today, the bikes built at the Ural factory differ little from those first BMW clones. Ural makes one basic bike, the boxer-powered Solo ($4,495), and sells four versions with sidecar rigs attached, ranging in price from $6,295 to $7,795. Owning a Ural requires a bit more dedication than owning a more modern bike, but Urals have developed a devoted following in this country.

Victory

Polaris Industries, the first American company to produce a brand-new line of motorcycles since the Great Depression, has caused quite a stir in the motorcycle world with its new Victory bikes.

Victory 92C   ($13,000 estimated)

The bike Polaris is using to lead its assault on the motorcycle market is a high-tech, big-inch cruiser that should inhale stock Harley-Davidsons and spit them out through its exhaust pipes, judging by the technical specifications.

Yamaha

Although Yamaha has long held the number-two spot among Japanese motorcycle manufacturers, losing the number-one slot to arch-rival Honda year after year, it builds some of the nicest, most dependable bikes you can buy.

Royal Star Tour Deluxe Solitaire   ($14,999)

This cross between a big cruiser and an ultimate behemoth touring bike has fans from both camps. It's a nice bike, but it's just too large for a new rider, as are all the Royal Stars.

Royal Star Tour Deluxe Deuce   ($15,149)

This is the dual-seat version of the Solitaire, which only has a solo saddle.

Royal Star Tour Classic   **($14,299)**

This is pretty much the same bike as the Tour Deluxe Deuce, but with leather saddlebags instead of the Deluxe's hard luggage.

Royal Star Tour Classic II   **($14,799)**

This version of the Tour Classic has a backrest and passing lamps.

Royal Star Silverado   **($13,949)**

This is as close to a basic Royal Star as you can get. While it's the only Royal Star without a windshield as standard equipment, it is loaded with things like billet-aluminum brake caliper accents and chrome fake cylinder fins.

Royal Star Boulevard   **($13,999)**

This is the Royal Star Elvis would have ridden had Elvis ridden a Royal Star. This bike has more studded leather than any other motorcycle not produced in Milwaukee.

Royal Star Cheyenne   **($13,749)**

The lowest-priced Royal Star makes do without studded leather, but it does have a windshield. It also has the same 1300cc liquid-cooled V-four that powers all Royal Stars.

V-Star Classic   **($5,899)**
(Best Buy) (Best First Bike)

This is only a 650, but you'd never guess by looking at it. It is a full-sized motorcycle with room for real people on board. The engine may be a bit weak for some people, but most novices should find it powerful enough.

V-Star Custom   **($5,599)**
(Best Buy) (Best First Bike)

This is the chopper version of the V-Star.

Virago 1100   **($7,799) (Best Buy)**

Photo not available

This bike was introduced as a 1000 back in 1984 and has had only detail changes since then. Which is not bad, since it has always been a lot of fun. It might have a bit too much power for some beginners, but it is a fairly small bike compared to other 1100s.

Virago 535   **($5,299)**

This is certainly an easy enough motorcycle to drive, but it's small for average-sized adults and underpowered even for a beginner. You'd be better off spending the extra $300 for the V-Star Custom.

Virago 250   **($3,999)**

While this makes an ideal bike for your first few weeks of riding, it is just too small for real-world use. It is a cute little thing, though.

V-Max   **($10,499)**

If this bike were a film, it would be rated XXX. Trying to learn to ride on this powerful beast would be like trying to learn to drive in a nitro-burning dragster. The V-Max is a fantastic motorcycle, but it is not for the novice or faint of heart.

YZF-R1   **($10,199)**

This is one of the most potent sportbikes you can buy, but while it may impress your friends, it will do little to help you develop your riding skills.

YZF750R   ($8,799)

While this bike may be a bit more comfortable than most 750cc repli-racers, it's still too race-oriented to make a useful all-around motorcycle.

YZF600R   ($7,399) (Best Buy)

This is the best all-around motorcycle in the 600cc sportbike class, but like any bike from that group, it's still ill-suited for a beginner.

FZR600   ($5,299) (Best Buy)

This was Yamaha's cutting-edge sportbike in 1988, and it is still competent enough to remain in Yamaha's lineup. While this bike offers more performance per dollar than any other 600 sportbike, it is even less well-suited for a beginner than the YZF600R.

Seca II   ($5,299)
(Best Buy) (Best First Bike)

This sporty 600cc four-cylinder bike combines good looks, comfort, and great handling with adequate power for even experienced riders, making it not just a great beginner's bike, but a great bike for anyone.

XT350   **($4,449) (Best First Bike)**

Photo not available

Yamaha's XT350 provides adequate, if not stellar, power for riding in traffic. The advantage 350s have over the bigger thumpers is that they are lighter and easier to ride, both on- and off-road. Personally, I'd spend the extra $350 and buy the bigger Kawasaki KLR 650, a more useful all-around motorcycle.

XT225   **($3,849)**

Photo not available

These are nice enough bikes and are easy to learn on, but in the long run, they are best left to the kids.

TW200   **($3,399)**

Photo not available

This is sort of a hybrid between a dual-sport bike and an all-terrain vehicle. It is not really suited for use on public roads.

Best First Bikes

BMW F650ST

BMW R1100R

Honda CB750 Nighthawk

Honda VT600D Shadow VLX Deluxe

Honda VT750C Shadow American Classic Edition

Honda VT750D Shadow American Classic Edition Deluxe

Honda XR650L

Kawasaki KLR650

Kawasaki Ninja 250R

Kawasaki Ninja 500R

Kawasaki Vulcan 500 LTD

Kawasaki Vulcan 750

Kawasaki Vulcan 800

Kawasaki Vulcan 800 Classic

MZ Skorpion Baghira

MZ Skorpion Mastiff

MZ Skorpion Sport Cup

MZ Skorpion Traveler

Suzuki DR350SE

Suzuki DR650SE

Suzuki GS500E

Suzuki GSF600S Bandit

Suzuki GSX600F Katana

Suzuki VS800GL Intruder

Suzuki VZ800 Marauder

Yamaha Seca II

Yamaha V-Star Classic

Yamaha V-Star Custom

Yamaha XT350

Best Buys

Harley-Davidson Dyna Super Glide

Harley-Davidson Electra Glide Standard

Honda CB750 Nighthawk

Honda PC800 Pacific Coast

Honda Valkyrie

Honda VT600D Shadow VLX Deluxe

Honda VT750D Shadow American Classic Edition

Honda VT750D Shadow American Classic Edition Deluxe

Honda VT1100C1 Shadow Spirit

Honda VT1100T Shadow Tourer

Honda XR650L

Kawasaki Concours

Kawasaki KLR650

Kawasaki Ninja 250R

Kawasaki Ninja 500R

Kawasaki Ninja ZX6

Kawasaki Vulcan 500 LTD

Kawasaki Vulcan 750

Kawasaki Vulcan 800

Kawasaki Vulcan 800 Classic

Kawasaki Vulcan 1500

Kawasaki Vulcan 1500 Classic

Kawasaki Vulcan 1500 Nomad

Suzuki DR350SE

Suzuki DR650SE

Suzuki GS500E

Suzuki GSF600S Bandit

Suzuki GSF1200S Bandit

Suzuki GSX600F Katana

Suzuki VL1500 Intruder

Suzuki VS800GL Intruder

Suzuki VS1400 Intruder GLP

Suzuki VZ800 Marauder

Triumph Sprint Executive

Triumph Thunderbird Sport

Triumph Trident 900

Yamaha FZR600

Yamaha Seca II

Yamaha V-Star Classic

Yamaha V-Star Custom

Yamaha Virago 1100

Yamaha YZF600R

Best First Bikes and Best Buys

Honda CB750 Nighthawk

Honda VT600D Shadow VLX Deluxe

Honda VT750D Shadow American Classic Edition

Honda VT750D Shadow American Classic Edition Deluxe

Honda XR650L

Kawasaki KLR650

Kawasaki Ninja 250R

Kawasaki Ninja 500R

Kawasaki Vulcan 500 LTD

Kawasaki Vulcan 750

Kawasaki Vulcan 800

Kawasaki Vulcan 800 Classic

Suzuki DR350SE

Suzuki DR650SE

Suzuki GS500E

Suzuki GSF600S Bandit

Suzuki GSX600F Katana

Suzuki VS800GL Intruder

Suzuki VZ800 Marauder

Yamaha Seca II

Yamaha V-Star Classic

Yamaha V-Star Custom

Give an old bike a good home

Biker's Buying Guide to Used Bikes

Appendix A listed just about every new streetbike sold in the United States, some of which can honestly be called bargains. But as you may have noted, even the so-called bargains will require you to lay out some serious cash before you can park one in your garage.

If the price of a new bike is beyond your means, you needn't worry much; the used-bike market can help get you on two wheels.

While some motorcyclists trash their machines, most keep them in fairly good condition. Many of the used bikes you'll find will be in nearly the same shape as a new bike.

In Chapter 7, "Buying Your First Bike," I told you how to make certain a used bike is in sound mechanical shape. In this appendix, I'll list some used bikes that will make exceptional first motorcycles.

Since prices of used bikes vary according to a variety of factors, from the condition of the bike to locale, I'm not including prices in this guide. Generally, bikes that cost more new tend to cost more used. Just as a new BMW costs more than a new Kawasaki, so will a used BMW cost more than a used Kawasaki.

As with the "Biker's Buying Guide to New Bikes" in Appendix A, I've listed the used bikes alphabetically, by make. I've only included bikes manufactured since 1982. There are some good, dependable motorcycles manufactured before that time, and if you find one that runs well and is in good shape, you shouldn't pass it up just because it's old. But be aware that you will have more mechanical trouble with older bikes than with newer bikes. In addition, technological advances from the early 1980s to the present make motorcycles manufactured since then safer and more practical.

For more information, The *AMA Official Motorcycle Value Guide* is one of the best sources I've found for accurate used-bike prices. An annual subscription costs $30, and you can purchase individual copies for $12.95. Call CPI, Ltd., the publishers of the guide, at 800/972-5312.

BMW

Like new BMWs, used Beemers tend to cost more than most other bikes, but they are well worth the extra money. The care with which these bikes are built means they tend to last longer than most other motorcycles.

R80GS/R100GS

These big Beemer dual sports, the original leviathans of the trail-bike world, might be a bit of a handful for a new rider, but their torquey, tractable engines and overall balance make them much easier to ride than other bikes of similar engine displacement. These are expensive motorcycles, but they tend to last a long time.

R80/R80ST

This is a street-only version of the original R80GS dual sport. The R80s are even easier for an inexperienced rider to learn on than the GS series, because they have lower seats—a factor that seems to make new riders feel more secure. The R80s are relative bargains, too. These are some of the few used Beemers you'll find priced under three grand.

K75/K75S/K75C

These bikes use three-cylinder versions of BMW's unique flat four-cylinder engine. They are rather large bikes for a beginner, but like the R80 and R100 boxer twins, their power-delivery characteristics make them easy to ride. And like the boxers, they tend to cost more than most other used bikes.

Honda

Honda motorcycles rival BMWs when it comes to quality, and you'll find a lot of nice, used Hondas out there. The fit and finish tends be of higher quality on Hondas than on most other bikes.

NX650

Back in the late 1980s, Honda decided to produce a dual sport that didn't look like a dual sport (or like anything else the motorcycling world had seen before). The result was the unique NX650, a streetbike based on Honda's XL600R dual sport. Honda created a rather interesting and useful street thumper, one that will cost you less than half of what the cheapest new 650 thumper will cost you.

XL350R/XL500R/XL600R

These bikes are rather crude compared to the newer XR650R dual sports, but in their day, they were the nicest trail bikes around. The dual-carburetion system of the XL600R can cause the power delivery to seem a bit abrupt, making that bike more difficult for a novice to master than some other thumpers, but considering that used XLs will only cost you between $750 and $1,500, you can probably learn to live with it.

XL600V Transalp

This V-twin dual sport, which was only imported into the United States in 1989 and 1990, is one of the best all-around motorcycles produced that year and very easy for a beginning rider to master. This model is very popular in Europe.

VTR250 Interceptor

While only a 250, this little V-twin sportbike is capable of freeway riding. It is also a fun, good-handling little bugger, and pretty, too.

CB650SC/CB700SC Nighthawks

If you're looking for a good inline four-cylinder Japanese motorcycle, I highly recommend Honda's original Nighthawk series. In fact, I (and many motorcyclists) prefer them to the newer 750 Nighthawks, simply because they have shaft drives, while the newer Nighthawks have chains. Even with shaft drives, they are some of the best-handling motorcycles of their day. Some riders take issue with their 16-inch front wheels, which make these bikes seem a bit twitchy in some circumstances, although I've found that many novices prefer the maneuverability those same wheels provide.

CB750 Nighthawk

While the newer Nighthawk hasn't won me over quite like the older version, it is still a fantastic all-around motorcycle, and a clean used example represents an even better value than a new one.

FT500/VT500 Ascots

These are two very different bikes—the FT uses an air-cooled, single-cylinder engine derived from the XL500 dual sport, while the VT uses a liquid-cooled V-twin lifted from the 500 Shadow—but both make excellent first bikes. For some reason, perhaps because of the increase in interest in thumper streetbikes, the price of an FT has actually climbed a bit in recent years.

NT 650 Hawk GT

These little V-twin sportbikes have become more popular since Honda stopped importing them to the United States. They are more fun on a twisty road than just about any motorcycle I've ever ridden, and one of my greatest regrets is not buying one. The only drawback is that they're a bit cramped for riders over six feet tall.

VF500C V30 Magna/VF500F Interceptor

Both these bikes use different versions of the same engine. The Magna surrounds the engine with one of history's most elegant little cruisers, while the Interceptor is the finest-handling motorcycle built in the mid-1980s.

VT500/VT600/VT700/VT750/VT800 Shadows

The Shadow cruiser line contains some of the most reliable motorcycles manufactured in the past couple of decades. I especially recommend the 1986–87 VT700 Shadows, which combine striking looks and genuine comfort with the low maintenance of shaft drive and hydraulically-adjusted valves. In my opinion, this model makes a better all-around motorcycle than any of the new mid-size cruisers. The 1988 VT800 looks much the same as the VT700, but it only comes with a four-speed transmission, detracting from its versatility.

Kawasaki

Because Kawasaki had a reputation as a high-performance company, many Kawasaki motorcycles will have seen hard use. But they were rugged bikes, and they could withstand a lot of abuse.

KLR600/KLR650/KL650-B2 Tengai/KLX650

Not much has changed in the KLR line since the 600 first appeared in 1984, which is a good thing, since it's such a good basic motorcycle. The Tengai is a funky rally-style version (one of the most unique-looking dual sports to come out of Japan), and the KLX is a more off-road-worthy machine. All make fine first bikes.

EL250 Eliminator

This nifty little power cruiser shares its engine with the EX250 Ninja, meaning that it is a snappy bike. These motorcycles are easy to ride, plenty fast, and with their small bikini fairings, just about the cutest bikes ever made.

EX250 Ninja

This is the same bike as the 250 Ninja that Kawasaki sells today, and it hasn't changed much since its introduction in 1986, except for graphics. If the new bike is a best buy, the used version is even better.

EN450 454 LTD/EN500 Vulcan 500

These ancestors to the new Vulcan 500 LTD are fast little cruisers, but many people question their styling. If you don't mind the way they look, they are useful bikes.

EX500/500 Ninja

Kawasaki has made incremental improvements to its 500 Ninja over its 11-year production run, but the original is still a very good bike, and a 1987 model will cost about two-thirds less than what you'll pay for a new model.

KZ550/KZ550 LTD/KZ550 GPz/KZ550 Spectre

Kawasaki's 550 four-cylinder bike was impressive when it first appeared, and it's still an impressive bike today. Reliable as a clawhammer, the 550 still has enough power to get you into serious trouble with legal authorities. The best of the bunch is the GPz, which practically created the current 600cc sportbike class.

ZR550 Zephyr

Although a very good bike, this isn't noticeably better than its predecessor, the KZ550, but it costs more. Still, if you can find a deal on a ZR550 Zephyr, you'll have a great motorcycle.

VN700/750 Vulcan

If you can get past the styling of this one, you'll find a great motorcycle underneath.

ZL600 Eliminator

This is a fun, easy-to-ride power cruiser. Its main drawback is a too-small fuel tank that can barely go 100 miles between fillups.

Suzuki

Suzuki has built some unique, often highly functional motorcycles, but throughout the company's history, designers have occasionally created bikes the buying public has not warmed up to. One such bike, the rotary-engined RE5, almost bankrupted the company. On the other hand, when Suzuki designers get the look of a bike right, they create some of the prettiest machines on the road.

DR350S/SE/DR650S/SE

Basically, these are the same as the current versions of Suzuki's dual sports, at lower prices.

GS500E

Everything I said about this bike in Appendix A goes for the used version, except the price. These bikes have been popular ultra-light racers, so if you buy a used GS500E, make certain that it hasn't been raced.

GS550E/ES/L/M/GS650G/GL/GS650M Katana

Any of Suzuki's air-cooled four-cylinder 550s and 650s make excellent, dependable bikes, but these are older, so expect them to need small repairs more frequently than newer motorcycles. The switch gear and electrical components are the items most likely to need some attention.

GSF400 Bandit

Some people consider the smallest Bandit, built between 1991 and 1993, one of the best-handling motorcycles ever made. You have to rev the snot out of its little four-cylinder engine, but when you do, it goes like stink.

GSX600F/GSX750F Katanas

These are high-performance sportbikes that require a rider with self control, but they are such good all-around motorcycles that if you think you can trust yourself, you might want to consider buying one.

VX800

This capable motorcycle might be a bit much for most new riders, but those who feel comfortable with a bike of this size will find it a best buy. It is one of the most versatile motorcycles built during the past decade.

Yamaha

I have a special fondness for Yamahas. My first real motorcycle was a Yamaha. I've owned more than one dozen Yamahas over the years, and currently own two of them. They are rugged, well-constructed bikes. The fit and finish aren't always up to Honda's standards. Don't be surprised to find chrome plating peeling off older Yamahas.

XT350/XT550/XT600

This bike traces its roots back to the original big Japanese thumper, the XT500 of the 1970s. Although it was a very nice dual sport, it wasn't competitive with the other thumpers from Japan and was discontinued in 1995.

XJ550 Seca/Maxim/XJ650 Seca/Maxim/XJ700 Maxim

Yamaha's first four-cylinder mid-sized engine series, which powers all these bikes, set new standards for performance when introduced in 1981 and has proven rugged and dependable over the years. The same basic engine design is still used in the 1998 Seca II.

FJ600

Although considered a sportbike in its day, the FJ seems like a standard today. With its frame-mounted half fairings and sporty riding position, this bike is still striking today. If you can find a clean example of this elegant bike, buy it.

YX600 Radian

The successor to the FJ600 had all that bike's mechanical virtues but lacked the FJ's style. It's still a good bike, though.

XJ600S Seca II

If a new Seca II costing $5,300 is a best buy, then buying a six-year-old version of the exact same machine for $3,000 less should earn the buyer a place in the bargain-hunter's hall of fame. Some models have cheap, tacky stickers marring the clean, elegant lines of the bike, but don't worry—they come off easily.

Resources

Throughout this book, I've discussed what a wonderful community of people you will meet when you become a motorcyclist. This appendix will tell you how to get in touch with that community. I'll list the addresses of some major clubs and organizations, and I'll also tell you where you can find all the books, videotapes, accessories, and other paraphernalia you'll want and need.

Motorcycle Safety Foundation (MSF)

The Motorcycle Safety Foundation is a national, nonprofit organization sponsored by the U.S. distributors of Honda, Kawasaki, Suzuki, Yamaha, and BMW motorcycles. I've tried to stress the value of taking a Motorcycle Safety Foundation RiderCourse, but in case I haven't made myself perfectly clear, taking such a course can save your life. No other action you can take will help you have a safer motorcycling career. To find a RiderCourse near you, contact

Motorcycle Safety Foundation
2 Jenner St., Suite 150
Irvine, CA 92718–3812
800/447-4700

American Motorcyclist Association (AMA)

Taking an MSF RiderCourse is the most important thing you can do to help make you a safer rider. Joining the AMA is the most important thing you can do to safeguard your rights as a motorcyclist. Contact the AMA today at

American Motorcyclist Association
33 Collegeview Rd.
Westerville, OH 43081-1484
800/AMA-JOIN
ama@ama-cycle.org
http://ama-cycle.org/

Clubs and Organizations

As I said in Chapter 19, "Join the Club: Motorcycle Clubs," joining a club can be your best way to get in touch with your local motorcycling community. The following list gives you the names and addresses of just a few of the thousands of clubs available.

American Sport Touring Riders Association (ASTRA)

Much controversy exists about what separates sport touring from regular touring, but in reality, it matters little. In the end, sport touring seems to be as much about your frame of mind as it is about what you ride, and the folks in ASTRA seem to agree—their members ride a wide variety of motorcycles. You can contact ASTRA at:

American Sport Touring Riders Association
P.O. Box 672051
Marietta, GA 30067-0035
770/222-0380
astra@info-gw.com

Bavarian Illuminati Motorcycle Club and Conspiracy

I don't know much about this club, except that it has a terrific suggested-reading list, and its web site has some interesting links. Contact Club Dominatrix and Co-President Ilsa Super Sexy at:

http://www.wilder.net/bimc/home.htm

Biker Scum

Biker Scum is a motorcycle group dedicated to the pursuit of happiness through riding and the neglect of personal hygiene. Their goal is to form a worldwide network of riders, connected via the Internet, that assist other motorcyclists when planning trips, specifically by giving them advice on local roads and brew pubs. So far, they have chapters in Pennsylvania; Texas; Virginia; California; Indiana; Ontario, Canada; and Okinawa, Japan. Other chapters are planned for Estonia and England. To contact Biker Scum, send e-mail to:

Dan Lubell
drlubell@cts.com

Blue Knights

The Blue Knights is a club specifically for law-enforcement officials, with chapters located in all 50 states, as well as in 12 countries. To find the chapter nearest you, contact:

Blue Knights International Law Enforcement Motorcycle Club, Inc.
International Headquarters
38 Alden St.
Bangor, ME 04401
207/947-4600
207/947-5814 (fax)

BMW Motorcycle Owners of America (BMWMOA)

I have to admit to being less than objective when it comes to BMW motorcycles. I think they are the finest motorcycles you can buy and worth the extra money. Plus, when you buy a BMW, you get to join BMWMOA, which in itself justifies spending a bit more for your bike. BMWMOA has chapters across the country and puts on some of the best rallies you'll find anywhere. Plus, it puts out an excellent monthly magazine. You can contact its national headquarters at:

BMW Motorcycle Owners of America
P.O. Box 89
Chesterfield, MO 63006
314/537-5511
bmwmoa@aol.com
http://www.bmwmoa.org/

Christian Motorcyclists Association (CMA)

As I said in Chapter 1, "The Motorcycle Mystique," motorcycling is a spiritual activity—so much so that some people like to formally combine it with their religion. If you would like to do the same, a great way to do so is by joining the CMA. These folks put on some terrific events and have chapters all across the country. Contact them at:

Christian Motorcyclists Association
P.O. Box 9
Hatfield, AR 71945
870/389-6196
http://www.cmausa.com/index.html

EasyRiders

EasyRiders is a California-based club for newcomers to the sport of motorcycling. For more information, contact:

G. David Lapin
EasyRiders
384 East 16th St.
Costa Mesa, CA 92627
714/650-4807

Gold Wing Road Riders Association (GWRRA)

GWRRA is the largest club in the world devoted to a single motorcycle—the Honda Gold Wing. Membership is open to owners of the ultimate behemoth, although the club is considering allowing owners of Honda Valkyries to join, too. You can contact GWRRA at:

Gold Wing Road Riders Association
P.O. Box 42450
Phoenix, AZ 85080-2450
http://www.gwrra.org/

Motor Maids

Motor Maids is not only one of the oldest clubs for female motorcyclists; it's one of the oldest motorcycle clubs, period. Some of the women still riding with Motor Maids were dispatch motorcyclists in World War II. Contact them at:

Motor Maids
P.O. Box 443
Chardon, Ohio 44024

Retreads Motorcycle Club International, Inc.

Retreads Motorcycle Club International boasts a membership of 24,000 motorcyclists, and all of them have at least two things in common: they have reached the age of 40, and they love to ride motorcycles. If you are interested in locating a club near you, contact one of the following addresses:

Arkansas Retreads
George Ayers
P.O. Box 443
Russelville, AR 72811

Bobby Thompson
213 Preston Dr.
Russellville, AR 72811
501/967-7175
bthomps@cswnet.com

Capital District Retreads, New York
Keith & Cindy Lamp
2102 William St.
Schenectady, NY 12036

Colorado Retreads
Bill & Phyllis Ranzinger
7694 South Madison Circle
Littleton, CO 80122
wranzinger@aol.com

Delmarva, Delaware Retreads
Larry & Debbie Wright
125 Belmont Ave.
Smyra, DE 19977

Eastern Pennsylvania Retreads
Dexter & Mary Lou Sturgis
dexter1810@aol.com

Kansas Retreads
Albert & Lois Bacon
905 Michigan St.
Leavenworth, KS 66048

Louisiana Retreads
Ed Campbell
139 Saunders St.
Mansfield, LA 71052

Mid Atlantic Regional
Howard & Ellen Outten
midretread@aol.com

Missouri Retreads
Pete & Sheila Wills
2301 East Parkwood
Springfield, MO 65803-4957

Nature Coast Florida Retreads
Henry Evarts, Director
7080 Wildfire Lane
Homosassa, FL 34448
goldwing@citrus.infi.net

NE Florida Retreads
Carmen & Brenda Varcadipane, Directors
3873 Tropical Terrace
Jacksonville Beach, FL 32250
904/246-7582
carmen57@mediaone.net

New York Retreads
Al Fuerst
19 Hillberry Lane
Holbrook, NY 11741
ghulse@suffolk.lib.ny.us

North Carolina Retreads
Jerry & Glenda Davis
1023-36 E. Gilbreath St.
Graham, NC 27253

North Country Retreads New York
Bill & Joan Blair
16420 Parker Rd.
Watertown, NY 13601

Oklahoma Retreads
Bill & Bobby Betts
2617 Cherokee Strip
Altus, OK 73521

Phoenix, Arizona
Charlie & Denise Wasserman
P.O. Box 55886
Phoenix, AZ 85078
602/368-1914
acftwrench@juno.com

Sunshine Regional Directors
Bob & Ginny Johnson
309 Daffodil St.
Inverness, FL 34452

Virginia Retreads
Andy & Sylvia Bradley
19 Grimes Drive
Madison Heights, VA 24572

Ontario Durham Retreads
Bob Smith
Oshawa, Ontario, CAN
rwsmith@spanit.com

Ontario Northern Triangle Retreads
Gord & Cleo Walker
58 Forest Circle, RR 3
Penetanguishene, Ontario, L9M1R3 CAN
705/533-2622
gwwalker@bconnex.net

Ontario Northwest Retreads
Merv & Laura Donohue
2036 E. Arthur St.
Thunder Bay, Ontario, P7E-5N8 CAN
onw_retreads@yahoo.com

Saskatchewan Estevan Retreads
Paul Currie
Estevan, Saskatchewan, CAN
pwc@sk.sympatico.ca

Turbo Motorcycle International Owners Association (TMIOA)

The TMIOA is a club for owners of all the factory turbocharged motorcycles. You can contact them at:

Turbo Motorcycle International Owners Association
P.O. Box 385
Westtown, PA 19395

E-mail addresses:

Bob Miller, President/Treasurer
brbob@bellatlantic.net

Steve Klose, Turbo News Editor
steve11@idt.net

Arlie Rauch, Membership Director
adarpub@servco.com

Bob Durrstein, technical help
durrstein@aol.com

Women On Wheels (WOW)

I've spent some time with members of this motorcycle club for women and have found them to be some of the most enjoyable motorcyclists I've ever ridden with. If you are a female motorcyclist, I highly recommend joining your local chapter of WOW. To find your nearest chapter, contact Women On Wheels at:

WOW International Headquarters
P.O. Box 0546
Sparta, WI 54656-0546
800/322-1969

Ronnie Cramer's Motorcycle Web Index—Clubs/Organizations

This site has the most complete listing I've found of motorcycle clubs and organizations. If there is a club—or even a type of club—you're looking for, you should be able to find it here. Check out Ronnie Cramer's Motorcycle Web Index—Clubs/Organizations at:

http://sepnet.com/cycle/clubs.htm

Books and Videotapes

You can learn anything you've ever wanted to know about motorcycles and motorcycling by reading one of the tens of thousands of books available on the subject.

Whitehorse Press

Whitehorse Press publishes and distributes nothing but motorcycle books. It's owned and operated by Dan and Judy Kennedy, both of whom are devoted motorcyclists as well as publishers, and that devotion to the sport shows in their books. Whitehorse publishes many excellent books on motorcycling, and their catalog contains one of the most complete selections of motorcycle-related books and products you'll find anywhere. To obtain the latest catalog, contact them at:

Whitehorse Press
3424 North Main St.
P.O. Box 60
North Conway, NH 03860-0060
800/531-1133
75030.2554@compuserve.com

Classic Motorbooks

Classic Motorbooks publishes and distributes books on all aspects of vehicular culture, from antique tractors to airplanes. In the process, it produces and distributes an incredibly diverse collection of motorcycle books. You can order a catalog at:

Classic Motorbooks
729 Prospect Ave.
P.O. Box 1
Osceola, WI 54020-0001
800/826-6600
mbibks@win.bright.net

Suggested Reading

The following list includes some of the most important books you can read when starting out as a motorcyclist. Everyone has their own preferences and individual tastes, so any suggested reading list has to be somewhat subjective, but whatever your tastes, you will find the following books useful:

How to Set Up Your Motorcycle Workshop: Designing, Tooling, and Stocking
Charles G. Masi
Whitehorse Press Softbound, 1996, 160 pp.
This book can save you a lot of headaches (as well as a lot of aches in other places) when doing your own motorcycle maintenance. Masi even manages to make the subject entertaining with his offbeat sense of humor.

Against the Wind—A Rider's Account of the Incredible Iron Butt Rally
Ron Ayres
Whitehorse Press Softbound, 1997, 240 pp.
This book gives you an inside look at what it is like to compete in one of the most demanding motorcycle endurance events in the world. Ayres' story-telling skills make what is already a fascinating story even more fun to read.

Pictorial History of Japanese Motorcycles
Cornelis Vanderheuvel
Elmar/Bay View Books Hardbound, 1997, 168 pp.
distributed by Classic Motorbooks
This book does an excellent job of chronicling the evolution of the Japanese motorcycle industry—an evolution that helped make motorcycling accessible to most of the people riding today. More than 375 color illustrations are included.

One Man Caravan
Robert Edison Fulton, Jr.
Whitehorse Press Softbound, 1996, 288 pp.
In this book, Fulton chronicles his 17-month around-the-world motorcycle trip, which he began in 1932. In this fascinating story, Fulton gives the reader an idea of what it was like to tour on a motorcycle in the days before electric starters and gas stations on every corner.

Motorcycle Owner's Manual: A Practical Guide to Keeping Your Motorcycle in Top Condition
Hugo Wilson
DK Publishing Softbound, 1997, 112 pp.
distributed by Whitehorse Press

This book won't replace a good repair manual specifically for your bike, as the author himself admits, but it will serve as an excellent additional source of information. General procedures are explained much more clearly than in most manuals, and the photos are easier to follow.

The Motorcycle Safety Foundation's Guide to Motorcycling Excellence: Skills, Knowledge, and Strategies for Riding Right
Motorcycle Safety Foundation
Whitehorse Press Softbound, 1995, 176 pp.
If you can't take a RiderCourse, at least buy the Motorcycle Safety Foundation's book, which is a collection of its instructional material. If I discovered that any idea, technique, or practice I discussed in this book differed from MSF practice, I deferred to them—these folks know what they're doing, and they know how to save lives.

World Superbikes: The First Ten Years
Julian Ryder, photographs by Kel Edge
Haynes Publishing Softbound, 1997, 160 pp.
distributed by Classic Motorbooks
When World Superbike racing first began in 1988, journalist Julian Ryder left the Grand Prix circuit to cover the new series. He's been doing so ever since, and now he's written a book chronicling the first decade of the immensely popular series. His in-depth knowledge of the racers and the sport in general make this a gripping book, and Edge's photography is superb.

Ducati Story: Racing and Production Models 1945 to the Present Day
Ian Falloon
Patrick Stephens Limited Hardbound, 1996, 160 pp.
distributed by Classic Motorbooks
Until recently, little information was available about this small Italian racing-savant manufacturer, but during the past decade, many books have been written on the subject. This is one of the best of those books. *Ducati Story* is a case study in how to build the finest high-performance motorcycles in the world and how *not* to conduct a business. Motorcyclists and business types alike should find this a fascinating book.

Zen and the Art of Motorcycle Maintenance: An Inquiry into Values
Robert M. Pirsig
Bantam Books Softbound, 1974, 380 pp.
distributed by Whitehorse Press
I try to reread Pirsig's motorcycle classic at least once a year, and each time, it is like reading a different book. It may prove a tough read for those without a philosophical bent, but it is worth the effort.

Hell's Angels: A Strange and Terrible Saga
Dr. Hunter S. Thompson
Ballantine Books Softbound, 1967, 276 pp.
distributed by Whitehorse Press
Hunter S. Thompson may be more famous for his excessive lifestyle than for his writing, but long after everyone has forgotten about his excesses, his writing will live on. His command of the English language rivals that of any author, living or dead, and when he chooses to write about motorcycles, so much the better.

Recommended Viewing

Street Smarts: The Advanced Course in Urban Survival video series
produced by Paul Winters and David West
distributed by Whitehorse Press
Nothing compares to taking an MSF RiderCourse, but if you choose not to do so, at least buy these three videos—they may save your life. Much of the material presented in the videos is covered in a RiderCourse, and while you won't benefit from individual instruction and instructor feedback, you'll at least be able to see how it's done. Ideally, you should take a RiderCourse and buy these videos. Considering what's at stake, the relatively low cost of these videos represents one of the best investments you can make.

Parts and Accessories

In the long run, you're better off buying as many motorcycle supplies as you can from your local dealers, but often you won't be able to find what you want locally, and you'll have to look elsewhere. The following list provides you with names, addresses, and phone numbers where you can find just about anything you need.

Aerostich Riderwear and RiderwearHouse

To get one of Aerostich's fantastic riding suits, you're going to have to go directly to the source and give owner Andy Goldfine a call. Even if you're not in the market for a riding suit, you should contact him anyway and get a copy of the Aerostich RiderwearHouse catalog, which contains the most useful collection of quality riding accessories you'll find anywhere. It is also the most entertaining catalog you'll ever read.

Aero Design
8 South 18th Ave. West
Duluth, MN 55806-2148
800/222-1994
aerostich@aol.com
74544,323@compuserve.com
http://www.aerostich.com/aerostich

Chaparral Motorsports

Chaparral has one of the widest selections of gear and accessories for both on- and off-road riding you'll find anywhere. Contact them at:

Chaparral Motorsports
555 South H St.
San Bernardino, CA 92410
800/841-2960

Dennis Kirk, Inc.

Dennis Kirk may not always have the lowest prices on all items, but they have an incredibly wide selection, and they get your stuff fast. Besides, on some items, they will match the best price you can find elsewhere. Contact them at:

Dennis Kirk, Inc.
955 South Field Ave.
Rush City, MN 55069
800/328-9280
info@denniskirk.com

Dynojet Research, Inc.

Many motorcycles come with their carburetion set too lean. Not only does this hinder performance, but it can cause your engine to run hot, especially if you install an aftermarket air filter. If your bike suffers from such problems, or if you just want to improve its overall performance, the helpful folks at Dynojet Research can set you up with just the carburetor jetting kit. Contact them at:

Dynojet Research, Inc.
200 Arden Dr.
Belgrade, MT 59714
800/992-4993

J&P Cycles

If you have a Harley-Davidson garbage wagon and want to chop it, if you have a basket-case Harley chopper and want to refurbish it, if you want to spiff up your Harley, or if you just want to build a complete motorcycle from spare parts, you'll find everything you need to do so in the J&P Cycles catalog. Contact them at:

J&P Cycles
P.O. Box 138
Anamosa, IA 52205
800/397-4844
www.j-pcycles.com
jpcycles@netins.net

JC Whitney

If you're a careful shopper, you can get some killer buys on motorcycle accessories from JC Whitney. Although inexpensive, some of the items JC Whitney carries are of surprisingly high quality. You can contact them at:

JC Whitney
1 JC Whitney Way
P.O. Box 3000
LaSalle, IL 61301-0300
312/431-6102

National Cycle, Inc.

National Cycle builds some of the finest aftermarket windshields and fairings you can buy. I've owned six of them, and have found them all to be of the highest quality. You can purchase their products from any shop or catalog, but if you call the folks at National Cycle and order direct, they can help you select the windshield or accessory that best fulfills your needs. It is a tremendous opportunity for you to benefit from their experience. Contact National Cycle at:

National Cycle, Inc.
2200 Maywood Drive
PO Box 158
Maywood, IL 60153-0158
708/343-0400
www.nationalcycle.com
info@nationalcycle.com

Sport Wheels

Ex-racer Denny Kannenberg owns more motorcycles than anybody—at least 10,000, at last count. He also owns the world's largest motorcycle salvage operation, meaning that he has more used parts to sell than anyone else. And even though he's located in Jordan, Minnesota, he does business with motorcyclists across the country. If you ever need something—whether it is a part or a complete motorcycle—and can't find it, give Denny a call. You can contact Sport Wheels at:

800/821-5975
sportwheel@aol.com
http.www.mm.com/swapmeet/swheels/swheels.htm

If you can't find what you're looking for at Sport Wheels, it may not exist. (Photo ®1998 Darwin Holstrom)

Tuners and Builders

As a new rider, you really don't need to make your motorcycle any faster than it is. I'm not trying to be a wet blanket; it's just that today's motorcycles are ultra-high performance machines right out of the crate. If you do want more power, the following people can help you out.

Graves Motorsports, Inc.

Chuck Graves knows a thing or two about building fast bikes—in 1993, he won the Formula USA championship, and he's a four-time Willow Springs Formula One champion. Contact him at:

Graves Motorsports, Inc.
7645 Densmore Ave.
Van Nuys, CA 91406
818/902-1942

Hahn Racecraft

Bill Hahn's claim to fame is building motorcycles for drag racing, but for a price, he'll help you build what will without a doubt be the quickest motorcycle in town. Contact him at:

Hahn Racecraft
1981 D Wiesbrook Dr.
Oswego, IL 60543
630/801-1417

HyperCycle

If, for some reason, you want a flat-out AMA superbike for the street, you should get a hold of the folks at HyperCycle. Contact them at:

HyperCycle
7712 Gloria Ave., #8
Van Nuys, CA 91406
818/998-8860

Mr. Turbo

Mr. Turbo builds turbo kits for a variety of motorcycles, from ZX11 Ninjas to Harley dressers. Contact them at:

Mr. Turbo
4002 Hopper St.
Houston, TX 77093
281/442-7113

Racing Clubs

The following is a list of clubs that can help you get started in motorcycle road racing.

American Federation of Motorcyclists
P.O. Box 5018-333
Newark, CA 94560
510/796-7005

American Historic Racing Motorcycle
Association
P.O. Box 882
Wausau, WI 54402-0882
715/842-9699
Fax 715/842-9545

California Mini Road Racing
Association
15023 Valencia Street
Lake Elsinore, CA 92530
909/674-5357

Central Motorcycle Roadracing
Association
P.O. Box 156
Richmond, TX 77469
800/423-8736

Central Roadracing Association, Inc.
P.O. Box 5385
Hopkins, MN 55343
612/332-4070
Fax 612/949-9465

Championship Cup Series
P.O. Box 447
Skyland, NC 28776
704/684-4297
Fax 704/684-3819

Championship Cup Series: Florida
16871 Hollow Tree Lane
Loxahatchee, FL 33470
407/793-3394

Hallett Road Racing Association
6105 New Sapulpa Rd.
Tulsa, OK 74131
918/446-6657

Mid-Atlantic Road Racing Club
P.O. Box 2292
Wheaton, MD 20915
301/933-2599

Motorcycle Roadracing Association
P.O. Box 4187
Denver, CO 80204
303/530-5678

Northern California Mini Road Racing
Association
P.O. Box 2791
Citrus Heights, CA 95611-2791
916/722-5517

Oregon Motorcycle Road Racing
Association
P.O. Box 6388
Portland, OR 97228
503/221-1487

Southeastern Sportbike Association
P.O. Box 420683
Atlanta, GA 30342
404/984-2606

Utah Sport Bike Association
P.O. Box 26791
Salt Lake City, UT 84126
801/535-4625

Washington Motorcycle Road Racing
Association
P.O. Box 94323
Seattle, WA 98124-5623
206/338-4686

Western Eastern Roadracers' Association
P.O. Box 440549
Kennesaw, GA 30144

Or:

3446 Bells Ferry Rd.
Kennesaw, GA 30144
770/924-8404
Fax: 770/924-1277

Willow Springs Motorcycle Club
P.O. Box 911
Rosamond, CA 93560
805/256-1234

High Performance Riding Schools

Besides taking the Experienced RiderCourse from the Motorcycle Safety Foundation, the best way to improve your riding skills (and your chances of having an injury-free riding career) is to take a course in high-performance riding. Whether you are going racing, or you just want to hone your street riding skills, taking a quality high-performance riding course can teach you things that can save your life. Usually these schools are expensive, but if they can make you a better (and safer) rider, they are worth the money.

Although most of these schools have their headquarters in the American southwest, many conduct classes at different racetracks around the country, making it easier for riders to attend. Call or write for a schedule of class dates and locations.

Keith Code's California Superbike School
P.O. Box 9294
Glendale, CA 91226
800/530-3350
Fax: 818/246-3307

Freddie Spencer's High Performance
Riding School
P.O. Box 36208
Las Vegas, NV 89133
702/643-1099

CLASS Motorcycle Schools
15599 West Telegraph Road, Suite C24
Santa Paula, CA 93060
805/933-9936
Fax: 805/033-9987

DP Safety School
P.O. Box 1551
Morro Bay, CA 93443
805/772-8301
Fax: 805/772-5929

Cycle Babble Glossary

ABS (Antilock Brake System)   The ABS detects when a wheel is not turning and releases pressure to the brake on that wheel, preventing a skid.

aftermarket   The sector of the market that sells parts and accessories other than OEM (Original Equipment Manufacturers).

Airheads   A term for older, air-cooled BMW Boxer Twins.

ape hangers   A term coined at the height of the custom-bike movement to describe tall handlebars that forced the rider to reach skyward to grasp the controls, making the rider adopt an ape-like posture.

bagger   A motorcycle equipped with saddlebags and other touring amenities.

belt-drive system   A final-drive system that transmits the power to the rear wheel via a drive belt.

Big Twins   The engines in the larger Harley-Davidson bikes.

bobbers   The custom bikes American riders built after World War II where the owners cut off, or "bobbed," much of the bodywork.

bottom end   The bottom part of the engine, where the crankshaft and (usually) the transmission reside.

Boxer   A two-cylinder engine with the pistons opposing each other, resembling fists flying away from each other.

brakes (disc and drum)   Disc brakes are located on the front tire and use stationary calipers that squeeze pads against the discs that rotate with the wheel. Drum brakes, on the other hand, are located on the rear wheel and use horseshoe-shaped brake shoes that expand against the inner surface of the wheel hub.

cafe chop   Converting a stock motorcycle into a cafe racer is known as doing a *cafe chop* on a bike.

cafe racer   Motorcycles modified to resemble racing motorcycles from the 1950s and '60s. They are called "cafe racers" because their owners supposedly raced from cafe to cafe in London, where the bikes first appeared in the 1960s.

cam   A rod with lobes on it that opens the valves.

carbon fiber   A high-tech material favored in many motorcycle applications because it is extremely strong, light, and expensive. The distinctive look of carbon fiber has become trendy.

carburetor   A device that mixes fuel with air to create the fuel charge burned in the combustion chamber.

cases   The two clam-shell–like halves in the bottom end of the engine surrounded by a metal shell.

centerstand   A stand that supports the motorcycle in an upright position.

centerstand tang   A small lever attached to the centerstand.

chain drive system   A final-drive system that transmits the power to the rear wheel via a chain.

chassis   The combined frame and suspension on a motorcycle.

chopper   Once used to describe a custom motorcycle that had all superfluous parts "chopped" off in order to make the bike faster, a chopper today is a type of custom bike that usually has an extended fork, no rear suspension, and high handlebars.

clip-ons   Handlebars that attach directly to the fork tubes, rather than to the top yoke, that hold the fork tubes together.

clutch   A device that disengages power from the crankshaft to the transmission, allowing a rider to change gears.

combustion chamber   The area at the top of the cylinder where the fuel charge burns and pushes the pistons down.

coming on the cam   The term used when a four stroke reaches its powerband.

coming on the pipe   The term used when a two stroke reaches its power band.

connecting rods   These attach the crankshaft to the pistons via the eccentric journals, and the rods' up-and-down movement is converted into a circular motion through the design of the journals.

constant-radius turn   A turn with a steady, nonchanging arc. In a decreasing-radius corner, the arc gets sharper as you progress through the curve, while in an increasing-radius corner, the arc becomes less sharp.

contact patch   The area of your tire that actually contacts the road while you ride.

counterbalancer   A weight inside an engine that cancels out some of the engine's vibration.

countersteering   The way you use the handlebar to lean the bike into a turn. If you want to turn right, you push the handlebars to the left, and vice versa.

cowlings   A piece of bodywork that covers the engine area.

crotch rocket   A term some people use to refer to sportbikes.

crowns   The tops of the pistons.

cycle   The up-and down motion of the piston. The terms *cycle* and *stroke* are used interchangeably when referring to engine types.

cylinders   The hollow shafts in the top end of an engine inside which internal combustion occurs.

cylinder block   The hunk of aluminum with holes bored through it, inside which the pistons move up and down.

decreasing-radius corner   A turn where the arc gets sharper as you progress through the curve.

dirtbike   Bikes intended for off-road use that aren't legal to ride on public roads. Sometimes the term *pure-dirt* is used to distinguish a dirtbike from a dual-sport motorcycle.

discs   These are the metal rotors the caliper presses the pads against to brake.

double-cradle frame   A bike frame with two steel tubes circling the engine from the front and "cradling" it.

dresser   A motorcycle set up for long-distance touring.

dual sport   Street-legal motorcycles with varying degrees of off-road capabilities. Also called *dual-purpose motorcycles*.

eccentric journals   These are used to attach the connecting rods to the crankshaft (also called *metal shafts*).

ergonomics   The science used to design devices, systems, and physical conditions that conform to the human body. A prime consideration when designing a motorcycle.

Evolution (Evo)   When Harley-Davidson began using aluminum to build its cylinder jugs, it called this new engine the Evolution.

fairings   The devices mounted at the front of a motorcycle to protect the rider from the elements. These range from simple, Plexiglas shields to complex, encompassing body panels.

false neutral   When you fail to engage gears and the transmission behaves as though it is in neutral, even though it isn't .

flat cylinders   Found in the flat-four- and flat-six-cylinder engines used in Honda's Gold Wings, the cylinders are arranged in a flat, opposing configuration.

foot paddling   The way an unskilled rider "walks" his or her motorcycle around at low speeds.

forks   The metal tubes holding the front wheel to the rest of the motorcycle.

four-cylinder bike   A motorcycle with four cylinders.

fuel-injection system   This mixes the fuel-air charges and forcibly injects them into the combustion chambers, unlike carburetors, which rely on the vacuum created by the engine to draw the charges into the combustion chambers.

garbage wagon   A scornful term used by some outlaw bikers to describe touring bikes.

gearhead   A person with a strong interest in all things mechanical; a motorcyclist.

gearset   A set of gears within a bike's transmission.

high siding   Pitching a bike over away from the direction you are turning. The most dangerous kind of crash.

horsepower   A measure of an engine's strength.

hydroplane   When your tires start to float on top of water, causing them to lose contact with the road's surface.

increasing-radius corner   A turn where the arc becomes less sharp as you go through the curve.

inline six   An engine with six cylinders in a row.

inline triple   An engine with three cylinders placed in a row.

Iron Butt Rally   The most grueling long-distance motorcycle rally in the world. To finish the rally requires that you ride at least 10,000 miles in 11 days.

Knucklehead   A term for Harley-Davidson's first overhead-valve Big Twin, introduced in 1936.

L-twin engine   A V-twin engine with its cylinders splayed apart at a 90-degree angle, which creates a smoother-running engine. These engines can either be placed transversely (crosswise), or longitudinally (lengthwise) in the motorcycle frame.

lane splitting   Riding between lanes of traffic on a freeway.

laying the bike down   A crash where you slide down on one side of the bike.

leviathan   Used to describe big, multicylinder dual sports.

lugging the engine   Letting the RPMs fall below the engine's powerband.

manual transmission   A device consisting of a set of gears (the gearset), that alter the final-drive ratio of a vehicle to enable an operator to get up to speed. Automatic transmissions do not have gearsets but rather use a complex system of fluid and metal bands to vary the final-drive ratio of a vehicle.

naked bikes   Bikes without any type of fairing.

Oilheads   Newer, air-and-oil-cooled BMW Boxer engines.

open-class   When referring to street-legal sportbikes, *open-class* designates motorcycles with engines that displace more than 800 cubic centimeters of volume.

Original Equipment Manufacturers (OEM)   The companies that build the bikes.

orphan bikes   Rare bikes that are no longer in production.

Otto cycle   The four-stroke engine is sometimes called the Otto cycle, in honor of its inventor, Otto Benz.

overbore   When you *overbore* your engine, you drill out the cylinders and then put oversized pistons in the holes, effectively increasing your engine capacity.

overhead cam system   A system where the cam rides directly on top of the valve stems.

Panhead   A term for Harley-Davidson's second-generation overhead-valve Big Twin, introduced in 1948.

parallel-twin engine   A two-cylinder engine with its cylinders placed side-by-side in an upright position.

pistons   The slugs moving up and down within the cylinders.

powerband   A certain RPM (*revolutions per minute*—how many times per minute an engine's crankshaft spins around) range in which an engine makes most of its power.

primary drive   A drive chain connecting the engine's crankshaft to its transmission.

production motorcycles   The bikes manufacturers produce to sell to the general public, rather than bikes built specifically for racers.

pushrod system   In a pushrod system, the cams are located below the cylinder heads and push on the rocker arms by moving long rods, called the *pushrods*.

radial   When used to describe a tire, refers to the way the cords of a tire are constructed. While radial tires have long been used with automobiles, they are just now being used on motorcycles.

rain grooves   Channels cut into a road's surface to help water run off the road during a rainstorm.

repair link   A link in some motorcycle chains that can be disassembled for chain repair.

repli-racers   Hard-edged sportbikes. These motorcycles are characterized by riding positions that tuck the rider into an extreme crouch, forcing him or her to practically lay down on the fuel tank.

revolutions per minute (rpm)   The number of times the crankshaft spins around each minute. Often, the term *revs* is used, especially in conversation.

riding two up   Carrying a passenger on your bike.

rocker arms   Devices that work like upside-down teeter totters and push on the valve stems.

rubber-mounted   Rubber-mounted engines use a system of rubber cushions and/or jointed engine mounts to isolate engine vibration from the rider.

shaft drive system   A final-drive system that transmits the power to the rear wheel via a drive shaft.

shaft jacking   Shaky or bumpy motion created by the impact of acceleration and then fed back into the bike's frame.

Shovelhead   A term for Harley's third-generation overhead-valve Big Twin engine, introduced in 1966.

sidecars   Small carriages attached to the side of a motorcycle to provide extra carrying capacity.

sissy bar   The backrest put behind the passenger's portion of the saddle.

snicking   The act of shifting a well-functioning transmission is often called *snicking*, because that's the sound the action makes. A transmission that doesn't snick into gear is described as *sloppy-shifting*.

solid-mounted   A bike with a solid-mounted engine has the engine bolted directly to the frame tubes.

splitting the cases   The metal shell surrounding the bottom end is composed of two clam-shell–like halves, called *cases*. Taking these apart to repair the motor is called *splitting the cases*. *See also* **bottom end**.

sport tourer   A motorcycle that combines the comfort and carrying capacity of a touring bike with the handling and power of a sportbike with larger fairings and hard, lockable luggage.

sportbike   A motorcycle designed for optimal speed and handling characteristics, often with extensive bodywork.

springer fork   Springer-type forks use large, exposed springs to dampen the impact of road irregularities.

squid   Someone who rides a sportbike on the street as if he or she were on a racetrack.

steering geometry   The geometrical relationship between the motorcycle frame, the angle of the fork, and the position of the front tire.

streetfighter   A bare-bones sportbike, stripped of all extraneous body work (also called a "hooligan" bike).

stroke   The up-and-down motion of the piston.

suspension   The forks, shocks, and to a degree, tires, of a motorcycle. The springs and fluids in these items that "suspend" the motorcycle frame off of the ground.

tappets   Small metal slugs between the cam and the pushrod or rocker arm.

Telelever system   The most successful alternate front suspension, made by BMW, which takes the shock-absorption function of a hydraulic fork and transfers it to a shock absorber located behind the steering head.

thumper   Bikes with large-displacement, single-cylinder, four-stroke engines.

top end   The upper part of the engine, which contains the pistons, cylinders, and valve gear, and the induction system consists of the apparati that mix an air-and-fuel charge and inject it into the combustion chamber, located in the top end.

torque   A twisting force, and in a motorcycle, it is a measure of the leverage the engine exerts on the rear wheel.

touring bike   A bike equipped for longer rides with fairings and lockable saddle bags.

traction   A tire's ability to grip the road.

travel   The distance that suspension components, the forks and shocks, move up and down when the bike rides over bumps.

twin spar-type frame   A bike frame with two steel or aluminum "spars" (flat beams) sandwiched around the sides of the engine.

two up   A term for carrying a passenger on your motorcycle.

two stroke engine   An engine (also called a "stroker") whose power cycle consists of just two movements, or strokes: The piston moves down, drawing in the fuel-air charge, and then up, combusting the charge.

unitized transmission   A transmission (often referred to as a "unit transmission") that is an integral part of the engine's bottom end.

Universal Japanese Motorcycle (UJM)   During the 1970s, the Japanese became so identified with the four-cylinder, standard-style motorcycle that this term was coined to describe them.

V-four   An engine with four cylinders arranged in a V-shaped configuration.

V-twin   A two-cylinder engine with its cylinders placed in a V shape.

valves   Devices consisting of metal stems with flat disks on one end that open and close to let fuel charges in and exhaust gases out.

valve guides   Metal tubes that house the valves.

valve train   The system of valves that let the fuel charges in and let the exhaust gases out.

Index

C

I

mounting, 137
preparing for races,
290-291
safety zone around,
157-158
shifting gears, 143-144
starting, 137-138
friction zone, 139-140
ignition, 138-139
kick-starting, 139-140
stopping, 141-143
brake practice, 142
parking, 142-143
throttle control, 145
types
500cc Honda NSR500V
V-twin, 271
cruisers, 30-32
dirtbikes, 34-35
dual-sports, 28-30
NSR500 Grand Prix
racer, 273
production-based,
275-279
sportbikes, 33-34
street standards, 35-37
touring bikes, 37-39
Motorcycling Amateur
Radio Club (MARC), 248
motorcycling, *see* riding
Motorcyclist, 293
motors, *see* engines
mounting motorcycles, 137
movies, 8-10
biker chic, 7-8
Mr. Turbo, 360
MSF (Motorcycle Safety
Foundation), 125-126, 347
RiderCourses, *see*
RiderCourses
mud, riding off-road,
192-194
Mudrats club, 247
MZ motorcycles
Silverstar Gespann, 321
Skorpion Baghira, 321
Skorpion Mastiff, 321

Skorpion Replica, 69, 320
Skorpion Sport Cup, 320
Skorpion Traveler, 321

N

National Cycle, Inc., 358
National Pony Express
Tour, 248
negotiating prices, 96
new bikers
buying motorcycles,
48-49
EasyRiders clubs, 249
night time, riding in
dark, 175
Nighthawk motorcycle, 36
Ninja (Kawasaki), 36, 50-51
Ninja 250R motorcycle, 317
Ninja 500R motorcycle, 316
Ninja ZX11 motorcycle, 315
Ninja ZX6 motorcycle, 316
Ninja ZX6R motorcycle, 316
Ninja ZX7R motorcycle, 316
Ninja ZX9R motorcycle, 315
Northern California
Mini Road Racing
Association, 361
Norton Owners Club, 244
NSR500 Grand Prix
racer, 273
NT 650 Hawk GT
motorcycle, 342
NX650 motorcycle, 341

O

O-ring chains, *see*
chain-drive systems
obstacles
riding off-road, 189-190
see also stationary objects
off-road riding, 185-186
clubs, 243
obstacles, 189-190
posture, 186-189

downhill, 188
embankments,
188-189
ledges, 188-189
uphill, 186-188
surface conditions,
191-194
rocks, 193-194
sand, 191-194
water/mud, 192-194
see also dirtbikes
oil, 201-205
changing, 202-205
disposing of used
oil, 199
checking oil level, 202
filters, 204
lubricating shafts, 209
storing bikes, 210-211
Oilheads, 244
Oregon Motorcycle Road
Racing Association, 361
organizations
American Motorcyclist
Association (AMA), 347
American Sport Touring
Riders Association
(ASTRA), 348
Motorcycle Safety
Foundation (MSF),
125-126, 347
see also clubs
origins of motorcycles,
14-15
see also history of
motorcycles
orphan bike clubs, 245
Otto cycle, 68
out-the-door prices, 95
outlaw bikers
BMW Riders Association
rally, 7
Hollister Invasion, 9
The Wild One movie,
15-16
overhead cam systems,
engines, 57

S

alpha
books

Business

The Complete Idiot's Guide to Assertiveness
ISBN: 0-02-861964-1
$16.95

The Complete Idiot's Guide to Business Management
ISBN: 0-02-861744-4
$16.95

The Complete Idiot's Guide to Dynamic Selling
ISBN: 0-02-861952-8
$16.95

The Complete Idiot's Guide to Getting Along with Difficult People
ISBN: 0-02-861597-2
$16.95

The Complete Idiot's Guide to Great Customer Service
ISBN: 0-02-861953-6
$16.95

The Complete Idiot's Guide to Leadership
ISBN: 0-02-861946-3
$16.95

The Complete Idiot's Guide to Managing People
ISBN: 0-02-861036-9
$18.95

The Complete Idiot's Guide to Managing Your Time
ISBN: 0-02-861039-3
$14.95

The Complete Idiot's Guide to Marketing Basics
ISBN: 0-02-861490-9
$16.95

The Complete Idiot's Guide to New Product Development
ISBN: 0-02-861952-8
$16.95

The Complete Idiot's Guide to Office Politics
ISBN: 0-02-862397-5
$16.95

The Complete Idiot's Guide to Project Management
ISBN: 0-02-861745-2
$16.95

The Complete Idiot's Guide to Speaking in Public With Confidence
ISBN: 0-02-861038-5
$16.95

The Complete Idiot's Guide to Starting a Home Based Business
ISBN: 0-02-861539-5
$16.95

The Complete Idiot's Guide to Starting Your Own Business
ISBN: 1-56761-529-5
$16.99

The Complete Idiot's Guide to Successful Business Presentations
ISBN: 0-02-861748-7
$16.95

The Complete Idiot's Guide to Terrific Business Writing
ISBN: 0-02-861097-0
$16.95

The Complete Idiot's Guide to Winning Through Negotiation
ISBN: 0-02-861037-7
$16.95

The Complete Idiot's Guide to Protecting Yourself from Everyday Legal Hassles
ISBN: 1-56761-602-X
$16.99

Personal Finance

The Complete Idiot's Guide to Buying Insurance and Annuities
ISBN: 0-02-861113-6
$16.95

The Complete Idiot's Guide to Managing Your Money
ISBN: 1-56761-530-9
$16.95

The Complete Idiot's Guide to Making Money with Mutual Funds
ISBN: 1-56761-637-2
$16.95

The Complete Idiot's Guide to Getting Rich
ISBN: 1-56761-509-0
$16.95

The Complete Idiot's Guide to Finance and Accounting
ISBN: 0-02-861752-5
$16.95

The Complete Idiot's Guide to Investing Like a Pro
ISBN:0-02-862044-5
$16.95

The Complete Idiot's Guide to Making Money After You Retire
ISBN:0-02-862410-6
$16.95

The Complete Idiot's Guide to Making Money on Wall Street
ISBN:0-02-861958-7
$16.95

The Complete Idiot's Guide to Personal Finance in Your 20s and 30s
ISBN:0-02-862415-7
$16.95

The Complete Idiot's Guide to Wills and Estates
ISBN: 0-02-861747-9
$16.95

The Complete Idiot's Guide to 401(k) Plans
ISBN: 0-02-861948-X
$16.95

Careers

The Complete Idiot's Guide to Changing Careers
ISBN: 0-02-861977-3
$17.95

The Complete Idiot's Guide to Freelancing
ISBN: 0-02-862119-0
$16.95

The Complete Idiot's Guide to Getting the Job You Want
ISBN: 1-56761-608-9
$24.95

The Complete Idiot's Guide to the Perfect Cover Letter
ISBN: 0-02-861960-9
$14.95

The Complete Idiot's Guide to the Perfect Interview
ISBN: 0-02-861945-5
$14.95

The Complete Idiot's Guide to the Perfect Resume
ISBN: 0-02-861093-8
$16.95

Education

The Complete Idiot's Guide to American History
ISBN: 0-02-861275-2
$16.95

The Complete Idiot's Guide to British Royalty
ISBN: 0-02-862346-0
$18.95

The Complete Idiot's Guide to Civil War
ISBN: 0-02-862122-0
$16.95

The Complete Idiot's Guide to Classical Mythology
ISBN: 0-02-862385-1
$16.95

The Complete Idiot's Guide to Creative Writing
ISBN: 0-02-861734-7
$16.95

The Complete Idiot's Guide to Dinosaurs
ISBN: 0-02-862390-8
$17.95

The Complete Idiot's Guide to Genealogy
ISBN: 0-02-861947-1
$16.95

The Complete Idiot's Guide to Geography
ISBN: 0-02-861955-2
$16.95

The Complete Idiot's Guide to Getting Published
ISBN: 0-02-862392-4
$16.95

The Complete Idiot's Guide to Grammar & Style
ISBN: 0-02-861956-0
$16.95

The Complete Idiot's Guide to an MBA
ISBN: 0-02-862164-4
$17.95

The Complete Idiot's Guide to Philosophy
ISBN:0-02-861981-1
$16.95

The Complete Idiot's Guide to Learning Spanish On Your Own
ISBN: 0-02-861040-7
$16.95

The Complete Idiot's Guide to Learning French on Your Own
ISBN: 0-02-861043-1
$16.95

The Complete Idiot's Guide to Learning German on Your Own
ISBN: 0-02-861962-5
$16.95

The Complete Idiot's Guide to Learning Italian on Your Own
ISBN: 0-02-862125-5
$16.95

The Complete Idiot's Guide to Learning Sign Language
ISBN: 0-02-862388-6
$16.95

Food/Beverage/Entertaining

The Complete Idiot's Guide to Baking
ISBN: 0-02-861954-4
$16.95

The Complete Idiot's Guide to Beer
ISBN: 0-02-861717-7
$16.95

The Complete Idiot's Guide to Cooking Basics
ISBN: 0-02-861974-9
$18.95

The Complete Idiot's Guide to Entertaining
ISBN: 0-02-861095-4
$16.95

The Complete Idiot's Guide to Etiquette
ISBN0-02-861094-6
$16.95

The Complete Idiot's Guide to Mixing Drinks
ISBN: 0-02-861941-2
$16.95

The Complete Idiot's Guide to Wine
ISBN: 0-02-861273-6
$16.95

Health and Fitness

The Complete Idiot's Guide to Beautiful Skin
ISBN: 0-02-862408-4
$16.95

The Complete Idiot's Guide to Breaking Bad Habits
ISBN: 0-02-862110-7
$16.95

The Complete Idiot's Guide to Eating Smart
ISBN: 0-02-861276-0
$16.95

The Complete Idiot's Guide to First Aid Basics
ISBN: 0-02-861099-7
$16.95

The Complete Idiot's Guide to Getting and Keeping Your Perfect Body
ISBN: 0-02-861276-0
$16.95

The Complete Idiot's Guide to Getting a Good Night's Sleep
ISBN: 0-02-862394-0
$16.95

The Complete Idiot's Guide to a Happy, Healthy Heart
ISBN: 0-02-862393-2
$16.95

The Complete Idiot's Guide to Healthy Stretching
ISBN: 0-02-862127-1
$16.95

The Complete Idiot's Guide to Jogging and Running
ISBN: 0-02-862386-X
$17.95

The Complete Idiot's Guide to Losing Weight
ISBN: 0-02-862113-1
$17.95

The Complete Idiot's Guide to Managed Health Care
ISBN: 0-02-862165-4
$17.95

The Complete Idiot's Guide to Stress
ISBN: 0-02-861086-5
$16.95

The Complete Idiot's Guide to Vitamins and Minerals
ISBN: 0-02-862116-6
$16.95

Home and Automotive

The Complete Idiot's Guide to Buying or Leasing a Car
ISBN: 0-02-861274-4
$16.95

The Complete Idiot's Guide to Buying and Selling a Home
ISBN: 0-02-861959-5
$16.95

The Complete Idiot's Guide to Decorating Your Home
ISBN: 0-02-861088-1
$16.95

The Complete Idiot's Guide to Gardening
ISBN: 0-02-861-096-2
$16.95

The Complete Idiot's Guide to Motorcycles
ISBN: 0-02-862416-5
$16.95

The Complete Idiot's Guide to Smart Moving
ISBN: 0-02-862126-3
$16.95

The Complete Idiot's Guide to Trouble-Free Car Care
ISBN: 0-02-861041-5
$16.95

The Complete Idiot's Guide to Trouble-Free Home Repair
ISBN: 0-02-861042-3
$16.95

Leisure/Hobbies

The Complete Idiot's Guide to Antiques and Collectibles
ISBN: 0-02-861595-6
$16.95

The Complete Idiot's Guide to Astrology
ISBN: 0-02-861951-X
$16.95

The Complete Idiot's Guide to the Beatles
ISBN: 0-02-862130-1
$18.95

The Complete Idiot's Guide to Boating and Sailing
ISBN: 0-02-862124-7
$18.95

The Complete Idiot's Guide to Bridge
ISBN: 0-02-861735-5
$16.95

The Complete Idiot's Guide to Chess
ISBN: 0-02-861736-3
$16.95

The Complete Idiot's Guide to Cigars
ISBN: 0-02-861975-7
$17.95

The Complete Idiot's Guide to Crafts with Kids
ISBN: 0-02-862406-8
$16.95

The Complete Idiot's Guide to Elvis
ISBN: 0-02-861873-4
$18.95

The Complete Idiot's Guide to Extra-Terrestrial Intelligence
ISBN: 0-02-862387-8
$16.95

The Complete Idiot's Guide to Fishing Basics
ISBN: 0-02-861598-0
$16.95

The Complete Idiot's Guide to Gambling Like a Pro
ISBN: 0-02-861102-0
$16.95

The Complete Idiot's Guide to a Great Retirement
ISBN: 0-02-861036-9
$16.95

The Complete Idiot's Guide to Hiking and Camping
ISBN: 0-02-861100-4
$16.95

The Complete Idiot's Guide to Needlecrafts
ISBN: 0-02-862123-9
$16.95

The Complete Idiot's Guide to Organizing Your Life
ISBN: 0-02-861090-3
$16.95

The Complete Idiot's Guide to Photography
ISBN: 0-02-861092-X
$16.95

The Complete Idiot's Guide to Reaching Your Goals
ISBN: 0-02-862114-X
$16.95

The Complete Idiot's Guide to the World's Religions
ISBN: 0-02-861730-4
$16.95

Music

The Complete Idiot's Guide to Classical Music
ISBN: 0-02-8611634-0
$16.95

The Complete Idiot's Guide to Playing the Guitar
0-02-864924-9
$17.95

The Complete Idiot's Guide to Playing the Piano and Electric Keyboards
0-02-864925-7
$17.95

Parenting

The Complete Idiot's Guide to Adoption
ISBN: 0-02-862108-5
$18.95

The Complete Idiot's Guide to Bringing Up Baby
ISBN: 0-02-861957-9
$16.95

The Complete Idiot's Guide to Grandparenting
ISBN: 0-02-861976-5
$16.95

The Complete Idiot's Guide to Parenting a Preschooler and Toddler
ISBN: 0-02-861733-9
$16.95

The Complete Idiot's Guide to Raising a Teenager
ISBN: 0-02-861277-9
$16.95

The Complete Idiot's Guide to Single Parenting
ISBN: 0-02-862409-2
$16.95

The Complete Idiot's Guide to Stepparenting
ISBN: 0-02-862407-6
$16.95

Pets

The Complete Idiot's Guide to Choosing, Training, and Raising a Dog
ISBN: 0-02-861098-9
$16.95

The Complete Idiot's Guide to Fun and Tricks with Your Dog
ISBN: 0-87605-083-6
$14.95

The Complete Idiot's Guide to Living with a Cat
ISBN: 0-02-861278-7
$16.95

The Complete Idiot's Guide to Turtles and Tortoises
ISBN: 0-87605-143-3
$16.95

Relationships

The Complete Idiot's Guide to Dating
ISBN: 0-02-861052-0
$14.95

The Complete Idiot's Guide to Dealing with In-Laws
ISBN: 0-02-862107-7
$16.95

The Complete Idiot's Guide to a Healthy Relationship
ISBN: 0-02-861087-3
$17.95

The Complete Idiot's Guide to a Perfect Marriage
ISBN: 0-02-861729-0
$16.95

The Complete Idiot's Guide to the Perfect Wedding
ISBN: 0-02-861963-3
$16.95

The Complete Idiot's Guide to Surviving Divorce
ISBN: 0-02-861101-3
$16.95

Sports

The Complete Idiot's Guide to Golf
ISBN: 0-02-861760-6
$16.95

The Complete Idiot's Guide to Pro Wrestling
ISBN: 0-02-862395-9
$17.95

The Complete Idiot's Guide to Skiing
ISBN: 0-02-861965-X
$16.95

The Complete Idiot's Guide to Tae Kwon Do
ISBN: 0-02-862389-4
$17.95

The Complete Idiot's Guide to Understanding Football Like a Pro
ISBN:0-02-861743-6
$16.95

The Complete Idiot's Guide to Yoga
ISBN: 0-02-861949-8
$16.95

Look for the Complete Idiot's Guides at your local bookseller, or call 1-800-428-5331 for more information.

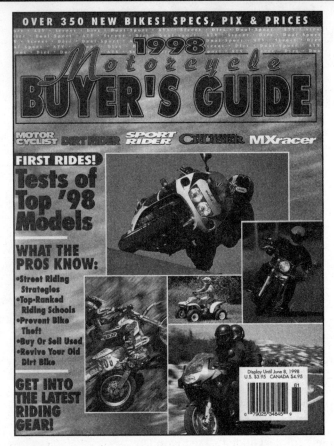